The BIG BOOK *of*
ONE POT
RECIPES

The BIG BOOK of
ONE POT
RECIPES

More Than 500 One Pot Recipes
for Easy, Flavorful Meals

Avon, Massachusetts

Published by
Adams Media, a division of F+W Media, Inc.
57 Littlefield Street, Avon, MA 02322. U.S.A.
www.adamsmedia.com

Contains material adapted and abridged from *The Everything® Cast Iron Cookbook* by Cinnamon Cooper, copyright ©
2010 by F+W Media, Inc., ISBN 10: 1-4405-0225-0, ISBN 13: 978-1-4405-0225-5; *The Everything® One-Pot Cookbook, 2nd
Edition* by Pamela Rice Hahn, copyright © 2009, 1999 by F+W Media, Inc., ISBN 10: 1-59869-836-2, ISBN 13: 978-1-59869-
836-7; *The Everything® Pressure Cooker Cookbook* by Pamela Rice Hahn, copyright © 2009 by F+W Media, Inc., ISBN 10:
1-4405-0017-7, ISBN 13: 978-1-4405-0017-6; *The Everything® Vegetarian Pressure Cooker Cookbook* by Amy Snyder and
Justin Snyder, copyright © 2010 by F+W Media, Inc., ISBN 10: 1-4405-0672-8, ISBN 13: 978-1-4405-0672-7; *The Everything®
Vegetarian Slow Cooker Cookbook* by Amy Snyder and Justin Snyder, copyright © 2012 by F+W Media, Inc., ISBN 10:
1-4405-2858-6, ISBN 13: 978-1-4405-2858-3; and *The Everything® Vegetarian Cookbook* by Jay Weinstein, copyright © 2002
by F+W Media, Inc., ISBN 10: 1-58062-640-8; ISBN 13: 978-1-58062-640-8.

ISBN 10: 1-4405-8147-9
ISBN 13: 978-1-4405-8147-2
eISBN 10: 1-4405-8148-7
eISBN 13: 978-1-4405-8148-9

Printed in the United States of America.

10 9 8 7 6 5 4 3 2 1

Library of Congress Cataloging-in-Publication Data
The big book of one pot recipes.
    pages cm
    Includes index.
    ISBN-13: 978-1-4405-8147-2 (pb)
    ISBN-10: 1-4405-8147-9 (pb)
    ISBN-13: 978-1-4405-8148-9 (ebook)
    ISBN-10: 1-4405-8148-7 (ebook)
    1. One-dish meals. 2. Quick and easy cooking. I. Adams Media.
    TX840.O53B54 2014
    641.82--dc23
                                        2014015638

Many of the designations used by manufacturers and sellers to distinguish their product are claimed as
trademarks. Where those designations appear in this book and F+W Media, Inc. was aware of a trademark claim,
the designations have been printed with initial capital letters.

Always follow safety and commonsense cooking protocol while using kitchen utensils, operating ovens and
stoves, and handling uncooked food. If children are assisting in the preparation of any recipe, they should always
be supervised by an adult.

Cover images © iStockphoto.com/Petegar; 123RF/ Peter Zijlstra.

This book is available at quantity discounts for bulk purchases.
For information, please call 1-800-289-0963.

CONTENTS

4 Soups, Stews, and Chilies 141

5 Pasta, Rice, Beans, and Grains 213

6 Poultry 267

7 Beef, Pork, and Lamb.......333

INTRODUCTION

TODAY IT SEEMS LIKE EVERYONE is always on the go. And whether you're working full time, raising a growing family, or are just plain busy, the thought of cooking dinner—let alone washing all those dishes after the fact!—can feel overwhelming. Fortunately, *The Big Book of One Pot Recipes* is here to make mealtime easier.

Throughout this book you'll find more than 500 one pot recipes devoted to making that kitchen cleanup as easy as possible. With recipes ranging from Baked French Toast with Toasted-Pecan Maple Syrup for breakfast to Chicken Breast Rotolo with Currant Stuffing for dinner to the Chocolate Chip Skillet Cookie for dessert, you'll find that cleanup is a breeze no matter what meal you're making.

And, in addition to being easy to clean up, the recipes found throughout are also easy to make. You'll find simple skillet recipes like the Shrimp and Artichoke Fettuccine, quick casserole dishes like the Ham and Sweet Potato Casserole, and pressure cooker and slow cooker dishes like Cashew Chicken and Slow-Cooked Mushroom Steak and Vegetables. You'll also find simple saucepan meals as well as dishes made in a Dutch oven or a deep fryer. But no matter what you're whipping up— or how—with *The Big Book of One Pot Recipes*, you'll have a no-mess dinner on the table in no time. Enjoy!

CHAPTER 1

BREAKFAST AND BRUNCH

CRUSTLESS COTTAGE CHEESE QUICHE

Vary the vegetables according to your family's tastes. You can use something as simple as peas and carrots or as varied as your favorite stir-fry vegetable mix. Just be sure to thaw the frozen vegetables before you add them to the egg mixture.

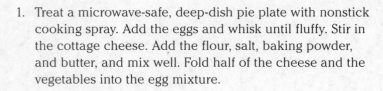

Yields 4–6 servings

Nonstick cooking spray

5 large eggs

½ pound cottage cheese

¼ cup all-purpose flour

⅛ teaspoon salt

½ teaspoon baking powder

¼ cup melted butter

½ pound Monterey jack cheese, grated

½ 10-ounce package frozen vegetables

3 green onions, chopped

1. Treat a microwave-safe, deep-dish pie plate with nonstick cooking spray. Add the eggs and whisk until fluffy. Stir in the cottage cheese. Add the flour, salt, baking powder, and butter, and mix well. Fold half of the cheese and the vegetables into the egg mixture.

2. Cover the filled pie plate with a paper towel to prevent splatters. Microwave for 6 minutes. Let rest for 1 minute, then remove the paper towel.

3. Top with the remaining cheese. Sprinkle the green onions over the cheese.

4. Microwave for an additional 5 minutes, or until the cheese is melted and the quiche is set.

"Eggsact" Measurement

A large egg typically is equal to ¼ cup or 2 ounces. Adjust the number of eggs if the ones you're using are smaller. Large eggs can be double the size of smaller ones. The egg carton will tell you whether your eggs are large or small.

BAKED CORNMEAL MUSH WITH CHEESE AND EGGS

This brunch dish is delicious topped with some salsa. For an Italian spin, substitute Parmigiano-Reggiano for the jack cheese and top it with some marinara sauce.

Yields 8 servings

4 tablespoons butter

3 cups cornmeal mush

1 cup sour cream

1 cup Monterey jack cheese, grated

1 cup Cheddar cheese, grated

8 large eggs

Salt to taste

Freshly ground black pepper

1. Preheat oven to 350°F.

2. Melt the butter and add it to a 9" × 13" nonstick baking pan, turning the pan to coat the bottom.

3. Cut the cornmeal mush into cubes and mix it with the sour cream until it reaches the consistency of thick cake batter. If it's too thick, add more sour cream or some heavy cream or milk. Add the jack cheese and half of the Cheddar cheese; mix to combine. Spread the mixture across the bottom of the baking pan. Bake for 15 minutes.

4. Remove the pan from the oven. Press a small glass into the mush to make 8 equally spaced indentations across the pan. Crack an egg into each indentation. Top each egg with salt, if using, and some pepper. Sprinkle the remaining Cheddar cheese over the top.

5. Bake for an additional 15 minutes, or until the eggs are set as desired and the cheese is melted. Cut into 8 wedges. Serve hot or at room temperature.

Cornmeal Mush by Any Other Name

"Cornmeal mush" is simply the countrified name for polenta. Like polenta, it's typically made with yellow cornmeal. Grits are a similar dish made with white cornmeal. Regardless of what you call it, Baked Cornmeal Mush with Cheese and Eggs is also a great way to use leftover cornmeal mush, polenta, or grits.

WELSH RAREBIT

Welsh Rarebit is a versatile dish. You can use more Worcestershire sauce and choose the beer based on the bread you'll serve it with; a hearty bread like pumpernickel, for example, goes better with stronger flavors than does a sweet challah or brioche.

Yields 6 servings

1 tablespoon butter

Pinch cayenne pepper or hot sauce to taste

1 teaspoon Worcestershire sauce

⅔ cup warm beer

1 pound sharp Cheddar cheese, grated

2 teaspoons cornstarch

1 teaspoon dry mustard

6 thick slices bread, toasted

Optional: tomato slices

Optional: bacon

Optional: 6 poached or fried eggs

1. In a nonstick saucepan, melt the butter and stir in the cayenne pepper or hot sauce and Worcestershire sauce over medium heat. Add the beer and bring to a simmer. Lower the heat to medium-low or low; melting the cheese over a low temperature prevents it from separating into a greasy mess.

2. Toss the cheese with the cornstarch and dry mustard. Add it to the beer mixture. Stir occasionally until the cheese is melted.

3. Place the toast on individual plates and top with the Welsh Rarebit.

4. To serve with the optional ingredients, place the toast on individual plates. Top each slice of toast with a tomato slice, crisscrossed bacon slices, and an egg. Top with the Welsh Rarebit.

BACON, BROCCOLI, AND CHEESE QUICHE

This quiche can easily be adapted to match whatever you happen to have in your fridge. Substitute other leftover vegetables or use American cheese slices instead of the Cheddar. Just keep in mind that the cooler the temperature of the filling, the longer it'll take the quiche to bake.

Yields 4–8 servings

1 9" deep-dish frozen pie crust, thawed

8 slices cooked bacon, chopped

½ cup Cheddar cheese, grated

1 cup cooked broccoli florets

6 large eggs

¼ cup milk or heavy cream

Salt and freshly ground black pepper to taste

1. Preheat oven to 350°F.

2. Spread the bacon evenly over the bottom of the pie crust. Top with the cheese. Place the broccoli over the bacon and cheese.

3. Whisk the eggs together with the milk or cream and seasoning. Carefully pour the egg mixture over the ingredients in the pie crust.

4. Bake for 35–45 minutes, or until the center of the pie is set. Let sit for 10 minutes before slicing. Serve warm or at room temperature.

QUICHE LORRAINE

The ham will already be salty, so be careful about how much salt you add to the egg mixture. The optional Dijon mustard and mayonnaise punch up the flavor.

Yields 4–8 servings

6 large eggs

1 tablespoon all-purpose flour

1 cup milk

Salt and freshly ground pepper to taste

Optional: dash of cayenne pepper to taste

Optional: ½ teaspoon Dijon mustard

Optional: 1 tablespoon mayonnaise

½ pound Swiss cheese, grated

½ pound cooked ham, cut into cubes

1 9" unbaked pie shell

1. Preheat oven to 350°F.

2. Beat the eggs with the flour, then stir in the milk. Add salt, pepper, cayenne, mustard, and mayonnaise, if using. Fold in the cheese and ham. Pour into the pie shell.

3. Place the pie shell on a baking sheet or jellyroll pan and put in the oven. Bake for 40–45 minutes, or until the eggs are set. Let rest for 10 minutes before cutting into wedges. Serve warm or at room temperature.

COTTAGE CHEESE CASSEROLE

This recipe was tested using a Birds Eye Steamfresh vegetable mixture of asparagus, gold and white corn, and baby carrots. The vegetables were microwave "steamed" for 5 minutes. If you prefer a vegetable mixture without corn, omit the cornmeal and use ¼ cup flour instead.

Yields 4–8 servings

Nonstick cooking spray

6 large eggs

1 pound cottage cheese

¼ cup unbleached all-purpose flour

⅛ teaspoon salt

½ teaspoon baking powder

¼ cup melted butter

1 pound Cheddar cheese, grated

1 12-ounce package frozen vegetables, thawed

Optional: chopped red onion, shallots, or green onions to taste

1. Preheat oven to 325°F if using a Pyrex pie pan or 350°F if using a metal pie pan.

2. Treat an ovenproof, deep-dish pie pan with nonstick cooking spray. Add the eggs and whisk until fluffy. Stir in the cottage cheese. Add the flour, salt, baking powder, and butter, and mix well. Fold the cheese and the vegetables into the egg mixture. Add the onion, shallots, or green onions, if using.

3. Bake for 40–45 minutes, or until the top is lightly browned. Let rest for 10 minutes before cutting into wedges for serving.

Serving Suggestions

The baked recipe will serve 4 as a standalone breakfast or brunch dish. To stretch it to 8 servings, serve it with some brown-and-serve sausages and toasted English muffins or bagels.

BAKED MONTE CRISTO BRUNCH CASSEROLE

The quality of the bread you use makes a big difference in how good the end result will taste. This recipe is traditionally made with classic white bread, but for a slightly sweeter, richer taste, use challah or brioche.

Yields 4–8 servings

4 large eggs

½ cup milk or heavy cream

Optional: salt and freshly ground black pepper to taste

Optional: dash of cayenne pepper

Optional: Dijon mustard to taste

8 teaspoons butter

8 slices bread

8 teaspoons mayonnaise

8 slices Swiss cheese

4 thick slices cooked ham

1. Preheat oven to 350°F.

2. Beat the eggs, milk, and optional ingredients, if using, together in a shallow bowl.

3. Spread butter over one side of each slice of bread, and spread the mayonnaise on the other side. Dip 4 slices of the bread in the egg mixture and assemble them butter side down in the baking pan.

4. Top each slice of bread with a slice of Swiss cheese, a slice of ham, and then another slice of Swiss cheese. Place the remaining 4 slices of bread on top, mayonnaise side down.

5. Pour the remaining egg mixture over the top of the bread. Bake for 40–45 minutes, or until the cheese is melted and the eggs are set. Let rest for 10 minutes before cutting into serving pieces.

HAM AND CHEESE CORNBREAD

The American cheese will satisfy younger tastes. Adults might prefer it made with Swiss or Cheddar cheese. You can either use chopped cooked ham or thinly sliced boiled ham.

Yields 4–8 servings

2 tablespoons butter or bacon grease

1 large yellow onion, thinly sliced

1 large clove garlic, minced

¼ teaspoon chili powder

½ cup unsalted peanuts, chopped

Freshly ground black pepper to taste

1 10-ounce package cornbread mix

1 large egg, beaten

½ cup milk

½ pound cooked ham

3 slices American cheese

Optional: sliced pimiento-stuffed olives

1. Preheat oven to 350°F.

2. Melt the butter or bacon grease in a 12" cast-iron or ovenproof skillet over medium heat. Add the onion, garlic, and chili powder, and sauté until the onion slices are transparent. Remove from the heat and stir in the peanuts and freshly ground pepper. Stir to mix well.

3. Once the pan has cooled, add the cornbread mix, egg, and milk; combine with the onion mixture. Spread evenly over the bottom of the pan and top with the ham.

4. Bake for 15 minutes, or until cornbread is still moist but a toothpick comes out clean. Top with the cheese and return to the oven; bake for an additional 5 minutes, or until the cheese is melted. Garnish with olive slices, if desired.

BASIC OMELET

Using milk in the batter makes an omelet runny, but if you want a richer-tasting dish, substitute an equal amount of heavy cream for the water. Heating the pan and then the oil and butter before you add the egg batter results in a lighter, fluffier omelet.

Yields 1 or 2 servings

3 large eggs, at room temperature

1 tablespoon water or heavy cream

Salt and freshly ground pepper to taste

½ tablespoon peanut or vegetable oil

½ tablespoon butter

Cheese, cooked meat, or vegetables for filling

1. Whisk the eggs with the water or cream and salt and pepper. Bring a 10" nonstick skillet to temperature over medium-high heat, and then add the oil and the butter. Once the butter is melted and starts to foam, pour in the egg mixture. Tilt the pan to distribute the egg mixture evenly around the pan.

2. Lower the heat to medium and continue to cook until the eggs are almost set, occasionally tilting the pan to move any uncooked egg mixture evenly across the omelet. Once the eggs are almost set, distribute the fillings across the half of the omelet that's opposite from the skillet handle.

3. If necessary, use a spatula to loosen the edges of the omelet from the skillet. Give the pan a shake to ensure the omelet will slide out of the pan, then slide it onto a serving plate, using the pan to fold the omelet in half. Top with some additional freshly ground pepper, if desired, and serve hot.

BASIC FRITTATA

A frittata is basically an unfolded omelet that's topped with precooked meat, vegetables, and cheese and then finished under the broiler. That finishing step allows you to add a bit more filling than you can to an omelet.

Yields 4 servings

6 large eggs, at room temperature

2 tablespoons water

Salt and freshly ground black pepper to taste

½ tablespoon peanut or vegetable oil

½ tablespoon butter

Cheese, cooked meat, or vegetables for toppings

1. Whisk the eggs with the water, salt, and pepper. Bring a 10" ovenproof, nonstick skillet to temperature over medium-high heat, then add the oil and butter. Once the butter is melted and starts to foam, pour in the egg mixture. Tilt the pan to distribute the mixture evenly around the pan.

2. Lower the heat to medium and continue to cook until the eggs begin to set, occasionally tilting the pan to move any uncooked egg mixture evenly across it. Once the eggs start to set, distribute the toppings across the entire top of the frittata.

3. Place the pan in the oven and broil until the eggs are set and the cheese is melted and begins to bubble. Remove from the broiler and let the frittata rest for 2 minutes. Slice as a pie and serve hot or at room temperature. You can stretch the frittata to 8 servings if you serve it with a salad.

ASPARAGUS FRITTATA

This recipe shows an alternative one pot way to make a frittata by first sautéing the vegetable fillings in the pan and then adding the egg mixture and topping it all with some cheese.

Yields 6 servings

6 large eggs

2 tablespoons whipping cream

½ teaspoon salt

¼ teaspoon freshly ground black pepper

1 tablespoon olive oil

1 tablespoon butter

1 pound asparagus, trimmed, cut into ¼" to ½" pieces

1 tomato, seeded, diced

3 ounces fontina cheese, diced

1. Whisk the eggs, cream, salt, and pepper together in a medium-size bowl and set aside until needed.

2. Bring a 10" ovenproof, nonstick skillet to temperature over medium heat, then add the oil and the butter. Once the butter is melted, add the asparagus and sauté until crisp-tender, about 2 minutes. Increase the heat to medium-high. Add the tomato and an additional pinch of salt, if desired, and sauté 2 minutes longer. Pour the egg mixture over the asparagus mixture and cook until the eggs begin to set. Sprinkle with the cheese. Reduce heat to medium-low and cook for an additional 2 minutes.

3. Place the skillet under the broiler. Broil until the eggs are set and the cheese is golden brown on top, about 5 minutes. Remove from the broiler and let the frittata rest for 2 minutes. Slice as a pie and serve.

HASH BROWNS WITH SAUSAGE AND APPLES

Depending on how the cooked sausage you're using is seasoned, you can substitute sage or fennel leaves or seeds for the thyme. Or, if you prefer, use a mixture of all of them.

Yields 4 servings

2 tablespoons olive oil

1 tablespoon butter

5 cups frozen shredded hash brown potatoes

Salt and freshly ground pepper to taste

1½ teaspoons snipped fresh thyme

6 ounces cooked smoked sausage, coarsely chopped

1 medium apple, cut into thin slices

Optional: 1–2 tablespoons toasted walnuts, chopped

Optional: 1–2 tablespoons maple syrup

1. Heat the oil and 1 tablespoon butter in a 10" seasoned cast-iron or nonstick skillet over medium heat. Add the hash brown potatoes and cook for 8–10 minutes, stirring occasionally, until they are thawed and beginning to brown. Stir in the salt, pepper, and thyme. Use a wide metal spatula to press the potatoes down firmly in the pan.

2. Add the sausage and apple over the top of the potatoes. Cover and cook for 10 minutes, or until the apple is tender. Top with the toasted walnuts and drizzle with the maple syrup, if using. Cook uncovered for an additional 10 minutes, or until the hash browns are lightly browned on the bottom.

3. Use a spatula to loosen the potatoes from the pan and slide the dish onto a serving platter or serve from the pan.

Recipe Tweaks to Suit Your Tastes

Instead of using the sliced apple, you can toss the sausage with some apple butter before you add it atop the potatoes. Then add another flavor dimension by sprinkling some cinnamon over the dish when you add the nuts.

SLOW-COOKED IRISH OATMEAL WITH FRUIT

Feel free to substitute other dried fruit according to your taste. Add a dried fruit mixture like a tropical mix of coconut, papaya, pineapple, and mango, or add strawberries, apples, and blueberries. It's even a way you can sneak some prunes into your diet.

Yields 8–10 servings

2 cups steel-cut Irish oats

5 cups water

1 cup apple juice

¼ cup dried cranberries

¼ cup golden raisins

¼ cup snipped dried apricots

¼ cup maple syrup

1 teaspoon ground cinnamon

½ teaspoon salt

Optional: brown sugar or maple syrup to taste

Optional: chopped toasted walnuts or pecans to taste

Optional: milk, half-and-half, or heavy cream to taste

1. Add the oats, water, apple juice, cranberries, raisins, apricots, maple syrup, cinnamon, and salt to a 4-quart slow cooker and stir to mix.

2. Cover and cook on the low-heat setting for 6–7 hours, or on high for 3–3½ hours.

3. Serve the oatmeal warm topped with brown sugar or additional maple syrup, chopped nuts, and milk, half-and-half, or heavy cream.

Cooking Ahead

Once the oatmeal has cooled, divide any leftovers into single-serving, microwave-safe containers and freeze. When you're ready to start a new day, put it in the microwave to defrost. Cover the container with a paper towel to catch any splatters, then microwave on high for 1–2 minutes!

SAUSAGE AND CHEESE SCRAMBLE

You can stretch this recipe to even more servings by increasing the amount of chopped peppers you sauté with the onion. In fact, a mixture of red, green, and yellow peppers makes for a delicious combo.

Yields 8 servings

1 tablespoon extra-virgin olive oil

1 large yellow onion, diced

1 green bell pepper, diced

1 pound ground sausage

4 cups frozen hash brown potatoes

8 large eggs

¼ cup water or heavy cream

Optional: a few drops hot sauce

Salt and freshly ground pepper to taste

½ pound Cheddar cheese, grated

1. Preheat an electric skillet to medium-high or heat a deep 3½-quart nonstick sauté pan over medium-high heat and add the oil. Once the oil is heated, add the onion and pepper and sauté until the onion is transparent, about 5 minutes. Add the sausage and cook for 5 minutes, or until browned, breaking it apart as it cooks. Remove any excess fat, if necessary, by carefully dabbing the pan with a paper towel. Add the hash browns and cook covered for 10 minutes, or until the hash browns are tender and the sausage is cooked through. Stir to combine well.

2. Whisk together the eggs, water or heavy cream, hot sauce (if using), and salt and pepper. Remove the lid from the pan and pour the eggs over the sausage-potato mixture. Stir to combine and scramble the eggs until they begin to set. Add the cheese and continue to scramble until the eggs finish cooking and the cheese melts. If you prefer, instead of stirring the cheese into the mixture, you can top it with the cheese; then cover the skillet and continue to cook for 1–2 minutes or until the cheese is melted. Serve immediately.

Cooking with Your Feet Up

As long as you can position it so the cord is safely out of the way, you can fix this meal in an electric skillet at the table. Chop the vegetables the night before and mix the eggs together in a jar with a tight lid. You'll be able to sit down to cook while you savor your first cup of coffee.

BAKED FRENCH TOAST WITH TOASTED-PECAN MAPLE SYRUP

You do most of the work for this dish the night before, so you can have it ready within an hour the next morning. Have maple or raspberry syrup available at the table for those who wish to add it.

Yields 8–10 servings

1 16-ounce loaf challah or brioche

Butter to cover baking dish plus ¾ cup butter for topping

8 large eggs

1 cup heavy cream

2 cups milk

2 tablespoons granulated sugar

1 tablespoon vanilla extract

½ teaspoon ground cinnamon

½ teaspoon ground nutmeg

Dash salt

1 cup packed light brown sugar

1 cup chopped pecans

2 tablespoons light corn syrup

½ teaspoon ground cinnamon

½ teaspoon ground nutmeg

1. Slice the bread into 20 1"-thick slices. Generously butter a 9" × 13" flat baking dish. Arrange the bread slices in two rows, overlapping the slices.

2. Whisk the eggs, cream, milk, sugar, vanilla, cinnamon, nutmeg, and salt until blended but not too bubbly. Pour the egg mixture evenly over all of the bread slices. Cover the pan with plastic wrap or foil and refrigerate overnight.

3. The next day, preheat the oven to 350°F. While the oven is coming to temperature, remove the baking pan from the refrigerator so that the French toast mixture begins to come to room temperature.

4. Melt the ¾ cup butter and mix with the brown sugar, pecans, corn syrup, cinnamon, and nutmeg. Remove the foil or plastic wrap from the baking pan, and spread the pecan mixture evenly over the bread. Bake uncovered for 45 minutes, or until puffed and lightly golden. Serve warm.

HOMEMADE GRANOLA

Coconut oil contains no trans fat, but it does contain lauric acid. When it is consumed, lauric acid transforms to monolaurin, which is believed to strengthen the immune system. Coconut oil proponents also claim it stimulates the metabolism.

Yields 12 servings

¾ cup cold-pressed, organic coconut oil

½ cup honey

4 cups old-fashioned rolled oats

2 cups sweetened shredded coconut

2 cups slivered or whole almonds

1 cup raw unsalted cashews

1½ cups small-diced dried apricots

1 cup small-diced dried figs

1 cup dried cherries

1 cup dried cranberries

1. Preheat the oven to 250°F.

2. Add the oil and honey to a large microwave-safe bowl. Microwave until the oil is liquid and can be whisked into the honey. Mix in the oats, coconut, almonds, and cashews using a wooden spoon to stir until all the dry ingredients are coated. Pour onto a 13" × 18" × 1" sheet pan. Stirring with a spatula every 15 minutes, bake for 75 minutes, or until the mixture turns a nice, even, golden brown. Remove the granola from the oven and allow to cool, stirring occasionally. Toss with the apricots, figs, cherries, and cranberries. Store in an airtight container for up to 2 weeks.

Alternate Recipe: Maple-Walnut Granola

Substitute chopped walnuts for half of the almonds and the cashews. Use ½ cup maple syrup and ¼ light brown sugar instead of the honey, and raisins instead of dried apricots.

RED FLANNEL HASH

The beets in this dish turn corned beef hash into red flannel hash.

Yields 4 servings

8 ounces salt pork or bacon, diced

2 tablespoons butter or vegetable oil

1 small yellow onion, diced

2½ cups frozen hash brown potatoes, thawed

8 ounces cooked corned beef, chopped

1 16-ounce can beets, drained and diced

1 tablespoon dried parsley

1 teaspoon Worcestershire sauce

¼ cup half-and-half or heavy cream

4 large eggs

Salt and freshly ground black pepper to taste

1. Add the salt pork or bacon to a large nonstick or well-seasoned cast-iron skillet; cook over medium heat until the fat begins to render from the meat. Add the butter or oil and stir in the onions; sauté for 5 minutes, or until the onion is transparent. Stir in the potatoes; stir-fry until the potatoes begin to brown. Add the corned beef, beets, parsley, Worcestershire sauce, and the half-and-half or cream. Mix well. Carefully stir-fry until the hash mixture is cooked through, or until the potatoes are done and the meat and beets are warm.

2. Lower the heat. Press the hash down into the pan to form a round cake. Fry over low without stirring for 10 minutes, or until the bottom begins to brown and forms a crisp crust. Use the back of a spoon to make 4 indentations in the hash; break an egg into each indentation. Cover the skillet and cook for 3 minutes, or until the eggs are done to your taste. Taste for seasoning and add salt and pepper, if needed.

APPLE PANCAKE

Serve this for a special occasion brunch along with some brown-and-serve sausages and some cinnamon ice cream on the side.

Yields 4 servings

4 tablespoons butter

2 tablespoons granulated sugar

⅛ teaspoon ground nutmeg

¼ teaspoon ground cinnamon

4 tart apples, peeled, cored, and sliced thin

4 eggs

1 cup milk

¼ teaspoon salt

½ cup all-purpose flour

1 teaspoon vanilla extract

1. Preheat oven to 375°F.

2. Melt butter in a 10" ovenproof skillet or German pancake pan over medium heat. Add 1 tablespoon of the sugar, the nutmeg, cinnamon, and apple slices to the pan; sauté and stir for 8 minutes, or until the apples start to soften and the sugar starts to brown.

3. Add the remaining 1 tablespoon of sugar, the eggs, milk, salt, flour, and vanilla to a bowl; whisk to combine. Gently pour the pancake batter into the pan, keeping the apples as a separate layer on bottom. Move to the oven and bake for 10 minutes, or until puffed and almost firm. Slide onto a large plate, cut into wedges, and serve.

HAM AND RED-EYE GRAVY

It's legend that General Andrew Jackson told his cook, who had been drinking the night before, that for breakfast he wanted ham with gravy as red as his eyes. This gave ham gravy a new name. Serve with biscuits, if you like.

Yields 4 servings

4 slices country ham, ¼" thick

1 cup hot coffee

2 tablespoons brown sugar

1. Place a skillet over medium heat. Place 1 or 2 ham slices in the skillet and cook each side for 3–5 minutes, or until the ham is browned and the fat has rendered. Remove ham from the skillet and keep warm; repeat with the remaining ham slices.

2. Add ½ cup coffee to the skillet with the brown sugar. Stir until it is melted. Add the ham slices back to the skillet, cover, and cook 3 minutes. Remove the ham to a plate and keep warm.

3. Discard any pieces of fat in the skillet. Add the rest of the coffee. Increase the heat to medium-high, and stir to remove any stuck-on bits. Simmer for 3 minutes.

4. Pour the gravy over the ham and serve while warm.

BIRD IN A NEST

To make this a one pot breakfast, you can fry a slice of bacon in the skillet and then cook the nest in the drippings. And to make it fancier you can garnish it with pesto, a sun-dried tomato, some chopped olives, or a roasted red pepper strip.

Yields 1 serving

1 tablespoon butter or vegetable oil

1 small garlic clove, peeled and smashed

1 piece thick-cut crusty bread

1 large egg

Pinch salt

Pinch pepper

1 tablespoon shredded cheese

1. Place a small skillet over medium-low heat. Add the butter and let it melt. Once the butter has melted, add the garlic to the skillet. Fry for 1 minute on each side and then remove from the skillet.

2. Use a biscuit cutter or small glass to cut a hole in the center of the bread. Place the slice of bread in the skillet and press slightly. Crack the egg and drop it in the hole. Season with a pinch of salt and pepper.

3. Cook for 3 minutes. Once the egg has started to firm up, flip the nest over. Sprinkle the cheese on top of the nest. Cook for 2 minutes, turn off the heat, and let the nest sit in the skillet until ready to serve.

CORNED BEEF HASH

If you happen to have any leftover Basic Beef Roast or Oven-Braised Pork Roast (see recipes in Chapter 7), you can use it to make this dish.

Yields 4–6 servings

1 tablespoon butter

3 tablespoons olive oil

1 medium onion, finely chopped

1 garlic clove, minced

2–3 cups chopped, cooked beef or pork roast

2–3 cups peeled, chopped potatoes

Salt to taste

Pepper to taste

1. Place a skillet over medium heat. Once it is heated through add the butter and oil. Stir in the onion and cook for 4–5 minutes. Add the garlic and cook for 1 minute.

2. Add the beef and potatoes to the skillet. Spread them evenly across the surface of the pan and increase the heat to medium-high. Press down on the mixture frequently with a spatula. Do not stir.

3. Cook the first side for 6–9 minutes. Lift a section in the middle up to see if the bottom is browning. Once it is browned, flip the contents over in sections so the other side can brown. Cook the second side for 4–7 minutes.

4. Remove it from the heat, season with salt and pepper, and serve with crusty bread and fried eggs for breakfast.

APPLE STREUSEL OATMEAL

Get creative and turn any of your favorite desserts into a breakfast oatmeal.

Yields 2 servings

¾ cup water

1 cup milk or soymilk

1 cup quick-cooking oats

2 apples, peeled, cored, and diced

2 tablespoons brown sugar

2 teaspoons cinnamon

2 tablespoons chopped pecans

1. Place all of the ingredients in a pressure cooker.

2. Lock the lid into place. Bring to high pressure and maintain for 5 minutes. Remove from the heat and allow pressure to release naturally.

3. Remove the lid and stir the oatmeal, adding more milk if desired.

IRISH OATMEAL WITH FRUIT

You can substitute other dried fruit according to your tastes. Try prunes, dates, or cherries for different flavors.

Yields 2 servings

3 cups water

1 cup toasted steel-cut oats

2 teaspoons butter

1 cup apple juice

1 tablespoon dried cranberries

1 tablespoon golden raisins

1 tablespoon snipped dried apricots

1 tablespoon maple syrup

¼ teaspoon ground cinnamon

Pinch salt

1. Place a rack in a pressure cooker; pour ½ cup water over the rack.

2. In a metal bowl that will fit inside the pressure cooker and rest on the rack, add the remaining 2½ cups water, oats, butter, apple juice, cranberries, raisins, apricots, maple syrup, cinnamon, and salt; stir to combine.

3. Lock the lid into place. Bring to low pressure. For chewy oatmeal, maintain the pressure for 5 minutes. For creamy oatmeal, maintain pressure for 8 minutes.

4. Remove from the heat and allow pressure to release naturally. Use tongs to lift the metal bowl out of the pressure cooker.

Cooking Ahead

If you're not a morning person, you can make Irish Oatmeal with Fruit the night before. Once it's cooled, divide between two covered microwave-safe containers and refrigerate overnight. The next morning, cover each bowl with a paper towel to catch any splatters and then microwave on high for 1–2 minutes or until heated through.

GRITS

Slowly adding grits to boiling water, while gently stirring, will help prevent clumping.

Yields 4 servings

4 cups water

1 teaspoon salt

½ teaspoon black pepper

1 cup stone-ground grits

1 tablespoon butter

1. Bring the water, salt, and pepper to a boil in a pressure cooker over high heat. Slowly stir in the grits.

2. Lock the lid into place. Bring to high pressure and maintain for 10 minutes. Remove from the heat and allow pressure to release naturally.

3. Remove the lid and stir in butter before serving.

Grits

Grits are a Southern breakfast staple that are served topped with butter or margarine, salt, pepper, and sometimes cheese. It's very similar to polenta, especially when polenta is served creamy.

HASH BROWNS

Let Waffle House inspire you to serve these hash browns any way you'd like—scattered, covered, or smothered.

Yields 4 servings

4 cups russet potatoes, peeled and grated

2 tablespoons olive oil

2 tablespoons butter

Salt and freshly ground pepper, to taste

1. Prepare the potatoes and set aside.

2. Add the oil and butter to a pressure cooker and bring to temperature over medium heat.

3. Add the hash brown potatoes; sauté for 5 minutes, stirring occasionally, until they are just beginning to brown. Season with the salt and pepper.

4. Use a wide metal spatula to press the potatoes down firmly in the pan.

5. Lock the lid in place and bring to low pressure; maintain pressure for 6 minutes. Remove from the heat and quick-release the pressure.

Preparing the Potatoes

Rinsing and thoroughly drying the grated potatoes will help you achieve a delicious crispy brown exterior on your hash browns. After grating the potatoes, pour them into a colander and let sit under running cold water for 1 minute. Once done, let the potatoes air-dry or use a towel to remove excess water before cooking.

HOME FRIES

Like hash browns, home fries can also be served with a variety of toppings or plain with a side of ketchup.

Yields 4 servings

2 tablespoons olive oil

4 cups red potatoes, diced

1½ teaspoons paprika

1 teaspoon chili powder

1½ teaspoons salt

1 teaspoon black pepper

1. Bring the olive oil to medium heat in a pressure cooker. Add the potatoes and sauté for about 3 minutes.

2. Add all remaining ingredients and stir. Lock the lid in place and bring to high pressure; maintain pressure for 7 minutes. Remove from the heat and quick-release the pressure.

TURKEY AND BELL PEPPER SCRAMBLE

Serve with toasted whole-grain bread or biscuits spread with some honey-butter. Experiment with different types of cheese to find your favorite.

Yields 8 servings

1 tablespoon olive oil or vegetable oil

1 large sweet onion, diced

1 green bell pepper, seeded and diced

1 red bell pepper, seeded and diced

1 yellow or orange bell pepper, seeded and diced

1 pound ground turkey

1 1-pound bag frozen hash browns, thawed

8 large eggs

¼ cup water or heavy cream

Salt and freshly ground pepper, to taste

½ pound Cheddar cheese, grated

1. Add the oil to a pressure cooker and bring it to temperature over medium-high heat.

2. Add the onion and diced bell peppers; sauté until the onion is transparent, about 5 minutes. Stir in the sausage and hash browns.

3. Bring to low pressure; maintain for 10 minutes. Remove from the heat and quick-release the pressure. Remove the lid. Drain and discard any excess fat.

4. Return the pan to medium heat. Whisk together the eggs, water or heavy cream, hot sauce (if using), and salt and pepper.

5. Pour the eggs over the sausage-potato mixture. Stir to combine and scramble the eggs until they begin to set.

6. Add the cheese and continue to scramble until the eggs finish cooking and the cheese melts.

7. If you prefer, instead of stirring the cheese into the mixture, you can top it with the cheese, then cover the pressure cooker and continue to cook for 1–2 minutes or until the cheese is melted. Serve immediately.

FRENCH TOAST

You can use any flavoring extract in place of the vanilla. You can also grate citrus zest and whisk it into the eggs to make flavored French toast. This recipe can easily be doubled.

Yields 2 servings

3 tablespoons vegetable oil

3 eggs

3 tablespoons milk

¼ teaspoon vanilla extract

6 slices bread

Butter, as needed for topping

Maple syrup, as needed for topping

1. Place a skillet over medium heat and add 1 tablespoon vegetable oil.

2. While the skillet heats, crack the eggs into a wide, shallow bowl and whisk in the milk and vanilla extract.

3. Once the skillet is heated and the egg mixture is thoroughly combined, dip the bread slices into the mixture so each side is coated. Swirl the oil in the skillet if necessary so the bottom is evenly coated. Place two slices of dipped bread in the skillet.

4. Let the bread cook for 2–3 minutes on each side, or until the bread is golden brown. Place on a plate and keep warm while repeating with the remaining slices of bread.

5. Serve warm with butter and maple syrup.

Is French Toast Really French?

The short answer is that no one really knows. There were mentions of this dish in medieval times in England and France. And the *Oxford English Dictionary* has an eggless version listed in 1660. But the name French Toast came about in the late 1800s alongside Egg Toast, Spanish Toast, and German Toast.

STUFFED FRENCH TOAST

The good thing about this dish is that you can use just about any berry in the stuffing. If your berries are large, like blackberries, cut them into halves or quarters.

Yields 4 servings

1 loaf Vienna bread

6 ounces cream cheese

2 tablespoons honey

¼ teaspoon salt

1 pint strawberries, stemmed and sliced

1 tablespoon butter

4 eggs, beaten well

1. Cut the ends off the bread to get a rectangular loaf. Cut four 1½"-thick slices from the bread. Cut the ends in half. Take a skinny knife and cut a pocket into the bread.

2. In a small bowl, mix the cream cheese, honey, and salt. Use a knife to spread ¼ of the cream cheese in each bread pocket. Place several strawberry pieces in each pocket. Take one of the chunks cut from the end of the loaf and wedge it into the pocket opening.

3. Heat a griddle over medium heat, and once it's heated melt the butter evenly across the surface of the griddle.

4. Carefully dunk each slice of bread into the egg, making sure all of the bread is coated. Carefully place the cut end of the bread on the griddle and cook for 2 minutes before laying the bread on its side. This seals the opening to prevent the cheese from leaking out. Repeat with each slice, cooking the bread for 3–4 minutes on each side until golden brown. Serve immediately.

BLINI

These thin, Russian-style pancakes are great served with sweet fruit jam or honey, or with sour cream and caviar. They're traditionally made from a yeast-based mix, but this quick-rising batter makes for faster cooking.

Yields 15 pancakes

2 eggs, beaten

1 tablespoon sugar

¼ teaspoon salt

½ cup all-purpose flour

½ teaspoon baking powder

2½ cups milk

2 tablespoons vegetable oil

¼ cup soft butter for spreading

1. Whisk together the eggs, sugar, and salt in a large bowl. Sift the flour and baking powder over the bowl and pour the milk on top. Mix until blended.

2. Place a skillet over medium heat and brush the surface of the pan with a little of the oil.

3. Pour 2 tablespoons of batter onto the skillet surface and gently rotate the skillet on a slight angle to spread it out evenly.

4. When the edges start to crisp and the center looks dry, use a spatula to flip the pancake. Cook 1 minute, or until the other side is lightly browned and then move it to a plate.

5. Spread butter on the pancakes and keep them warm in a stack until ready to serve.

PERFECT SUNNY-FRIED EGG

Eggs come in different sizes. Most baking recipes call for large eggs, but any size will work here.

Yields 1 serving

2 eggs

2 tablespoons olive oil

Pinch salt

Pinch pepper

Optional: 2 tablespoons shredded
  Parmesan cheese

Optional: pinch red pepper flakes

1. Place a small skillet over low heat. Let it warm up for 5 minutes. Crack the eggs into a small bowl.

2. Add the oil to the skillet; swirl the skillet to coat the bottom and the sides. Wait 1 minute and then slowly pour the eggs into the skillet. Sprinkle salt, pepper, and, if using, cheese or red pepper flakes over the egg.

3. Cover the skillet and cook for 2–3 minutes to get a set white and a runny yolk, 3–4 minutes for a set white and a partially set yolk, 4–5 minutes for a set white and yolk.

4. Run a butter knife or spatula along the edges of the skillet and then slide the egg onto a plate.

ASPARAGUS AND LEEK FRITTATA

A 4" or 5" skillet works perfectly for this dish. Smaller skillets may be harder to find, but they're great for single servings and for when you just need to make a small amount of food.

Yields 1 serving

1 stalk of cooked asparagus, chopped

1 teaspoon unsalted butter

¼ cup chopped leeks

2 large eggs

2 tablespoons Parmesan cheese, shredded

2 tablespoons Gruyère, shredded

1 teaspoon chives, minced

Pinch salt

Pinch pepper

1. Steam the piece of asparagus if it isn't already cooked. Place a skillet over medium heat. Once it is warm add the butter and the leeks. Cook the leeks slowly and stir frequently for 8–10 minutes. Add the asparagus to the skillet.

2. Turn on the broiler. In a separate bowl, whisk together the eggs, cheese, chives, salt, and pepper. Once the leeks are soft and the asparagus is warmed, pour the egg mixture into the skillet. Let the eggs cook for 5–6 minutes without stirring.

3. Once the bottom and sides of the eggs are firm, place the skillet under the broiler about 4" from the heat. Let the frittata cook until the top of the eggs are lightly browned, about 4–5 minutes.

4. Remove the pan from the oven and while it is still hot, run a thin knife along the edges of the skillet to loosen the frittata. Slide the frittata onto a plate and serve immediately.

Frittatas, the Lazy Man's Omelet

Frittatas are the perfect way to use up small amounts of leftovers. A handful of leftover chicken, or any leftover vegetable, can be substituted in this recipe. Just make sure the filling is warm when the eggs are added. It's traditional in Naples for leftover pasta to be added to a frittata. Frittatas are almost always served well done, or firm.

EARLY AMERICAN JOHNNYCAKES

Historically these would have been fried in bacon fat, but vegetable oil will work just fine.

Yields 6–8 servings

1 cup cornmeal

1 teaspoon salt

1 teaspoon sugar

1½ cups boiling water

¼ cup vegetable oil or bacon drippings

1. Stir the dry ingredients in a bowl and whisk in the boiling water.

2. Place a griddle over medium-high heat. Once it's heated, add 2 tablespoons of the vegetable oil.

3. Drop the mixture onto the pan a few tablespoons at a time. Cook for 5 minutes before flipping and cooking the other side. Place them on a warmed plate until ready to serve with butter, maple syrup, or hot sauce.

Unleavened Bread

Baking powder and baking soda are the two most frequently used leaveners for dough. They create air pockets that give dough a lighter texture. But since baking soda wasn't common until the mid-1800s and baking powder wasn't invented until then, this recipe is probably very close to what would have been common fare before the Civil War.

PANCAKES

Pancake-like sweets have been eaten for thousands of years. The form we're used to became popular in Europe during medieval times.

Yields 8 4" pancakes

1½ cups flour

2 tablespoons sugar

2 teaspoons baking powder

½ teaspoon salt

1 large egg, beaten

1 cup milk

2 tablespoons vegetable oil

1. Stir together the flour, sugar, baking powder, and salt in a large bowl. Whisk together the egg, milk, and 1 tablespoon of oil in a small bowl.

2. Pour the liquid mixture into the dry ingredients. Stir together until all the flour is incorporated but the mixture is still lumpy.

3. Place a griddle over medium heat. Once it's heated through drizzle 1 teaspoon of oil over the pan and swirl to coat. Pour ¼ cup of batter for each pancake, and add more oil as needed.

4. Cook until the bottom is golden brown and bubbles appear on the top surface. Flip and cook until the bottom is golden. Place on a plate and keep warm.

SCONES

These Scottish baked goods take their name from the Stone of Destiny, also called Scone, where Scottish kings were once crowned. The traditional triangular shape is believed to resemble the crown.

Yields 8–10 servings

2 cups all-purpose flour

1 tablespoon baking powder

3 tablespoons sugar

¾ teaspoon salt

4 tablespoons butter, cold and cubed

½ cup dried fruit or nuts, chopped

¾ cup heavy cream

1 large egg, lightly beaten

1. Preheat oven to 400°F and place a griddle on a rack in the middle of the oven. Mix the flour, baking powder, sugar, and salt either in a food processor or by hand until well combined.

2. Add the butter and mix until it is coarse crumbs with a few larger chunks of butter, 12–14 pulses if using a food processor. Add the fruit or nuts and pulse quickly until combined.

3. Use a rubber spatula to stir in the cream and egg until a dough starts to form. Dump the mixture onto a floured surface and knead until it has come together but has a rough and sticky texture.

4. Pat the dough into a circle and use a sharp knife to cut it into eight triangular wedges. Place on the griddle and bake for 12–15 minutes. The tops should be golden brown when ready. Cool for 10 minutes before serving with butter, jam, or clotted cream.

WELSHCAKES

These cakes are a traditional treat served on March 1, St. David's Day. They are a cross between a scone, a pancake, and a cookie. They can be flavored with cinnamon, honey, or dried fruit.

Yields 20 cakes

½ cup cold butter, diced

1⅔ cups self-rising cake flour

¼ cup sugar, plus 2 tablespoons

¼ teaspoon allspice

¼ teaspoon cinnamon

1 large egg, beaten

1 tablespoon butter or vegetable oil

1. Cut the butter into the flour until it's a crumbly mix. Stir in ¼ cup of sugar and spices. Add the egg to make a dough that is soft, but not sticky. If the dough is sticky, add a tablespoon or two of flour.

2. Shape the dough into a disc, cover it with plastic wrap, and refrigerate for at least 30 minutes.

3. Flour a surface and roll the dough until it is ¼" thick. Use a biscuit cutter to make small cakes. Re-roll the scrap and cut more biscuits until you have used all the dough.

4. Place a griddle over medium heat. Once it's heated, grease the pan lightly. Add a few of the cakes and cook on each side for 3 minutes until golden brown. Keep them warm and sprinkle them with the remaining sugar. Serve while warm.

BACON AND SAUERKRAUT PANCAKES

The sauerkraut in this recipe can also be substituted with jarred kim chi if you like. Or you can add a diced chili pepper to make it spicy.

Yields 4 medium-size pancakes

1 cup sauerkraut

1¼ cups all-purpose flour

⅓ cup rice flour

1½ cups water

1 small potato, peeled and shredded

1 small onion, skinned and shredded

4 slices cooked bacon, crumbled

3 tablespoons vegetable oil

½ cup mustard or Sour Cream Mustard Dipping Sauce (see recipe in sidebar)

1. Place the sauerkraut in a small strainer and let it sit over a bowl for 30 minutes. Squeeze it regularly to remove as much of the moisture as possible. Combine the flours in a medium bowl. Slowly stir in the water until it is thoroughly mixed. Add the drained sauerkraut, potato, onion, and bacon to the batter. Stir until it is combined.

2. Place the griddle over medium-high heat. Add half of the oil to the pan and swirl so it is evenly coated.

3. Pour ¼ of the batter slowly onto the griddle. Cook for 3 minutes, or until the bottom is golden and bubbles have risen to the top. Flip it over, press against the pancake with the back of your spatula, and cook for 3 minutes. Press firmly. If batter comes through on the top, flip and cook for 1 minute before pressing to make sure the center is cooked. Repeat with the rest of the batter.

4. Transfer to a serving platter and serve with mustard or Sour Cream Mustard Dipping Sauce (see recipe in sidebar).

Sour Cream Mustard Dipping Sauce

This sauce is great with these pancakes and can also be served with Oven-Braised Pork Roast (see recipe in Chapter 7). Combine 1 cup sour cream, 2 teaspoons Dijon mustard, 2 minced scallions, and ½ teaspoon Worcestershire sauce in a small bowl. Let it sit for at least 30 minutes and up to 24 hours before serving. Leftovers will keep for 1 week.

CHAPTER 2

SAUCES AND SPREADS

GARLIC CONFIT

The garlic should be stored separately from the oil, in the refrigerator, for no more than one week. Botulism spores, which are odorless and tasteless, can be present on the garlic and will thrive in the oil.

Yields ½ cup

1 head of garlic

½ cup olive oil

1. Preheat oven to 350°F.

2. Peel all of the garlic cloves and place them in a small skillet. Pour the olive oil on top of the garlic cloves.

3. Bake the garlic for 45–60 minutes, or until the garlic is soft and golden brown.

The Many Uses of Garlic

Spread the garlic on bread, or use in any dish in which you want an intense garlic flavor. Use the oil when cooking, making vinaigrette, or dipping when you want a lighter garlic flavor.

CAJUN ROUX

This recipe makes enough roux to thicken a large pot of gumbo. Leftovers can be refrigerated for a week, or frozen for three months.

Yields 3 cups

1 cup vegetable oil or peanut oil

1¼ cups all-purpose flour

1 onion, chopped

1 bell pepper, chopped

3 celery stalks, chopped

2 carrots, chopped

1. Place a skillet over medium heat. Once it is heated add the oil. Stir the oil with a whisk in one hand while you slowly add the flour with the other. Once all of the flour is added, stir continuously for up to 25 minutes. Use the whisk to scrape the edges of the skillet to prevent the roux from browning.

2. Once the roux looks just darker than peanut butter, turn off the heat and add the vegetables. The sugars in the vegetables, and the residual heat from the hot skillet, will permit the roux to get darker and finish cooking.

History of Roux

Roux comes in three colors: white, blonde, or brown. It thickens sauces and adds flavor. The longer a roux is cooked, the darker, more flavorful, and less thickening it becomes. Most French roux is light-colored, but in Cajun cuisine a darker roux is used. Creole food is more likely to use a white or blonde roux to make a sauce.

BEURRE BLANC

Beurre Blanc (white butter) is great when served over fish fillets that are lightly seasoned. Because lemon juice is used in this recipe, it should only be made in a well-seasoned or an enameled pan.

Yields 4 tablespoons

1 shallot, minced

2 tablespoons white wine

4 tablespoons butter, cut into
   1-tablespoon sections

Juice from 1 lemon

Salt to taste

Pepper to taste

1. Place a skillet over medium heat. Once it is heated, add the shallot and wine. Stir continually until the liquid has reduced by half and is starting to get a syrupy consistency.

2. Reduce the heat to low and add 1 tablespoon of butter. Whisk the sauce continually until the butter is almost melted. Add the next pat while there are bits of butter in the skillet. Repeat until all of the butter is melted and the sauce can easily coat the back of a spoon.

3. Whisk in the lemon juice and taste before seasoning with salt and pepper. Serve immediately.

CHIPOTLE ORANGE SAUCE

Chipotle in adobo sauce can often be found in small cans. If you can't find canned chipotle peppers, you can substitute with jalapeño peppers.

Yields 1 cup

1 teaspoon vegetable oil

½ small onion, finely chopped

1 7-ounce can chipotle in adobo sauce

1 cup orange juice

Juice from 1 lime

1 teaspoon ground cumin

2 garlic cloves, minced

2 tablespoons brown sugar

Salt to taste

1. Place a skillet over medium-high heat. Once it is heated, add the oil and the onion. Cook for 5–7 minutes or until the onion has softened and has started to turn brown.

2. Stir in the remaining ingredients and simmer for 10 minutes, or until it has reduced and thickened. Taste and season with salt as necessary. Use as a condiment.

TOASTED PEANUT SAUCE

This Thai condiment is often served as a sauce for satay, spring rolls, potstickers, or brushed on vegetables. For a quick meal or snack, pour on cooked pasta and sprinkle sesame seeds or chopped scallion on top.

Yields 3 cups

1 13-ounce can coconut milk

2 ounces red curry paste or Green Curry Paste (see recipe in this chapter)

¾ cup unsweetened peanut butter

½ tablespoon salt

½ cup sugar

2 tablespoons apple cider vinegar

½ cup water

¼ teaspoon spicy red pepper flakes

1 teaspoon toasted sesame oil

1. Place an enameled pot over medium heat. Add all ingredients and bring to a boil, whisking continually.

2. Reduce the heat to low and simmer for 4 minutes, stirring occasionally.

3. Remove from the heat and serve immediately or place in an airtight container in the refrigerator for up to 1 month. (Refrigerated sauce will be thick, but will thin when heated.)

STRAWBERRY UN-PRESERVES

This recipe will work with any type of berry as long as the fruit is chopped. This dessert topping is great on ice cream, sponge cake, or as a filling or topping in layered cakes.

Yields 2 cups

1 quart strawberries, stems removed, chopped

½ cup sugar

Juice from 1 lemon

Pinch salt

1. Place a skillet over medium-high heat. Add all ingredients and stir frequently until the mixture begins to bubble.

2. After 10 minutes, once bubbles cover the surface and the mixture has thickened, turn off the heat.

3. Pour the mixture into a sealable glass jar and let the mixture cool to room temperature. Refrigerate for up to 2 weeks.

CLARIFIED BUTTER

To "clarify" butter is to remove milk solids and water to give a clear golden liquid with a higher smoke point than regular butter.

Yields 1 cup

1¼ cups unsalted butter

1. Place a skillet over the lowest heat possible. Cut the butter into smaller chunks and sprinkle it over the bottom of the skillet. Do not stir.

2. The butter will separate into three layers as it melts. The top layer is foam. Use a large spoon to skim it off slowly and discard.

3. Let the butter cook for about 10 minutes, skimming as necessary.

4. Place two plain paper towels in a fine mesh strainer. Over a heatproof container, slowly pour the butter through the towels to remove the remaining foam. Stop pouring before the brown milk solids can make it into the dish. Put a tight lid on the container and store in the refrigerator.

Butter by Another Name

Most people use clarified butter, or drawn butter, for dipping lobster or crabmeat. But it is also known as ghee in India where it is often flavored with spices and used for high-heat frying, cooking flatbreads, and even making desserts.

MANGO CHUTNEY

This condiment originated in Southeast Asia. It blends spicy, sweet, and tart flavors and is served with many meals in India as a condiment. Because of the acid in this recipe, use an enameled pan.

Yields 1½ pints

1 cup sugar

½ cup apple cider vinegar

3 fresh mangoes, peeled and chopped in ¾" pieces

1 small onion, chopped

¼ cup golden raisins, or chopped dates

1 garlic clove, minced

½ teaspoon whole mustard seeds

½ teaspoon red chili flakes

1. Place a large skillet or Dutch oven over medium heat. Add the sugar and vinegar, and stir continually until the sugar dissolves. Lower the heat to the lowest setting.

2. Add the remaining ingredients and simmer uncovered for 45 minutes. It should be syrupy and thick.

3. Pour into a clean, airtight jar and store in the refrigerator for up to 1 month.

FIG BALSAMIC DESSERT SAUCE

If you made the Fresh Fig Muffins (see recipe in Chapter 9), use the apple juice left over and supplement with fresh apple juice to get 2 cups.

Yields 1–1½ cups syrup

8 dried figs, stemmed and minced

2 cups apple juice

¼ cup sugar

¼ cup balsamic vinegar

1. Place a skillet over medium heat. Once it is heated, place everything but the vinegar in the skillet and bring to a boil. Lower the heat to medium-low and simmer for 10–15 minutes. It should be frothy and reduced by half.

2. Add the vinegar and increase the heat to medium-high. Stir frequently for 5 minutes. The sauce is ready when it sticks to the back of the spoon.

3. Use a stand or stick blender to purée the sauce. Serve hot or warm. Refrigerate any leftovers for 2 weeks.

VIETNAMESE CHILI GARLIC SAUCE

This Vietnamese condiment is great stirred into noodle soups, served on meats, used as a dipping sauce for egg rolls, or stirred into any sauce that you would like to be spicier. It will keep in an airtight jar in the refrigerator for at least 1 month.

Yields 1 cup

6 ounces Thai, serrano, cayenne, or red jalapeño peppers

4 garlic cloves, chopped

1 teaspoon salt

2 teaspoons honey

2 tablespoons apple cider vinegar or rice wine vinegar

Optional: 1–2 tablespoons water

1. Place all of the ingredients in a blender or food processor. Pulse until the mixture is smooth. Add 1–2 tablespoons of water if necessary.

2. Place a skillet over medium heat. Once it is heated, pour the mixture into the skillet and bring to a simmer.

3. Reduce the heat to low and simmer uncovered for 10 minutes. It should lose its raw smell and develop a richer smell. Transfer to an airtight jar.

AMERICAN PICCALILLI

There is a dish by this name in Britain that is more mustardy and less sweet. Use the American version on cold meats, sausages, roasts, or even mixed into rice or vegetable dishes.

Yields 1 pint

2 green tomatoes

½ green bell pepper

½ red bell pepper

1 small onion, peeled

1 cup cabbage

¼ cup salt

½ cup brown sugar

¼ teaspoon celery seed or celery salt

¼ teaspoon mustard seed

2 whole cloves

½ teaspoon ground cinnamon

½ teaspoon ground allspice

⅓ cup apple cider vinegar

1. Chop all vegetables. Sprinkle them with salt and place in a covered bowl overnight.

2. The next day, lightly rinse the vegetables with cold water to remove the salt.

3. Combine the vegetables with the remaining ingredients and place in a skillet. Bring to a boil and reduce the heat to low.

4. Simmer for 15 minutes. If desired, purée with a stick blender or run through a stand blender after it has cooled. Store in an airtight jar for up to 1 month.

CARAMELIZED ONION AND FENNEL

Raw fennel has a fairly strong anise flavor. But when it cooks, that flavor almost disappears.

Yields 1 quart

2 heads fennel

2 tablespoons olive oil

2 large sweet onions, peeled and thinly sliced

2 small tomatoes, cored and sliced

1 teaspoon salt

1. Cut off the green part of the fennel and the base. Discard. Separate the pieces and rinse well to remove any dirt. Slice thinly.

2. Place a Dutch oven over medium heat. Once it is warmed, add the olive oil and the vegetables. Sprinkle the salt across the top and stir to combine. Cover the pan with a lid and reduce the heat to low. Stir the vegetables every 3 minutes, three times.

3. Add a little more oil if the pan seems dry and let it cook for about an hour, stirring every 15 minutes. The mixture should be very juicy. Turn the heat to high and stir frequently for 5 minutes, or until the liquid evaporates.

Caramelized Fennel and Onion Tart

To make a quick appetizer, mix 2 cups of this mixture with ¼ cup of grated Parmesan cheese. Spread it on a premade pie shell. Place it in a 350°F oven for 20–30 minutes or until the crust and top have browned.

GREEN CURRY PASTE

This is a fairly mild curry paste. If you prefer a hot paste, use serrano chilies instead of jalapeños. This paste can be used in the Toasted Peanut Sauce (see recipe in this chapter).

Yields ½ cup

2 stalks lemongrass

1 2" piece ginger, peeled and sliced

½ bunch cilantro

4 jalapeños, seeded

1 small yellow onion, peeled and quartered

3 garlic cloves, peeled

Zest from 1 lime

1 teaspoon ground coriander

1 tablespoon ground cumin

1 teaspoon honey

1 tablespoon soy sauce

3 tablespoons peanut oil

1. Remove the bottom 3" from the lemongrass and the dried fibrous tops. Cut into 1" pieces. Add to a food processor with the ginger, cilantro, peppers, onion, garlic, and lime zest. Pulse for several minutes until it is a smooth paste.

2. Add the coriander, cumin, honey, soy sauce, and oil, and pulse until it is combined.

3. Place a skillet over medium heat. Add the curry paste, spreading it out evenly. Cook for 7–10 minutes, stirring frequently, until the pepper smell is overpowering. If the mixture sticks, add a tablespoon of oil.

4. Once the paste is ready, remove from the skillet. Store refrigerated for 2 weeks or frozen for up to 6 months.

CHICKEN GRAVY

Gravy requires practice and repetition to make it perfectly. If you use a whisk, keep a spoon nearby so you can test for your preferred thickness and flavor.

Yields 6 servings

2 tablespoons chicken drippings, or other oil

1 cup chicken broth (or juice, or beer, or wine)

1–2 tablespoons flour

Salt and pepper as needed

1. Place a skillet over medium-high heat and add the drippings. Pour in ½ cup of the broth. In a separate container, stir 1 tablespoon of flour into the remaining ½ cup of liquid and whisk until it is lump-free.

2. Once the liquid in the skillet starts to boil, slowly pour the flour and liquid mixture into the skillet, whisking continually. Once it returns to a boil it will start to thicken. Reduce the heat to medium and keep stirring.

3. After 3–4 minutes, if it isn't thick enough, sprinkle 1 teaspoon of flour across the top of the gravy, stirring continually to prevent lumps. Cook for another 2 minutes before adding more flour.

4. If the gravy gets too thick, add a few tablespoons of liquid to thin it, and boil again before removing. If you keep the gravy in the pan, it will continue to cook even if the burner is turned off, so stir frequently. Add salt and pepper to taste.

Reheating Leftover Gravy

You can refrigerate leftover gravy in a sealed container for 2–3 days. It will become solid when cold. Reheat it in a pan over medium heat or in the microwave for 2–3 minutes. Whisk in a tablespoon or two of chicken broth or other liquid to get the desired consistency.

BOLOGNESE SAUCE

This dish comes from Bologna, Italy, and is most often served on a wide noodle called tagliatelle. It is wider than fettuccine and is easier to find fresh than dried. The width makes sauce stick more easily.

Yields 6–8 servings

3 tablespoons butter

3 tablespoons olive oil

½ small yellow onion, chopped

½ celery stalk, chopped

½ carrot, chopped

¾ pound lean ground beef

1 cup dry white wine

½ cup whole milk

⅛ teaspoon ground nutmeg

1 28-ounce can chopped Italian tomatoes

1 teaspoon salt to taste

1. Place a Dutch oven over medium heat and add the butter and oil. Once the butter has melted, add the onion, stirring continually for 1 minute until slightly translucent. Stir in the celery and carrot and cook for 2 minutes.

2. Add the ground beef and stir continually, breaking the meat into small pieces while it cooks. Once the meat is slightly more brown than red, turn the heat up to medium-high and add the wine. Leave uncovered and simmering vigorously. Stir occasionally for 10 minutes to prevent it from sticking while the wine evaporates.

3. Add the milk and the nutmeg and lower the heat to medium. Stir continually until it stops boiling vigorously. Continue to stir it frequently for about 6–8 minutes until the milk evaporates. Add the tomatoes and reduce the heat to low. You want it to bubble occasionally, but barely simmer.

4. Cooking time will vary between 3½ and 5 hours. Once all of the liquid has evaporated you'll be left with a meaty, gravylike sauce. Taste and add salt if necessary.

KANSAS CITY–STYLE BARBECUE SAUCE

Because this recipe uses a lot of acidic tomato sauce, use a well-seasoned or enameled Dutch oven.

Yields 3–4 pints

1 large yellow onion, chopped

4 garlic cloves, minced

1 teaspoon salt

2 tablespoons vegetable oil

1 26-ounce can tomato sauce

1 6-ounce can tomato paste

¼ cup dark molasses

1 cup mango juice

3 tablespoons cocoa powder

1 can dark beer

1 can cola (or other soda with caramel coloring)

2 tablespoons Worcestershire sauce

1 pinch cayenne powder

¼ cup cider vinegar

1 tablespoon cumin

1 tablespoon paprika

1 tablespoon coriander

1 tablespoon dried oregano

1 tablespoon dried mustard powder

1 teaspoon ground black pepper

1 teaspoon ground cinnamon

1. Place a Dutch oven over medium-high heat and when it is heated, add the onion, garlic, salt, and oil. Stir frequently and cook for 5 minutes until the onions are translucent. Turn the heat to low and cook for 15 minutes. Stir occasionally. When the onions start to caramelize and turn a light brown, add the remaining ingredients, stirring after every few items are added. Once everything is incorporated, cover with a lid and cook for 30 minutes. Stir occasionally to prevent from burning.

2. Remove the lid and simmer for 1½ hours. Some of the liquid will evaporate to create a thicker sauce. Taste and add extra salt, spice, vinegar, or sugar if desired.

ETHIOPIAN BERBERÉ RED PEPPER PASTE

Berberé is the official language of Ethiopia, where this intensely spicy sauce is used as a condiment. To reduce the heat, use less or omit the cayenne pepper. You can also use this paste as a rub on meat before grilling.

Yields 1½ cups

1 teaspoon ground ginger

1 teaspoon ground cardamom

1 teaspoon ground coriander

¼ teaspoon ground nutmeg

⅛ teaspoon ground cloves

⅛ teaspoon ground allspice

½ teaspoon ground cinnamon

2 tablespoons onion, minced

2 garlic cloves, minced

2 tablespoons salt

1½ cups water

1 cup sweet paprika

½ cup smoky paprika

2 teaspoons ground cayenne pepper

½ teaspoon black pepper

1. Place a dry cast-iron skillet over medium heat. Once it is hot, add the ginger, cardamom, coriander, nutmeg, cloves, allspice, and cinnamon and cook for 1 minute. They should start to smell nutty.

2. Pour the spices into a blender and add the onion, garlic, salt, and ¼ cup of water. Blend into a paste.

3. Reduce the heat on the skillet to low. Add the paprika, cayenne pepper, and black pepper in the skillet. Toast for 1–2 minutes. Stir in the rest of the water, ¼ cup at a time. Once the water is combined, stir in the blended mixture.

4. Stir continuously for 10–15 minutes. Transfer the paste to a jar and cool to room temperature. Store in the refrigerator for several weeks, as long as there is a film of oil on top of the paste.

ROASTED TOMATILLO AND GREEN CHILI SAUCE

You can either purée this sauce until smooth and use in a dish like the Enchilada Casserole (see recipe in Chapter 3), or you can keep it chunky and use it like salsa with chips.

Yields 1 pint

10 tomatillos

1 tablespoon olive oil

1 small onion, quartered

2 cloves garlic, peeled

2 Anaheim chilies, seeded

Juice from 2 limes

Salt to taste

1. Preheat oven to 350°F. Remove the papery husks from the tomatillos and wash them. Remove the core and cut into quarters.

2. Place a large skillet over medium heat and once it is heated, add the olive oil, vegetables, garlic, and chilies. Shake the pan frequently to keep ingredients from sticking. Cook for about 10 minutes. Place the skillet in the middle of the oven.

3. Roast for 30 minutes. Remove the pan from the oven and cool.

4. Place the vegetables in a blender or food processor. Add the lime juice. Pulse several times to get the desired texture. Taste and add salt as needed. Place in a tightly sealed container and refrigerate for up to 1 week.

Tomatillos, the Distant Tomato Cousin

Tomatillos look like green tomatoes wrapped in a green, papery husk. The Aztecs in Mexico domesticated the tomatillo around 800 B.C. They're generally smaller than apricots. They have a tart, slightly bitter taste when raw, but roasting them brings out the sugars and the tartness mellows to a refreshing flavor.

ONION MARMALADE

Even though this dish makes quite a bit of food, it stores well. You can keep it in your refrigerator in a tightly sealed glass jar for up to 2 months. Or you can freeze it for up to 4 months.

Yields 1 pint

2 tablespoons olive oil

2 large white or yellow onions, thinly sliced

½ teaspoon salt

1 bay leaf

¼ cup sherry, brandy, or a sweet white wine

1. Place a Dutch oven over low heat. Once it's warm add the olive oil and stir in the onions with the salt and bay leaf. Cover and cook for 15 minutes.

2. Stir it a few times to prevent sticking. Once the onions are translucent, remove the lid. Add the sherry and stir. Let the liquid evaporate and stir every few minutes to prevent burning.

3. Replace the lid and cook for 1–1½ hours. If more liquid accumulates, remove the lid and let the liquid evaporate. Once there is no liquid in the pan and the onions are a light golden color, remove the bay leaf, and the marmalade is ready to serve.

VANILLA-SPICE PEAR BUTTER

Bartlett pears are light green and are especially prevalent in the Pacific Northwest. Serve on scones or toasted English muffins.

Yields about 2 cups

6 medium Bartlett pears

¼ cup dry white wine

1 tablespoon fresh lemon juice

¾ cup sugar

2 orange slices

1 lemon slice

2 whole cloves

1 vanilla bean, split lengthwise

1 cinnamon stick

¼ teaspoon ground cardamom

Pinch salt

1. Rinse, peel, and core the pears, and cut them into 1" dice. Add the pears, wine, and lemon juice to a pressure cooker. Lock the lid into place and bring to low pressure; maintain pressure for 8 minutes.

2. Remove from heat and allow pressure to release naturally for 10 minutes. Quick-release any remaining pressure and remove the lid. Transfer the fruit and juices to a blender or food processor and purée.

3. Return the purée to the pressure cooker. Add the sugar. Stir and cook over low heat until sugar dissolves. Stir in the remaining ingredients. Increase the heat to medium and boil gently, cooking and stirring for about 30 minutes or until mixture thickens and mounds slightly on a spoon.

4. Remove and discard the orange and lemon slices, cloves, and cinnamon stick. Remove the vanilla pod; use the back of a knife to scrape away any vanilla seeds still clinging to the pod and stir them into the pear butter. Cool and refrigerate covered for up to 10 days or freeze for up to 4 months.

CHAPTER 3

SALADS, APPETIZERS, AND SIDES

WARM CHICKEN SALAD

You can increase this recipe to 8 servings by using all of the meat from the chicken and doubling the other ingredients.

Yields 4 servings

2 medium oranges

6 cups torn romaine lettuce

1 medium red sweet pepper, seeded and diced

½ small red onion, halved and thinly sliced

½ cup slivered or sliced almonds, toasted

Breast meat from a rotisserie chicken, cut into thin bite-size strips

⅓ cup orange juice

1 tablespoon red wine vinegar

1 tablespoon extra-virgin olive oil

1 teaspoon Dijon mustard

Optional: coarsely ground black pepper to taste

1. Peel and section the oranges; cut each section into 4 pieces. Add the orange pieces to a large salad bowl and toss them with the romaine, red pepper, onion, almonds, and chicken. Set aside.

2. Add the orange juice and vinegar to a microwave-safe bowl. Microwave on high for 1 minute, or until heated through. Whisk in the olive oil and mustard. Pour the warm dressing over the salad and toss to mix. Season to taste with coarsely ground black pepper if desired. Serve immediately.

HOT CHICKEN FAJITA PASTA SALAD

You can easily stretch this recipe to 8 servings by serving the pasta salad over lettuce or along with baked corn tortilla chips.

Yields 6 servings

1 3-pound rotisserie chicken

12 ounces dried egg noodles

2 tablespoons extra-virgin olive oil

1 medium yellow onion, halved and thinly sliced

1 medium red sweet pepper, seeded and cut into thin strips

1 fresh Anaheim chili pepper, seeded and cut into thin strips

1 8-ounce carton sour cream

½ cup chipotle liquid meat marinade

2 tablespoons lime juice

1 teaspoon chili powder

1 teaspoon ground cumin

½ teaspoon dried red pepper flakes, crushed

Optional: fresh cilantro, chopped, to taste

1. Remove and discard the skin from the chicken; remove the meat from the bones and shred it. Set aside.

2. In a Dutch oven, cook the pasta according to the package directions; drain and keep warm. Wipe out the Dutch oven, add the oil, and bring it to temperature over medium heat. Add the onion, sweet pepper, and Anaheim pepper; sauté for 5 minutes, or until crisp-tender. Add the sour cream, marinade, lime juice, chili powder, cumin, and crushed red pepper to a bowl; stir to mix. Add the cooked noodles, chicken, and sour cream mixture to the sautéed vegetables; toss to coat. Leave on the heat long enough to reheat the noodles and warm the chicken, if necessary. Garnish with cilantro, if using. Serve warm.

Heat Hints

The dried red pepper flakes and Anaheim chili pepper will add heat to this Hot Chicken Fajita Pasta Salad, which will be somewhat tempered by the cooked noodles and sour cream. If you prefer a milder taste, reduce the amount you add at first, taste the salad, and then add more, if needed.

ROTISSERIE CHICKEN SALAD

You can substitute some of the melted chicken fat from the rotisserie chicken for the oil in the dressing.

Yields 4 servings

1 3-pound Italian-seasoned rotisserie chicken

8 cups salad mix

2 tablespoons red wine vinegar

1 tablespoon Dijon mustard

1 clove garlic, minced

¼ teaspoon sea salt

¼ teaspoon freshly ground black pepper

4 tablespoons extra-virgin olive oil

Optional: Parmigiano-Reggiano, grated to taste

1. Cut the legs, thighs, and wings from the chicken. Remove and discard the skin from the rest of the chicken; remove the remaining meat from the chicken and shred it.

2. Divide 2 cups of salad mix between 4 plates. Divide the shredded chicken between the plates, placing it atop the salad mix. Place a leg or thigh on each plate.

3. Add the vinegar, mustard, garlic, salt, pepper, and oil to a jar; cover and shake vigorously to emulsify. Pour the dressing evenly over the chicken-topped salad mix on each plate. Top each salad with grated cheese if desired.

SHRIMP SALAD WITH LOUIS DRESSING

You can prepare the shrimp, the hard-boiled eggs, and the dressing the night before so that your salad is ready to assemble for lunch the next day.

Yields 4 servings

1 cup mayonnaise

½ cup fresh spinach leaves

5 watercress sprigs

½ small yellow onion

1 clove garlic, minced

1 tablespoon fresh lemon juice

1½ teaspoons granulated sugar

4 cups lettuce or salad mix

4 small tomatoes, sliced

4 hard-boiled eggs, peeled and sliced

1 pound cooked shrimp, peeled, deveined, and cooled

Salt and freshly ground pepper to taste

1. To make the Louis dressing, add the mayonnaise, spinach, watercress, onion, garlic, lemon juice, and sugar to a blender or food processor; pulse until smooth. Cover and chill until ready to assemble the salad.

2. For each salad serving, put 1 cup of salad mix on a serving plate and top with 1 sliced tomato, 1 sliced hard-boiled egg, and ¼ of the shrimp. Season with salt and pepper to taste, and top with the Louis dressing.

HAM AND BEANS SALAD

This recipe turns some leftover cooked ham into a delicious luncheon salad.

Yields 4 servings

¼ cup extra-virgin olive oil

3 tablespoons balsamic vinegar

1 tablespoon red onion or shallots, minced

1 clove garlic, minced

1 tablespoon fresh parsley, minced

2 stalks celery, diced

2 large carrots, peeled and shredded

1 cup cooked ham, diced

1 15-ounce can cannellini or white beans, rinsed and drained

Salt and freshly ground black pepper to taste

4 or more cups lettuce or salad mix

In a mixing bowl, make the dressing by whisking together the oil and vinegar; then stir in the onion or shallots, garlic, parsley, celery, carrots, ham, and beans. Cover and let stand for at least 1 hour. Taste for seasoning, and add salt and pepper, if needed. Divide the lettuce or salad mix between 4 plates and top with equal amounts of the dressing.

QUINOA SALAD

You can make this quinoa salad the night before and then assemble the salad for lunch that day.

Yields 2 servings

2 cups quinoa

4½ cups water

1 teaspoon sea salt

2 tablespoons extra-virgin olive oil

½ cup sliced marinated artichoke hearts

¼ cup sliced, pitted kalamata olives

2 tablespoons fresh spinach, finely chopped

1 cup cherry tomatoes, cut in half

2 tablespoons flat-leaf parsley, finely chopped

1 tablespoon freshly grated lemon zest

¼ cup balsamic vinegar, or more to taste

¼ cup orange juice

¼ cup extra-virgin olive oil, or more to taste

1 teaspoon dried oregano

1 teaspoon dried mint

1 teaspoon dried fresh basil

Sea salt and freshly ground black pepper to taste

2 cups fresh baby spinach

2 tablespoons toasted pine nuts

½ cup feta cheese, crumbled

1. Cover the quinoa with water; rub the grains between the palms of your hands for several seconds, drain, and repeat the process once.

2. Bring the water to a boil in a saucepan; add the quinoa, salt, and oil. Lower heat, cover, and simmer for 20 minutes, or until all of the water is absorbed. Remove the pan from the heat and allow the cooked quinoa to cool, and then fluff with a fork. Stir in the artichoke hearts, olives, spinach, tomatoes, and parsley.

3. To make the citrus vinaigrette, whisk together the lemon zest, balsamic vinegar, orange juice, oil, oregano, mint, basil, salt, and pepper. Taste for seasoning and adjust, if necessary, by adding more vinegar, oil, or salt and pepper. Divide the salad between 2 plates of the baby spinach leaves. Dress with the citrus vinaigrette and serve with the pine nuts and crumbled feta cheese sprinkled over the top.

TACO SALAD

You can use canned or leftover chili for this recipe. Choose the salsa according to how it is seasoned and how spicy your family likes taco-style dishes.

Yields 4 servings

2 cups chili

1 1-pound bag salad mix

1 cup salsa

2 avocados, peeled, seeded, and sliced

4 ounces Cheddar cheese, grated

4 ounces Monterey jack cheese, grated

Baked corn tortilla chips

Heat the chili on the stovetop or in the microwave. Divide the salad mix between 4 large plates or salad bowls. Spoon ½ cup hot chili over the top of each salad and top that with ¼ cup of the salsa. Arrange the avocado slices around each salad. Sprinkle 1 ounce each of the Cheddar and Monterey jack cheese over the top of each salad. Serve with baked corn tortilla chips.

Stretching the Chili

You can stretch the chili by stirring a 15-ounce can of refried beans into it when you heat it. Increase the remaining ingredients according to how many servings you need to fix. This dish can be expanded to serve as many people as you want, or you can make the servings as big as you want.

BEEF AND ROASTED VEGETABLES WITH PROVENÇAL VINAIGRETTE

Use leftover roast or steak and roasted potatoes to make this salad transport you and your family to the south of France.

Yields 4 servings

3 tablespoons extra-virgin olive oil

1 tablespoon sherry, red wine, or champagne vinegar

1 tablespoon chopped fresh parsley

2 teaspoons minced shallot

1 teaspoon Dijon-style mustard

Salt to taste

¼ teaspoon pepper

1 12-ounce package steam-in-the-bag green beans

4 small baked or oven-roasted potatoes, quartered

2 cups leftover steak or roast beef, cubed or shredded

4 cups mixed baby salad greens

1 cup grape tomatoes

¼ cup thinly sliced red onion

16 niçoise olives, pitted

1. Add the oil, vinegar, parsley, shallot, mustard, salt, and pepper to a glass jar; screw on the lid and shake the jar to combine the dressing. Set aside to allow flavors to meld.

2. Prepare the green beans in the microwave according to package directions; set aside. Add the potatoes and steak or roast to a large microwave-safe bowl; cover and microwave at 70 percent power for 2 minutes, or until heated through. Add the green beans to the bowl and mix with the potatoes and steak or roast. Shake the dressing jar to remix the dressing and then pour it into the bowl; stir to cover the warm meat and vegetables in the dressing. Add the salad greens, tomatoes, onion, and olives; toss to combine. Serve immediately.

CHICKEN SALAD WITH TOASTED PECANS AND GREEN GRAPES

The presentation for this salad is a bit more attractive if you use cubed cooked chicken breast, and it tastes delicious when it's made with both dark and white meat.

Yields 4 servings

⅔ cup sour cream

⅓ cup mayonnaise

½ teaspoon champagne or white wine vinegar

1 teaspoon granulated sugar

1 small red onion, diced

8 bread and butter pickle slices, minced

2 cups cooked chicken, cubed or shredded

1 cup grape tomatoes

1 cup green seedless grapes

1 cup pecans, toasted and chopped (see instructions in sidebar)

4 cups salad mix

1. Add the sour cream, mayonnaise, vinegar, sugar, onion, and pickles to a large bowl; stir to combine. Fold in the chicken, tomatoes, grapes, and half of the pecans.

2. To serve, put 1 cup of salad greens on each of 4 plates. Spoon equal amounts of the chicken salad over the tops of each plate of salad greens, and sprinkle the remaining pecans over the top of the chicken salad.

Toasting Pecans

To toast pecans, either dry-fry them for 5 minutes in a skillet over medium heat or bake them at 300°F for 10–15 minutes in a single layer on a baking sheet. Either way, be sure to stir them often and only toast them until they just begin to turn brown. Watch the nuts closely because they go from toasted to burned within seconds, and they'll continue to roast after they've been removed from the heat.

NEW ORLEANS–STYLE OYSTERS AND SHRIMP SALAD

You can serve the pasta and the salad separately, but the contrast between the warm, soft pasta and the cool, crisp salad makes for a delightful dish.

Yields 8 servings

1 pound dried penne pasta

2 tablespoons peanut or vegetable oil

2 tablespoons all-purpose flour

1 large yellow onion, diced

1 teaspoon anchovy paste

1 cup milk

1 cup heavy cream

Hot sauce to taste

1 teaspoon Worcestershire sauce

Pinch dried thyme

2 pints small oysters

2 pounds medium shrimp, cooked, peeled, and deveined

Salt and freshly ground black pepper to taste

8 cups salad mix

8 green onions, chopped

1. In a Dutch oven, cook the penne according to package directions; drain, set aside, and keep warm.

2. Wipe out the Dutch oven; add the oil and bring it to temperature over medium heat. Stir in the flour and cook it until it begins to turn light brown. Add the onion; sauté for 3 minutes, or until limp. Whisk in the anchovy paste, milk, and cream. Bring to a simmer and stir in the hot sauce, Worcestershire sauce, and thyme; simmer for 10 minutes.

3. Drain the oysters and stir them and the shrimp into the cream sauce. Simmer just long enough to bring the seafood to temperature; then stir in the pasta. If the pasta mixture is too thick, stir in a little extra milk, cream, or the liquid drained from the oysters. Taste for seasoning and add salt and pepper if needed.

4. To serve, spread 1 cup of salad mix over the top of a plate, ladle the pasta mixture over the salad greens, and garnish with the chopped green onion.

INDIAN SPINACH SALAD

The assortment of nuts in this dish takes the place of meat. If you don't have all the nut varieties on hand, substitute an equal amount of what you do have. You can use more or fewer nuts according to your taste.

Yields 8 servings

1½ cups plain yogurt

½ cup sour cream

1 teaspoon ground cumin, pan-toasted

1 teaspoon ground coriander, pan-toasted

¼ teaspoon freshly ground black pepper

Cayenne pepper to taste

Salt to taste

1 10-ounce package frozen spinach, thawed and squeezed dry

2 large cucumbers, peeled and grated

2 tablespoons fresh mint, finely chopped

2 tablespoons fresh cilantro, finely chopped

½ cup currants or raisins

¼ cup walnuts, toasted and chopped

½ cup roasted cashews

¼ cup almonds, toasted and chopped

¼ cup pistachios, toasted

¼ cup macadamia nuts, chopped

8 cups fresh baby spinach

1. In a large bowl, mix together the yogurt, sour cream, cumin, coriander, black pepper, cayenne, salt, frozen spinach, cucumbers, mint, cilantro, currants or raisins, and nuts. Taste for seasoning and add more salt, pepper, or spices, if desired. The moisture remaining in the spinach and cucumbers will determine the final texture of the salad; if it's too thick, add additional sour cream to thin it.

2. For each serving, put 1 cup of baby spinach on a plate or in a salad bowl and top with a helping of the salad.

Pan-Toasting Spices

To toast spices on the stovetop, add them to a skillet and dry sauté them over medium heat until they just begin to release their aromas. Pan-toasting the spices gives them a unique flavor. Be careful not to burn the spices.

TABOULEH

This Middle Eastern dish is a meatless departure from the usual luncheon salad.

Yields 4 servings

1 cup fine bulgur wheat

2 cups cold water

8 green onions

2 large bunches fresh parsley

1 small red bell pepper, seeded and quartered

2 stalks celery, cut into quarters

2 tablespoons fresh mint

¼ cup extra-virgin olive oil

¼ cup fresh lemon juice

¼ teaspoon ground allspice

¼ teaspoon ground cinnamon

Salt to taste

¼ teaspoon freshly ground black pepper

4 medium tomatoes, diced

Optional: 4 cups salad mix or baby spinach

1. In a large bowl, pour the cold water over the bulgur wheat; let soak for 15 minutes. Drain off any excess water, and pour the bulgur out onto a clean cotton towel and squeeze dry.

2. Cut off the root end and remove the outer membrane of each green onion and slice the white part of each green onion into 2 1" pieces; discard the remaining green tops. Remove the parsley from the stems. Add the green onions, parsley, bell pepper, celery, and mint to a food processor; pulse until finely chopped.

3. Add the oil, lemon juice, allspice, cinnamon, salt, and black pepper to the large bowl. Whisk to mix, and then whisk in the mixture from the food processor. Fold in the bulgur wheat and tomatoes. Serve over salad mix or baby spinach, if desired.

SWEDISH HERRING SALAD

This isn't your everyday style of potato salad. If you're uncertain about the herrings, only use one jar and increase the amount of cooked roast beef. For a milder taste, use creamed herring.

Yields 4 servings

½ pound new potatoes, unpeeled, diced small

½ cup water

1 1-pound can pickled beets

2 hard-boiled eggs

2 6-ounce jars wine-flavored pickled herring

1 Granny Smith apple, cored and diced small

½ cup cooked roast beef, shredded

2 tablespoons yellow onion, finely diced

⅓ cup dill pickle, finely chopped

6 tablespoons reserved beet liquid

2 tablespoons white or white wine vinegar

2 tablespoons granulated sugar

Salt and freshly ground black pepper to taste

½ cup heavy cream

Optional: 4 cups salad mix

1. Add the diced potatoes and water to a large microwave-safe bowl; cover and microwave on high for 5 minutes, or until the potatoes are tender. Drain in a colander and then return to the bowl. Drain the beets, reserving 6 tablespoons of the liquid; finely dice the beets and add to the bowl. Peel the hard-boiled eggs and set aside the yolks; dice the whites and add them to the bowl. Drain and finely chop the herring; add to the bowl along with the apple, beef, onion, dill pickle, beet liquid, vinegar, 1 tablespoon of the sugar, the salt, and black pepper. Mix well; taste for seasoning and add the remaining sugar, if desired. Whip the heavy cream until soft peaks form; fold it into the salad.

2. Serve over salad mix, if desired. Garnish with the reserved, chopped hard-boiled egg yolk.

THAI BEEF SALAD

This salad takes leftover beef to a whole new level. You can punch it up with store-bought dressing.

Yields 4 servings

1 small yellow onion, thinly sliced

¼ cup fresh lime juice

¼ cup fish sauce

10 fresh mint leaves, chopped

½ teaspoon granulated sugar

½ teaspoon red chili paste

2 cloves garlic, minced

2 cups cooked beef, cubed

4 cups salad mix

2 large cucumbers, thinly sliced

Fresh chopped cilantro to taste

4 green onions, chopped

1. Add the yellow onion, lime juice, fish sauce, mint, sugar, red chili paste, garlic, and beef to a bowl; stir to mix. Cover and chill for 30 minutes.

2. For each serving, place 1 cup of salad mix on a plate or in a salad bowl. Arrange the cucumber slices over the top of the salad mix. Spoon the beef mixture over the cucumber slices. Garnish with fresh cilantro and chopped green onion.

MACADAMIA AND AVOCADO CHICKEN SALAD

If you don't have macadamia nut oil, you can substitute extra-virgin olive oil or a mild vegetable oil. If you use a substitute, start with half the oil called for in the recipe, taste, and then add more oil, if desired.

Yields 4 servings

½ cup macadamia nut oil

2 tablespoons white balsamic vinegar

½ tablespoon whole-grain mustard

2 green onions, white part only, chopped

Salt and freshly ground black pepper to taste

2 cups cooked chicken, shredded

1 red bell pepper, seeded and diced

1 yellow bell pepper, seeded and diced

4 ounces macadamia nuts, chopped

4 cups mesclun greens or salad mix

2 avocados, peeled, pitted, and sliced

Add the oil, vinegar, mustard, onion, salt, and pepper to a large bowl; whisk to combine. Add the chicken, red and yellow bell pepper, nuts, and mesclun greens or salad mix; toss to mix. Spoon the salad onto 4 individual plates and arrange ¼ of the avocado slices decoratively on the side of each plate.

CHICKEN AND CELLOPHANE NOODLE SALAD

You can substitute 2 cups of water and 2 chicken bouillon cubes for the chicken broth.

Yields 4 servings

1 8-ounce package cellophane noodles

2 cups chicken broth

4 tablespoons peanut butter

2 tablespoons hot water

5 tablespoons soy sauce

Red chili paste or cayenne pepper to taste

2 large cucumbers

1 tablespoon rice wine vinegar

½ teaspoon granulated sugar

2 teaspoons sesame oil

4 cups salad mix

2 cups cooked chicken, shredded

¼ cup dry-roasted peanuts, chopped

1. Add the noodles and chicken broth to a saucepan; soak the noodles for 1 hour. Place the saucepan over medium heat and bring to a simmer; simmer for 10 minutes, or until the noodles are tender. Drain off the broth. Cover and cool in the refrigerator.

2. Add the peanut butter, hot water, soy sauce, and red chili paste or cayenne to a small bowl; whisk to mix, adding more water if necessary to bring the mixture to the consistency of heavy cream. Pour the mixture over the noodles; toss to mix.

3. Peel, seed, and cut the cucumbers into julienne strips. In a small bowl, mix the cucumber strips together with the vinegar, sugar, and sesame oil.

4. To assemble each salad, arrange 1 cup of salad mix on a plate or in a salad bowl. Top with ¼ of the cellophane noodles, ¼ of the chicken, ¼ of the cucumber, and 1 tablespoon of chopped peanuts, in that order.

A Noodle by Any Other Name

Cellophane noodles—sometimes referred to as bean threads, glass noodles, and sai fun—are commonly made from bean starch. These delicate noodles easily absorb the flavors they are cooked with. You can find them in the Asian foods aisle in most supermarkets.

CHICKEN WALDORF SALAD

This salad is better if it's refrigerated for 1 hour before serving. The lime juice prevents the apples from turning brown.

Yields 4 servings

¼ cup mayonnaise

½ cup sour cream

½ tablespoon fresh lime juice

1 teaspoon granulated sugar

¼ teaspoon fresh ginger, grated

1 large Granny Smith apple, cored and diced

1 large Red Delicious apple, cored and diced

1 large Yellow Delicious apple, cored and diced

2 stalks celery, diced

½ cup walnuts, toasted and chopped

2 cups cooked chicken, shredded

Salt and freshly ground black pepper to taste

4 cups salad mix

Add the mayonnaise, sour cream, lime juice, sugar, and ginger to a bowl large enough to hold the salad; stir to combine, then fold in the apples, celery, walnuts, and chicken. Before serving, check for seasoning and add salt, pepper, and more sugar, if needed. To serve, spoon ¼ of the chicken salad over 1 cup of salad mix.

CHINESE CHICKEN SALAD

Start this meal the night before you plan to serve it. Complete step 1 the night before, step 2 1–2 hours before serving, and step 3 immediately before the dish hits the table.

Yields 6 servings

1 3-pound rotisserie chicken

½ cup tamari sauce

½ cup macadamia nut oil

⅓ cup rice wine vinegar

1 teaspoon fresh ginger, grated

½ teaspoon garlic powder

1 teaspoon honey

4 cups raw broccoli florets

6 cups salad mix

4 stalks celery, diced

4 green onions, sliced on a slant

5 large radishes, thinly sliced

1 red bell pepper, seeded and sliced

½ cup unsalted macadamia nuts, toasted and chopped

1. Remove the skin from the chicken and discard; remove the meat from the bones and shred it. Put the chicken in a large salad bowl. To make the dressing, put the tamari sauce, oil, vinegar, ginger, garlic powder, and honey in a jar with a tight-fitting lid; shake well to mix. Pour ¼ cup dressing over the chicken; cover and chill overnight. Cover and refrigerate the remaining dressing.

2. The next day, 1–2 hours before serving, add the broccoli florets and ⅓ cup of the dressing; stir to mix and chill. Cover and refrigerate the remaining dressing.

3. To serve, add the salad greens, celery, green onions, radishes, and red pepper to the salad bowl. Pour the remaining dressing over the salad; toss lightly to mix. Divide the greens equally among individual chilled salad plates. Top each serving with toasted macadamia nuts.

BACON-SPINACH SALAD

You can use a combination of melted bacon grease and oil for the dressing.

Yields 4 servings

1 cup vegetable oil

1 small yellow or red onion, diced

¾ cup granulated sugar

¼ cup apple cider vinegar

⅓ cup ketchup

1 teaspoon Worcestershire sauce

8 cups baby spinach, stems removed

8 ounces fresh button mushrooms, cleaned and sliced

4 hard-boiled eggs, peeled and chopped

8 slices bacon, cooked crisp and crumbled

Optional: fresh bean sprouts

4 ounces Cheddar cheese, grated

1. Add the oil, onion, sugar, vinegar, ketchup, and Worcestershire sauce to a blender or food processor; pulse to mix.

2. To assemble each salad, arrange 2 cups of spinach on a plate and top with the mushrooms, chopped egg, bacon, and bean sprouts (if using). Drizzle a generous amount of dressing over the salad, and top with grated cheese. Refrigerate any leftover dressing.

Hot Bacon Dressing

In a nonreactive or nonstick skillet, fry 1 pound of bacon until crisp. Remove the bacon and crumble it. Remove the pan from the heat and stir ¼ cup apple cider vinegar, ¼ cup granulated sugar, 1 diced small yellow or red onion, and ⅓ cup ketchup into the bacon fat. If desired, stir the bacon back into the dressing.

CHEF'S SALAD

This salad is an easy one to pack for lunch. Put the salad in an empty container with a lid, the cheese in a snack-size baggie, and enough dressing for your salad in a small plastic container.

Yields 4 servings

8 cups salad mix

1 small red onion, sliced or diced

2 stalks celery, diced

1 cup frozen baby peas, thawed

4 hard-boiled eggs, peeled and chopped

1 pound boiled ham, diced

8 ounces Cheddar cheese, grated

Salad dressing to taste

1. Add the salad mix, onion, celery, peas, eggs, and ham to a large salad bowl; toss to mix.

2. Divide the salad between 4 plates or salad bowls. Top each salad with grated cheese and salad dressing.

The Best Blue Cheese Dressing Ever!

In a small bowl, stir together ⅔ cup sour cream, ⅓ cup mayonnaise, 1 teaspoon champagne vinegar, 2 teaspoons (or to taste) granulated sugar, and 1 ounce (or to taste) crumbled blue cheese. Store leftovers in the refrigerator.

TUNA-MACARONI SALAD

This salad tastes best if it's refrigerated overnight before serving. Wait until after it's completely chilled to taste for seasoning.

Yields 4 servings

7 ounces dried elbow macaroni

4 ounces Cheddar cheese, cut into cubes

1 7-ounce can tuna, drained

¾ cup candied sweet pickles, chopped

1 small red onion, diced

1 cup salad dressing or mayonnaise

1 tablespoon granulated sugar, or to taste

Salt and freshly ground black pepper to taste

Optional: iceberg lettuce or salad mix

1. Cook the macaroni according to package directions; drain well. Add the cooked macaroni to a large bowl. Add the cheese, tuna, sweet pickles, onion, salad dressing or mayonnaise, sugar, salt, and pepper. Stir to combine.

2. Cover and refrigerate overnight. Taste for seasoning before serving, and add additional sugar, salt, and pepper, if needed. Serve the salad on top of lettuce leaves or salad mix.

FRIED TOMATO AND CORN SALAD

This dish is good served cold, which makes it great for taking to a summer barbecue.

Yields 4–6 servings

1 pint cherry or grape tomatoes

1 poblano pepper

1 tablespoon olive oil

Kernels from 2 ears of sweet corn or 2 cups frozen corn

1 small onion

2 teaspoons sherry or rice wine vinegar

Salt to taste

Pepper to taste

⅓ cup chopped cilantro

1. Place the tomatoes in the freezer for at least 2 hours, or overnight.

2. Use long tongs to hold the pepper over a burner set on high heat. Rotate and move the pepper until all of the skin has blackened and bubbled. Wrap it in a paper towel and roll it tightly in foil for 2 minutes. Remove the foil and use the paper towel to rub the skin off the pepper. Be careful not to burn yourself. Remove the stem and the seeds from the pepper and dice it finely.

3. Place a skillet over high heat and add the oil. Once it starts to smoke, add the tomatoes to the skillet. Wear an oven mitt around your wrist or use a splatter screen to protect yourself if the tomatoes pop. Shake the skillet back and forth frequently. Once the tomatoes start to thaw and release their juice, drain them and add the corn. Toss to combine and cook for 2–3 minutes. Drain again if necessary and add the onion and poblano pepper and cook for an additional 2–3 minutes. The onions should be soft.

4. Stir in the vinegar and season with salt, pepper, and the fresh cilantro, and serve either hot, warm, or cold.

BULGUR SALAD WITH ROASTED CHICKPEAS AND LEMON

Bulgur is whole pieces of wheat that have been cleaned, parboiled, dried, and sorted into sizes. It's healthier than rice or pasta, and just as easy.

Yields 4 servings

1¼ cups water

1 cup coarse bulgur

1 medium red onion, thinly sliced

2 tablespoons olive oil

Juice from 1 lemon

2 bay leaves

1 teaspoon cumin seeds

½ teaspoon ground turmeric

½ teaspoon ground paprika

1 pinch cayenne pepper

1 15-ounce can chickpeas, rinsed and drained

Salt to taste

Pepper to taste

1. Preheat oven to 400°F.

2. Bring the water to a boil in a saucepan and add the bulgur and a pinch of salt. Remove from heat and let it sit for 20 minutes until all of the water has been absorbed.

3. Place a skillet over medium heat. Once it is heated, add the onion, oil, lemon juice, bay leaves, cumin, turmeric, paprika, and cayenne. Stir until the onions are coated with the spices. Cook the onions for 5–7 minutes until they're soft and the spices smell toasted. Stir the chickpeas into the onions and cook until they start to sizzle.

4. Place the skillet into the middle of the oven for 20 minutes and stir halfway through. Remove the skillet from the oven, discard the bay leaves, and season with salt and pepper as necessary. Pour over the bulgur and serve while hot.

CHICKEN ENCHILADAS

For 6 servings, allow 2 enchiladas per person along with a tomato salad. To stretch it to 12 servings, allow 1 enchilada per person along with a generous serving of tossed salad.

Yields 6–12 servings

1 rotisserie chicken

¼ teaspoon freshly ground black pepper

1 10-ounce package frozen chopped spinach, thawed and well drained

6 green onions, thinly sliced

1 cup tomato salsa

4 ounces Cheddar or Monterey jack cheese, shredded

Nonstick cooking spray

12 7" flour or corn tortillas

1¼ cups sour cream

2 tablespoons all-purpose flour

Salt and freshly ground black pepper to taste

½ teaspoon ground cumin

½ cup milk

1 4-ounce can diced green chili peppers, drained

Optional: fresh tomato, diced

Optional: fresh cilantro, chopped

1. Preheat oven to 350°F.

2. Remove and discard the skin from the chicken; remove the meat from the bones and shred it. For the filling, mix together the shredded chicken, black pepper, spinach, green onions, salsa, and half of the cheese in a bowl. Treat a 9" × 13" nonstick baking pan with nonstick spray. Soften the flour or corn tortillas by placing them on a microwave-safe plate; cover with a damp paper towel and microwave on high for 1 minute. Spoon the filling down the centers of the tortillas, roll them, and place seam side down in the baking pan.

3. To make the sauce, add the sour cream, flour, salt, pepper, cumin, milk, and chili peppers to a small bowl; stir to mix. Spoon the sauce over the tops of the rolled tortillas in the baking pan. Cover and bake for 20 minutes. Uncover and bake for an additional 20 minutes, or until heated through. Sprinkle with remaining cheese; bake for another 5 minutes, remove from the oven, and let stand for 5 minutes before serving. Garnish with chopped tomato, cilantro, or additional salsa if desired.

The Traditional Way to Soften Corn Tortillas

Heat 1" of corn oil or lard in a skillet over medium heat until the fat is hot enough that a drop of water splatters when dropped in the oil. Holding a tortilla with tongs, immerse it in the oil, turning it over a few times until it becomes pliable. Drain on paper towels.

CRANBERRY TURKEY QUESADILLA

Mixing fruit with salsa adds a twist to a Southwestern dish. You can substitute tart cherry juice concentrate for the cranberry sauce or use dried cranberries or other dried fruit and a bit more salsa.

Yields 1 serving

2 teaspoons extra-virgin olive oil

2 flour tortillas

1 tablespoon cranberry sauce

1 tablespoon salsa

½ cup Monterey jack or Cheddar cheese, grated

¼ cup chopped cooked turkey

Optional: 1 teaspoon chopped jalapeño pepper

1. Pour the oil into a small nonstick skillet. Add one of the tortillas and coat one side with oil. Remove and repeat with the second tortilla. Mix together the cranberry sauce, salsa, cheese, turkey, and jalapeño (if using). Spread the mixture over the tortilla in the pan. Top with the other tortilla, oiled side up. Press gently but firmly to keep the quesadilla together.

2. Place the pan over medium heat. Cook for about 2 minutes, or until the bottom is lightly browned. Flip the quesadilla and cook for another 2 minutes, or until that side is lightly browned and the cheese is melted.

STUFFED GRAPE LEAVES

This dish is often used as an appetizer, but it's also good as a light supper.

Yields 4–6 servings

1 pound lean ground lamb

1 cup uncooked long-grain rice

¼ teaspoon ground cinnamon

¼ teaspoon ground allspice

Salt and freshly ground pepper to taste

1 1-pound jar grape leaves

Nonstick cooking spray

Water or chicken broth as needed

Juice of 2 lemons

1. In a bowl, mix together the lamb, rice, cinnamon, allspice, salt, and pepper.

2. Drain the grape leaves. Use any small leaves to line the bottom of a heavy saucepan or Dutch oven treated with nonstick spray. Lay each larger leaf on a flat surface, vein side up; trim off any stem. Spoon some of the lamb mixture onto the center of each grape leaf. To form each roll, fold the stem end over the filling, fold the sides over each other, and fold down the tip. Carefully place each roll, seam side down, in the saucepan. Place the rolls close together in the pan to prevent them from unrolling while they cook. You may end up with several layers of rolls, depending on the size of the pan.

3. Place a plate over the rolls and then add enough water or broth to cover the plate. Bring to a boil over medium-high heat, then reduce the heat, cover, and simmer for 30 minutes. Add the lemon juice; cover and continue to simmer for an additional 30 minutes. The stuffed grape leaves (dolmas or dolmades) are done when they're tender when pierced with a fork. You can serve them warm, at room temperature, or cool.

SHRIMP RISOTTO

A fresh tomato salad is a nice complement to this rich, creamy dish.

Yields 4 servings

2 tablespoons extra-virgin olive oil

1 small Vidalia onion, diced

1 teaspoon fennel seeds

3 cloves garlic, minced

1½ cups arborio rice

2 tablespoons tomato paste

Pinch saffron threads

¼ cup dry white vermouth

3 cups chicken broth

1 pound medium shrimp, peeled and deveined

Salt and freshly ground black pepper to taste

1. Add the oil to a pressure cooker and bring to temperature over medium-high heat. Add the onion and fennel seeds; sauté for 5 minutes, or until the onions are softened. Add the garlic, rice, tomato paste, and saffron; stir until the rice is evenly colored. Stir in the vermouth and broth.

2. Close and lock the pressure cooker lid; bring to high pressure and maintain it for 3 minutes. Remove from heat and use the cooker's quick-release method to release the pressure. Carefully remove the lid. Put the cooker back on the burner over medium heat and stir in the shrimp; simmer for 2 minutes, or until the shrimp are pale pink and cooked through. Taste for seasoning and add salt and pepper, if needed. Serve immediately.

Add a Veggie!

Add a vegetable to the Shrimp Risotto by stirring in 1 cup of thawed frozen baby peas when you add the shrimp.

SPANAKOPITA

Serve these as an appetizer or as a main course with a tossed salad. If you like, you can add a piece of cooked chicken, lobster, or crabmeat to each triangle.

Yields 10 servings

3 tablespoons olive oil

1 large yellow onion, diced

8 green onions, white and 1" of green parts diced

3 cloves garlic, minced

2 pounds fresh baby spinach, trimmed, washed, and roughly chopped

1½ tablespoons fresh lemon juice

2 large eggs, lightly beaten

12 ounces crumbled feta

1 tablespoon coriander seeds, toasted and ground

½ teaspoon freshly grated nutmeg

½ pound unsalted butter, melted

1 pound package of phyllo pastry sheets

¼ cup fresh oregano, finely chopped

¼ cup fresh chives, finely chopped

½ cup freshly grated Parmigiano-Reggiano

1. Add the oil and yellow and green onions to a large microwave-safe bowl; cover and microwave on high for 1 minute. Stir and microwave for 1 more minute, or until the onions are transparent. Stir in the garlic and spinach; cover and microwave on high for 2 minutes. Set aside to cool, and then stir in the lemon juice, eggs, feta, coriander, and nutmeg.

2. Preheat oven to 350°F.

3. Brush 2 baking sheets with some of the melted butter. Unroll the phyllo dough; prevent the dough from drying out and becoming brittle by keeping it covered with a damp towel until you are ready to work with it. Lay out a piece of the dough flat on a work surface; brush it with melted butter, then evenly spread some oregano and chives over it. Repeat the butter and herb step with 2 more sheets of phyllo, stacking them on top of each other. Use a sharp knife or pizza cutter to cut the sheets lengthwise into thirds to form 2½" strips. Repeat with all the remaining sheets of dough.

4. Put 1 heaping teaspoon of the spinach filling near 1 corner of each layered phyllo strip. Fold the end at an angle over the filling to form a triangle and continue to fold along the strip until you reach the end, in a manner similar to folding up a flag. Brush the top of the resulting triangle packet with butter and dust with Parmigiano-Reggiano. Place each triangle on one of the prepared baking sheets; cover while preparing the remaining pastries. Repeat until all the filling and phyllo strips are used up. Bake for 20–30 minutes, or until crisp and golden. Serve hot, warm, or cold.

CHEDDAR AND JALAPEÑO CORN STICKS

If you like the jalapeño flavor but don't want the crunchy texture in your sticks, heat the milk till it is not quite boiling and then add jalapeño rings to the milk. Refrigerate overnight and discard the jalapeño before cooking.

Yields 14 sticks

1 cup yellow cornmeal

1 teaspoon sugar

½ teaspoon baking soda

½ teaspoon salt

1 cup milk

1 egg

1 cup shredded Cheddar cheese

2 scallions, finely chopped

2 jalapeños, seeded and minced

2 tablespoons melted butter

1. Preheat oven to 425°F. Place the corn stick pans on the middle rack.

2. Combine the dry ingredients in a large bowl. Whisk the milk and egg together. Add the milk mixture, cheese, scallions, and the jalapeños to the dry mixture and stir gently until everything is combined.

3. Remove the pans from the oven and use a brush to apply the melted butter. Pour the batter into the pans, being careful not to get any batter on the outside of the pans.

4. Bake for 12–15 minutes, or until golden brown. Remove the sticks from the pan and let them cool for 5 minutes.

DEEP-FRIED CALAMARI

This dish is often served with Cocktail Sauce (see Deep-Fried Shrimp and Oysters recipe in Chapter 8), but it can also be served with a spicy or garlicky mayonnaise or a rémoulade sauce.

Yields 2 or 3 servings

1 pound frozen calamari, cleaned

¼ cup fine cornmeal

2 tablespoons cornstarch

2 teaspoons Old Bay Seasoning

½ teaspoon salt

1 quart canola or safflower oil

1. Thaw the calamari. Slice off the tentacles. Slice the tubes into ½"-wide rings. Pat dry with paper towels. Combine the cornmeal, cornstarch, Old Bay Seasoning, and the salt in a plastic bag. Add the calamari to the bag and shake till coated evenly.

2. Preheat oven to 175°F. Place a wire rack over a baking sheet in the middle of the oven. Place the oil in a fryer over medium-high heat. Once the oil is heated, carefully add a handful of calamari pieces. Cook for 2–3 minutes or until they're lightly golden brown.

3. Remove the cooked calamari with a fryer basket or wire skimmer and place on the wire rack to drain.

CRISPY BUFFALOED CHICKEN BITES

This football-season classic gives you the feeling of having eaten fried wings without the mess or calories.

Yields 6–8 servings as an appetizer

1½ pounds boneless, skinless chicken breast

¼ cup butter, melted

¼ cup Tabasco sauce

1 tablespoon garlic powder

1 tablespoon apple cider vinegar

1 teaspoon salt

4 cups corn flakes, crushed

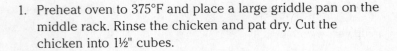

1. Preheat oven to 375°F and place a large griddle pan on the middle rack. Rinse the chicken and pat dry. Cut the chicken into 1½" cubes.

2. Whisk the butter, Tabasco sauce, garlic powder, vinegar, and salt together in a wide, shallow bowl. Place the corn flakes into another wide, shallow bowl.

3. Dip a handful of chicken pieces into the liquid mixture. Shake off the excess and drop them into the corn flakes. Roll them until coated and set aside. Repeat with the rest of the chicken.

4. Once the oven and griddle are hot, place the chicken on the griddle, spreading them out evenly so they barely touch. Cook for 6 minutes on the first side. Flip them and cook for another 6 minutes.

5. Remove them from the oven and let them cool; place them on a serving platter with celery sticks and blue cheese dressing.

FRIED RAVIOLI APPETIZER

This recipe works best with ravioli that are about 1½–2" across. Larger ravioli won't cook through and smaller ravioli will break up in the fryer.

Yields 8–10 servings

1 large egg

½ cup panko or bread crumbs

1 teaspoon dried oregano

1 teaspoon garlic powder

¼ teaspoon black pepper

½ teaspoon salt

2 tablespoons shredded Parmesan cheese

1 package frozen ravioli, thawed

2 cups vegetable oil

1 cup marinara sauce, warmed

1. Whisk the egg in a small bowl. In a separate bowl combine the panko, spices, and cheese.

2. Dip each ravioli in the egg with one hand. Dip the ravioli in the panko mixture with the other hand.

3. Place a Dutch oven over medium heat and fill it with vegetable oil. Drop the ravioli in the oil and cook for 2 minutes on each side till they're lightly golden.

4. Remove them from the skillet and drain on paper towels. Serve with a bowl of warmed marinara sauce for dipping.

BAKED ONIONS

These onions make a great appetizer or side with grilled meats or fish. If you prefer, you can sprinkle them with tarragon, basil, or rosemary.

Yields 4 servings

1 pound small sweet onions, peeled and stem trimmed

4 tablespoons butter, in wrapper

1 teaspoon salt

½ teaspoon ground black pepper

1 teaspoon dried thyme

1. Preheat oven to 350°F and place a rack in the middle of the oven.

2. Rub the onions with the stick of butter until they're completely coated. Place them in the skillet and sprinkle with salt, pepper, and thyme.

3. Place the skillet in the middle of the oven and bake for 45 minutes. They should be very soft. Serve while hot.

PAN-SEARED SCALLOPS AND CHORIZO

Chorizo comes in many varieties. Spanish varieties are more like a firm, cured sausage, while the Mexican varieties are soft with a texture more like that of breakfast sausage. Both varieties will work in this dish.

Yields 4 servings

6 ounces chorizo sausage

1 pound scallops, cut in half if large

Juice from 1 lemon

Fresh ground pepper to taste

¼ cup chopped fresh parsley

1. If using a firm sausage in casing, slice into ¼" rounds.

2. Place a skillet over medium heat. Once heated, add the chorizo. If cooking rounds of sausage, cook 3 minutes or until lightly crispy on each side. If using loose sausage, spread the sausage evenly over the bottom of the skillet and cook 5–7 minutes or until the sausage is cooked through. Break up the sausage into bite-size chunks.

3. Remove the chorizo and place in a bowl. Drain off all but 1 tablespoon of oil from the skillet. Add the scallops to the skillet and cook for 1 minute on each side.

4. Return the chorizo to the skillet, pour the lemon juice over, and sprinkle with ground pepper while stirring to coat.

5. Remove the chorizo and scallops to plates and sprinkle fresh parsley on top.

PAN-ROASTED TURKEY WINGS

Turkey wings come in three parts. The tips are inedible but are great for creating stock and aren't needed for this dish.

Yields 4 servings

8 turkey wings, tips removed and sections separated

1 teaspoon salt

2 tablespoons olive oil

3 cups ketchup

3 cups apple juice

2 teaspoons Tabasco sauce

1 large onion, chopped

8 garlic cloves, smashed

2 teaspoons fresh thyme leaves

1. Preheat oven to 300°F. Place a rack in the middle of the oven.

2. Sprinkle the wing pieces lightly with salt. Place a skillet over medium heat. Once it is heated, add the oil and the wings to the skillet. Cook on each side for 3 minutes, or until they're lightly browned.

3. Whisk the ketchup, apple juice, Tabasco sauce, onion, garlic, and thyme in a small bowl. Pour the sauce over the wings, and place the pan in the middle of the oven.

4. Cook 30 minutes. Use tongs to turn them over and continue cooking them for another 15–20 minutes, or until the meat is tender and the sauce has thickened.

5. Serve the sauce in a small bowl alongside the wings.

MARYLAND CRAB CAKES

The crab flavor and spices are dominant in these cakes. Serve with tartar sauce, Cocktail Sauce (see Deep-Fried Shrimp and Oysters recipe in Chapter 8), Spicy Mayonnaise (see recipe in sidebar), and lemon wedges.

Yields 4 servings

½ cup mayonnaise

1 large egg

1 tablespoon mustard

1 tablespoon Old Bay Seasoning

1 pound jumbo lump crabmeat, shells and cartilage removed

1 tablespoon vegetable oil

1. Preheat oven to 400°F and place a skillet on a rack in the middle.

2. Whisk together the mayonnaise, egg, mustard, and Old Bay. Once the egg is completely incorporated, gently stir in the crabmeat. Be careful not to break up the lumps.

3. Divide the mixture into 4 even pieces. Form each piece into a patty.

4. Add the oil to the skillet and add the patties. Bake the patties for 12 minutes and flip. Bake for 5–8 minutes on the second side. Remove immediately from the skillet and let sit for 5 minutes before serving.

Spicy Mayonnaise

If everyone eating crab cakes likes spicy food, you can add a ¼ teaspoon of cayenne pepper to the crab cake mixture. But if only some of your dinner guests like it spicy, you can mix ½ cup of mayonnaise with 2 tablespoons of chili sauce and juice from half of a lemon.

LEEK, MUSHROOM, AND GOAT CHEESE QUESADILLA

A 6" skillet fits a small corn tortilla perfectly.

Yields 2 servings

1 tablespoon plus 1 teaspoon olive oil

¼ cup leek, chopped

¼ cup mushrooms, chopped

½ teaspoon garlic powder

Salt to taste

Pepper to taste

2 corn tortillas

¼ cup goat cheese, crumbled

Optional: ½ cup salsa and sour cream

1. Place a small skillet over medium heat. Once heated, add 1 tablespoon olive oil and leek. Cook for 3–4 minutes or until the leek is just starting to soften. Add the mushrooms, garlic powder, and salt and pepper to taste, and stir frequently for 4–5 minutes. The mushrooms should reduce and the leeks should start to turn golden.

2. Remove the contents of the skillet to a small bowl. Wipe out the skillet and add 1 teaspoon olive oil. Place 1 corn tortilla in the skillet and add the leek and mushroom mixture on top of it. Add the cheese on top, being careful to keep it from touching the sides of the skillet. Place another tortilla on top and press down.

3. Cook for 3–4 minutes, or until the bottom tortilla is crispy. Carefully remove the quesadilla from the skillet and flip over. Cook the second side for 2–3 minutes or until crispy.

4. Remove from skillet and let it rest for 3 minutes before slicing in half and serving with or without salsa and sour cream.

BACON-WRAPPED, CHEESE-STUFFED JALAPEÑOS

If you leave in the peppers' ribs, it will make the dish spicy. If you remove all of it, it will be fairly mild.

Yields 14 pieces

7 jalapeños

4 ounces cream cheese

14 slices bacon (approximately 1 pound)

1. Trim the woody part of the stem from the jalapeños. Cut the peppers open lengthwise and scoop out the seeds and the white veins. Spread a teaspoon or two of cream cheese onto each jalapeño half.

2. Starting at the thick end, wrap the bacon slice around the pepper. Spear with a toothpick to hold it in place. If the slice of bacon is too long, trim off the extra instead of wrapping it further.

3. Preheat oven to 375°F. Place a grill pan in the middle of the oven. Add the peppers and cook for 12–15 minutes, or until the bottom of the bacon is crispy.

4. Turn on the broiler and cook for 4–6 minutes until the cheese is bubbling and the bacon is crispy. Remove to a plate and let them rest before serving.

Alternate Option

The flavor of the bacon and the pepper are dominant. But if you'd like the cheese to be more prominent, you can mix 2 tablespoons shredded Cheddar cheese, 1 teaspoon garlic powder, and 1 teaspoon cumin in the cheese.

BEEF AND CHICKEN FAJITAS

Even though you're using the same marinade for the chicken and the beef, you can't marinate them together. Chicken has to cook at a higher temperature than beef to kill any potential salmonella.

Yields 6–8 servings

12 ounces beer

½ cup vegetable oil, plus more as needed

Juice from 2 limes

5 garlic cloves, smashed

2 tablespoons Worcestershire sauce

1 tablespoon chili powder

1 teaspoon ground black pepper

1 teaspoon ground cumin

1 pound skirt or flank steak

1 pound boneless, skinless chicken breasts

Salt to taste

2 small onions, quartered

1 green pepper, cut into ½" strips

1 red or yellow pepper, cut into ½" strips

Corn or flour tortillas for 6–8 people

Chopped fresh cilantro

Lime wedges

Bottled hot sauce or salsa to taste

1. Combine the beer, ½ cup vegetable oil, lime juice, garlic, Worcestershire sauce, chili powder, pepper, and cumin and divide into 2 large sealable bowls.

2. Trim any excess fat off the steak and chicken. Use a meat tenderizer to pound the chicken to ⅜" thick. Sprinkle the meat lightly with salt and place the beef in one container and the chicken in the other. Refrigerate for 3–8 hours.

3. Place a grill pan over medium-high heat and brush the ridges with oil. Place the onions on the pan and cook until translucent. Move to a bowl and keep warm. Scatter the peppers across the grill pan and cook until soft. Place them in the bowl with the onions.

4. Apply another coating of oil on the grill pan ridges. Cook the flank steak for 4–5 minutes on each side. Let it rest on a plate. Slice the steak into strips.

5. Apply another coating of oil on the grill pan ridges. Cook the chicken breasts for 6–7 minutes on each side. Let them rest on a plate. Slice the chicken into strips. Serve meat and vegetables with warm tortillas, chopped cilantro, lime wedges, and hot sauce or salsa.

CHIPOTLE BLACK BEAN QUESADILLA

If you have leftover black beans from the Stewed Black Beans (see recipe in this chapter), you can use those and omit the chipotle if desired.

Yields 4 servings

1 15-ounce can black beans, drained and rinsed

2 tablespoons canned chipotle

1 cup diced tomato, seeded

8 flour or corn tortillas

1 cup shredded cheese

1. Place the beans in a bowl and mash them with a fork. Stir in the chipotle and tomato.

2. Place a griddle over medium heat. Once it's heated place 2 or 4 tortillas on the griddle. Don't overlap them. Sprinkle ¼ cup of cheese on each tortilla. Spoon ¼ of the bean mixture on top of the cheese. Top with another tortilla and press down slightly.

3. Cook for 4–6 minutes on the first side, or until the tortilla is slightly browned. Press the top tortilla to make it stick to the cheese. Carefully flip the tortilla.

4. Cook on the second side for 4–6 minutes, or until the tortilla is slightly browned. Cut into wedges and serve with salsa and sour cream.

Perfect Cheese for Quesadilla

Any cheese that will melt is suitable for quesadillas. But some cheeses melt better and are less likely to clash with the black beans. If you don't have Mexican Chihuahua cheese at your grocery, use Monterey jack or a mild Cheddar. These cheeses will melt easily without getting too greasy, and without clashing with the strong flavor of the beans.

ENCHILADA CASSEROLE

Enchilada translates from Spanish to mean "in chili." But it is possible to regulate the heat to get a flavorful sauce that isn't too spicy.

Yields 2–4 servings

½ teaspoon corn or vegetable oil

2 corn tortillas

1 cup enchilada sauce

¼ cup shredded Cheddar cheese

2 tablespoons minced onion

2 tablespoons sliced black olives

1. Preheat oven to 350°F. Add the oil to a small skillet.

2. Cut the corn tortillas into 8 wedges and soak them in the enchilada sauce for 15 minutes.

3. Place half of the tortilla wedges in the bottom of the skillet. Sprinkle half of the cheese on top. Add the remaining tortillas, the rest of the cheese, and sprinkle the onion and olives on top. Pour the sauce over the wedges. Place the skillet in the middle of the oven and bake for 15 minutes. Cool for a few minutes before serving.

MIGAS

If you don't have corn tortillas, you can use flour tortillas, although the texture won't be quite the same. For this dish, canned green chilies are perfect.

Yields 2–4 servings

2 large eggs

1 tablespoon chunky salsa

1 teaspoon water

1 tablespoon butter

1 tablespoon olive oil

4 6" corn tortillas

¼ small onion, finely chopped

2 tablespoons chopped green chilies

½ small tomato, chopped

½ avocado, sliced

1 teaspoon fresh cilantro

3 tablespoons grated Monterey jack cheese

Dollop sour cream

1. Place skillet over medium heat.

2. Crack the eggs into a small bowl and mix in the salsa and water. Set aside.

3. Once the skillet is heated, add the butter and olive oil. Once the foaming stops, tear up 2 corn tortillas and sauté them until they're soft. Add the onion to the skillet. Cook and stir for 5 minutes, or until the onion is translucent and soft. Stir in the green chilies.

4. Pour the egg mixture in the skillet and slowly fold until the eggs are cooked through. Sprinkle the tomato over the top of the eggs.

5. Remove the skillet from the heat and stir in the avocado, cilantro, and cheese. Turn out onto a plate and serve with sour cream and 2 remaining warmed corn tortillas.

Eat Every Crumb

Migas is a Tex-Mex dish in America, but it started and remains popular in Spain. *Migas* means "crumbs" and refers to the use of scraps of tortillas or bread. In Spain, you're likely to have spinach, chorizo, or grapes mixed in your migas. The recipes vary from one area of Texas to the next, but this version is popular in Austin.

SOUR CREAM CHILI BAKE WITH CHICKEN

Because of the tomato sauce in this dish, this isn't a good recipe for a fairly new skillet. Tomato sauces can remove seasoning from a new skillet.

Yields 4–6 servings

1 pound lean ground chicken

½ small onion, finely chopped

1 teaspoon ground cumin

1 10-ounce can enchilada sauce

1 8-ounce can tomato sauce

1 15-ounce can pinto beans

6 ounces crushed tortilla chips

2 cups shredded Cheddar cheese

Salt to taste

6 ounces tortilla chips

1 cup sour cream

1. Preheat oven to 350°F. Place a skillet over medium heat. When the skillet has warmed, crumble the ground chicken into the skillet, breaking it into chunks. Cook for several minutes using a wooden spoon or spatula to cut and toss the meat.

2. Sprinkle in the onion and cumin. Continue stirring and chopping until the meat is more brown than pink. Drain any excess fat. Add the enchilada sauce, tomato sauce, beans, crushed chips, and 1½ cups cheese. Stir to combine so the cheese melts evenly. Taste and add salt and cumin if desired. Place the skillet in the middle of the oven and bake for 30 minutes.

3. When the edges of the casserole are crispy and the mixture is lightly bubbling, sprinkle the remaining cheese across the top and bake for 2–3 minutes or until the cheese melts.

4. Serve with chips and sour cream as a garnish.

Spice It Up!

This is a weeknight, easy dish that can be made to suit your family's spice level. Mild enchilada sauce will result in a tame dish. You can also use spicy enchilada sauce, or double the mild sauce and leave out the tomato sauce. You could also substitute 1 cup of salsa for the plain tomato sauce to add even more flavor and texture to the dish.

GRILLED DIJON TOMATOES

This is a simple and delicious side dish to serve with the Basic Hamburger (see recipe in Chapter 7).

Yields 4 servings

1 tablespoon Dijon mustard

1 teaspoon salt

Large pinch black pepper

3 tablespoons melted butter

¼ cup panko bread crumbs

¼ cup Parmesan cheese, shredded

2 medium tomatoes, cut in half lengthwise and seeded

1 teaspoon olive or vegetable oil

Paprika to taste

1. Preheat broiler on high and place grill pan in middle of oven. In a small bowl combine the mustard, salt, pepper, butter, bread crumbs, and Parmesan cheese.

2. Once the grill pan is hot, brush the cut side of each tomato lightly with the oil and place cut side down. Cook for 2–3 minutes. If the skin on the uncut side starts to blacken, remove tomatoes from the oven.

3. Carefully turn the tomato halves over. Place a quarter of the mustard mixture onto each tomato half and sprinkle lightly with paprika. Return the skillet to the oven and cook for 3–5 minutes until the mustard mixture is golden brown. Serve immediately.

CUBAN BLACK BEANS

As with almost any bean dish, you can add chopped celery and carrots if you like.

Yields 4–6

1 pound dried black beans

4 cups water, or more, as needed

3 cloves garlic, minced

1 green pepper, seeded and chopped

1 large yellow onion, chopped

½ pound salt pork or bacon, chopped

1 pound smoked ham hocks

2 teaspoons paprika

1 tablespoon ground cumin

2 bay leaves

4 cups chicken broth

¼ teaspoon chili powder

1 tablespoon red wine vinegar

Salt and freshly ground black pepper to taste

1. Rinse the beans and put them in a 6-quart Dutch oven with the 4 cups water. Bring to a boil over medium-high heat; cover and boil for 2 minutes. Turn off the heat and let set for 1 hour.

2. Add the garlic, green pepper, onion, salt pork or bacon, ham hocks, paprika, cumin, bay leaves, chicken broth, and chili powder. Add enough additional water so that the beans are completely covered. Cover and simmer for 2 hours over low heat, or until the beans are tender. Remove the ham hocks and take the meat off of the bones; return the meat to the pot. Remove and discard the bay leaves. Add the vinegar, salt, and pepper, and stir to mix.

Using Leftovers

It's easy to turn Cuban Black Beans into a satisfying soup. Once the beans are tender, simply add more chicken broth and bring to temperature. After you've added the vinegar, salt, and pepper, taste for seasoning and adjust by adding more vinegar and other seasonings if needed.

PUERTO RICAN RICE AND PIGEON PEAS

If you want to serve this as a main dish, increase the amount of ham called for in the recipe.

Yields 8 servings

½ pound dried gandules (pigeon peas)

3 cups water

1 tablespoon extra-virgin olive oil

1 ounce salt pork or bacon, chopped

2 ounces cooked ham, chopped

2 cloves garlic, minced

1 red bell pepper, seeded and diced

1 green pepper, seeded and diced

1 large yellow onion, diced

1 medium tomato, finely chopped

1 tablespoon Annatto Oil (see Filipino Pork with Rice Noodles recipe in Chapter 5)

2 cups chicken broth or water

1 cup instant white rice

Salt and freshly ground black pepper to taste

1. Add the gandules and water to a 6-quart Dutch oven; bring to a boil over medium heat. Cover and turn off the heat; allow to sit for 1 hour. Drain, reserving 1½ cups of the water.

2. Add the oil, salt pork or bacon, and ham to the Dutch oven and sauté over medium heat for 3 minutes. Add the garlic, red pepper, green pepper, and onion; sauté until the onion is transparent. Add the tomato, drained gandules, and reserved water. Bring to a boil; cover and lower the heat, and simmer 15 minutes or until the gandules are almost tender and have absorbed most of the liquid.

3. Stir in the Annatto Oil and broth or water. Bring to a boil over medium heat. Add the rice, cover, turn off the burner, and let set for 30 minutes, or until the liquid is absorbed and the rice is tender. Stir to fluff the rice. Taste for seasoning and add salt and pepper to taste.

SCALLOPED POTATOES WITH HAM

This is almost a cook-without-a-recipe recipe, which makes it easy to customize. For example, you can add more cheese or onion if you like. Or change the type of cheese or add some diced bell pepper along with the onion. Make it your own.

Yields 8 servings

6 tablespoons butter, plus more for buttering pan

8 large russet potatoes, peeled and very thinly sliced

Salt and freshly ground black pepper to taste

1 large yellow onion, diced

6 tablespoons all-purpose flour

2 cups cooked ham, cubed

3 cups Cheddar or American cheese, grated

4 cups milk or more as needed, heated to almost boiling

1. Preheat oven to 350°F.

2. Generously butter the bottom of a 9" × 13" nonstick baking pan. Evenly spread ⅓ of the potatoes across the bottom of the pan and sprinkle lightly with salt and pepper. Evenly sprinkle ⅓ of the onion over the potatoes, 2 tablespoons of the flour over the onion, and dot the flour with 3 tablespoons of butter. Add 1 cup of the cooked ham in an even layer, and top that with 1 cup of the cheese. Add another layer of potatoes, salt, pepper, onion, flour, butter, ham, and cheese. Top with the remaining potatoes. Slowly pour the hot milk over the potatoes, adding enough milk to bring the liquid level to just below the top of the potatoes. Cover with foil and bake for 1 hour.

3. Remove the foil, top with the remaining 1 cup of cheese, and bake for an additional 15 minutes, or until the potatoes are cooked through, the sauce is thickened, and the cheese is melted and bubbling.

Cheese and Saltiness

Cheddar and American cheese are saltier than are most Swiss cheeses, so adjust how much you salt the potatoes according to the type of cheese you're using. Cheese is an excellent source of calcium, but you may want to opt for low-fat options if you are watching your fat intake.

OVEN-FRIED POTATOES

Almost everyone likes crispy, fried potatoes, but deep-frying is messy and unhealthy. This method gets you the same texture with a fraction of the oil needed for deep-frying.

Yields 4 servings

2 medium Yukon gold potatoes

1 tablespoon olive oil

Salt to taste

Pepper to taste

1. Preheat oven to 400°F. Place a skillet in the middle of the oven.

2. Scrub the potatoes clean and pat dry with a lint-free towel. Cut each potato into ¼" or ⅜" slices. Cut the slices into strips the same width. Cut those strips into cubes. Place into a bowl and drizzle with olive oil. Sprinkle with salt and pepper and toss so they're evenly coated.

3. Pour potatoes into the warm skillet so there is one even layer on the bottom. Place the skillet in the middle of the oven and bake for 30 minutes. Stir once or twice. The potatoes should be soft in the middle with crispy edges. Serve while hot.

DOWN-HOME CLASSIC GREEN BEANS

This dish is great hot or warm, and it can be made ahead of time and warmed later when ready to serve.

Yields 4–6 servings

3 slices bacon, diced

1 small onion, diced

1 pound fresh green beans, trimmed

1 russet potato, diced

½ cup chicken broth

1 garlic clove, minced

1 teaspoon salt

¼ teaspoon pepper

1. Place a large skillet over medium heat. Once the skillet is warmed, add the bacon and the onion and cook until bacon is brown but not crispy, about 5 minutes.

2. Add the green beans, potato, chicken broth, garlic, salt, and pepper and cook for 3–4 minutes.

3. Reduce the heat to medium-low and cover. Cook for 5 minutes. The potatoes should be almost soft and the green beans should be bright green. Remove the lid and increase the heat to medium-high. Let the broth evaporate. Serve immediately.

STIR-FRIED ASPARAGUS

Asparagus is tasty, but often expensive, even during the spring when it's in season. If you can't get asparagus, substitute green beans. Choose smaller beans, remove the stem ends, and cook them whole.

Yields 4 servings

1 pound thin asparagus

2 tablespoons olive oil

Pinch salt

Pinch pepper

2 tablespoons water or chicken broth

1. Wash the asparagus and snap off the bottoms. Cut them into 1" slices on an angle.

2. Place a skillet over medium heat. Once it has heated, add the oil and the asparagus. Sprinkle them with salt and pepper and stir continually for 2 minutes until they're coated.

3. Add 2 tablespoons of water or chicken broth and cover. Cook for 2 minutes.

4. Turn off the heat but keep the skillet covered for 3 minutes, or until tender. Serve while hot.

FRIED GREEN TOMATOES

If you have any leftover batter, try dredging some pickle slices in it and frying them. They'll cook in about 1½ minutes and are just as tasty as fried green tomatoes.

Yields 6–8 servings

1½ cups all-purpose flour

½ cup cornmeal

½ teaspoon salt, plus 1 pinch

¼ teaspoon ground black pepper

¼–½ cup milk

3 or 4 large green tomatoes

¼ cup vegetable oil

¾ cup ranch dressing

1. Mix together the flour, cornmeal, ½ teaspoon salt, and pepper in a large bowl. Pour ¼ cup milk into the bowl and stir to combine. If mixture looks dry, add more milk until you get a thick batter. Slice the tomatoes into ¼" slices. Pat dry with paper towels.

2. Place a skillet over medium heat and add the oil. Dip each tomato slice into the batter and let the excess drip off. Slide them into the skillet so they're not touching. Cook each side for 1½–2 minutes. Remove them and place on a rack over paper towels to keep them from getting soggy.

3. While they're still hot, sprinkle with a pinch of salt. Serve them with ranch dressing as a dipping sauce.

SAUTÉED MUSHROOMS

Even white button mushrooms can have a lot of flavor if they're cooked right. These mushrooms can also be served over steaks, with eggs, or with polenta.

Yields 4 servings

3 tablespoons butter

3 tablespoons olive oil

1 pound mushrooms, sliced

Pinch salt

Pinch pepper

4 large shallots, minced

1. Place a large skillet over medium heat. Add 1 tablespoon butter and 1 tablespoon oil.

2. Once the butter has stopped foaming, add 1 large handful of mushrooms. Sprinkle them lightly with salt and pepper. Cook for several minutes on each side, or until they've shrunk in size and turned dark brown. Remove from skillet and keep them warm.

3. Repeat with the rest of the butter, oil, and mushrooms until all of the mushrooms are cooked.

4. If the skillet is dry, add a small amount of oil. Add the shallots and stir frequently for 5 minutes, or until they're soft and starting to brown.

5. Return the mushrooms to the skillet and stir occasionally for 3 minutes, or until the mushrooms are hot again. Serve hot.

ZUCCHINI PANCAKES

To preserve your zucchini bounty, you can freeze it. Follow these steps to shred, salt, and squeeze them dry. Spread them onto a cookie sheet, freeze, and then break them into chunks to put in a freezer-safe container for up to 3 months.

Yields 24–30 pancakes

1½ pounds zucchini (3 large zucchini), shredded

1 teaspoon plus 1 pinch salt

¼ Vidalia onion, thinly sliced and separated

1 large egg

¾ cup fine bread crumbs

½ cup vegetable oil

Pinch pepper

1. Place the zucchini in a colander. Sprinkle with 1 teaspoon salt and toss to coat evenly. Let this sit in your sink for half an hour to 1 hour if it is humid.

2. Preheat oven to 200°F so you can keep cooked pancakes warm before serving.

3. Squeeze as much of the water out of the zucchini as you can. Place them in a bowl. Sprinkle the onion over the zucchini and mix in the egg and bread crumbs.

4. Place a skillet over medium-high heat and add the oil. If it starts to smoke, lower the temperature. Use your hands to scoop up a heaping tablespoon of the mixture and flatten it into a pancake. Place it in the skillet and fry 2 or 3 at a time. Cook on each side for about 3 minutes until they're light brown.

5. Remove them from the skillet and place on a rack over a cookie sheet in the middle of the oven. Sprinkle with salt and pepper. Repeat with the remaining mixture until they're all cooked. Serve while warm.

SWEET POTATO LATKES

Latkes are traditionally served for Jewish holidays, specifically Passover (provided all the ingredients are kosher) and Hanukkah. This is a variation on the traditional dish, but is tasty anytime.

Yields 4–6 servings

1 cup flour

4 teaspoons sugar

2 teaspoons brown sugar

2 teaspoons baking powder

½ teaspoon cayenne powder

4 teaspoons curry powder

2 teaspoons ground cumin

1 teaspoon plus 1 dash salt

¼ teaspoon ground black pepper

4 eggs, beaten

½ cup milk

2 pounds sweet potatoes, peeled, trimmed, and grated

½ cup vegetable oil

1. Stir together the flour, sugars, baking powder, and spices in a large bowl. Whisk together the eggs and milk in a smaller bowl. Pour the egg mixture into the dry ingredients. Stir till it is barely combined. Add the grated sweet potatoes to the mix and stir till evenly coated.

2. Place a skillet over medium heat. Once it is heated, add ¼ cup of the oil to the skillet.

3. Once the oil has come to temperature, drop the potato mixture into the hot oil by the tablespoonful and flatten slightly. Cook for 2 minutes on each side. Repeat until remaining mixture is used, adding more oil to the skillet as needed.

4. Place latkes on a wire rack over paper towels and let them drain. Sprinkle them while they're hot with a dash of salt.

QUINOA AND BEEF-STUFFED ACORN SQUASH

Make the Quinoa Pilaf (see recipe in Chapter 5) before making this dish. If you don't have leftovers, you can use any leftover flavored rice or grain dish in its place.

Yields 2 servings

1 acorn squash

Pinch salt

Pinch pepper

2 ounces ground beef

1 serving Quinoa Pilaf

¼ cup vegetable broth

2 teaspoons Parmesan cheese

1. Preheat oven to 350°F. Remove the stem and cut the squash in half lengthwise. Use a spoon to remove the seeds and strings to create a hollow in each half. Sprinkle each half lightly with salt and pepper.

2. Place a small skillet over medium heat. Once it is warm add the ground beef and stir continually with a fork, breaking the beef into small pieces. When cooked, drain off any excess grease and add the beef to a bowl with the pilaf. Stir to combine and place half of the mixture in each hollow of squash.

3. Pour half the vegetable broth and sprinkle half the cheese on each squash half. Place the squash in a small skillet in the middle of the oven for 40–50 minutes. It is ready when you can pierce the flesh with a fork through to the skin easily. Let each half cool for 5 minutes before serving.

Make Your Own Frozen Dinners

If you're trying to eliminate some of the sodium and preservatives in your diet, but like the convenience of frozen dinners, many of the recipes in this chapter can be doubled and the second portion can be stored in a sealable container for later. In most cases, you'll save money, eat healthier, and still have quick meals.

SOUR CREAMED GREENS

Most people make creamed greens dishes with a lot of heavy cream. But you can substitute sour cream (even the fat-free variety) to get a similar and healthier dish.

Yields 4 servings

1½ pounds fresh mustard greens, spinach, or chard

½ cup chicken broth

1 tablespoon butter

1 tablespoon olive oil

1 medium onion, chopped

2 cloves garlic, minced

Salt to taste

Pepper to taste

½ cup sour cream

1. Rinse the greens well and cut out tough stems if necessary. Tear the leaves into smaller pieces. Place a skillet over medium heat. Add the greens and the chicken broth. Boil for about 10 minutes. They should be bright green. Place the greens in a bowl temporarily.

2. Add the butter and oil to the skillet. Once the butter is melted, add the onion and garlic. Cook for about 5–7 minutes or until the onions are soft and starting to brown. Add the greens back into the skillet and season with salt and pepper.

3. Cook for 1–2 minutes until warmed through. Slowly stir in the sour cream. Cook for 1 minute. Serve hot.

SAUTÉED OKRA AND TOMATOES

Okra cooked with tomatoes is a classic Southern dish, and by pan-frying the okra first before mixing in the tomatoes, you prevent them from becoming sticky.

Yields 6–8 servings

1 pound okra pods, stemmed and sliced into rings

3 tablespoons vegetable oil

1 small yellow onion, chopped

3 large fresh tomatoes, seeded and chopped

2 garlic cloves, minced

1 tablespoon apple cider vinegar

Salt to taste

Pepper to taste

1. Wash the okra pods, cut off the stem ends, and slice the pods into ¼" slices. Pat them dry to prevent oil splatters. Place a skillet over medium-high heat. Once it is heated, add the oil, onion, and okra. Cook them for several minutes on each side. The onion should be golden brown about the same time that the okra is crispy on the cut sides.

2. Add the tomatoes and garlic, stirring continually for 2–3 minutes, or just until the tomatoes are cooked through. Pour into a bowl and sprinkle with the apple cider vinegar. Stir to combine and taste before adding salt and pepper.

SAUTÉED RADISHES WITH SCALLIONS

Radishes are members of the mustard and horseradish family. Their pungent flavor turns off many people, but when cooked their flavor becomes very mild.

Yields 4 servings

1 tablespoon butter

2 bunches red radishes, cleaned, stemmed, and quartered

1 scallion, chopped into rings

½ cup chicken stock

Salt to taste

1. Place a skillet over medium heat. When it is heated, add the butter. Once the butter has melted, add the radishes and stir frequently for 2–3 minutes, or until the radishes have started to soften.

2. Sprinkle the scallion over the radishes and pour the chicken stock into the skillet. Cover the skillet and let the radishes cook for about 4 minutes.

3. Once the radishes are tender, uncover and increase the heat. Boil rapidly until the liquid has evaporated. Stir frequently to keep them from sticking. Sprinkle lightly with salt and serve immediately.

CARAMELIZED CARROTS

Parsnips can be substituted in this dish. If using parsnips, cut them into long, skinny strips instead of rings so they cook evenly.

Yields 6–8 servings

1 pound carrots, peeled and cut into ¼"-thick slices

½ cup apple juice

Water, as needed

1 lemon

2 tablespoons butter

2 tablespoons olive oil

¼ cup brown sugar

¼ cup slivered or sliced almonds

1. Place a skillet over medium heat. Add the carrots and apple juice. Add enough water to just cover the carrots. Simmer for about 5–7 minutes, or until the thickest pieces can be pierced with a fork. Drain off the water.

2. Use a microplane or zester to remove about 1 tablespoon of peel from the lemon. Squeeze the lemon to get 2 tablespoons of juice. Place the skillet back over medium heat and add the lemon zest, lemon juice, butter, oil, and brown sugar. Stir to combine. Once it starts to bubble, reduce the heat slightly and stir frequently to keep the carrots from sticking. Cook for about 5 minutes. They should be soft and glazed. Serve while hot and garnish with the almonds.

ROASTED BROCCOLI WITH PARMESAN

This is a great recipe for using up a head of broccoli that may be slightly past its prime.

Yields 6 servings

3 pounds broccoli stems

6 tablespoons olive oil

¾ teaspoon red pepper flakes

Pinch salt

Pinch pepper

¾ cup grated Parmesan cheese

⅓ cup white wine vinegar

1. Preheat oven to 450°F. Place a skillet in the middle of the oven. Trim the bottoms off the broccoli stems. Peel the stems and cut them into skinny florets. Place in a bowl and toss with the oil, pepper flakes, salt, and pepper. Spread the broccoli throughout the skillet. Sprinkle the cheese over the broccoli.

2. Place the pan in the middle of the oven and cook for 20–25 minutes, or until the stems have softened.

3. Place the broccoli on a serving platter. Pour the vinegar into the skillet and stir, scraping the caramelized bits off the bottom. Pour the pan juices over the broccoli and serve.

CAULIFLOWER WITH CHICKPEAS AND MUSTARD SEEDS

This dish makes a lot of food, but the leftovers can easily be substituted in Lamb Shepherd's Pie (see recipe in Chapter 7).

Yields 6–8 servings

1 medium white onion, chopped

1 tablespoon olive oil

5 tablespoons yellow or black mustard seeds

1 head cauliflower, divided into florets

Pinch salt

1 can chickpeas, drained and rinsed

¼ cup white wine

1. Place a skillet over medium heat. Once the skillet is heated add the onion, olive oil, and mustard seeds. Stir frequently and let the onion cook until it starts to turn brown.

2. Add the cauliflower florets to the skillet with a sprinkle of salt.

3. Stir to combine and cook for 4 minutes. Add the chickpeas to the skillet with the white wine. Stir to combine.

4. Cover the skillet and cook for 3–4 minutes. Remove the lid and let the liquid evaporate. Serve when the cauliflower is fork-tender.

ASIAN POTATOES WITH CHILI AND SHALLOTS

Serve these potatoes with fried chicken. Your guests will thank you!

Yields 4 servings

3 shallots, or 1 small yellow onion

2 serrano chilies

½ teaspoon plus 1 pinch salt

¼ cup peanut oil

1½ pounds Yukon gold potatoes, cut into 6 wedges

1 teaspoon apple cider vinegar

1. Mince the shallots and chilies finely. Place in a bowl, sprinkle ½ teaspoon salt, and toss to combine. Let sit for 10 minutes. Smash the vegetables into a slight paste.

2. Place a skillet over medium-high heat. Add the oil, then add the potatoes when the oil is warmed. Nudge them for 3 minutes to keep from sticking. Turn them over and cook for 3–5 minutes. Once the outsides are crispy, place on paper towels to drain.

3. Drain off most of the oil. Place over medium heat and add the paste. Stir continually for 4–5 minutes. Once it smells toasty, add the potatoes and toss until they're well coated and warmed. Sprinkle vinegar and pinch of salt over the potatoes and serve immediately.

ICELANDIC SUGAR-GLAZED POTATOES

This dish is fantastic only on the day it's made. Leftovers can be chopped up and served in another dish, but are disappointing if you try to reheat them.

Yields 8–10 servings

Water as needed

2 pounds waxy potatoes

4 tablespoons sugar

3 tablespoons butter

1. Place a large pan of water over high heat. Boil the potatoes whole for 20 minutes. When you can insert a knife to the middle of the potato, it is ready. Remove them to cool; reserve ½ cup of the cooking water. Peel skins and cut into thick slices.

2. Place a skillet over medium heat. Add the sugar and butter. If the sugar starts to smoke, lower the temperature. Whisk them together. Add 1–3 tablespoons of water that the potatoes were boiled in.

3. Place the potatoes in the skillet one at a time and stir to coat. If the mixture won't coat, increase the temperature slightly and add 1–2 tablespoons of water. When all of the potatoes are coated in sugar and warm, serve.

POMMES FONDANTES

It's best to use potatoes that are no larger than 2" across for this dish.

Yields 4–6 servings

2 pounds baby red potatoes

2 cups chicken or vegetable broth

2 tablespoons olive oil

1 tablespoon butter

1 tablespoon chopped sorrel or thyme

½ teaspoon salt

1. Wash the potatoes and remove the eyes. Arrange as many as possible in a 10" or 12" skillet. Add all of the remaining ingredients. Bring the pan to a boil, reduce the heat to medium, then cover with a lid that is slightly ajar. Cook the potatoes for 15–20 minutes or until a fork can be inserted easily.

2. Make sure the liquid covers half of the potatoes and add more broth if necessary. Use the bottom of a sturdy drinking glass to lightly smash the potatoes so the skins barely crack. Place the pan over medium-high heat and cook until all of the liquid has evaporated and the potatoes are brown on one side, about 10–12 minutes.

3. Use a pair of tongs to gently turn the potatoes. Cook for 5–7 minutes until brown on the other side. If necessary, add another tablespoon of olive oil.

4. Remove the pan from the heat and let the potatoes rest for about 5 minutes before sprinkling with a little extra salt to serve.

What Happens When You "Melt" Potatoes

Pommes Fondantes translates from French as "melted potatoes." Slow cooking these potatoes makes the inside creamy, and then frying them in butter makes the outside crispy. These are likely to stick so use a well-seasoned skillet for this dish.

POTATOES AU GRATIN

Cooking this dish in a cast-iron skillet should give you crunchier edges and crust. Use a very well-seasoned skillet when making this dish to prevent sticking.

Yields 6 servings

2 tablespoons olive oil

1 tablespoon butter

1 small onion, finely chopped

1 large clove garlic, minced

1 tablespoon flour

1¼ cups milk

1½ cups heavy cream

1 cup Gruyère cheese, shredded

Salt to taste

Pepper to taste

2½ pounds potatoes sliced ⅛" thick

¼ cup Parmesan cheese, shredded

1. Preheat oven to 350°F and place a rack in the center of the oven.

2. Place a skillet over medium heat. Once it is heated add the olive oil, butter, and onion. Cook for 3–5 minutes until translucent but not brown. Add the garlic and cook for 1 minute.

3. Add the flour to the skillet and stir for 1 minute. Slowly add the milk, stirring continually to prevent lumps. Slowly add the cream, stirring continually, until it just comes to a simmer. Reduce the heat to low and simmer until slightly thickened.

4. Add the Gruyère cheese and stir until it melts. Turn off the heat. Sprinkle the salt and pepper on the potatoes. Slowly add them to the pan, a few at a time. Use the spoon to push the potatoes to the bottom of the skillet and make even layers.

5. Once all of the potatoes are in the skillet, sprinkle the Parmesan cheese on top and bake for 45 minutes. Let it rest for 10 minutes before serving.

Melty Cheese Substitutes

Gruyère and Emmenthaler are great cheeses to use in dishes like this when you want a subtly complex flavor and smooth melting. But if you can't find Gruyère cheese, or are looking for a more economical substitute, you can substitute Monterey jack for a milder flavor or a mixture of provolone and Cheddar cheese for a stronger flavor.

BASIC SAUTÉED SWISS CHARD

Swiss chard is a hardy green with large leaves and a thick stem. It has a much milder and less bitter taste than mustard or collard greens. Avoid leaves that are wilted, yellow, or that have holes in the spines.

Yields 2 or 3 servings

1 pound Swiss chard

1 tablespoon olive oil

½ small onion, chopped

1 garlic clove, minced

Pinch crushed red pepper flakes

1 tablespoon cider or balsamic vinegar

Pinch nutmeg

½ cup chicken stock

Salt to taste

Pepper to taste

1. Run the chard under cold water to remove any leftover dirt. Cut the thick part of the stem out of the leaves and set aside. Tear the leaves into several pieces and place on a towel. Chop the stems into ½" pieces.

2. Place a skillet over medium heat. Once it is hot, add the oil, the stem pieces, and the onion. Cook for 5–7 minutes, or until the onion is translucent and just starting to brown.

3. Add the garlic, pepper flakes, vinegar, nutmeg, and stock. Stir to combine and bring to a boil.

4. Add the leaves and stir, cooking for 2–3 minutes before covering. They should be starting to wilt. Cook for 4–5 minutes, or until the leaves are cooked through and limp.

5. Remove the lid and stir frequently as the liquid evaporates. Taste and add more vinegar, salt, or pepper as needed. Serve immediately.

KALE WITH BACON AND TOMATOES

If you can't find kale, substitute spinach or Swiss chard and reduce the cooking time from 15 minutes to 5. You can also keep more of the bacon fat and omit the olive oil to get a truly flavorful dish. Be sure to taste the dish before adding more salt.

Yields 6–8 servings

2 pounds kale

4 slices bacon

1 tablespoon olive oil

1 small onion, chopped

2 garlic cloves, minced

Salt to taste

Pepper to taste

2 Roma tomatoes, seeded and chopped

2 tablespoons balsamic vinegar

1. Strip all the stems from the leaves and discard. Wash the leaves thoroughly and shake or drain until fairly dry. Chop or tear the leaves into large pieces and set aside.

2. Place a large skillet over medium-high heat and when heated, add the strips of bacon. Cook till crisp, remove from the pan, and let cool. Pour off all but 1 tablespoon of the bacon fat.

3. Add the olive oil to the skillet with the bacon fat and the chopped onion. Cook for 5–7 minutes, or until the onion is soft and starting to brown. Stir in the minced garlic clove.

4. Add a large bunch of kale to the skillet and sprinkle with salt and pepper. Cover with a lid for 1 minute to wilt the kale. Use a spoon to move the wilted kale to the outsides of the skillet. Repeat until all of the kale has been added. Stir frequently and cook for 15–20 minutes till tender.

5. Crumble the cooked bacon and sprinkle on top with the tomato. Sprinkle the balsamic vinegar over the kale and toss to combine. Remove to a bowl and serve immediately.

All Hail Kale

Kale has been cooked in so many parts of the world, and for so long, that food historians don't know where it originated. Because it grows easily in all climates, it has migrated with travelers throughout most of the world. It's incredibly high in vitamins and minerals and has helped sustain people during rough times.

SPICY MUSTARD GREENS

Mustard greens are less bitter than kale or collard greens, and have a much more peppery flavor, similar to arugula. But a splash of spicy vinegar will help combat any remaining bitter flavor.

Yields 6 servings

2 large bunches mustard greens

3 tablespoons olive oil

2 medium onions, chopped

6 garlic cloves, minced

1 teaspoon ground cumin

1 teaspoon dried crushed red pepper flakes

1 cup chicken or vegetable broth

Salt and pepper to taste

Spicy vinegar as condiment

1. Remove the veins from the greens and rinse them thoroughly in cold water. Shake dry and tear into large pieces.

2. Place a skillet over medium-high heat and once heated, add the oil and onion. Stir frequently until they're soft and starting to turn brown, about 10 minutes.

3. Stir in the garlic, cumin, and crushed red pepper and cook for 3 minutes.

4. Add one batch of the greens and cover for 1–2 minutes until the greens wilt. Repeat with the other batches until all the greens have been added and have wilted.

5. Add the broth, cover, and reduce the heat to low. Let the greens cook for 30–45 minutes. They should be very tender. Taste before adding salt and pepper. Serve while hot with spicy vinegar for people to garnish as they wish.

GRILLED SWEET POTATO STICKS

Scotch bonnet peppers are native to Africa and are one of the spiciest peppers. If you prefer a less spicy dish, you can use a serrano or a jalapeño.

Yields 6–8 servings

3 pineapple slices

1 Scotch bonnet pepper

¼ cup rum

2 tablespoons vegetable oil

½ teaspoon salt

1½ pounds fresh sweet potatoes

1–2 tablespoons peanut oil

1. Place everything except the sweet potatoes and peanut oil in a blender or food processor and pulse till well combined. Pour into a saucepan or small skillet over medium-high heat and boil for 10 minutes until it has reduced slightly.

2. Peel the sweet potatoes and cut them into 1" slices lengthwise. Cut slices in 1" strips. Dip them into the glaze and toss to combine.

3. Place a grill pan over moderate direct heat. Brush with peanut oil. Cook sweet potatoes on each side for 5–7 minutes. Baste with the glaze as you turn them. Serve while warm.

BASIC GRILLED VEGETABLES

These vegetables are delicious in their simplicity. But if you prefer a little more tang, sprinkle them with a little flavored oil and vinegar.

Yields 8–12 servings

2 bunches asparagus

16 ounces button mushrooms

3 zucchinis

Salt to taste

6 cubanelle peppers

2 eggplants

¼ cup olive oil

Pepper to taste

1. Trim the bottoms off the asparagus. Cut thick stalks in half lengthwise. Slice the button mushrooms in half through the stem.

2. Cut the zucchini in half lengthwise, and then into ½" slices. Place on top of two layers of paper towels. Sprinkle lightly with salt. Let sit for 10 minutes. Flip over, sprinkle with salt, and let sit for another 10 minutes.

3. Remove the stems and seeds from the peppers. Cut in half and make small cuts as needed in the bottom of the peppers so they will lie flat.

4. Cut the stems off the eggplants, then cut ½" slices along their length. Cut in half lengthwise if desired. Salt the same way as the zucchini, but let rest for 20 minutes on each side.

5. Place a griddle over medium-high heat on a stovetop. Toss the asparagus and mushrooms in a tablespoon of olive oil separately. Sprinkle them lightly with salt and pepper. Brush the grill lightly with oil. Cook the asparagus for 2–4 minutes on each side. Place them on a warmed platter.

6. Cook the mushrooms for 2–4 minutes on each side and add them to the platter. Pat the eggplant and zucchini dry and place several slices on the pan. Cook for 4–6 minutes on each side. Place them on the platter.

7. Brush both sides of the peppers with oil. Place them on the pan skin side up. Grill for 2–4 minutes on each side. Sprinkle with salt and pepper and add to the platter. Keep the platter warm until ready to serve.

BOSTON BAKED BEANS

The molasses in this recipe has made this dish a Boston specialty since the colonial days, when the city was part of the rum trade.

Yields 6–8 servings

1 pound small white or pink beans

Water, as needed, plus 9 cups

4 ounces salt pork, rind removed and cut into ½" cubes

3 slices bacon, cut into matchsticks

1 medium onion, finely chopped

½ cup molasses

2 tablespoons stone-ground or brown mustard

1 tablespoon apple cider vinegar

Pinch salt

Pinch pepper

1. Rinse the beans and remove any bad beans or debris. Cover the beans with 3" of water and soak overnight. Place the salt pork in water in the refrigerator.

2. Preheat oven to 300°F. Place the salt pork and bacon in a Dutch oven over medium-high heat. Cook for 7–9 minutes until the bacon is crispy. Drain off almost all pork fat. Add the onion and cook for 7–8 minutes.

3. Stir in the molasses, mustard, drained beans, and 9 cups water. Turn the heat to high and boil. Stir, cover, and cook in the middle of the oven for 3 hours.

4. Remove the lid and stir. Cook for another 1–1½ hours. The liquid should thicken to a syrup consistency. Stir in the vinegar, salt, and pepper. Serve hot or warm.

STEWED BLACK BEANS

It is easier to sort beans if you pour them onto a white surface. The contrast makes it easier to see anything that isn't a bean, or any beans that look inedible. Black beans are hard to sort since they're smaller and dark.

Yields 8–10 servings

8 ounces black beans

Water, as needed

¼ cup olive oil

2 yellow onions

2 red or yellow bell peppers

4 garlic cloves

1½ tablespoons ground cumin

¼ teaspoon baking soda

1 dried chipotle pepper, stemmed and seeded

1 tablespoon dried oregano

3 bay leaves

1 teaspoon ground coriander

2 teaspoons salt

¼ cup orange juice

Juice from 1 lime

2 tablespoons apple cider vinegar

Chopped cilantro to taste

1. Sort and rinse the beans. Cover them with 2" of water in a large container and soak overnight.

2. Place a Dutch oven over medium heat. Add the oil, onion, and bell pepper. Sauté until the pepper starts to turn soft. Stir in the garlic and cumin.

3. Drain the beans and add them to the pot with enough water to cover them by 2". Add in the baking soda, dried pepper, oregano, bay leaves, and the coriander. Bring to a boil. Reduce the heat to a simmer, cover, and cook until beans are soft, but not mushy, for 1–1½ hours.

4. Remove and reserve the water so there is just ½" of water above the beans. Simmer for 1 hour, uncovered, until the beans have soaked up the remaining water. Stir occasionally. Remove the dried pepper and bay leaves.

5. Add the salt, orange juice, lime juice, and vinegar. Taste and add more salt or more hot sauce if desired. Garnish with chopped cilantro and serve with rice or tortillas.

MATAR PALAK: PEAS AND SPINACH INDIAN STYLE

This dish tends to be fairly spicy. If you prefer a mild dish, you can use 1 jalapeño instead of several of the green chilies.

Yields 4–6 servings

16 ounces frozen spinach, thawed

3 or 4 green chilies, with or without the seeds

1 cup chicken broth

1 potato, peeled and chopped

1 tomato, seeded and chopped

1 tablespoon oil

1 medium onion, chopped

1 tablespoon ground cumin

1 garlic clove, minced

2 cups frozen peas

1 teaspoon turmeric

Salt to taste

Pepper to taste

1. Place the spinach and chilies in a food processor. Cut out the seeds to reduce the spiciness. Pulse until you get a paste, scraping the sides of the bowl when necessary.

2. Place a skillet over medium heat. Once it is heated add the chicken broth and potato. Simmer for 10 minutes, or until potatoes can be pierced with a fork but are not soft. Pour off the remaining broth and add the chopped tomato.

3. Add the oil, onion, cumin, and garlic. Stir until combined and cook for 5 minutes, or until the onion is soft and the cumin smells toasted. Stir in the spinach and chili mixture, and let it cook for 10 minutes.

4. Add the peas to the skillet and cook for 5 minutes. They should be warmed and tender. Stir in the turmeric and season with salt and pepper.

PALAK PANEER: INDIAN SPINACH WITH FRESH CHEESE

This Indian dish may also be called saag paneer. Palak and saag are often used to mean "spinach" or a similar green. Paneer is an unsalted and unaged cheese. If you can't find paneer, you can substitute feta or firm tofu.

Yields 4 servings

1 tablespoon vegetable oil

1 small yellow onion, chopped

½ teaspoon ground turmeric

1 teaspoon ground cumin

1 teaspoon garam masala powder

1 pound frozen spinach, thawed, squeezed, and chopped

Optional: 1 green jalapeño, seeded and chopped

1 garlic clove, minced

1 small tomato, chopped

¼ cup chopped cilantro

1 teaspoon salt

12 ounces chicken broth

1 cup plain Greek yogurt

8 ounces paneer

1. Place a skillet over medium heat. Once it is warm, add the oil and the onion. Stir the onion frequently for 4–5 minutes, or until translucent.

2. Add the dried spices and stir continually for 2 minutes. The spices should be very fragrant.

3. Add the spinach to the skillet and stir, scraping any bits of spice off the bottom if necessary. Add the jalapeño (if using), garlic, tomato, and cilantro. Cook for 10 minutes.

4. Add the salt and broth to the skillet and stir to combine. Let the liquid evaporate before stirring in the yogurt and cheese. Stir for 1–2 minutes until the cheese and yogurt are warmed. Serve immediately over cooked basmati rice.

ROMANESCO WITH MUSHROOM AND WINE SAUCE

If you can't find romanesco you can substitute cauliflower or broccoli. If you substitute broccoli, skip the steps related to boiling the vegetable. To turn this side into an entrée, just serve this dish over rice or egg noodles.

Yields 4–6 servings

1 head romanesco

1 teaspoon salt

Water, as needed

1 pound button mushrooms, sliced

3 shallots or 1 small yellow or red onion, sliced

3 tablespoons butter or olive oil

½ cup port, or other heavy red wine

½ teaspoon Dijon mustard

1. Rinse the romanesco and break the clusters, or curds, off the stalks. Add salt to a pot of water with a steamer basket and bring to a boil over high heat. Once the water comes to a boil, add the romanesco and cover. Cook for 5 minutes. Remove from the water and drain well.

2. Place a skillet over medium heat and add the mushrooms, shallots, and butter or olive oil. Cook for 10–12 minutes, stirring every few minutes, until the shallots and mushrooms have softened and browned. Add the wine and mustard and reduce the heat to low.

3. After the romanesco has drained, add it to the skillet. Cook uncovered for an additional 5–10 minutes until the romanesco has reached the desired tenderness and the wine sauce has reduced.

Romanesco, a Cousin of Cabbage

The Italians call it *broccolo romanesco* and the French call it *chou romanesco*. Like broccoli and cauliflower, it is a cousin of cabbage. Pick heads that are very firm with densely packed curds. Avoid any that are more yellow than green, or that have mold on them. The stalks are inedible, but the curds can be eaten raw.

CHAPTER 4

SOUPS, STEWS, AND CHILIES

GREEK MEATBALL, EGG, AND LEMON SOUP

This recipe is adapted from a Greek soup (youvarlakia avgolemono). The traditional version doesn't have the vegetables added to the broth, but it's those vegetables that make this soup a one pot meal. Serve it with some feta cheese sprinkled over the top and crusty bread on the side.

Yields 6 servings

1 pound lean ground beef

¼ pound ground pork

1 small yellow onion, minced

1 clove garlic, minced

6 tablespoons uncooked long-grain white rice

1 tablespoon dried parsley

2 teaspoons dried dill or mint

1 teaspoon dried oregano

Salt and freshly ground black pepper to taste

3 large eggs

4–6 cups chicken or vegetable broth

1 medium yellow onion, chopped

1 cup baby carrots, each sliced into thirds

2 large russet potatoes, peeled and cut into cubes

1 stalk celery, finely chopped

2 tablespoons corn flour

⅓ cup fresh lemon juice

1. In a large bowl, mix together the meat, minced onion, garlic, rice, parsley, dill or mint, oregano, salt, pepper, and 1 of the eggs. Shape into small meatballs and set aside.

2. Add 2 cups of the broth to a 4-quart slow cooker. Add the meatballs, chopped onion, carrots, potatoes, and celery, then pour in enough of the remaining broth to cover the meatballs and vegetables. Cook on low for 6 hours.

3. In a small bowl or measuring cup, beat the 2 remaining eggs and then whisk in the corn flour. Gradually whisk in the lemon juice, and then ladle in about 1 cup of the hot broth from the slow cooker, doing so in a slow, steady stream, beating continuously until all of the hot liquid has been incorporated into the egg mixture. Stir this mixture into the slow cooker, being careful not to break the meatballs. Continue to cook on low for 1 hour, or until mixture is thickened.

RUSSIAN BORSCHT

If fresh tomatoes are available, you can substitute about a pound of diced vine-ripened tomatoes for the canned.

Yields 6–8 servings

1½ tablespoons extra-virgin olive oil

1 clove garlic, minced

½ pound lamb, cut into ½" pieces

1 small yellow onion, diced

1 pound red beets

1 small head cabbage, cored and chopped

1 15-ounce can diced tomatoes

7 cups beef broth

¼ cup red wine vinegar

2 bay leaves

1 tablespoon lemon juice

Salt and freshly ground black pepper to taste

6–8 tablespoons sour cream

6–8 teaspoons fresh dill

1. Add the oil, garlic, and lamb to a 6-quart Dutch oven or stockpot. Brown the lamb over medium heat, stirring frequently to keep the garlic from burning. Add the onion and sauté until transparent.

2. Peel and dice the beets. Rinse the beets well and cover them with cold water until needed.

3. Add the beets, cabbage, tomatoes, beef broth, vinegar, bay leaves, and lemon juice to the pot. Bring to a boil; cover, reduce the heat, and simmer for 2 hours.

4. Chop the reserved beet greens and add to the soup; cover and simmer for another 15 minutes. Remove bay leaves. Taste for seasoning and add salt and pepper to taste. Ladle the soup into bowls and garnish each bowl with sour cream and fresh dill.

SCOTTISH BROTH

This is an adaptation of a recipe sometimes referred to as Scotch broth. The people who love it insist it's as therapeutic and comforting as chicken soup.

Yields 6–8 servings

¼ cup butter or extra-virgin olive oil

1 large yellow onion, diced

2 stalks celery, diced

3 large carrots, peeled and finely chopped

½ cup leeks (white part only), well rinsed and chopped

½ teaspoon salt

¼ teaspoon ground black pepper

2 pounds lamb neck bones or lamb shanks

4 cloves garlic, minced

2 bay leaves

½ cup Scotch whiskey or chicken broth

½ cup pearl barley, rinsed and drained

½ small head cabbage, cored and shredded

1 cup turnip, diced

Water as needed

½ cup frozen peas

¼ cup minced fresh parsley

1. Melt the butter over medium heat in a 6-quart Dutch oven or stockpot. Add the onion, celery, carrots, leeks, salt, and pepper; sauté for 5 minutes, or until the onion is transparent and the other vegetables are soft.

2. Cut away any excess fat from the lamb. Use a cleaver to cut the bones and meat into pieces. Add several pieces of the lamb and sauté until browned on all sides. Add the garlic and bay leaves; sauté for 1 minute. Turn off the heat under the pan and remove the pan from the burner. Deglaze the pan with the Scotch or broth.

3. Add the remaining lamb, barley, cabbage, and turnip; pour in enough water to cover all the ingredients in the pan by 2". Return the pan to the burner and bring to a boil over medium-high heat; lower the heat to medium-low and simmer uncovered for 2 hours, or until thickened and the meat is tender. Periodically skim off any fat from the top.

4. Use tongs or a slotted spoon to remove the meat from the pot. When it's cool enough to handle, cut the meat away from the bone; discard the bones. Stir the meat into the broth along with the peas and parsley. Bring to temperature, and taste for seasoning, adding additional salt and pepper if needed. Remove bay leaves. Ladle into bowls to serve.

Scottish Broth Options

You can substitute a cup of coleslaw mix for the shredded cabbage. For a richer soup, substitute chicken broth for some of the water. Add extra flavor by putting a few tablespoons of blue cheese into the bottom of each serving bowl before you ladle in the soup. The cheese will melt into the soup and give it a rich, hearty flavor.

SALMON SOUP

Smoked salmon will add another flavor dimension to this soup, but it is usually very salty. Therefore, either use reduced-sodium chicken broth or taste before you salt the soup to be sure that it needs it.

Yields 4 servings

4 cups chicken broth

1 pound fresh or smoked salmon

1 medium yellow onion, thinly sliced

Salt to taste

⅛ teaspoon freshly ground black pepper

1 bunch fresh spinach, well washed and chopped

Add the broth, salmon, onion, salt, and pepper to a 3-quart saucepan. Bring to a boil over high heat. Reduce the heat and simmer, covered, for 15 minutes. Add the spinach, cover, and cook for another 5 minutes.

Smoked Salmon Alternatives

If you use fresh salmon in the Salmon Soup recipe but still want to add a smoky flavor to the dish, garnish each serving with some finely chopped crisp bacon. You can find smoked salmon everywhere from Costco to Whole Foods.

BEEF AND BLACKBERRY SOUP

Serve this soup with cornbread or corn muffins. Have honey at the table for those who want to spread it on their cornbread or muffins, or want to use it to sweeten their soup.

Yields 6–8 servings

3 tablespoons peanut or extra-virgin olive oil

2 stalks celery, diced small

2 large carrots, peeled and diced small

1 large yellow onion, diced

1½ pounds boneless chuck roast

2 cups beef broth

2 cups water

1 tablespoon honey

1 cup blackberries

2 large sweet potatoes, peeled and diced

Salt and freshly ground black pepper to taste

Optional: 2 large russet potatoes, peeled and diced

1. Add the oil to a 6-quart Dutch oven and bring to temperature over medium heat. Add the celery and carrots; sauté for 3–5 minutes, or until tender. Add the onions and sauté until the onions are transparent.

2. Trim the fat from the roast and cut it into bite-size pieces. Add the meat to the Dutch oven and brown it for a few minutes. Add the broth, water, honey, blackberries, sweet potatoes, salt, and pepper. Bring to a boil. Lower the heat and simmer, covered, for 1 hour, or until the meat is tender. Taste for seasoning and add more honey, salt, and pepper, if needed.

3. Add the potatoes, if using. Cover and simmer for an additional 30 minutes, or until the potatoes are cooked.

Name Game

A boneless "English cut" chuck roast is the perfect cut to use in a slow-cooked beef dish; it cooks up to pull-apart tender. The boneless cut is sometimes called an English roll. That cut of chuck roast also can be referred to as a cross rib roast, cross rib pot roast, Boston cut, English cut roast, English roast, thick rib roast, bread and butter cut, or beef chuck cross rib pot roast.

MOCK TURTLE SOUP

This soup is the perfect opportunity to use up leftover meat you have stored in the freezer. Served with a salad and crusty bread or toast, it makes a hearty meal.

Yields 8–10 servings

¼ pound salt pork or bacon, diced

2 stalks celery, finely diced

2 large carrots, peeled and finely diced

1 medium yellow onion, diced

3 cloves garlic, minced

¼ cup butter

½ cup all-purpose flour

3 cups beef broth

1 cup chicken broth

1 15-ounce can diced tomatoes

½ teaspoon dried basil

½ teaspoon dried marjoram

½ teaspoon dried thyme

1 bay leaf

1 teaspoon freshly ground black pepper

1 tablespoon dried parsley

1 4-ounce halibut fillet

1 cup cooked roast beef, shredded

1 cup cooked chicken, shredded

½ cup cooked crabmeat, shredded

2 tablespoons fresh lemon juice

¼ teaspoon hot sauce, or to taste

1½ tablespoons Worcestershire sauce

⅛ teaspoon ground cloves

½ cup dry sherry

4 hard-boiled eggs, peeled and finely diced

1. Add the salt pork or bacon to a Dutch oven and sauté it over medium heat long enough to render the fat. Add the celery and carrots, and sauté for 3–5 minutes, or until tender. Add the onion and sauté until transparent. Add the garlic and sauté another 30 seconds. Melt the butter into the sautéed vegetables. Stir in the flour and cook until the roux turns the color of peanut butter, stirring constantly.

2. Gradually add the beef broth, whisking it in to mix thoroughly with the roux. Stir in the chicken broth and tomatoes. Stir in the basil, marjoram, thyme, bay leaf, pepper, and parsley. Bring to a boil, and boil for 1 minute. Reduce the heat and simmer until the mixture begins to thicken.

3. Add the halibut. Cover and simmer for 10 minutes. Remove the halibut and flake it. Stir in the fish, beef, chicken, crabmeat, lemon juice, hot sauce, Worcestershire sauce, and ground cloves. Reduce the heat; simmer until the meat reaches serving temperature. Stir in the sherry and diced eggs. Serve hot.

CHICKEN AND CORN SOUP WITH MINI DUMPLINGS

This is a simplified version of a Pennsylvania Dutch soup. In that version, the mini dumplings are known as rivels. *The literal meaning of* rivel *is "lump."*

Yields 4–6 servings

2 tablespoons butter

1 stalk celery, finely chopped

1 large carrot, peeled and finely chopped

1 small yellow onion, chopped

1 clove garlic, minced

4 cups chicken broth

1 17-ounce can creamed corn

1 large egg, beaten

Pinch salt

¾–1 cup all-purpose flour

1 cup cooked chicken, shredded

2 hard-boiled eggs, peeled and sliced

Optional: fresh chopped parsley for garnish

1. Melt the butter in a deep 3½-quart nonstick skillet or large saucepan over medium heat. Add the celery and carrot; sauté for 3–5 minutes, or until soft. Add the onion and sauté until transparent. Add the garlic and sauté for an additional 30 seconds. Stir in the broth and corn. Lower the temperature and allow the soup to simmer while you mix up the dumplings.

2. In a small bowl, mix the beaten egg together with the salt and enough flour to make a dry dough. Working with 1 tablespoon of the dough at a time, rub it between your hands over the pan so that pieces of the dough drop into the soup. After all of the mini dumplings have been added to the pan, add the chicken and simmer the soup for an additional 10 minutes, or until the dumplings are tender and the chicken is warmed through. Serve with slices of hard-boiled egg floating on top of the soup. Garnish with parsley, if desired.

Chicken and Corn Egg Drop Soup

In step 2, omit the flour and use 2 large eggs instead of 1. Beat the eggs together with a pinch of salt. A little at a time, drizzle the eggs into the simmering soup and cook until the eggs are set.

ARTICHOKE SOUP

With this soup, you almost spend more time opening cans than you do cooking. It doesn't get simpler than this, but it tastes like you worked on it all day.

Yields 8 servings

1 10¾-ounce can condensed cream of mushroom soup

1 10¾-ounce can condensed cream of celery soup

3¼ cups milk

1 5-ounce can shrimp, drained

1 cup carrots, peeled and finely shredded

1 14-ounce can artichoke hearts, drained and chopped

½ teaspoon curry powder

Pinch allspice

¼ teaspoon onion powder

Salt and freshly ground black pepper to taste

Add all ingredients except the salt and pepper to a large saucepan. Stir to combine. Bring to a simmer over medium heat; reduce the heat and simmer, uncovered, for 15 minutes. Taste for seasoning and add salt and pepper, if needed.

SAUERKRAUT SOUP

To save time, get frozen small white onions. Thaw them before you add them to the soup.

Yields 8–10 servings

3 cups water

½ teaspoon caraway seeds

½ teaspoon dried chervil

16 small white onions

4 stalks celery, diced

4 large carrots, peeled and thinly sliced

1 14-ounce can sauerkraut, undrained

1 tablespoon granulated sugar

1 8-ounce package frozen green beans, thawed

2 pounds hot dogs or fully cooked smoked sausage

1 large tomato, diced

2 10¾-ounce cans cream of potato soup

Salt and freshly ground black pepper to taste

1. Bring the water to boil in a 4-quart Dutch oven over medium-high heat. Add the caraway seeds, chervil, onions, celery, carrots, sauerkraut, and sugar. Reduce the heat and simmer, covered, for 15 minutes.

2. Stir in the green beans. Slice the hot dogs or smoked sausage into ½" pieces and stir into the soup along with the tomato and potato soup. Cook, covered, for 15 minutes, stirring occasionally. Taste for seasoning and add salt and pepper, if needed.

BUTTERNUT SQUASH SOUP WITH KIELBASA AND WILD RICE

If you prefer, you can substitute cooked pork, chicken, or turkey for the kielbasa.

Yields 6–8 servings

1 1½–2-pound butternut squash

2 tablespoons extra-virgin olive oil

6 cups chicken broth

1 large yellow onion, diced

1 cup uncooked wild rice

1 pound kielbasa, cut into ¼" slices

1 12- or 16-ounce package frozen whole kernel corn, thawed

Salt and freshly ground black pepper to taste

Water as needed

1 cup heavy cream

Optional: 1 tablespoon fresh parsley, chopped

1. Preheat oven to 400°F.

2. Cut the squash in half and remove the seeds. Place the squash halves skin side down on a baking sheet and drizzle the meat with 1 tablespoon of the olive oil; bake for 1 hour. Remove from the oven and let cool completely. Peel the squash and add it to a blender or food processor along with 2 cups of the chicken broth; purée until smooth and set aside.

3. Add the remaining 4 cups of the broth and ½ of the diced onions to a Dutch oven and bring to a simmer over medium heat. Stir in the rice; cook for 1 hour, or until the rice is tender and most of the liquid is absorbed, stirring occasionally with a fork. Remove the rice from the pan and set aside.

4. Add the remaining 1 tablespoon of oil to the Dutch oven and bring it to temperature over medium heat. Add the kielbasa slices; brown them for 3 minutes. Add the remaining onions and corn; season with salt and pepper and sauté for 3 minutes. Add the squash purée; reduce the heat to medium-low, cover, and simmer for 20 minutes, checking occasionally and adding water, if needed. Skim off any fat on the surface, stir in the rice, and continue to cook for 10 minutes. Remove from the heat and stir in the cream. Taste for seasoning, and add salt and pepper, if needed. Serve garnished with parsley, if desired.

Microwave-Roasted Butternut Squash

Instead of baking the butternut squash, you can fix it in the microwave. Wash the squash, slice in half lengthwise, remove the seeds, and place it cut side down in a shallow microwave-safe pan. Add water to about ¾" deep. Microwave on high for 8–10 minutes, or until the squash is tender.

PUMPKIN SOUP

Canned pumpkin actually packs more nutrients than raw fresh pumpkin, so this is one shortcut you absolutely shouldn't feel guilty about! Serve with cornbread or peanut butter sandwiches.

Yields 4–6 servings

2 tablespoons butter

1 stalk celery, finely diced

1 large carrot, peeled and finely diced

1 medium yellow onion, minced

1 medium apple, peeled, cored, and minced

1 15-ounce can pumpkin purée

3 cups chicken broth

1 10-ounce package frozen whole kernel corn, thawed

Optional: diced cooked ham, to taste

Salt and freshly ground pepper to taste

Optional: toasted pumpkin seeds, shelled

1. Melt the butter in a small Dutch oven over medium heat. Add the celery and carrot; sauté for 3–5 minutes, or until tender. Add the onion and apple; sauté until the onion is transparent. Stir in the pumpkin and chicken broth. Bring to a boil; reduce heat and simmer for 10 minutes. Use a stick blender to purée the soup if you wish.

2. Add the corn and the ham (if using); simmer for 8 minutes, or until the corn is tender. Taste for seasoning and add salt and pepper if needed. Garnish with pumpkin seeds, if desired.

Pumpkin Soup Variations

Omit the corn in the Pumpkin Soup recipe and stir in ½ cup of peanut butter and a little brown sugar instead. Or, season the soup by adding 1 teaspoon smoked paprika, ⅛ teaspoon ground cumin, and a pinch of cayenne pepper. Turn any variation into a cream soup by stirring in ½ cup of heavy cream, or more to taste.

SWEET POTATO SOUP WITH GINGER

This soup is hearty enough to serve as a meal, or serve it alongside a ham or turkey sandwich for a soup and sandwich lunch.

Yields 6–8 servings

2 tablespoons extra-virgin olive oil

2 stalks celery, finely diced

1 large carrot, peeled and finely diced

1 large yellow onion, minced

1 clove garlic, minced

2 teaspoons fresh ginger, grated

5 cups chicken broth

4 medium sweet potatoes, peeled and diced

1 cup heavy cream

Salt and freshly ground pepper to taste

Optional: ¼ cup dry sherry

Optional: fresh chives, chopped, to taste

1. Heat the oil in a deep 3½-quart nonstick skillet or large saucepan over medium heat. Add the celery and carrot; sauté for 3–5 minutes, or until soft. Add the onion and sauté until transparent. Add the garlic and ginger, and sauté for an additional 30 seconds.

2. Pour 3 cups of the chicken broth into the pan along with the diced sweet potatoes. Bring to a boil; reduce heat, cover, and simmer for 10 minutes, or until the sweet potatoes are cooked through. Periodically check the simmering pot to make sure it doesn't boil dry. Mash the sweet potatoes with a fork or blend them with a stick blender.

3. Stir the remaining broth and cream into the soup. Bring to temperature. Taste for seasoning and add salt and pepper if needed. Stir in the sherry and garnish with chopped chives, if desired.

Taking the Blender to the Pot

A stick blender is also sometimes referred to as an immersion blender or a hand blender. They're available in electric and cordless rechargeable battery models. You can purée soups with ease, and they're also excellent for making sauces. To clean, simply put the blades into some soapy water and run the appliance, then run in clear water.

PORK STEAK AND CABBAGE SOUP

You can ladle this soup over some shredded Cheddar or American cheese, allow time for the cheese to melt, and stir everything together.

Yields 8–10 servings

3 tablespoons extra-virgin olive oil

1 1-pound bag baby carrots

2 stalks celery, finely diced

1 large yellow onion, diced

1 clove garlic, minced

2 pounds boneless pork steak

4 large russet or red potatoes, peeled or unpeeled, and diced

4 cups chicken broth

1 large head of cabbage, cored and shredded

Optional: 1½ teaspoons juniper berries

Optional: ½ cup dry white wine or beer

Optional: shredded Cheddar cheese, to taste

1. Add the oil to a 6-quart Dutch oven and bring to temperature over medium heat. Mince or shred 4 or 5 of the baby carrots and add them to the pan along with the celery; sauté for 3–5 minutes, or until soft. Add the onion and sauté until transparent. Add the garlic and sauté for an additional 30 seconds. Trim the pork of most of the fat; cut into small strips or dice. Add the pork and potatoes; stir-fry for 3–5 minutes, or until the potatoes just begin to take on a golden brown color.

2. Deglaze the pan with some of the chicken broth, and then add the remaining broth. Bring the broth to a boil; reduce the temperature and simmer, covered, for 45 minutes. Cut the remaining carrots into 3 or 4 pieces each and add to the pan.

3. Add the cabbage in stages. Stir in ½ cup, cover the pan and allow to steam for 5 minutes, stir the cabbage into the soup, and repeat until all the cabbage has been added. Add the juniper berries and wine or beer, if using. Cover and simmer for 45 minutes, stirring occasionally. Add water if additional cooking liquid is needed. Serve topped with some shredded Cheddar cheese, if desired.

Best Options

This hearty soup tastes even better after it's been refrigerated overnight and warmed up the next day. The traditional version doesn't have the extra carrot pieces in it; omit them if you wish. Serve the soup with pumpernickel or whole-grain bread and beer.

MULLIGATAWNY SOUP

This soup is traditionally served garnished with lots of freshly ground black pepper along with the chopped cilantro.

Yields 8 servings

8 chicken thighs

1 stalk celery, cut in half

1 large carrot, peeled and cut in 4 pieces

1 small yellow onion, quartered

8 cups water

1 tablespoon ghee

2 stalks celery, finely diced

4 large carrots, peeled and finely diced

1 medium yellow onion, diced

2 cloves garlic, minced

¼ teaspoon turmeric

½ teaspoon ground coriander

¼ teaspoon dried red pepper flakes

½ teaspoon dried cumin

½ teaspoon ground cardamom

½ teaspoon ground dried ginger

Salt and freshly ground black pepper to taste

4 cups chicken broth

Optional: fresh chopped cilantro, to taste

1. Add the chicken thighs, celery and carrot pieces, onion quarters, and 4 cups of the water to a Dutch oven. Bring to a simmer over medium heat; reduce the heat, cover, and simmer for 1 hour. Strain the broth into a bowl and set aside. Discard the cooked vegetables. Once the chicken has cooled enough to handle it, remove the meat from the bones, discarding the skin and the bones; set aside.

2. Meanwhile, melt the ghee in the Dutch oven over medium heat. Add the diced celery and carrots; sauté for 3–5 minutes, or until soft. Add the diced onion and sauté until transparent. Add the garlic and sauté for an additional 30 seconds.

3. Stir the turmeric, coriander, red pepper flakes, cumin, cardamom, ginger, salt, and pepper into the sautéed vegetables. Stir in the chicken broth and the remaining 4 cups of water. Bring to a boil; reduce the heat, cover, and simmer for 30 minutes. Add the cooked chicken; simmer uncovered, stirring occasionally, for an additional 5 minutes to bring the meat to temperature. Taste for seasoning and add additional salt, if needed. Serve garnished with additional freshly ground black pepper and chopped cilantro if desired.

Fat Adds Flavor—and Calories

Fat is tasty, but it adds extra calories to a dish. If you favor lean over flavor, you can either remove the skin before you cook the thighs or refrigerate the broth to make it easier to skim the fat off the top.

PHO

This is a simplified, Americanized version of this recipe, substituting brown sugar for the yellow rock sugar found in Asian markets.

Yields 8–10 servings

3-pound English-cut chuck roast

3 medium yellow onions

1 4" piece ginger

5 star anise

6 whole cloves

1 3" cinnamon stick

¼ teaspoons salt

2 cups beef broth

Water as needed

1½–2 pounds small dried banh pho noodles

4 tablespoons fish sauce

1 tablespoon light brown sugar

3 or 4 green onions, green part only, cut into thin rings

⅓ cup fresh cilantro, chopped

Freshly ground black pepper to taste

1. Trim the roast of any fat; cut the meat into 2" × 4" pieces and add them to a 4-quart slow cooker. Peel and quarter 2 of the onions. Cut the ginger into 1" pieces. Add the onion and ginger to the slow cooker along with the star anise, cloves, cinnamon stick, salt, broth, and enough water to cover the meat by about 1". Cook on low for 6–8 hours, or until the beef is pull-apart tender.

2. About 30 minutes before serving, peel the remaining onion; cut it into paper-thin slices and soak them in cold water. Cover the noodles with hot water and allow to soak for 15–20 minutes, or until softened and opaque white; drain in colander.

3. Remove the meat from the broth with a slotted spoon; shred the meat. Strain the broth through fine strainer, discarding the spices and onion; return the strained broth to the slow cooker along with the shredded meat. Set the slow cooker on the high setting and bring the broth to a rolling boil. Stir the fish sauce and brown sugar into the broth.

4. Taste and adjust seasoning if necessary. If you desire a stronger, saltier flavor, add more fish sauce. Add more brown sugar to make the broth sweeter, if desired. If the broth is too salty, add some additional water.

5. Blanch the noodles in stages. Add ¼ of the noodles to a strainer and submerge in the boiling broth, being careful not to allow the slow cooker to boil over. The noodles will collapse and lose their stiffness in about 15–20 seconds. Pull the strainer from the broth, letting the excess broth drain back into cooker, and empty the noodles into bowls, allowing each serving to fill about ⅓ of the bowl.

6. Ladle some of the hot broth and beef over each serving of noodles. Garnish with the onion slices, green onions, and chopped cilantro, and finish with freshly ground black pepper.

COCK-A-LEEKIE

This is the Scottish version of a chicken soup. Feel free to add carrots to the soup if you desire more vegetables with your meal. Serve it alongside or over buttered biscuits for true comfort food goodness.

Yields 6–8 servings

3–4 pounds bone-in chicken pieces

1 pound beef shanks, sawed into 1" cubes

4 slices thick-cut bacon, diced

4 cups chicken broth

1 tablespoon dried thyme

1 bay leaf

Water as needed

¾ cup pearl barley

1½ cups leeks (white part only), well rinsed and chopped

Salt and freshly ground black pepper to taste

Optional: fresh chopped parsley, to taste

1. Add the chicken, beef shanks, bacon, broth, thyme, and bay leaf to a large Dutch oven. Add enough water to cover the meat. Bring to a boil over medium-high heat; cover, reduce heat, and simmer for 1 hour, or until the chicken is cooked through and tender.

2. Use a slotted spoon to remove the chicken from the pot. Set aside and allow to cool. Bring the broth to a boil over medium heat. Add the barley. Boil for 10 minutes, stirring occasionally.

3. Remove the chicken from the bones. Discard the skin and bones, and shred the chicken. Use a slotted spoon to remove the beef shanks from the pot; set aside and allow to cool.

4. Add the leeks to the pan. Reduce heat, cover, and simmer for 10 minutes. Remove the beef from the bones, discarding the bones and any fat. Add the chicken and beef to the pan. Cover and simmer for 5 minutes to bring the meat to temperature. Remove the bay leaf. Taste for seasoning and add salt and pepper, if needed. Garnish with parsley if desired.

Matzo Balls

Matzo balls are good in almost any chicken soup. To make 6 servings, mix 2 tablespoons of chicken fat, 2 large eggs, ½ cup matzo meal, 1 teaspoon salt, and 2 tablespoons chicken broth. Cover and refrigerate for at least 20 minutes. Roll the mixture into 12 balls. Cook, covered, in boiling water or broth for 30–40 minutes.

FISH SOUP WITH LETTUCE

Pick up some spring or California rolls and serve them alongside this soup for a complete, light meal. Tastes vary, so have the salt, soy sauce, toasted sesame oil, and green onions at the table and let each person season his or her own soup.

Yields 4 servings

1 tablespoon peanut oil

2 cloves garlic, minced

4 cups chicken broth

1 ½" piece fresh ginger, thinly sliced

1 pound whitefish fillet, sliced thin

1 head iceberg lettuce, chopped

Salt to taste

Soy sauce to taste

Toasted sesame oil to taste

3 green onions, chopped

Add the peanut oil to a deep 3½-quart nonstick skillet or wok and bring to temperature over medium heat. Add the garlic and stir-fry for 30 seconds. Add the broth and bring to a simmer. Add the ginger and fish, cover, and simmer for 5 minutes. Use a slotted spoon to remove the ginger slices, and stir in the lettuce. Cook for another 2 minutes. Add the salt, soy sauce, and toasted sesame oil to taste. Garnish with the chopped green onions.

THAI-INSPIRED CHICKEN SOUP

This soup is an excellent use for leftover cooked chicken breast. If you don't have any on hand and want to add raw meat, allow extra simmering time to let the chicken cook through.

Yields 6–8 servings

6 cups chicken broth

1 ½" piece fresh ginger, thinly sliced

2 cloves garlic, minced

3 shallots, sliced

7 dried Kaffir lime leaves

3 stalks fresh lemongrass

1 teaspoon Thai red curry paste

1 tablespoon granulated sugar

1 14-ounce can coconut milk

3 tablespoons Thai fish sauce

2 cups cooked chicken breast, diced

2 small jalapeño peppers, seeded and thinly sliced

2 tablespoons fresh lime juice

Salt and freshly ground black pepper to taste

Optional: fresh chopped cilantro to taste

1. Add the chicken broth, ginger, garlic, shallot, and lime leaves to a 6-quart Dutch oven. Bring to a boil over medium heat. Peel the bottom 5" of the lemongrass stalks, chop, and add to the broth. Reduce the heat, cover, and simmer for 10 minutes. Strain the broth and discard the solids.

2. Return broth to the pan. Stir in the curry paste, sugar, coconut milk, and fish sauce. Bring to a simmer over low heat. Add the chicken, peppers, and lime juice. Cover and simmer for 10 minutes, or until the peppers are tender. Taste for seasoning and add salt and pepper if needed. Serve garnished with the chopped cilantro, if desired.

PERSIAN LENTIL AND RICE SOUP

If you prefer to have meat in your soup, add boiled chicken before simmering.

Yields 8–10 servings

2 tablespoons extra-virgin olive oil

1 large yellow onion, thinly sliced

1 tablespoon dried parsley

4 cups chopped tomatoes

10 cups chicken broth

2 teaspoons dried mint, crushed

1 cup lentils

⅛ cup fresh lemon juice

¼ cup uncooked basmati rice

½ cup bulgur wheat, medium grind

2 tablespoons tomato paste

½ teaspoon granulated sugar

2 teaspoons sumac

2 teaspoons Advieh (see recipe in sidebar)

Salt and freshly ground black pepper to taste

1. Add the oil to a 6-quart Dutch oven and bring to temperature over medium-high heat. Add the onion, and sauté until transparent. Stir in the parsley and tomatoes; sauté a few minutes and then add the chicken broth, mint, lentils, and lemon juice. Bring to a boil; reduce the heat, cover, and simmer for 30 minutes.

2. Add the rice to a blender or food processor; pulse several times to break it into a coarse powder. Add the broken rice and bulgur; cover and simmer for 75 minutes.

3. Stir in the remaining ingredients. Simmer until the soup is heated through. Taste for seasoning, adding more salt and pepper if necessary.

Advieh

To make this Persian seasoning mix, add 1 tablespoon edible dried rose petals, 1 tablespoon ground cinnamon, ¼ teaspoon cardamom seeds, ¼ teaspoon black peppercorns, ⅛ teaspoon turmeric, ½ teaspoon freshly ground nutmeg, ½ teaspoon cumin seeds, and ¼ teaspoon coriander seeds to a blender or spice grinder; grind to a powder. Store in an airtight container.

SAUERKRAUT AND BEAN SOUP

Keep with Eastern Europe tradition and serve this dish with hearty dark or whole-grain bread.

Yields 6–8 servings

2 tablespoons bacon fat, lard, or peanut oil

1 celery stalk, finely diced

1 large carrot, peeled and shredded

1 large yellow onion, diced

3 cloves garlic, minced

1 pound boneless pork butt, trimmed of fat and cut into bite-size pieces

1 14-ounce can reduced-sodium beef broth

Water as needed

2 teaspoons paprika

1 2-pound bag sauerkraut, rinsed and drained

2 15-ounce cans of pink or pinto beans, rinsed and drained

Salt to taste

Freshly ground black pepper

Optional: sour cream to taste

1. Add the bacon fat, lard, or oil to a Dutch oven and bring it to temperature over medium heat. Add the celery and carrot; sauté for 3–5 minutes, or until soft. Add the onion and sauté until transparent. Add the garlic and sauté for an additional 30 seconds.

2. Brown some of the pork butt. Add the remaining meat, the broth, and enough water to bring the liquid level to just above the meat. Stir in the paprika and bring to a simmer; reduce heat, cover, and simmer for 1 hour.

3. Mash half of the beans. Add the sauerkraut and beans into the meat. Add water, if needed; cover and simmer for 1 hour, or until the meat is tender. Season with salt and pepper. Serve with a dollop of sour cream, if desired.

SPANISH BEAN SOUP

Many claim that the leftovers taste even better than the original servings. You can add a ham bone before simmering to enhance the flavor.

Yields 12 servings

½ pound dried white beans

Water as needed

¼ pound salt pork or bacon, diced

½ pound Spanish chorizo, diced or thinly sliced

1 stalk celery, finely chopped

1 large carrot, peeled and shredded

1 large yellow onion, diced

3 cloves garlic, minced

½ pound smoked ham, diced

4 chicken thighs

1 cup chicken, pork, or ham broth

4 cups water

2 teaspoons Worcestershire sauce

Hot sauce to taste

4 large russet potatoes, peeled and diced

4 turnips, quartered and sliced

1 small head cabbage, cored and shredded

2 cups kale, tough stems removed and thinly sliced

Salt and freshly ground pepper to taste

1. Put the dried beans in an 8-quart stockpot or Dutch oven. Add enough water to cover the beans; cover and let soak overnight.

2. Drain the beans in a colander. Wipe out the pot and add the salt pork or bacon; cook over medium heat to render the fat. Add the chorizo, celery, and carrot; sauté for 3–5 minutes, or until soft. Add the onion and sauté until transparent. Add the garlic and sauté for an additional 30 seconds. Stir in the smoked ham. Add the beans and chicken. Stir in the broth, water, Worcestershire, and hot sauce. Bring to a simmer; cover and simmer for 1 hour, stirring occasionally. Add more water, if needed to keep the pot from boiling dry.

3. Remove the chicken and set aside. Stir the soup well and then stir in the potatoes and turnips. Add the cabbage and kale; cover and simmer for 15 minutes. Shred the chicken, discarding the skin and bones. Stir the chicken into the soup. Add additional water, if needed. Bring to a simmer, cover, and simmer for 45–60 minutes, or until the beans are tender. Taste for seasoning and add salt and pepper if desired.

Try This with Leftover Bean Soup

Add ½ teaspoon (or more) of cider vinegar and granulated sugar to taste to a bowl of reheated soup. If you want an improvised baked beans effect, stir in a little ketchup, too. Top with minced onion.

MUSHROOM AND BARLEY SOUP

To stretch this recipe to 10 servings instead of 8, use all 10 cups of beef broth. Either way, the final result will be a rich soup that, when served along with a salad and a dinner roll or toasted whole-grain bread, is a worthy main course.

Yields 8–10 servings

1 ounce dried porcini or oyster mushrooms

1 cup warm water

2 cups water

1 cup pearl barley

¼ cup butter

8–10 cups beef broth

2 large carrots, peeled and diced

2 large russet potatoes, peeled and diced

1 stalk celery, diced

1 10-ounce package cut frozen green beans, thawed

1 teaspoon dried parsley

Salt and freshly ground pepper to taste

Optional: sour cream to taste

1. Put the dried mushrooms in a small bowl and pour the 1 cup warm water over them. Set aside to soak for 30 minutes.

2. Add the 2 cups water to a 6-quart Dutch oven or stockpot and bring to a boil over medium-high heat. Stir in the barley; reduce the heat, cover, and simmer for 15 minutes, or until all liquid is absorbed. Stir in the butter.

3. Use a slotted spoon to remove the mushrooms from the soaking liquid; dice the mushrooms and then stir them into the butter-barley mixture.

4. Add the broth, carrots, potatoes, celery, green beans, and parsley. Stir well to separate the grains of barley. Bring to a simmer, cover, and cook for 1 hour, or until the barley is tender. Season with salt and pepper to taste. Ladle the soup into bowls and top each serving with a dollop of sour cream, if desired.

ITALIAN BARLEY SOUP

This is a meatless soup, but you can add leftover beef to it if you wish. With or without the meat, serve it with a salad and some dinner rolls to make it a complete meal.

Yields 8 servings

6 cups beef broth

2 cups water

¾ cup barley

4 stalks celery, finely diced

4 large carrots, peeled and grated

1 large yellow onion, diced

4 cloves garlic, minced

½ cup dry red wine

1 1" × ½" piece of lemon peel

½ teaspoon freshly ground black pepper

Salt to taste

1 teaspoon dried basil

½ teaspoon dried oregano, crushed

1 tablespoon dried parsley

2 bay leaves

½ teaspoon dried rosemary

2 tomatoes, diced, or 1 15-ounce can diced tomatoes, drained and juices reserved

4 tablespoons tomato paste

Water as needed

Freshly grated Parmigiano-Reggiano or Romano cheese to taste

1. Add the broth and water to a Dutch oven or stockpot; bring to a boil over medium-high heat. Reduce the heat, and stir in the barley, celery, carrots, onion, garlic, wine, lemon peel, pepper, and salt. Cover and simmer for 2 hours, stirring frequently to prevent the barley from sticking to the bottom of the pot.

2. Stir in the basil, oregano, parsley, bay leaves, rosemary, tomatoes, and tomato paste. Cover and simmer for 1 hour, stirring occasionally. Add the drained tomato juice (if using canned diced tomatoes) or water if needed to keep the pot from boiling dry. Remove the bay leaves and discard. Taste for seasoning and adjust, if necessary. Serve topped with the grated cheese to taste.

Instead of Wine

To give gravy a fruity taste reminiscent of wine, stir in some red currant jelly or a little balsamic vinegar and sugar before you thicken it. Currants are small berries, similar to gooseberries. If you go the balsamic route, adding a little sugar moderates the intense taste of the vinegar.

TUSCAN BEAN SOUP

Beans that are soaked overnight are supposed to be easier to digest. This recipe shows an alternative to soaking the beans overnight.

Yields 8–10 servings

8 ounces dry white kidney, cannellini, or Great Northern beans

10 cups water, or more as needed

1 tablespoon extra-virgin olive oil

2 stalks celery, diced

3 large carrots, peeled and diced

3 medium yellow onions, diced

4 cloves garlic, minced

1 pound crosscut beef shanks, 1"–1½" thick

1 14-ounce can reduced-sodium beef broth

4 smoked ham hocks

1 bay leaf

½ teaspoon dried thyme, crushed

½ teaspoon dried rosemary, crushed

¼ teaspoon freshly ground black pepper

Salt to taste

4 cups torn fresh spinach leaves

1. Rinse the beans and add them to a 6-quart Dutch oven along with 6 cups of the water. Bring to a boil; reduce the heat and simmer, uncovered, for 2 minutes. Remove from the heat, cover, and let stand for 1 hour. Drain the beans in colander; set aside.

2. Wipe out the pan. Add the oil and bring to temperature over medium heat. Add the celery and carrot; sauté for 3–5 minutes, or until soft. Add the onion and sauté until transparent. Add the garlic and sauté for an additional 30 seconds.

3. Add the beef and cook it in the hot oil for about 5 minutes, or until browned. Add the drained beans and the remaining 4 cups water, the beef broth, ham hocks, bay leaf, thyme, rosemary, pepper, and salt; bring to a boil. Reduce the heat, cover, and simmer for 1½ hours, stirring occasionally and adding more water if necessary.

4. Remove the bay leaf, ham hocks, and beef; set aside to cool. Remove the meat from the bones, cut it into bite-size pieces, and stir it into the soup. Discard the bones and bay leaf. Cover and simmer for another 30 minutes, or until the beans and meats are tender. Skim off any fat from the surface of the soup. Stir in the spinach. Heat through and serve.

ITALIAN PASTA AND BEAN SOUP

This recipe calls for more carrots than are traditionally used in Italian bean soup. You can cut that number if you prefer.

Yields 8–10 servings

2 cups dried cannellini or small white beans

6 cups water

2 pounds smoked ham hocks

1 bay leaf

2 cloves garlic, minced

1 small yellow onion, diced

1 1-pound bag baby carrots, cut into thirds

¼ cup lovage or celery leaves, chopped

½ cup tomato sauce

Pinch dried red pepper flakes

¼ teaspoon dried oregano

Pinch dried rosemary

½ teaspoon dried basil

1 teaspoon dried parsley

½ teaspoon granulated sugar

6 cups water

1 cup chicken broth

Salt and freshly ground black pepper to taste

Optional: 1 cup cooked pork, shredded

1 cup dried small pasta, such as orzo or stars

1. Add the beans and water to a 4-quart Dutch oven or stew pot and bring to a boil; cover, turn off the heat, and let sit for 1 hour. Drain the beans, discarding the water.

2. Return the beans to the pan along with all of the other ingredients except the cooked pork (if using) and the pasta. Bring to a simmer over medium heat; reduce the heat, cover, and simmer for 1½–2 hours, or until the beans are very tender. Remove the bay leaf and discard. Remove the ham hocks and set aside to cool.

3. Remove the meat from the ham hocks and cut it into bite-size pieces. Add the ham hock meat along with the cooked pork (if using) and the pasta to the pan. Cover and cook for 15 minutes, stirring occasionally, or until the pasta is tender.

MEATBALL AND VEGETABLE SOUP

Serve this soup with Texas toast, garlic bread, or toasted cheese sandwiches.

Yields 6–8 servings

3 14-ounce cans beef broth

1 16-ounce package frozen cooked meatballs, thawed

1 15-ounce can Great Northern or cannellini beans, rinsed and drained

1 14½-ounce can diced tomatoes with Italian herbs, undrained

1 10-ounce package frozen mixed vegetables, thawed

1 cup dried small pasta, such as orzo

Optional: freshly grated Parmigiano-Reggiano to taste

Add the broth, meatballs, beans, undrained tomatoes, and vegetables to a 4-quart Dutch oven over medium-high heat. Bring to a boil and stir in the pasta. Return to boiling; reduce heat and simmer, uncovered, for about 10 minutes, or until the pasta is cooked. To serve, ladle the soup into bowls. If desired, serve sprinkled with freshly grated Parmigiano-Reggiano cheese.

TORTELLINI SOUP

Opening a few cans is the most labor involved in making this dish. The result tastes like you've been cooking all day.

Yields 4–6 servings

1 tablespoon extra-virgin olive oil

1 small yellow onion, finely chopped

2 14-ounce cans chicken broth

1 can stewed Italian-style tomatoes, coarsely chopped

1 13½-ounce can chopped spinach, drained

1 16-ounce package fresh or frozen tortellini

Optional: freshly grated Parmigiano-Reggiano cheese

Add the oil to a large saucepan or Dutch oven; bring to temperature over medium heat. Add the onion and sauté for 3 minutes, or until transparent. Stir in the broth, tomatoes, and spinach; bring to a boil. Stir in the tortellini; lower the heat, cover, and simmer for the amount of time suggested on the tortellini package. Serve topped with grated cheese, if desired.

DELUXE POTATO SOUP

There's lots of fat (which adds lots of flavor) in this recipe, so it's not an everyday meal. But it's delicious for an occasional indulgence, especially when served over a warm buttermilk biscuit. This wonderfully thick soup freezes well, too.

Yields 12 servings

1 3-pound whole chicken

Salt and freshly ground black pepper to taste

1 large yellow onion, quartered

4 cloves garlic, crushed

2 stalks celery, cut in half

2 large carrots, peeled and cut in 1" pieces

Water as needed

1 1-pound package bacon, cut into small pieces

1 stalk celery, finely chopped

1 large carrot, peeled and shredded

1 small yellow or white onion, finely diced

8 large russet potatoes, peeled and diced

1 1-pound bag baby carrots, diced

1 7-ounce ham slice, diced

1 7-ounce package Canadian bacon, diced

1 8-ounce package cream cheese, cut into cubes

16 ounces medium Cheddar cheese, shredded

1 cup heavy cream

1. Rinse the chicken inside and out in cold, running water. Add the chicken to a Dutch oven or stockpot along with the salt, pepper, quartered onion, garlic, halved celery, and carrot pieces. Add enough water to cover the chicken. Bring to a simmer over medium heat; cover, lower the heat, and simmer for 1 hour, or until the chicken is cooked through.

2. Use tongs to move the chicken to a cutting board or platter; allow to sit until cool enough to handle. Remove and discard the bones and skin. Strain the broth, discarding the vegetables.

3. Add the bacon to the Dutch oven or stockpot and cook it over medium heat until it begins to render some of its fat. Add the chopped celery, shredded carrot, and diced onion; sauté for 5 minutes, or until the onion is transparent and the celery is tender. Stir in the potatoes and baby carrots. Fry until the potatoes just begin to brown, then stir in the cooked chicken, ham, and Canadian bacon. Measure the reserved chicken broth and add enough water to bring it to 6 cups. Pour the broth into the pan; bring to a simmer. Lower the heat, cover, and cook for 5 minutes, or until the potatoes and carrots are cooked through.

4. Add the cream cheese and Cheddar cheese, stirring gently to melt the cheeses into the broth. Stir in the heavy cream and cook about 3 more minutes to bring the cream to temperature. Taste for seasoning and add salt and pepper, if desired.

TURKEY DRUMSTICKS AND VEGETABLE SOUP

Measure the turkey drumsticks to make sure they'll fit in your pressure cooker. It's okay if the end of the bone touches the lid of the cooker, as long as it doesn't block the vent.

Yields 6 servings

1 tablespoon extra-virgin olive oil

1 clove garlic, minced

2 15-ounce cans diced tomatoes

6 medium russet potatoes, peeled and cut into quarters

6 large carrots, peeled and sliced

12 pearl onions, peeled

2 stalks celery, finely diced

½ ounce dried mushrooms

¼ teaspoon dried oregano

¼ teaspoon dried rosemary

1 bay leaf

2 strips orange zest

Salt and freshly ground black pepper to taste

2 1¼-pound turkey drumsticks, skin removed

1 10-ounce package frozen green beans, thawed

1 10-ounce package frozen whole kernel corn, thawed

1 10-ounce package frozen baby peas, thawed

Salt and freshly ground pepper to taste

Fresh chopped parsley or cilantro to taste

1. Add the oil to the pressure cooker and bring to temperature over medium heat. Add the garlic and sauté for 10 seconds. Stir in the tomatoes, potatoes, carrots, onions, celery, mushrooms, oregano, rosemary, bay leaf, orange zest, salt, and pepper. Stand the two drumsticks meaty side down in the pan.

2. Lock the lid and bring to high pressure; maintain it for 12 minutes. Remove from the heat and allow the pressure to drop naturally, and then use your cooker's quick-release method to release the remaining pressure, if needed. Remove the drumsticks, cut the meat from the bone into bite-size pieces, and return it to the pot. Stir in the green beans, corn, and peas; cook over medium heat for 5 minutes. Remove and discard the orange zest and bay leaf. Taste for seasoning and add salt and pepper, if needed. Serve garnished with chopped parsley or cilantro, if desired.

INDONESIAN CHICKEN SOUP

Indonesia is one of the Spice Islands, where many of the spices we use daily were discovered. Most of their dishes use a flavorful spice paste for seasoning.

Yields 6–8 servings

1 3–3½-pound chicken

2 quarts water

2 stalks lemongrass

Zest from 1 lime

1 teaspoon salt

2 jalapeño peppers or 1 serrano pepper

1 teaspoon ground coriander

1 teaspoon ground cumin

3 shallots, peeled

3 garlic cloves

1 teaspoon ground turmeric

1 2" piece ginger, peeled

1 package glass noodles

Juice from 1 lime

¼ cup chopped cilantro

1. Place a large Dutch oven over medium-high heat. Rinse the chicken and place breast down in the pan. Add the water. Cut off the base and the tips of the lemongrass and cut the stalks into 4" pieces. Tuck around the chicken. Sprinkle the zest in the water. Bring to a boil and skim the foam off the surface.

2. Once it boils, reduce the heat to low and cover the pan with a lid. Cook for 45 minutes and skim the foam off the top. Meanwhile, combine all of the remaining ingredients except noodles, lime, and cilantro in a food processor. Pulse for several minutes to create a creamy paste.

3. Once the chicken is cooked so the legs are loose, remove the chicken to a platter or bowl. Increase the heat to medium and stir in the flavoring paste.

4. Remove the skin from the chicken and discard. Cut off the chicken in large chunks and discard the bones. Return the chicken to the pot and cook for 10 minutes. Cook the glass noodles according to package directions and serve in bowls topped with the soup, with lime juice and cilantro as garnish.

FRENCH ONION SOUP

To make your soup even more flavorful, cook the onions for more than 1 hour.

Yields 6 servings

2 tablespoons olive oil

1 tablespoon butter

3 pounds yellow onions, thinly sliced

1 teaspoon salt

5 cups water

4 cups chicken or beef broth

1 thumb-size bundle of thyme

1 bay leaf

¼ cup red wine

Pepper to taste

6 slices baguette, cut 1" thick

8 ounces Gruyère or other soft cheese, shredded

1. Place a Dutch oven over medium heat. Add the oil and butter. Once the butter has melted add the onions and salt. Stir to coat. Cover and steam for 10 minutes.

2. Uncover and cook for 20–30 minutes or until the oil has evaporated and the onions are translucent. Reduce the heat to low and cook, stirring frequently, for 1 hour until the onions are brown and there is a crust on the bottom of the pan.

3. Preheat oven to 350°F. Stir in ¼ cup of water and scrape the crust off the bottom of the pan. Cook until the water has evaporated. Scrape the bottom of the pan as you add the remaining water, broth, thyme, and bay leaf. Simmer for 10 minutes. Add the wine and simmer for 10 minutes. Remove from the heat and discard the herbs. Taste before seasoning with salt and pepper.

4. Once the oven has warmed to temperature, place the bread slices on the oven rack and toast for 7–10 minutes. Remove and set the oven to broil.

5. Place 6 broiler-safe dishes on a baking sheet. Fill each about two-thirds with the soup. Place a bread slice on top and sprinkle the cheese on the dishes evenly. Broil for 5–7 minutes, or until the cheese is brown and bubbly. Remove bay leaf. Cool for 5 minutes before serving.

GARLIC SOUP

In France this dish is called aigo bouido, *which translates as "boiled water." It is a classic peasant dish because the ingredients are so basic and inexpensive.*

Yields 4 servings

2 tablespoons olive oil

3 small yellow onions, peeled and thinly sliced

2 large heads garlic, peeled and smashed

2 quarts water

2 teaspoons salt

Large pinch pepper

2 whole cloves

1 bay leaf

1 teaspoon ground sage

1 teaspoon dried thyme

1 teaspoon ground marjoram

4 slices stale bread

1. Preheat oven to 350°F. Place a Dutch oven over medium heat. Once it's warmed, add the olive oil and onions. Stir frequently. If the onions start to stick, add more oil, and if they start to brown, reduce the heat.

2. Add the garlic to the pot. Stir to combine and cook for 3 minutes. Once you start to smell a warm garlic aroma, and before the garlic browns, turn off the heat.

3. Add the water and dried spices to the pot. Stir to combine. Cover and place in the middle of the oven. Cook for 2 hours.

4. Remove the bay leaf and cloves from the pot and either use a stick blender or carefully pour the soup into a heat-safe blender and purée. Taste and season accordingly. Toast the bread and then add one slice to each dish. Ladle soup over the bread to serve.

Plump Up Your Soup

If you prefer a heartier soup, you can use this as a soup base and add a number of items after the soup has been puréed, such as: 2 cups cooked rice, 2 cups chopped potatoes, ½ cup oatmeal or barley, 1 cup dried pasta, 1 pound chopped whitefish, ½ cup shredded Parmesan cheese, 4 poached eggs, 1 cup cooked and shredded chicken or turkey, 1 strip crumbled bacon, or 1 package baked tofu cut into cubes.

SLOW-COOKED BEEF STEW WITH PARSNIP AND RAISINS

With this recipe, you have a choice: You can either stir the olives and raisins in just before serving, or you can have them at the table as condiments.

Yields 4–6 servings

2 tablespoons vegetable oil

1½-pound beef chuck roast, cut into 1" cubes

2 tablespoons all-purpose flour

1 1-pound bag baby carrots

2 large parsnips, peeled and sliced into ½" pieces

1 large yellow onion, roughly chopped

1 14½-ounce can diced tomatoes, undrained

1 14-ounce can beef broth

2 cloves garlic, minced

1 bay leaf

1 teaspoon dried thyme, crushed

¼ teaspoon freshly ground black pepper

½ cup almond- or pimiento-stuffed green olives

⅓ cup golden raisins

1. Add the oil to a 4-quart slow cooker and bring to temperature over high heat. Toss meat in flour. Add half of the meat to the slow cooker and sauté until brown; push the meat to the side and add remaining meat, stirring to coat all the meat in the hot oil. Wipe out any excess fat.

2. Add the carrots, parsnips, onion, tomatoes, broth, garlic, bay leaf, thyme, and pepper to the cooker; stir to combine. Reduce the heat setting to low; cover and cook for 8–10 hours.

3. Remove and discard the bay leaf. Stir in the olives and raisins. Serve warm.

SLOW-COOKED PORK STEW

This stew is good served over cooked rice and garnished with strips of green onion. Only add the poblano and jalapeño peppers if you want a hot, spicy stew; otherwise, omit them entirely or substitute chopped green pepper.

Yields 6–8 servings

2 pounds boneless pork shoulder

1 tablespoon vegetable oil

1 pound tiny new potatoes, washed and quartered

1 cup chopped yellow onions

Optional: 2 fresh poblano peppers, seeded and cut into 1" pieces

Optional: 1 fresh jalapeño pepper, seeded and chopped

4 cloves garlic, minced

1 2" cinnamon stick

2 cups chicken broth

1 14½-ounce can diced tomatoes

1 tablespoon chili powder

1 teaspoon dried oregano, crushed

¼ teaspoon black pepper

Optional: ¼ cup snipped fresh cilantro or parsley

1. Trim the fat from the pork and cut the meat into 1" cubes. Add the oil to a 4-quart or larger slow cooker and bring it to temperature over high. Add the pork; cover and let brown for 15 minutes. Stir the pork and brown for another 15 minutes. Drain off fat. Add the remaining ingredients except the cilantro or parsley (if using); stir to combine. Reduce the heat to low; cover and cook on low for 8 hours.

2. Discard the cinnamon stick. Stir in additional chicken broth if the stew is too thick and bring it to temperature. Stir in the cilantro or parsley, if desired. Serve warm.

Hot Pepper Precautions

Wear gloves or sandwich bags over your hands when you clean and dice hot peppers. It's important to avoid having the peppers come into contact with your skin or your eyes. As an added precaution, wash your hands (don't forget underneath your fingernails) thoroughly with hot soapy water after you remove the gloves or sandwich bags.

HUNGARIAN GOULASH

Hungarian Goulash is often served with prepared spaetzle (German dumplings) and Cucumber Salad (see recipe in sidebar). Make the cucumber salad before you prepare the goulash so the cucumbers marinate in the dressing while you make the stew.

Yields 4–6 servings

2 strips bacon

1 large yellow onion, diced

1 tablespoon extra-virgin olive oil

2½ pounds stewing beef, cut into ½" cubes

1 clove garlic, minced

Pinch caraway seeds, chopped

2 tablespoons sweet paprika

2 cups beef broth

Water as needed

1 15-ounce can diced tomatoes

1 green bell pepper, seeded and diced

4 large russet potatoes, diced

2 tablespoons sour cream, plus more for serving

1. Add the bacon to a 6- to 8-quart stewing pot; fry over medium heat until the fat is rendered, then discard the bacon slices. Sauté the onion in the bacon fat and olive oil until the onion is transparent. Add the beef; sauté with the onions about 10 minutes, or until the meat is browned. Stir in the garlic and caraway seeds and sauté for 1 more minute.

2. Remove the pot from the heat and quickly stir in the paprika. Add the beef broth; if needed, add enough water to cover the meat. Cover and simmer over low heat for 1½ hours.

3. Add the can of tomatoes with juice and green pepper. Add more water, if needed to cover the beef. Cover and simmer for 1 more hour, or until the meat is tender. Add the potatoes; cover and cook for an additional 30 minutes, or until the potatoes are fork-tender. Stir the 2 tablespoons of sour cream into the goulash. Serve with additional sour cream on the side if desired.

Cucumber Salad

Thinly slice 2 cucumbers; put the slices in a bowl and sprinkle with salt. Let rest for 30 minutes. Drain off the excess moisture and add a small, thinly sliced yellow onion; 1 or 2 tablespoons dry white wine or cider vinegar; ¼ cup heavy or sour cream; 2 teaspoons granulated sugar; ⅛ teaspoon sweet paprika; a pinch of dried or fresh dill; and freshly ground black pepper to taste. Mix well, cover, and refrigerate until ready to serve.

MOROCCAN LAMB STEW

Preserved lemon and orange blossom water are available at Middle Eastern markets or from specialty spice shops, like the Spice House (www.thespicehouse.com). They add the authentic flavors to this dish, which is traditionally served with couscous.

Yields 6 servings

2 pounds boneless lamb shoulder, trimmed of fat

1 teaspoon salt

2 teaspoons freshly ground black pepper

½ teaspoon saffron

1 teaspoon ground ginger

2 cloves garlic, minced

1 large yellow onion, diced

1 tablespoon dried parsley

4 tablespoons ghee or extra-virgin olive oil

2½ cups water, or more as needed

½ preserved lemon, diced (no pulp)

2 teaspoons ground cinnamon

¼ cup honey

2 tablespoons orange blossom water

Optional: 1 tablespoon sesame seeds

Optional: ¾ cup blanched slivered almonds

1. Cut the lamb into 1" cubes and add to a 6-quart Dutch oven along with the salt, pepper, saffron, ginger, garlic, onion, parsley, and 3 tablespoons of the ghee or oil. Add the water, increasing the amount if necessary to completely cover the meat. Bring to a boil over medium-high heat; lower the heat and simmer, covered, for 1½ hours, or until the meat is very tender.

2. Add the lemon and cinnamon; cover and simmer for 15 minutes. Add the honey and orange blossom water; simmer, stirring frequently, until the sauce is reduced and thickened.

3. If desired, add the remaining 1 tablespoon ghee or oil to a nonstick skillet and bring to temperature over medium heat. Add the sesame seeds and almonds; stir-fry until toasted to a light brown. Garnish each serving with the seed and nut mixture.

Couscous Consciousness

Couscous is a pasta made from semolina wheat granules that are coated in finely ground wheat flour. Regular couscous requires a multistage process of boiling, hand rubbing, and steaming. Quick-cooking couscous is also available. Another option is to substitute orzo, a semolina flour pasta shaped like grains of rice.

SHRIMP AND CRAB BISQUE

Adding carrots and potatoes to this dish turns it into a one pot meal. It may be stretching it to continue to call it "bisque," but when you consider the cost of the ingredients, it still deserves an expensive-sounding name.

Yields 6–8 servings

2 tablespoons plus ½ cup butter

4 stalks celery with leaves, finely chopped

1 1-pound bag baby carrots

1 large yellow onion, finely chopped

2 cloves garlic, minced

3 cups fish or shrimp stock, or chicken broth

4 large russet potatoes, peeled and diced

2 whole cloves

1 bay leaf

6 peppercorns

2 cups whole milk

½ cup all-purpose flour

1 pound raw shrimp, peeled and deveined

1 pound cooked crabmeat, broken apart

2 cups heavy cream

Optional: salt

Optional: white pepper to taste

Optional: dry sherry to taste

Optional: fresh parsley or 2 green onions (green part only), chopped

1. Melt 2 tablespoons of the butter in a 6-quart Dutch oven or stockpot over medium heat. Add the celery and stir into the butter. Finely dice 6 of the baby carrots and stir them into the butter and celery; sauté for 2 minutes. Add the onion and sauté until transparent. Stir the garlic into the sautéed mixture. Chop the remaining carrots into thirds, and then add them along with the stock or broth and the potatoes. Wrap the cloves, bay leaf, and peppercorns in cheesecloth or put them in a muslin cooking bag; add to the broth. Bring to a boil; lower the temperature, cover, and simmer for 10 minutes.

2. Add the milk. Bring to a boil over medium heat. Mix ½ cup butter and flour together to form a paste and stir it into the broth, 1 teaspoon at a time. Once all of the butter-flour mixture is added, boil for 1 minute, then lower the temperature and let simmer until the mixture begins to thicken and the raw flour taste is cooked out of the broth. Remove the cheesecloth or cooking bag.

3. Add the shrimp and cook just until they begin to turn pink; do not overcook. Stir in the crabmeat and cream. Bring to temperature. Taste for seasoning, and, if desired, season with salt, white pepper, and/or dry sherry. Remove from the heat and serve immediately. Garnish with chopped parsley or chopped green onion, if desired.

CLAM CHOWDER

Canned clams are salty, so chances are you won't need to add any salt to the chowder. Also, be sure to read the label on the cans if anyone in your family has food sensitivities; some canned clams have monosodium glutamate.

Yields 8–10 servings

½ cup butter

2 cloves garlic, minced

1 stalk celery, finely chopped

2 baby carrots, grated

1 large yellow onion, diced

½ teaspoon white pepper

⅛ teaspoon dried thyme, crushed

½ cup all-purpose flour

3 cups chicken broth or water

3 cups whole milk

1 bay leaf

4 large russet or red potatoes, peeled or unpeeled, and diced

2 6½-ounce cans chopped or minced clams

2 cups heavy cream

1. Melt the butter in a 6-quart Dutch oven over medium heat. Add the garlic, celery, and carrots; sauté for 2 minutes. Add the onion and sauté until transparent. Stir in the pepper, thyme, and flour. Whisk until the butter is absorbed into the flour. Slowly add the broth or water, whisking continuously to blend it with the butter-flour roux. Add the milk, bay leaf, and potatoes. Bring to a boil; reduce heat, cover, and simmer for 10–15 minutes, or until the potatoes are tender. Check and stir the chowder frequently to prevent it from burning.

2. Stir in the clams and cream. Bring to temperature, remove the bay leaf, taste for seasoning, and serve immediately.

Clam Salad

Chop leftover steamed clams and add them to a macaroni salad. For a complete quick and easy lunch, serve it over lettuce and garnish the clam-macaroni salad with chopped fresh parsley or dill.

OYSTER STEW

This stew is rich enough for a meal. Serve it with bread or crackers and a tossed salad. In the Midwest, it's served with butter-style crackers.

Yields 4 servings

2 pints fresh oysters

4 tablespoons butter

1 tablespoon yellow onion or shallot, finely chopped

1 cup whole milk

1 cup heavy cream

Salt and white pepper to taste

Optional: fresh parsley, chopped, to taste

1. Shuck the oysters. Start by folding a thick cloth several times to create a square. Use the cloth to steady each oyster firmly on a flat surface as you shuck it; the cloth will also help protect your hand. Insert the tip of an oyster knife between the shell halves and work it around from one side to the other as you pry the shell open. Use a sharp fillet or paring knife to cut away the muscles from the flat shell. Bend the shell back, break it off, and discard it. Run the knife underneath the oyster to detach it completely and pour it and the oyster juices into a measuring cup. Discard the bottom shell. Repeat until you have 3 cups.

2. Melt the butter in a heavy 2-quart saucepan over medium heat. Add the onion and sauté until transparent. Reduce the heat to low, and add the milk, cream, salt, and pepper; bring to a light simmer.

3. Add the oysters and juices. Heat only until the oysters are hot; do not overcook. Ladle into bowls and serve immediately. Garnish with parsley, if desired.

HEARTY BEEF STEW

Serve this stew with crackers or dinner rolls and you have an easy, complete comfort-food meal.

Yields 6 servings

- 1 pound cooked roast beef, cut into bite-size pieces
- 1 10¾-ounce can condensed tomato soup
- 1 10½-ounce can condensed French onion soup
- 1 tablespoon Worcestershire sauce
- 2 cups water
- 4 cups frozen vegetables of your choice
- 1 tablespoon butter
- 1 tablespoon all-purpose flour
- Salt and freshly ground black pepper to taste

1. Add the roast beef, soups, Worcestershire sauce, water, and vegetables to a 6-quart or larger Dutch oven. Bring to a boil over high heat. Lower the heat, cover, and simmer for 6 minutes.

2. In a small bowl, mix the butter into the flour to make a paste. Ladle about ½ cup of the soup broth into the bowl and whisk into the paste, then pour it into the stew.

3. Increase the heat to medium-high and return the pot to a boil; boil for 2 minutes, stirring occasionally. Reduce the heat, cover, and simmer for an additional 2 minutes, or until the vegetables are tender and the stew is thickened. Taste for seasoning, and add salt and pepper, if needed.

BRUNSWICK STEW

This stew is made with chicken or rabbit. The cooking times are the same whether you use fresh or thawed frozen vegetables.

Yields 6 servings

2 slices bacon, diced

3 tablespoons all-purpose flour

1 teaspoon salt

½ teaspoon pepper

Pinch cayenne pepper

1 4-pound chicken or rabbit, cut into serving pieces

3 small yellow onions, thinly sliced

1½ cups boiling water

4 tomatoes, diced

1 red bell pepper, seeded and diced

½ teaspoon dried leaf thyme, crushed

2 cups lima beans

2 cups corn kernels

½ cup okra, sliced

2 tablespoons fresh parsley, chopped

1 tablespoon Worcestershire sauce

Add the bacon to a slow cooker; cook on the high setting to render the fat. Remove the bacon and set aside. Put the flour, salt, pepper, and cayenne in a gallon-size food storage bag; add the chicken or rabbit, close the bag, and shake to coat the pieces with the seasoned flour. Add the meat to the pan and brown in the rendered fat. Add the onion, cover, and steam until the onions are transparent, about 5 minutes. Add the water, tomatoes, red pepper, and thyme to the slow cooker. Cover; cook on low for 6–8 hours, or until the meat is cooked through and tender. Add the remaining ingredients along with the reserved bacon; cover and cook on high for 25 minutes, or until the vegetables are tender.

POT-AU-FEU

Pot-au-feu *is French for "pot on the fire." This recipe is a slow-cooker adaptation of the French boiled dinner, with ingredients added so that the potatoes sit atop the meat and steam during the cooking process.*

Yields 8 servings

2 tablespoons butter

1 1-pound bag baby carrots

2 large yellow onions, sliced

4 stalks celery, finely diced

2 cloves garlic, left whole

1 bouquet garni (see instructions in sidebar)

1 2-pound boneless chuck roast, cut into 1" pieces

8 chicken thighs

1 pound Western-style pork ribs

1 tablespoon coarse sea salt

4 small turnips, peeled and quartered

1 medium rutabaga, peeled and cut into eighths

Water as needed

8 medium red or Yukon gold potatoes, cut into quarters

1. Add the butter to a 6½-quart slow cooker set on high heat. Finely dice 10 of the baby carrots and 2 of the onion slices. Add the diced carrots and onion and the celery to the slow cooker; cover and cook for 15 minutes. Add the garlic, bouquet garni, beef, chicken, and pork; sprinkle the salt over the meat and then layer in the remaining onion slices, remaining carrots, turnips, and rutabaga. Add enough water so that the water level comes just to the top of the vegetables. Arrange the potatoes on top of the rutabaga. Reduce the heat setting to low, cover, and cook for 8 hours.

2. For a casual supper, you can ladle servings directly from the crock. For a more formal dinner, use a slotted spoon to arrange the vegetables and potatoes around the outside of a large serving platter with the meats arranged in the center; ladle a generous amount of the broth over all. Strain the remaining broth; pour the strained broth into a gravy boat to have at the table.

3. Serve with toasted French bread rubbed with garlic and have coarse sea salt, cornichons, Dijon mustard, grated horseradish, pickled onions, sour cream, and whole-grain mustard at the table.

Bouquet Garni

Create the bouquet garni by wrapping 2 bay leaves, 1 teaspoon dried thyme, 1 tablespoon dried parsley, 1 teaspoon black peppercorns, and 4 cloves in cheesecloth or in a muslin spice bag.

SEAFOOD STEW

You can add a Portuguese touch to this dish by substituting linguiça or chorizo sausage for the smoked sausage. Regardless, serve the stew with warm garlic bread so you can sop up the broth.

Yields 8 servings

2 tablespoons extra-virgin olive oil, plus extra for serving

2 medium yellow onions, diced

4 garlic cloves, minced

1 pound smoked sausage, sliced into chunks

½ teaspoon dried thyme

¼ teaspoon dried oregano, crushed

1 bay leaf

8 large Yukon gold potatoes, diced

8 cups chicken broth

1 pound kale, chopped

2 pounds perch, cod, or bass fillets, skin and pin bones removed

Optional: Water as needed

2 28-ounce cans boiled baby clams, drained

Sea salt and freshly ground black pepper to taste

Optional: ¼ cup fresh flat-leaf parsley, chopped

1. Bring the oil to temperature in a 4- to 6-quart Dutch oven over medium heat. Add the onions, garlic, and sausage; stirring frequently, sauté for 5 minutes, or until the onions are transparent. Add the thyme, oregano, bay leaf, and potatoes, stirring everything to mix the herbs and coat the potatoes in the oil. Pour in the chicken broth; bring to a simmer. Add the kale; cover and simmer for 10 minutes, or until the potatoes are nearly tender.

2. Add the fish; cook for another 3 minutes. Add water if additional liquid is needed to cover the fish. Add the drained clams, and cook for an additional 3 minutes, or until the fish is cooked and the clams are brought to temperature. Taste for seasoning, and add salt and pepper if needed. Garnish with chopped parsley, if desired, and drizzle with extra-virgin olive oil.

Why Water Is Optional

The heat at which you cook a dish makes a difference in how much of the liquid will evaporate during the cooking process. Some vegetables in a dish also sometimes absorb more liquid than do others. If such evaporation or absorption occurs, the broth will become concentrated. Thus, water only reintroduces more liquid; it doesn't dilute the taste.

SOUTHERN CHICKEN STEW

The sugar in this dish offsets the acidity of the tomatoes. If you're using apple juice instead of wine, you may want to wait until the dish is cooked to see if the sugar is needed.

Yields 8 servings

3 tablespoons bacon fat

1 3-pound chicken, cut into serving pieces

2 cups water

1 28-ounce can diced tomatoes

2 large yellow onions, sliced

½ teaspoon granulated sugar

½ cup dry white wine or apple juice

1 10-ounce package frozen lima beans, thawed

1 10-ounce package frozen whole kernel corn, thawed

1 10-ounce package frozen okra, thawed and sliced

1 cup bread crumbs, toasted

3 tablespoons Worcestershire sauce

Salt and freshly ground black pepper to taste

Optional: hot sauce to taste

1. Bring the bacon fat to temperature in a 6-quart Dutch oven over medium heat. Add the chicken pieces and fry them until lightly browned. Add the water, tomatoes, onions, sugar, and wine or apple juice. Bring to a simmer; cover and simmer for 75 minutes, or until the chicken is cooked through. Use a slotted spoon to remove the chicken and set it aside until it's cool enough to handle. Then, remove the chicken from the bones and discard the skin and bones. Shred the chicken meat and set aside.

2. Add the lima beans, corn, and okra to the pot. Bring to a simmer and cook uncovered for 30 minutes. Stir in the shredded chicken, bread crumbs, and Worcestershire sauce. Simmer for 10 minutes, stirring occasionally, to bring the chicken to temperature and thicken the stew. Taste for seasoning and add salt and pepper, if needed, and hot sauce, if desired.

PRESSURE COOKER SOUTHERN CHICKEN STEW

For a milder dish, substitute green bell pepper for the jalapeño or Scotch bonnet chili.

Yields 6 servings

2 tablespoons vegetable oil

1 medium yellow onion, sliced

2 bay leaves

2 teaspoons ground allspice

1 teaspoon dried thyme

⅓ cup tomato paste

8 bone-in chicken thighs

Salt and freshly ground black pepper to taste

3½ cups water

1 jalapeño or Scotch bonnet chili pepper, pierced

8 ounces fresh okra, trimmed and cut in half crosswise

3 large sweet potatoes, peeled and cut into large dice

1 1-pound bunch collard greens, stems removed and chopped

1. Add the oil to the pressure cooker and bring it to temperature over medium heat. Stir in the onion, bay leaves, allspice, and thyme; sauté for 5 minutes, or until the onion is soft. Increase the heat to high, stir in the tomato paste, and cook for 2 minutes, stirring and scraping until it turns brick red.

2. Remove and discard the skin on the chicken. Season the thighs with salt and black pepper to taste, and add them to the cooker; turn them to coat with the tomato and onion. Stir in the water. Add the chili pepper, okra, potatoes, and collard greens in that order. Lock the pressure cooker lid; bring to high pressure and maintain it for 7 minutes.

3. Remove the cooker from the heat. Use the pressure cooker's quick-release method to release the pressure. Carefully open the pot. Remove and discard the bay leaves and chili pepper. Stir and then ladle the stew into bowls and serve.

AFRICAN PEANUT AND CHICKEN STEW

When served with all of the optional condiments, this African Peanut and Chicken Stew is a one pot meal and dessert rolled into one.

Yields 6 servings

2 tablespoons peanut oil

2 3-pound chickens, cut into serving pieces

1 large yellow onion, sliced

½ teaspoon dried dill

2 bay leaves

Water as needed

½ cup peanut butter

3 tablespoons cornstarch

½ cup cold water

Salt and freshly ground pepper to taste

Optional: 3–6 cups cooked long-grain rice

Optional: 5 bananas, peeled and cut lengthwise, then browned in butter

Optional: unsweetened pineapple chunks

Optional: 4 ounces unsweetened coconut, toasted (see instructions in sidebar)

½ cup roasted peanuts, finely chopped

1. Add the oil to a 6-quart Dutch oven and bring it to temperature over medium heat. Add the chicken pieces, skin side down, and brown them for 5 minutes. Add the onion, dill, bay leaves, and enough water to almost cover the chicken. Bring to a boil, reduce heat, and simmer, covered, for 45 minutes. Remove the chicken from the pot and keep warm; discard the skin, if desired. Remove and discard the bay leaves.

2. Add ½ cup of the hot liquid from the Dutch oven to the peanut butter; mix well, and then pour the resulting peanut butter sauce into the pan. In a small bowl, mix the cornstarch and cold water together; remove any lumps. Whisk the cornstarch mixture into the broth in the pan, continuing to stir or whisk until the broth thickens. If you prefer a thicker sauce, mix more cornstarch in cold water and repeat the process.

3. Taste the sauce for seasoning and add salt and pepper, if needed. The traditional way to serve this dish is to place the chicken over some cooked rice. Ladle the thickened pan juices over the chicken and rice. Top with fried bananas, pineapple, toasted coconut (if using), and chopped peanuts.

Toasted Coconut

To toast coconut, preheat oven to 350°F. Spread the coconut out over a jellyroll pan. Place the pan in the oven and, watching it carefully, bake the coconut for 5 minutes, or until it's a very light golden brown.

GREEN CHILI STEW

Serve this stew with a salad and corn chips. It also works as an enchilada filling. To accommodate different tastes, use mild green chili peppers in the stew and have hot green salsa at the table.

Yields 6–8 servings

½ cup butter

1 large yellow onion, diced

½ teaspoon dried oregano

½ tablespoon granulated garlic

1 tablespoon chili powder

¼ cup all-purpose flour

4 cups chicken broth

1 28-ounce can heat-and-serve pork

3 7-ounce cans mild or hot green chilies, drained and chopped

Salt and freshly ground black pepper to taste

Melt the butter in a 4-quart Dutch oven over medium heat. Add the onion and sauté for 5 minutes, or until the onion is transparent. Stir in the oregano, garlic, and chili powder. Whisk in the flour to make a roux, and cook it until it's lightly browned. Whisk in the chicken broth a little at a time, whisking until smooth. Bring to a boil and boil for 1 minute. Reduce heat, and stir in the pork and canned chilies. Simmer gently, stirring occasionally, until thickened. Taste for seasoning and add salt and pepper if desired.

SPICED ARMENIAN LAMB STEW

Serve this rich stew over rice or couscous along with a Cucumber Salad (see Hungarian Goulash recipe in this chapter) and your choice of bread.

Yields 4–6 servings

2 tablespoons butter

1 large yellow onion, diced

2 pounds lean, boneless leg of lamb, cut into 1" cubes

½ teaspoon paprika

½ teaspoon freshly ground black pepper

½ teaspoon ground allspice

¼ teaspoon ground cinnamon

Salt to taste

¼ cup tomato paste

1 cup water

2 tablespoons dry red wine

1. Melt the butter in a 6-quart Dutch oven and bring to temperature over medium heat. Add the onions; sauté for 3 minutes. Pushing the onions to the side of the pan, add the lamb and brown the meat in the butter. Stir the paprika, pepper, allspice, and cinnamon into the meat and onions. Add salt to taste.

2. Push the meat and onions to the side and sauté the tomato paste for 2 minutes, then stir it into the meat and onions. Slowly pour the water into the pan. Stir to dissolve the tomato paste into the water. Bring the water to a boil, then reduce the heat, cover, and simmer for 45 minutes, or until the meat is tender. Add the red wine, cover, and simmer for 15 more minutes. Taste for seasoning and add salt and pepper, if needed.

UNSTUFFED TOMATOES AND PEPPERS

Rather than taking the time to make a filling and then filling the peppers and tomatoes, this dish is prepared layered in a slow cooker.

Yields 8 servings

1 cup uncooked long-grain rice

1 cup tomato juice

1 pound ground beef

½ pound ground lamb or pork

1 large yellow onion, diced

1 tablespoon dried parsley

1 teaspoon salt

Freshly ground black pepper to taste

1 teaspoon paprika

⅛ teaspoon ground allspice

Pinch ground cinnamon

1 teaspoon granulated sugar

2 14½-ounce cans diced tomatoes

4 green bell peppers, seeded and diced

1 cup beef broth

2 tablespoons lemon juice

Water or additional broth, as needed

1. In a large mixing bowl, combine the rice, tomato juice, beef, lamb or pork, onion, parsley, salt, black pepper, paprika, allspice, cinnamon, and sugar. Set aside.

2. Add 1 can of the diced tomatoes to a 4-quart or larger slow cooker. Add half of the meat-rice mixture. Spread the diced green peppers over the top of the meat mixture, and top the peppers with the rest of the meat. Add the remaining can of diced tomatoes. Pour in the beef broth and add the lemon juice. If needed, add additional water or broth to bring the liquid to almost the top of the solid ingredients.

3. Cook for 6–8 hours on low. If too much liquid remains in the slow cooker, cook uncovered long enough to allow some of the liquid to evaporate.

IRISH LAMB STEW

This is the type of dish that's easy to expand if extra people show up for dinner. Simply add extra broth, carrots, and potatoes as needed.

Yields 6–8 servings

4 tablespoons extra-virgin olive oil or bacon fat

1 large yellow onion, chopped

1 clove garlic, minced

2½ pounds lean lamb shoulder, cut in bite-size pieces

2 tablespoons all-purpose flour

1½ cups chicken broth

Salt to taste

¼ teaspoon pepper

1 bay leaf

¼ teaspoon dried marjoram

2 teaspoons lemon juice

1 cup frozen pearl onions, thawed

4 large carrots, peeled and cut in chunks

4 large russet potatoes, peeled and diced

Optional: 1½ tablespoons fresh parsley, finely chopped

1. Bring the oil or fat to temperature over medium heat in a Dutch oven. Add the onion and sauté for 3–5 minutes, or until the onion is transparent. Add the garlic and sauté for an additional 30 seconds. Add the lamb; brown it for about 5 minutes, or until it begins to release some of its juices and some of the pieces are browned.

2. Sprinkle the flour over the lamb, and stir to toss the flour with the meat and fat in the pan. Stir in the broth, salt, pepper, bay leaf, marjoram, and lemon juice. Bring to a simmer, cover, and simmer for 30–60 minutes, or until the meat begins to get tender. If needed, skim off any excess fat from the top of the broth. Add the small onions, carrots, and potatoes; cover and simmer for 30 minutes, or until the carrots and potatoes are cooked through. Serve sprinkled with parsley, if desired.

PUERTO RICAN CHICKEN STEW

The consistency of this dish is a compromise: It's thicker than a stew but moister than a paella.

Yields 4 servings

2 teaspoons dried oregano, crushed

¼ teaspoon freshly ground black pepper

2 teaspoons paprika

¼ teaspoon salt

1 3½-pound chicken, cut into serving pieces

4 tablespoons extra-virgin olive oil

1 ounce salt pork or bacon, diced

1 medium yellow onion, diced

1 medium green bell pepper, seeded and diced

2 ounces ham, diced

1 medium tomato, diced

½ pound chorizo or smoked sausage

¼ cup small pimiento-stuffed olives

1 tablespoon capers, rinsed and drained

1 tablespoon Annatto Oil (see Filipino Pork with Rice Noodles recipe in Chapter 5)

2 cups converted rice

3 cups water

½ cup frozen peas

1. Add the oregano, black pepper, paprika, and salt to a large resealable plastic bag; shake to mix the spices. Add the chicken and shake to coat the chicken in the spices.

2. Add the olive oil to a large Dutch oven and bring to temperature over medium heat. Add the salt pork or bacon, onion, and green pepper. Sauté for 3–5 minutes, or until the onion is transparent and the green pepper begins to get tender. Stir in the ham and tomato; reduce heat to low, cover, and simmer for 10 minutes. Stir in the chorizo or smoked sausage, and then add the chicken, skin side down, with as many of the chicken pieces touching the pan bottom as possible. Cover and simmer for 30 minutes.

3. Add the olives, capers, Annatto Oil, rice, and water; bring to a simmer, cover, and simmer for 15 minutes. Add the peas; cover and simmer for another 5 minutes, or until the chicken is cooked through and the rice is tender. Taste for seasoning and add salt and pepper, if needed.

ROMANIAN VEAL WITH VEGETABLES STEW

This recipe lets you stretch a small amount of expensive veal into lots of servings. This stew is especially good if each bowl is garnished with a dollop of drained yogurt or sour cream.

Yields 8 servings

3 tablespoons all-purpose flour

½ teaspoon salt

¼ teaspoon freshly ground black pepper

1 pound boneless veal shoulder, cut into 1" cubes

2 tablespoons butter

1 medium yellow onion, sliced

2 small cloves garlic, minced

½ cup beef broth

½ cup dry red wine

1 small head cabbage, cored and thinly sliced

2 teaspoons dried parsley

1 tablespoon tomato paste

2 large carrots, peeled and sliced

1 14½-ounce can diced tomatoes

1 large green pepper, seeded and cut into strips

2 cups eggplant, diced

2 cups zucchini, diced

1 cup leeks (white part only) well rinsed and thinly sliced

2 small turnips, diced

1 cup celery root, diced

2 small parsnips, diced

1 14½-ounce can French-style green beans, drained

¼ cup seedless green grapes

¼ teaspoon dried thyme

¼ teaspoon dried marjoram

1. Add the flour, salt, and pepper to a large food storage bag; shake to mix. Add the veal cubes and toss to coat in the seasoned flour. Melt the butter in an ovenproof 6-quart Dutch oven over medium heat. Add the veal, and brown for 5 minutes. Add the onions and sauté, stirring frequently, for 5 minutes, or until the onions are transparent. Add the garlic and sauté for an additional 30 seconds.

2. Preheat oven to 350°F.

3. Add the beef broth, wine, and half of the cabbage; cover and simmer until the cabbage wilts, then add all the remaining ingredients. Bring to a boil, cover, and bake for 1 hour, stirring the stew about every 20 minutes. The stew is done when the meat and all of the vegetables are cooked through and tender.

FRENCH VEAL STEW

This stew is sometimes served over rice cooked with lots of onions in it, but a tossed salad with lemon vinaigrette will complement the gremolata's citrus addition to the stew.

Yields 6–8 servings

4 pounds veal stew meat, cut into 2" pieces

1 pound veal bones, sawed into pieces

Water as needed

8 tablespoons butter

1 large carrot, peeled and finely diced

1 celery stalk, finely diced

2½ cups veal or chicken broth

1 large white onion, peeled and stuck with a whole clove

1 tablespoon dried parsley

½ bay leaf

Pinch dried thyme, crushed

8 ounces fresh button or cremini mushrooms, cleaned and sliced

5 tablespoons all-purpose flour

1 tablespoon lemon juice

1 1-pound bag frozen white pearl onions, thawed

3 egg yolks

½ cup heavy cream

Optional: Gremolata (see recipe in sidebar)

Gremolata

Gremolata is a garlic-citrus condiment for stews. Remove the zest from an orange and a lemon; blanch in 4 cups of water for 10 minutes. Drain and rinse in cold water. Pat dry, then finely chop it along with 1 garlic clove and ¼ cup fresh flat-leaf parsley. Sprinkle over the stew, to taste.

1. Add the veal and veal bones to a 4-quart Dutch oven. Add enough cold water to cover the meat; bring to a boil over high heat. Reduce temperature and simmer for 3 minutes, or until a heavy scum rises to the top of the pan. Drain the meat and bones in a colander and rinse to remove the scum.

2. Wipe out the Dutch oven. Melt 2 tablespoons of the butter over medium heat. Add the carrot and celery; sauté for 5 minutes, or until tender. Add the veal and veal bones back into the pan along with the broth and onion studded with a clove, parsley, bay leaf, and thyme. If needed, add enough water to bring the liquid level up to the top of the meat. Bring to a boil; reduce heat, cover, and simmer for 1½ hours, or until the veal is tender. Skim any scum from the surface and discard. Taste for seasoning and add salt, if needed; let the meat rest in the broth, uncovered, for 30 minutes. Pour the contents of the pan into a colander set over a large bowl to hold the broth.

3. Melt 2 tablespoons of the butter in the Dutch oven over medium heat. Add the mushrooms to the pan and sauté for 5 minutes, stirring occasionally. Return the broth to the pan, adding water if necessary to bring the broth to 4 cups.

4. Melt the remaining 4 tablespoons of butter in a small microwave-safe bowl. Whisk in the flour and lemon juice. Once the broth begins to boil, whisk in the flour mixture, stirring constantly for 2 minutes, or until the broth begins to thicken. Stir in the pearl onions. Reduce the heat and simmer uncovered while you prepare the final touches.

5. Discard the clove-studded onion and veal bones. Add the veal meat to the Dutch oven. In a small bowl, whisk the egg yolks together with the cream. Slowly whisk in a cup of the thickened broth from the pan to temper the eggs. Remove the pan from the heat, then slowly whisk the egg mixture into the remaining thickened broth in the pan. Set the pan back over low heat and stir gently to allow the egg yolks to cook into the sauce, being careful not to allow the sauce to return to a simmer. Remove ½ bay leaf. Taste for seasoning; add salt and pepper, if needed. If desired, stir some of the gremolata into the stew before you garnish each serving with it.

LOBSTER CHOWDER

Serve this rich chowder alongside a green salad and buttered biscuits, dinner rolls, or common crackers.

Yields 4 servings

2 ounces smoked slab bacon, cut into ¼" dice

2 medium leeks, white part only, rinsed and cut to ½" dice

4 medium russet or red potatoes, peeled and diced

4 cups water, lobster or fish stock, or chicken broth

2 tablespoons unsalted butter

Freshly ground black pepper to taste

1 pound cooked lobster, cut into bite-size pieces

1 cup heavy cream

Sea salt to taste

Optional: pinch cayenne pepper or dash of hot sauce

Optional: fresh chives, snipped

1. Add the diced bacon to a 4-quart Dutch oven and fry it over moderate heat until golden and nearly crisp. If the bacon renders more than 2 tablespoons of fat, pour off the excess. Add the leeks, stir to coat them in the bacon fat, and sauté for 2 minutes. Stir in the potatoes and reduce the heat to low; cover, and cook for 10 minutes, stirring frequently to prevent browning, or until the potatoes are tender. Mash some of the potatoes with a fork, if desired. Add the water, stock, or broth; bring to a simmer, cover, and cook for 5 minutes.

2. Whisk the butter into the broth. Once the butter is melted, add the pepper, lobster, and cream. Stir gently and cook on low to bring all the ingredients to temperature. Taste for seasonings, and add sea salt, additional black pepper, and a pinch of cayenne pepper or a dash of hot sauce, if desired. Remove the pan from the stove, cover, and allow the chowder to ripen for 15–20 minutes before serving. Ladle into warmed shallow soup bowls; sprinkle with snipped chives, if desired.

Healthy Alternatives

If you don't want to use heavy cream in this recipe, decrease the amount of water, stock, or broth by 1 cup and add 2 cups of milk. Do not use half-and-half because it has a tendency to curdle.

SIMPLIFIED BOUILLABAISSE

Using tomato juice or chicken broth lets you customize this simple fish stew without the tedium of creating fish stock, cleaning and steaming clams, and all of those other steps the purists insist you go through.

Yields 8 servings

⅓ cup extra-virgin olive oil

1 large yellow onion, sliced

1 bunch green onions (4 or 5 stalks), sliced

1 clove garlic, minced

2 cups tomato juice or chicken broth

1 14½-ounce can diced tomatoes

1 cup Chardonnay or other dry white wine

2 cups water

1 bay leaf

½ teaspoon freshly ground black pepper

1 teaspoon dried tarragon, crumbled

½ teaspoon thyme, crushed

1 tablespoon parsley, crushed

1 pound whitefish, cut into 1" pieces

1 pound frozen cooked shrimp, thawed

2 3½-ounce pouches of whole baby clams

1 10-ounce can boiled mussels, drained

Optional: Garlic Toast (see recipe in sidebar)

1. Add the oil to a Dutch oven and bring to temperature over medium heat. Add the yellow and green onions; sauté for 5 minutes, or until transparent. Add the garlic and sauté for another 30 seconds. Add the tomato juice or broth, tomatoes, wine, water, bay leaf, pepper, tarragon, thyme, and parsley; bring to a boil. Reduce the heat, cover, and simmer for 1 hour. Remove the bay leaf. At this point, this broth can be refrigerated and reheated later to finish the dish.

2. Add the fish pieces; simmer for 10 minutes, or until the fish is opaque and cooked through. Stir in the shrimp, clams, and mussels; simmer for 2–3 minutes to bring all the ingredients to temperature. Serve with garlic toast, if desired.

Garlic Toast

Preheat the oven to 400°F. Slice French bread into ¼"-thick slices. Brush both sides of the bread with extra-virgin olive oil, place flat on a baking sheet, and bake for 10 minutes, or until crisp and lightly browned. While the toast is still warm, rub a cut clove of garlic over the top of each slice. Allow 2 slices per serving.

MARSALA BEEF STEW

Serve this rich stew over cooked rice, polenta, mashed potatoes, or toast alongside a tossed salad.

Yields 8 servings

2 tablespoons extra-virgin olive oil

1 tablespoon butter or ghee

3 pounds English-cut chuck roast, cut into bite-size pieces

1 large carrot, peeled and finely diced

1 celery stalk, finely diced

1 large yellow onion, diced

3 cloves garlic, minced

8 ounces button or cremini mushrooms, cleaned and sliced

½ cup dry white wine

1 cup Marsala wine

½ teaspoon dried rosemary

½ teaspoon dried oregano

½ teaspoon dried basil

Water as needed

Salt and freshly ground black pepper to taste

1. Add the oil and melt the butter in a 4-quart Dutch oven over medium-high heat. Add 10 pieces of the beef to the pan and brown for 5 minutes, or until the meat takes on a rich dark outer color. Reduce the heat to medium and add the carrot and celery; sauté for 3–5 minutes, or until soft. Add the onion and sauté until the onion is transparent. Add the garlic and sauté for an additional 30 seconds. Stir in the mushrooms; sauté until tender.

2. Add the remaining meat, the wines, rosemary, oregano, and basil to the pan. Add water, if needed, to bring the liquid level to just over the top of the meat. Reduce the heat, cover, and simmer for 1½ hours or until the meat is tender. Taste the broth. Simmer uncovered long enough to reduce the broth if it tastes weak. Add salt and pepper, if needed. Allow the stew to rest, uncovered, off of the heat for 30 minutes, then return it to the stovetop over low heat to bring it back to temperature.

Contrary to Popular Opinion

Searing meat does not seal in the juices, but it does intensify the flavor of a dish by adding another flavor dimension. Therefore, while it isn't necessary to sear all of the meat, it is a good idea to do so with some of it before you add the liquid and begin to simmer a stew.

NEW ENGLAND FISH STEW

To add even more impact and make this a special occasion dish, float a pat of butter on top of each portion. Using heavy cream obviously makes this a richer stew, but you can substitute milk if you prefer.

Yields 4 servings

2 tablespoons butter

1 large Vidalia onion, diced

2 stalks celery, diced

4 large carrots, peeled and diced

4 medium russet or red potatoes, peeled and cut in ½" cubes

1 pound firm-fleshed whitefish fillets (like cod), cut in ½" pieces

2 cups fish stock or clam juice

1 cup cold water

1 bay leaf

½ teaspoon dried thyme

1 cup heavy cream or milk

1 cup fresh or thawed frozen corn kernels

Salt and freshly ground white or black pepper to taste

Optional: additional butter to taste

Optional: fresh chopped parsley to taste

1. Add the butter to a pressure cooker and bring it to temperature over medium heat. Add the onions; sauté for 3 minutes, or until soft. Stir in the celery, carrots, and potatoes; sauté for 1 minute. Add the fish, fish stock or clam juice, water, bay leaf, and thyme.

2. Lock the lid in place; increase to high heat and bring the pressure cooker to high pressure. Adjust the heat to maintain the high pressure and cook for 4 minutes. Reduce the pressure with your cooker's quick-release method. Remove the lid, tilting it away from you to allow any excess steam to escape.

3. Remove and discard the bay leaf. Stir in the cream or milk and corn. Taste for seasoning and add salt and pepper to taste. Simmer until the corn is cooked and the chowder is hot. Transfer to a serving tureen or individual bowls and top with additional butter, if desired. Garnish with parsley, if desired.

SIMPLIFIED CHICKEN STEW

Serve this stew with warm, buttered buttermilk biscuits.

Yields 4 servings

4 large carrots, peeled and sliced

1 stalk celery, finely diced

1 large yellow onion, diced

4 large russet potatoes, peeled and diced

4 long strips lemon zest

1 teaspoon dried dill

2 tablespoons extra-virgin olive oil

2 cups chicken broth

4 bone-in chicken breast halves

Salt and freshly ground black pepper to taste

1. Put the carrots, celery, onions, potatoes, lemon zest, dill, and oil in a pressure cooker. Pour the broth into the pot. Remove and discard the skin on the chicken, then nestle the chicken pieces meat side down on top of the vegetables.

2. Lock the pressure cooker lid and bring to high pressure and maintain it for 10 minutes. Remove the cooker from the heat. Use the pressure cooker's quick pressure release. Carefully open the pot. Taste for seasoning and add salt and pepper to taste. Put 1 chicken breast in each of 4 large soup bowls and ladle some carrots, potatoes, and broth over each one.

TEX-MEX BEEF STEW

This stew can easily be stretched to serve more than 8 if you serve it with an avocado salad and over rice, in tacos or burritos, or with whole kernel corn or baked corn chips.

Yields 8 servings

2 tablespoons extra-virgin olive or vegetable oil

1 4-pound English or chuck roast, trimmed of fat and cut into 1" cubes

1 7-ounce can green chilies

2 15-ounce cans diced tomatoes

1 8-ounce can tomato sauce

1 large sweet onion, diced

1 green bell pepper, seeded and diced

6 cloves garlic, minced

1 tablespoon ground cumin

1 teaspoon freshly ground black pepper

Cayenne pepper to taste

2 tablespoons lime juice

2 jalapeño peppers, seeded and diced

Beef broth or water as needed

1 bunch fresh cilantro, chopped

1. Add the oil to the pressure cooker and bring it to temperature over medium-high heat. Add the beef and stir-fry for 8 minutes, or until it's well browned. Stir in the chilies, tomatoes, tomato sauce, onion, bell pepper, garlic, cumin, black pepper, cayenne, lime juice, and jalapeño peppers. If needed, add enough beef broth or water so that all the ingredients in the cooker are covered by liquid.

2. Lock the lid, lower the heat to medium, and bring to high pressure; maintain for 45 minutes. Let the pan remain on the burner and allow 15 minutes or more for the pressure to drop on its own. Remove the lid and stir in the cilantro. Serve immediately.

SARDINIAN MINESTRONE STEW

Until the 1900s, Italy was divided into regions and people from each area ate different foods, or ate the same foods differently. The contents of minestrone vary by region, but there are some similarities. They all tend to have chunky vegetables, beans, and a rich broth.

Yields 4–6 servings

2 tablespoons olive oil, plus more as needed

1 celery stalk, chopped

1 carrot, chopped

1 medium white onion, chopped

2 quarts vegetable or chicken stock

2 16-ounce cans chickpeas, rinsed and drained

1 15-ounce can chopped tomatoes

½ pound arugula, washed and chopped roughly

1 head of endive, sliced in long, thin strips

8 ounces small pasta

Salt to taste

Pepper to taste

1. Place a Dutch oven over medium-high heat. Once the pan is heated, add 2 tablespoons olive oil, celery, carrot, and onion. Cook for 10 minutes. Add 1 cup of stock and scrape the bottom of the pan.

2. Add the rest of the stock, the chickpeas, the tomato, and the greens and stir to combine.

3. Reduce the heat to low and cover. Cook for 1 hour. Add the pasta and cook for 10 minutes. Taste and add salt and pepper as needed. Once the pasta is al dente, serve it in large bowls with a drizzle of olive oil floating on top.

GUMBO

The Cajun Roux (see recipe in Chapter 2) makes the right amount of roux for this dish. If you can't find andouille sausage, a spicy Italian sausage would also work.

Yields 6–8 servings

2 teaspoons paprika

1 teaspoon garlic powder

½ teaspoon dried oregano

½ teaspoon black pepper

½ teaspoon dried thyme

½ teaspoon onion powder

¼ teaspoon cayenne powder

1 teaspoon salt

1 small frying chicken, cut into 10 pieces

1 pound andouille sausage

2 bay leaves

3 garlic cloves, chopped

2 quarts chicken stock

½ pound okra, cut into ½" rounds

1 pound shelled shrimp

8 ounces crabmeat

½ cup cooked long-grain rice per person

½ cup fresh parsley, chopped

1. Preheat oven to 350°F. Mix all the spices together and rub over the pieces of chicken. Place in a Dutch oven. Cut the sausage at an angle into ¼" thick slices. Sprinkle the sausage over the chicken. Cook in the oven for 40 minutes. Pour off all the fat.

2. Save the sausage on a platter. Lay the chicken pieces out to cool. Once it is cool to the touch, remove all the meat from the bones and set the bones and skin aside for making stock.

3. Place the chicken meat and sausage back in the Dutch oven. Add the bay leaves and any leftover seasoning mix to the pan. Tuck the garlic cloves around the meat with the bay leaves. Cover with chicken stock by 2". Turn the heat to medium-high, cover, and boil. Lower the heat to a simmer and cook for 45 minutes. Stir to prevent sticking.

4. Add the okra and cook for 30 minutes. Sprinkle the shrimp on top; cut up the crabmeat and add to the pan. Cook for 6–8 minutes. Remove bay leaves. Taste and salt if necessary. Ladle the gumbo over rice in a bowl. Garnish with parsley. Serve with Tabasco and crusty bread.

Gumbo: Variety and Myth

Some gumbo recipes only use seafood, some focus more on poultry, others are heavy with sausage. All gumbo is thickened and served over rice. Because there is no original recipe, it's hard to determine where it was invented. It may be a descendant of a French seafood soup called bouillabaisse, but it is also similar to West African stews.

BASIC BEEF STEW

The vegetables recommended here are just a suggestion. You could use sweet potato, parsnip, rutabaga, or even celery root for a different flavor.

Yields 6–8 servings

2–4 tablespoons vegetable oil

2½ pounds beef chuck, cut into 2" cubes

Pinch salt, plus 2 teaspoons

Pinch pepper

2 tablespoons butter

2 medium onions, peeled and quartered

5 garlic cloves, crushed

2 tablespoons tomato paste

⅓ cup all-purpose flour

10 cups beef or chicken broth

1 tablespoon dried thyme

2 bay leaves

4 medium red potatoes, cut into large cubes

4 carrots, peeled and cut into 2" pieces

2 celery stalks, cut into 2" pieces

1 can whole, peeled tomatoes

3 tablespoons red wine or balsamic vinegar

1. Place a large Dutch oven over medium-high heat. Once it's heated, add 1 tablespoon of oil. Season the meat with a pinch of salt and pepper and add one layer to the pan. Cook for about 8 minutes, turning so all of the beef is browned. Remove and set aside. Repeat with the rest of the beef, adding more oil as necessary.

2. Add the butter. Once it has melted, add the onion and stir frequently for 5 minutes. Add garlic and cook for 1 minute. Add the tomato paste and cook for 1 minute.

3. Return the beef to the pan and stir until it is coated evenly. Sprinkle the flour over the beef. Stir and cook for 4 minutes.

4. Add the broth and simmer. Add the thyme, bay leaves, and 2 teaspoons of salt. Reduce the heat to low, cover, and simmer for 1½ hours. Add the potatoes, carrots, celery, and tomatoes. Cook for 1 hour. Discard the bay leaves. Stir in the vinegar. Taste and season with salt and pepper as needed. Serve warm.

Beef Stew Meat Isn't the Best for Stew

Meat labeled "beef stew meat" tends to be small, odd-shaped pieces from different cuts. They're apt to have fat and sinew that requires trimming, and will not cook uniformly. Chuck comes from the shoulder of the cow. It is a flavorful but tough cut that is best when braised, as in stew.

CHICKEN CHILI

Serve this chili with an avocado salad and baked flour or corn tortilla chips.

Yields 4 servings

3 tablespoons extra-virgin olive oil

1 large yellow or white onion, diced

2 jalapeño peppers, seeded and diced

1 green bell pepper, seeded and diced

1 teaspoon cumin seeds

4 cloves garlic, minced

4 boneless, skinless chicken thighs, cut into bite-size pieces

1 15-ounce can diced tomatoes

1 15-ounce can kidney beans, rinsed and drained

2 cups chili sauce

1 tablespoon Worcestershire sauce

1 cup red wine

Salt and freshly ground black pepper to taste

1. Add the oil to a deep 3½-quart nonstick skillet and bring it to temperature over medium heat. Add the onion, jalapeño peppers, bell pepper, and cumin seeds; sauté for 5 minutes, or until the onion is transparent. Add the garlic and chicken; stir-fry until chicken is lightly browned.

2. Stir in the tomatoes, kidney beans, chili sauce, Worcestershire, and red wine. Bring to a simmer; lower the heat and simmer for 1 hour. Taste for seasoning and add salt and pepper if needed.

SLOW COOKER TEXAS CHILI

Texas chili is traditionally made without kidney beans. You can add some if you prefer it that way. Serve this dish with cornbread and a tossed salad.

Yields 6–8 servings

¼ pound bacon, diced

1 stalk celery, finely chopped

1 large carrot, peeled and finely chopped

2-pound chuck roast, cubed

2 large yellow onions, diced

6 cloves garlic, diced

6 jalapeño peppers, seeded and diced

Salt and freshly ground pepper to taste

4 tablespoons chili powder

1 teaspoon Mexican oregano

1 teaspoon ground cumin

Optional: 1 teaspoon light brown sugar

1 28-ounce can diced tomatoes

1 cup beef broth

Add all the ingredients to a 4-quart slow cooker, and stir to combine. The liquid in your slow cooker should completely cover the meat and vegetables. If additional liquid is needed, add more crushed tomatoes, broth, or water. Cook on low for 6–8 hours. Taste for seasoning, and add more chili powder if desired.

CHILI CON CARNE

Chili powder is available in mild, regular, and hot varieties. If the chili still isn't spicy enough to suit your tastes, you can punch up the dish by adding some chopped jalapeño peppers or hot sauce.

Yields 4–6 servings

2 tablespoons peanut oil

1 pound lean hamburger

1 large yellow onion, chopped

3 tablespoons chili powder

1 teaspoon ground cumin

3 cloves garlic, diced

1 tablespoon Worcestershire sauce

1 28-ounce can chopped tomatoes

1 large green pepper, seeded and chopped

1 15-ounce can kidney beans, rinsed and drained

Salt and freshly ground pepper to taste

Optional: 1 teaspoon granulated or light brown sugar

Bring the oil to temperature over medium heat in a Dutch oven. Add the hamburger, onion, chili power, and cumin. When the meat is cooked and the onions are transparent, drain any excess fat from the pan. Add the remaining ingredients and stir to combine. Lower the heat, cover, and simmer for 1–2 hours, stirring occasionally. Taste and adjust seasoning if necessary before serving.

Fiesta Chili Buffet

Have bowls of these condiments lined up so that family and guests can top their chili: crushed corn chips, shredded Cheddar cheese, cooked rice, shredded lettuce, chopped green pepper, sliced black olives, chopped tomatoes, diced onion or chopped green onions, toasted pecans or chopped peanuts, shredded coconut, and salsa.

ENCHILADA CHILI

This chili can be served as a dip. After step 2, reduce the heat to low and stir in the cheese; continue to stir until the cheese is melted. Reduce the heat setting to warm. Serve with baked corn tortilla chips.

Yields 6 servings

1½-pound boneless beef chuck roast, cut into bite-size pieces

1 15-ounce can pinto and/or red kidney beans, rinsed and drained

1 14½-ounce can diced tomatoes, undrained

1 10½-ounce can condensed beef broth

1 10-ounce can enchilada sauce

1 large yellow onion, chopped

2 teaspoons bottled minced garlic

½ cup water

2½ tablespoons fine cornmeal

2 tablespoons fresh cilantro, snipped

2 ounces queso blanco or Monterey jack cheese, shredded

1. Add the beef, beans, tomatoes, broth, enchilada sauce, onion, and garlic to a 4-quart slow cooker. Cover and cook on low for 8 hours.

2. In a small bowl, whisk the water and cornmeal together; stir into the chili. Cover and cook on high for an additional 15–30 minutes, or until the chili is thickened.

3. Top each serving with the snipped cilantro and cheese.

LAMB CHILI

Serve this chili with a tossed salad that includes avocado slices, papaya pieces, and goat cheese. A little drizzle of extra-virgin olive oil is the only dressing it needs.

Yields 6–8 servings

2 pounds ground lamb

3 tablespoons extra-virgin olive oil

1 large yellow onion, diced

4 cloves garlic, crushed

2 tablespoons chili powder

1 tablespoon whole cumin seeds

¼ teaspoon dried oregano, crushed

2 jalapeño or red peppers, seeded and diced

2 green bell peppers, seeded and diced

1 28-ounce can diced tomatoes

1 8-ounce can tomato sauce

1 tablespoon Worcestershire sauce

2 15-ounce cans red kidney beans, rinsed and drained

Salt and freshly ground black pepper to taste

Water, if necessary

Add the lamb, oil, onion, garlic, chili powder, and cumin seeds to a large Dutch oven over medium heat. Sauté until the meat is brown and the onion is transparent, and then add the remaining ingredients. Add water, if needed, so that all the ingredients are covered by liquid. Continue to cook on medium for about 15 minutes to bring all the ingredients to temperature, then lower the heat, cover, and simmer for 1½ hours. Check the pot periodically to stir the chili and to make sure that it doesn't boil dry. Add more water, if necessary.

Make Your Own Chili Powder

Add 5 dried poblano peppers, 1 dried ancho chili pepper, ⅜ teaspoon ground cumin, ¾ teaspoon dried oregano, and 1 teaspoon garlic powder to a spice grinder, food processor, or blender. Process until fine. Add cayenne pepper to taste if you wish to make it hotter. Store in the freezer in a tightly covered container and it'll keep indefinitely.

CHIPOTLE CHILI

This chili is also good if you use leftover roast beef or pork instead of the hamburger. Serve the chili with crackers and cheese, peanut butter or toasted cheese sandwiches, or cornbread.

Yields 4 servings

1 pound lean ground beef

1 tablespoon chili powder

1 medium yellow onion, diced

2 cloves garlic, minced

1 15-ounce can red kidney beans, rinsed and drained

1 cup chipotle salsa

1 cup frozen whole kernel corn

1 14-ounce can beef broth

Salt and freshly ground pepper to taste

Add the ground beef and chili powder to a deep 3½-quart nonstick skillet; brown the meat over medium-high heat, breaking it apart as it cooks. When the meat is almost cooked through, add the onion; lower the heat to medium and sauté the onion until transparent. Drain off any excess fat. Add the garlic and sauté for 30 seconds. Stir in the kidney beans, salsa, corn, and broth. Bring to temperature and simmer for 15 minutes. Taste for seasoning and add salt and pepper if desired.

SWEET AND HOT CHILI

The longer you simmer chili, the richer the flavor.

Yields 8–10 servings

1 pound ground chuck

1 pound ground pork

2 large yellow onions, diced

6 cloves garlic, minced

1 teaspoon whole cumin seeds

2 tablespoons chili powder

¼ teaspoon oregano

1 28-ounce can diced tomatoes

¼ cup ketchup

¼ teaspoon cinnamon

¼ teaspoon ground cloves

2 tablespoons light brown sugar

2 15-ounce cans kidney beans, rinsed and drained

1 14-ounce can reduced-sodium beef broth

Optional: 1 tablespoon Worcestershire sauce

Water, if needed

Salt and freshly ground black pepper to taste

Optional: hot sauce to taste

1. Add the ground chuck, pork, onion, garlic, cumin seeds, chili powder, and oregano to a Dutch oven; cook over medium heat until the beef and pork are browned and cooked through. Drain off any excess fat and discard.

2. Stir in the tomatoes, ketchup, cinnamon, cloves, brown sugar, kidney beans, beef broth, and Worcestershire sauce (if using). Bring to a simmer; reduce the heat, cover, and simmer for 1 hour. Stir the chili occasionally, and add water if needed. Taste for seasoning and add salt and pepper, if needed, and hot sauce, if desired. You may also wish to add more brown sugar or chili powder according to your taste.

Use a Slow Cooker

If you want to make the chili in a slow cooker, follow step 1, and then add the cooked meat mixture, tomatoes, ketchup, cinnamon, cloves, brown sugar, kidney beans, beef broth, and Worcestershire sauce (if using) to the slow cooker. Add water if needed to bring the liquid level to the top of the beans and meat. Cook on low for 6–8 hours.

CINCINNATI CHILI

Cincinnati Chili is served like a sauce over cooked pasta, and then topped with onion and cheese.

Yields 8 servings

2 pounds lean ground beef

3 large yellow onions, diced

3 cloves garlic, minced

1 16-ounce can tomato sauce

1 cup beef broth

2 tablespoons chili powder

2 tablespoons semisweet chocolate chips

2 tablespoons red wine vinegar

2 tablespoons honey

1 tablespoon pumpkin pie spice

1 teaspoon ground cumin

½ teaspoon ground cardamom

¼ teaspoon ground cloves

Salt and freshly ground black pepper to taste

2 16-ounce cans kidney beans, rinsed and drained

1 pound cooked pasta of your choice

4 cups American or Cheddar cheese, shredded

1. Add the ground beef and ¾ of the diced onions to a 4½-quart Dutch oven over medium-high heat; stir-fry until the beef is browned and the onion is transparent. Drain off and discard any excess fat. Stir in the garlic and stir-fry for 30 seconds. Add the tomato sauce, broth, chili powder, chocolate chips, vinegar, honey, pumpkin pie spice, cumin, cardamom, cloves, salt, and pepper; mix well. Bring to a simmer; lower the heat to maintain the simmer, and cook for at least 30 minutes to let the flavors mix. Shortly before serving, add the kidney beans and cook until they're heated through.

2. Serve the Cincinnati Chili meat sauce over cooked pasta, then top the chili with the remaining diced onions to taste and a generous amount of grated cheese.

PRESSURE COOKER CHICKEN CHILI

Serve this chili with an avocado or tossed salad, sour cream, and baked corn tortilla chips.

Yields 4 servings

2 tablespoons vegetable oil

2 pounds boneless, skinless chicken thighs, cut into bite-size cubes

1 jalapeño pepper, seeded and minced

1 small red bell pepper, seeded and diced

1 small yellow onion, diced

1 clove garlic, minced

1 15-ounce can diced tomatoes

1 16-ounce can red kidney beans, rinsed and drained

1 tablespoon paprika

1 tablespoon tomato paste

1 cup chicken broth

¼ teaspoon dried thyme

¼ teaspoon dried oregano

1 teaspoon chili powder

Salt and freshly ground black pepper to taste

1. Add oil to a pressure cooker and bring it to temperature over medium heat. Add the chicken and stir-fry for 5 minutes. Add the jalapeño and red peppers; stir-fry with chicken for 2 minutes. Stir in the onion; sauté for 3 minutes, or until tender. Stir in the garlic, tomatoes, kidney beans, paprika, tomato paste, broth, thyme, oregano, chili powder, salt, and pepper.

2. Lock the lid in place. Bring to low pressure, lower the heat, and maintain pressure for 10 minutes. Remove the pan from the burner and use the quick-release method to release the pressure. Stir the chili and taste for seasoning; add additional salt, pepper, spices, or herbs, if needed.

WHITE BEAN CHILI

If you like the idea of making this dish but don't have 4–5 hours, substitute 3 15-ounce cans of white beans for the dried, and cook for 20 minutes on medium low.

Yields 4–6 servings

1 pound cannellini or Great Northern beans

Water, as needed

1 tablespoon olive oil

1 medium onion, finely chopped

2 garlic cloves, minced

1 teaspoon ground cumin

1 smoked turkey leg, meat removed and chopped

6 cups vegetable stock

1 teaspoon cayenne powder

½ teaspoon chili powder

1. Sort the beans and remove any debris. Place them in a large bowl and cover them with water by several inches and soak overnight. Drain and rinse the beans.

2. Place a Dutch oven over medium-high heat. Once it's heated through, add the oil and the onion. Cook the onions for 8–10 minutes.

3. Lower the heat to medium and stir in the garlic and the cumin. Cook for 1 minute before adding the turkey meat and the stock.

4. Bring to a simmer before adding the beans, cayenne powder, and chili powder. Reduce the heat to low and simmer for 4–5 hours, or until the beans are tender.

CHAPTER 5

PASTA, RICE, BEANS, AND GRAINS

LOBSTER RAGU

Tasso is a Cajun ham that comes from the shoulder (pork butt), which makes it a fattier cut of meat with a great deal of flavor. If you're not sure how to cook a whole lobster, refer to the Lobster Bake recipe in Chapter 8.

Yields 6–8 servings

1½ pounds dried pappardelle or fettuccine

3 tablespoons extra-virgin olive oil

3 stalks celery, diced

3 large carrots, peeled and diced

2 medium red onions, sliced

8 ounces tasso, salt pork, or bacon, diced

8 ounces cremini mushrooms, cleaned and sliced

8 ounces portobello mushrooms, cleaned and sliced

8 ounces button mushrooms, cleaned and sliced

2 tablespoons tomato paste

2 teaspoons dried oregano

2 teaspoons dried thyme

1 tablespoon dried parsley

1 cup red wine

4 cups beef broth

2 1¼-pound cooked lobsters

¼ cup fresh basil, chopped

1. In a Dutch oven or deep pot, cook the pasta in boiling water according to the package directions until al dente. Drain in a colander, set aside, and keep warm.

2. Wipe out the Dutch oven; add the oil and bring to temperature over medium heat. Add the celery and carrots; sauté for 3–5 minutes, or until soft. Add the onion and sauté until transparent. If using tasso, sauté for 1 minute; if using salt pork or bacon, sauté for 3 minutes, or until it renders some of its fat. Add all the mushrooms; stirring frequently, cook until all of the mushroom liquid is rendered out. Push the mushrooms to the sides of the pan; add the tomato paste and sauté for 2 minutes, then stir it into the mushrooms along with the oregano, thyme, parsley, wine, and broth, scraping the bottom of the pot to loosen any browned bits as you stir. Reduce the heat and simmer for 20 minutes. Toss the drained pasta into the reduced ragu sauce.

3. Remove the meat from the lobster shells; chop into large pieces. Gently stir the lobster meat into the pasta and ragu sauce. Garnish with the chopped basil.

Lobster Shell Uses

Freeze the lobster shells and use them later to make a broth to add to your favorite seafood stew or soup. Lobster broth is delicious, and it's easy to make—just simmer the shells with a roughly chopped onion, a few bay leaves, and enough water to cover everything for about 45 minutes.

LAMB AND PASTA SALAD

Tomatoes are essential for this Greek-inspired salad. If you don't have fresh ones on hand, you can use 1 cup of drained canned diced tomatoes or use cherry tomatoes cut in half.

Yields 8–10 servings

1 pound dried penne pasta

3 tablespoons olive oil

2 medium yellow onions, peeled and thinly sliced

½ cup green onions, chopped

½ cup green olives, pitted and chopped

½ cup feta cheese, crumbled

2 large ripe tomatoes, diced

3 tablespoons fresh parsley, chopped

1 pound leftover roast lamb, cut into thin strips

1 cup extra-virgin olive oil

2 tablespoons mayonnaise

2 cloves garlic, minced

1½ teaspoons fresh dill, minced

Salt and freshly ground black pepper to taste

1. Cook the pasta according to the package directions. Drain and transfer to a large bowl.

2. Add the 3 tablespoons oil to a small skillet and bring to temperature over medium heat. Add the yellow onion and sauté for 3–5 minutes, or until transparent. Add the onion to the bowl with the pasta along with the green onions, olives, cheese, tomato, parsley, and lamb. Toss to combine.

3. In a small bowl, whisk together the 1 cup of extra-virgin olive oil, mayonnaise, garlic, and dill; add this mixture to the large bowl, and toss with the pasta and lamb. Taste for seasoning and add salt and pepper to taste. Chill for at least 1 hour before serving.

SOUPED-UP SPAGHETTI

Spaghetti is a classic dish, and this variation retains the characteristic taste but mixes up the textures.

Yields 6–8 servings

1 pound lean ground beef

1 medium yellow onion, chopped

1 small green sweet pepper, seeded and chopped

1 stalk celery, chopped

1 medium carrot, peeled and chopped

4 cloves garlic, minced

2 15-ounce cans diced tomatoes, undrained

2½ cups water

1 13- to 15-ounce jar spaghetti sauce

1 tablespoon granulated sugar

½ teaspoon dried Italian seasoning, · crushed

Dash dried red pepper flakes

2 ounces dried spaghetti, broken into 2" pieces

Salt and freshly ground black pepper to taste

Optional: fresh chopped parsley to taste

1. Add the ground beef, onion, sweet pepper, celery, carrot, and garlic to a 4-quart Dutch oven. Cook over medium heat until the vegetables are tender and the meat is no longer pink, stirring frequently. Drain off and discard excess fat.

2. Stir in the undrained tomatoes, water, spaghetti sauce, sugar, Italian seasoning, and red pepper flakes; bring to a boil. Add the spaghetti. Reduce the heat to a gentle boil and cook uncovered for 12–15 minutes, or until the spaghetti is tender.

3. Taste for seasoning and add salt and pepper, if desired. Serve immediately, garnished with parsley, if desired.

Sneaky Additions

Thanks to the spaghetti sauce, you can add a bag of frozen vegetables to the Souped-Up Spaghetti; add the vegetables 10 minutes into the pasta cooking time in step 2. This is a great trick for anyone who has a picky eater at the table.

PEPPERONI PASTA

To keep this a one pot meal, this recipe uses the same pot to cook the pasta, sauté the mushrooms and other ingredients, and mix it all together before plating.

Yields 4 servings

6 ounces dried spaghetti, broken in half

1 tablespoon butter

8 ounces fresh button or cremini mushrooms, cleaned and sliced

3 ounces pepperoni, thinly sliced or cubed

6 cups lightly packed fresh spinach, stems removed and torn

¼ cup Parmigiano-Reggiano cheese, grated

2 tablespoons fresh basil, chopped

1 teaspoon lemon juice

Salt and freshly ground pepper to taste

1. Prepare the pasta according to the package directions. Drain, set aside, and keep warm. Wipe out the pan. Add the butter and cook over medium heat until melted; add the mushrooms and pepperoni and sauté for 5 minutes, or until the mushrooms are just tender. Drain off and discard any excess fat. Stir in the spinach and cook for 1 minute or until spinach begins to wilt, stirring occasionally. Remove from heat.

2. Add the pasta to the pan and toss to combine with the pepperoni mixture, half of the cheese, the basil, and lemon juice. Taste for seasoning and add salt and pepper, if desired. Divide between 4 plates and sprinkle with the remaining cheese.

ONE POT KIELBASA DINNER

If fresh Roma tomatoes aren't available, you can use a 15-ounce can of diced tomatoes instead. Just add the undrained canned tomatoes and cook for 5 minutes before you add the pasta; this will reduce and thicken the sauce.

Yields 6 servings

2 cups dried rotini or rotelle pasta (about 6 ounces)

1 tablespoon olive oil

1 medium yellow onion, cut into wedges

1 pound cooked kielbasa, halved lengthwise and sliced diagonally

2 cloves garlic, minced

1 small zucchini, cut into matchstick-size strips

1 yellow or orange pepper, seeded and diced

1 teaspoon dried Italian seasoning, crushed

Pinch cayenne pepper

8 Roma tomatoes (about 1 pound), cored and chopped

Salt and freshly ground black pepper to taste

1. Cook the pasta according to the package directions. Drain, set aside, and keep warm.

2. Wipe out the pan, add the oil, and bring to temperature over medium-high heat. Add the onion and sauté for 1 minute. Add the kielbasa, stirring often to keep the onion from burning. Cook for 5 minutes, or until the onion is transparent. Add the garlic and sauté for an additional 30 seconds. Stir in the zucchini, yellow or orange pepper, Italian seasoning, and cayenne pepper; cook and stir for 5 minutes. Stir in the tomatoes and cooked pasta. Cook until heated through, stirring occasionally. Taste for seasoning and add salt and pepper, if desired.

SHRIMP AND FETTUCCINE

You can cut some of the fat in this dish by using 1 cup of evaporated skim milk instead of the chicken broth and heavy cream. Pattypan squash is a small summer squash with lovely scalloped edges.

Yields 4 servings

8 ounces garlic-basil- or tomato-basil-flavored dried fettuccine

1 tablespoon extra-virgin olive oil

6 ounces baby pattypan squash, halved or quartered

1 small red onion, diced

1 clove garlic, minced

8 ounces small shrimp, peeled and deveined

½ cup chicken broth

½ cup heavy cream

Optional: ½ teaspoon hot sauce

4 ounces cream cheese, cut up into small pieces

3 tablespoons fresh basil, chopped

2 teaspoons lemon peel, grated

1 teaspoon fresh mint, chopped

Salt and freshly ground black pepper to taste

1 small head radicchio, torn

1 cup cherry tomatoes, cut in half

Freshly grated Parmigiano-Reggiano to taste

1. Cook the fettuccine according to package directions. Drain, set aside, and keep warm. Wipe out the pan; add the oil and bring to temperature over medium heat. Add the squash, onion, and garlic; sauté for 3 minutes, or until the onion and squash begin to soften. Add the shrimp; sauté for 3 minutes, or until the shrimp are opaque.

2. Reduce the heat and stir in the chicken broth, cream, and hot sauce (if using). Remove from heat; whisk in the cream cheese, stirring until the cheese is melted into the sauce. Stir in the cooked fettuccine, basil, lemon peel, mint, salt, and black pepper. Add the radicchio and cherry tomatoes; stir until the radicchio is wilted. Serve topped with freshly grated Parmigiano-Reggiano to taste.

Herb Help

Fresh herbs, especially basil, are the most tasty and aromatic when they're raw or only exposed to heat for a short time. On the other hand, dried herbs take some time to draw out the flavor. Therefore, if you're using dried herbs in the Shrimp and Fettuccine recipe, consider adding them when you sauté the shrimp.

MEXICAN-STYLE BAKED PASTA

This dish is a salsa-spiked, macaroni and cheese–style dish. Use mild or hot salsa, according to your preference.

Yields 6 servings

12 ounces dried bow tie pasta

3 tablespoons butter

1 medium yellow onion, diced

1 red sweet pepper, seeded and chopped

⅓ cup all-purpose flour

½ teaspoon salt

1 teaspoon dried cilantro, crushed

½ teaspoon ground cumin

3 cups milk

6 ounces Colby cheese, cubed

6 ounces Monterey jack cheese, grated

1 cup bottled salsa

⅔ cup halved pitted green and/or ripe olives

Chili powder to taste

1. Preheat oven to 375°F.

2. Cook the pasta. Wipe out the pan; melt the butter over medium heat. Add the onion and sweet pepper and sauté for 5 minutes. Stir in the flour, salt, cilantro, and cumin. Whisk in the milk and cook until thickened and bubbly.

3. Reduce heat to low; add the Colby cheese and half of the Monterey jack cheese. Stir until the cheese is melted. Add the drained pasta, salsa, and olives to the pan; stir to combine. Sprinkle with the remaining Monterey jack cheese. Sprinkle lightly with chili powder. Bake, uncovered, for 20 minutes, or until bubbly around edges and heated through. Let stand 5 minutes before serving.

SKILLET RAVIOLI

Simply change the type of pasta sauce that you use and you easily change the taste of this dish. Try roasted red pepper or roasted garlic sauce instead of the traditional marinara.

Yields 4 servings

2 cups pasta sauce of your choice

¼ teaspoon granulated sugar

⅓ cup water

Salt and freshly ground pepper to taste

1 9-ounce package frozen ravioli

1 large egg, lightly beaten

1 15-ounce carton ricotta cheese

½ cup grated Romano or Parmigiano-Reggiano cheese, or more, if desired

1 10-ounce package frozen chopped spinach, thawed and drained

1. Add the pasta sauce, sugar, and water to a 10" skillet. Bring to boil over medium-high heat. Taste and add salt and pepper, if desired. Stir in the ravioli. Reduce the heat; cover and cook, stirring occasionally, for about 5 minutes or until the ravioli are tender.

2. Add the egg, ricotta cheese, and ½ cup grated cheese to a bowl and stir to combine. Top the ravioli with the spinach and then spoon the cheese mixture on top of the spinach. Cover and cook over low heat for about 10 minutes, or until the cheese layer is set.

SLOW-COOKED CHICKEN AND MUSHROOMS

Serve this dish with a tossed or spinach salad and garlic bread.

Yields 4–6 servings

2 cups cleaned and sliced fresh button or cremini mushrooms

1 14½-ounce can diced tomatoes with Italian herbs

1 red sweet pepper, seeded and diced

1 medium yellow onion, thinly sliced

¼ cup dry red wine or beef broth

2 tablespoons quick-cooking tapioca

2 tablespoons balsamic vinegar

3 cloves garlic, minced

2½ pounds chicken breasts, skin removed

¼ teaspoon salt

¼ teaspoon paprika

¼ teaspoon freshly ground black pepper

1 9-ounce package fresh or frozen cheese tortellini or ravioli

Optional: freshly grated Parmigiano-Reggiano cheese to taste

1. Add the mushrooms, undrained tomatoes, red pepper, onion, wine or broth, tapioca, balsamic vinegar, and garlic to a 4- or 6-quart slow cooker. Stir to combine. Place the chicken pieces on top of the sauce. Sprinkle the salt, paprika, and black pepper over the chicken. Cover and cook on low for 8–9 hours.

2. Remove the chicken pieces and keep warm. Add the tortellini or ravioli to the sauce; cover and cook on high for 10–15 minutes, or until the pasta is done. Arrange the chicken pieces on a serving platter and top with the pasta and sauce. Top with grated cheese, if desired.

SEAFOOD PASTA

Herbs can add a distinctive touch to your cooking. Try a variety of fresh herbs in this recipe to create a wide range of different flavors.

Yields 4–6 servings

1 pound dried linguini

2 tablespoons extra-virgin olive oil

2 celery stalks, diced

1 small yellow onion, diced

4 cloves garlic, minced

½ teaspoon dried basil

¼ teaspoon dried dill

¼ teaspoon dried fennel

Salt to taste

½ teaspoon freshly ground black pepper

Pinch dried red pepper flakes

1 16-ounce can diced tomatoes

½ cup white wine or chicken broth

4 tablespoons butter

1 pound grouper, salmon, or snapper, cut into bite-size pieces

1 10-ounce can of boiled baby clams or 6½-ounce can of whole shelled mussels

½ pound shrimp, peeled and deveined

¼ cup fresh parsley, chopped

1. In a Dutch oven or stockpot, cook the pasta to al dente according to package directions. Drain, set aside, and keep warm.

2. Wipe out the pan. Add the oil and bring to temperature over medium heat. Add the celery; sauté for 3–5 minutes, or until soft. Add the onion and sauté until transparent. Add the garlic and sauté for an additional 30 seconds. Stir in the dried herbs, salt, pepper, red pepper flakes, and tomatoes. Add the wine or broth; bring to a simmer and then add the butter, fish, and clams or mussels. Cover and simmer for about 5 minutes. Add the shrimp; simmer until the shrimp are firm and pink in color. Serve over the pasta, topped with chopped parsley.

SPAGHETTI PIZZA

If you prefer, you can bake this pizza in a 9" × 13" nonstick baking pan or 14" nonstick deep-dish pizza pan.

Yields 10–12 servings

1 pound spaghetti

2 cups pasta sauce

½ teaspoon granulated sugar

6 large eggs, lightly beaten

1 pound mozzarella cheese, grated

6 ounces soppressata sausage, cut into ¼" dice

4 ounces freshly grated Parmigiano-Reggiano cheese

¼ cup heavy cream

1 tablespoon dried parsley

Salt to taste

½ teaspoon freshly ground pepper

8 ounces fresh button or cremini mushrooms, cleaned and sliced

6 ounces pepperoni, thinly sliced

1. Preheat oven to 375°F.

2. In an ovenproof Dutch oven, cook the spaghetti according to package directions. Drain the pasta and return it to the pan. Stir the pasta together with the pasta sauce, sugar, eggs, half of the mozzarella cheese, the soppressata, Parmigiano-Reggiano, heavy cream, dried parsley, salt, and pepper. Arrange the mushroom slices over the top of the spaghetti mixture, and arrange the pepperoni over the top of the mushrooms. Sprinkle the remaining mozzarella cheese over the top.

3. Cover and bake for 45 minutes. Remove the cover, and bake for an additional 20 minutes, or until the cheese on top is melted, bubbling, and lightly browned. Remove from the oven and let set for 10 minutes before serving.

SIMPLIFIED BAKED LASAGNA

This recipe requires a stovetop pan and a separate baking pan, but you don't have to cook the lasagna noodles before you bake them in the lasagna, nor do you have to peel and dice the onions or garlic.

Yields 8–10 servings

1 pound lean ground beef

1 tablespoon dried minced onion

1 teaspoon dried oregano, crushed

1 teaspoon dried minced garlic

Salt and freshly ground black pepper to taste

1 2-pound, 13-ounce jar pasta sauce

½ teaspoon granulated sugar

½ cup water

1 pound mozzarella cheese, grated

1 16-ounce container cottage cheese

Optional: freshly grated Parmigiano-Reggiano cheese

1 pound dried lasagna noodles

1. Add the hamburger, onion, oregano, garlic, salt, and pepper to a Dutch oven; brown the hamburger over medium heat, stirring it with the other ingredients in the pan and breaking apart the hamburger as it cooks. When the hamburger is cooked through, drain off any excess fat. Stir in the pasta sauce and sugar. Pour the water in the emptied pasta sauce jar; cover and shake to rinse out the jar. Add the water to the pan and stir into the hamburger-sauce mixture. Remove the pan from the heat; stir in half of the grated mozzarella cheese and the cottage cheese.

2. Preheat oven to 350°F.

3. To assemble the lasagna, ladle in enough of the sauce to cover the bottom of a 9" × 13" nonstick baking pan. Sprinkle grated Parmigiano-Reggiano cheese over the top of the sauce, if desired. Add a layer of uncooked lasagna noodles, being careful not to let the noodles overlap. Repeat layering noodles and sauce until all of the noodles are in the pan and covered. Sprinkle the remaining grated mozzarella cheese over the top, along with some additional Parmigiano-Reggiano cheese, if desired.

4. Cover with foil and bake for 45 minutes. Remove the foil and bake for an additional 15 minutes, or until the cheese on top is melted, bubbling, and lightly browned. Remove from the oven and let set for 10 minutes before serving.

Sausage Lasagna

If you prefer to skip the "browning the hamburger" step, you can instead substitute a pound of diced cooked smoked sausage. Use all of the other ingredients; however, because you will not be heating the pasta sauce before you assemble the lasagna, bake the lasagna covered for 1 hour and then uncovered for 15 minutes.

BEEF WITH WHOLE-GRAIN SPAGHETTI

If you don't have leftover roast beef on hand, you can cut up a pound of sirloin steak and sauté it along with the onions in the olive oil before you add the rest of the sauce ingredients.

Yields 4 servings

4 ounces dried whole-grain or whole-wheat spaghetti

1 tablespoon extra-virgin olive oil

1 medium yellow onion, diced

4 cloves garlic, minced

¼ teaspoon dried crushed red pepper flakes

12 ounces cooked roast beef, cut into bite-size pieces

1 14½-ounce can diced tomatoes with Italian herbs

1 cup bottled roasted red sweet peppers, drained and coarsely chopped

1 tablespoon balsamic vinegar

Salt to taste

½ teaspoon freshly ground black pepper

2 cups fresh baby arugula or spinach leaves

1 tablespoon snipped fresh Italian flat-leaf parsley

1 ounce Romano cheese, grated or shaved

1. In a large saucepan, cook the pasta according to the package directions. Drain the pasta in a colander; transfer to a covered oven-safe bowl, and keep warm in the oven.

2. Add the olive oil to the same saucepan, and bring to temperature over medium heat. Add the onion, garlic, and crushed red pepper flakes; sauté for 5 minutes or until the onion is tender, stirring occasionally.

3. Add the beef, undrained tomatoes, red peppers, balsamic vinegar, salt, and pepper to the pan. Heat through. Add the hot pasta to the pan along with the arugula or spinach and parsley; toss to combine. Top with the Romano cheese. Serve immediately.

SLOW-COOKED PORK LO MEIN

You can steam the noodles by adding them along with the other ingredients in your slow cooker. If you prefer, you can prepare the noodles according to the package directions and add them already cooked to the dish.

Yields 6–8 servings

1½ pounds boneless pork shoulder

2 medium yellow onions, sliced

2 cups frozen sliced carrots

1 12-ounce jar teriyaki glaze

1 cup thinly bias-sliced celery

1 8-ounce can sliced water chestnuts, drained

1 5-ounce can sliced bamboo shoots, drained

1 teaspoon grated fresh ginger

1 6-ounce package frozen sugar snap peas

1 cup broccoli florets

8 ounces dried egg noodles

½ cup cashew halves

1. Trim the fat from the pork and cut the meat into ¾" pieces. Add the pork, onions, carrots, teriyaki glaze, celery, water chestnuts, bamboo shoots, and ginger to a 4-quart slow cooker. Cover and cook on low for 7 hours.

2. Turn the cooker setting to high; add the sugar snap peas and broccoli. Cover and cook for 10–15 minutes, or until the snap peas are crisp-tender. Add the egg noodles and stir to mix. Reduce the setting to warm and cover; let steam for 30 minutes or until the pasta is done. Serve immediately. Sprinkle cashews over each serving.

FILIPINO PORK WITH RICE NOODLES

Annatto seeds are available at Asian markets or specialty spice shops. If the seeds aren't available, you can substitute toasted sesame oil for the annatto oil.

Yields 6–8 servings

1 8-ounce package rice noodles

¼ cup peanut oil

2 cloves garlic, minced

½ pound pork tenderloin, cut into thin strips

½ pound sweet Chinese sausage, cut into thin slices

1 large yellow onion, diced

1 cup napa cabbage, chopped

2 tablespoons soy sauce

1½ cups chicken broth

2 tablespoons fish sauce

¼ cup chopped leeks, well rinsed

1 tablespoon Annatto Oil (see recipe in sidebar)

Fresh chopped cilantro to taste

1. Put the rice noodles in a bowl and pour tepid (105°F) water over them. Allow to soak while you prepare the rest of the dish.

2. Heat a wok over medium-high heat; and add the oil, garlic, and pork. Stir-fry until the pork is done. Add the sausage, onion, and cabbage. Stir-fry for several minutes, and then add the soy sauce, broth, fish sauce, leeks, and annatto oil. Stir-fry until the cabbage is tender. Add the drained rice noodles; reduce the heat to medium and stir-fry until the noodles are tender. Serve garnished with the chopped cilantro.

Annatto Oil

Put ½ cup of peanut, sesame, or vegetable oil in a small heavy saucepan and heat until the oil smokes or reaches about 350°F. Remove the pan from the heat and stir ¼ cup of annatto seeds into the oil. Cool and strain the seeds from the oil. Store in a covered jar in the refrigerator.

LEBANESE BAKED KIBBE

Serve with a Greek salad or cucumber and yogurt salad. If you are serving the yogurt salad, omit the dill and garnish it with chopped fresh mint.

Yields 8 servings

2 cups fine-grain bulgur

¼ cup dried onion flakes

4 cups water

2½ pounds ground lamb

2 teaspoons dried parsley

½ teaspoon salt

¼ teaspoon plus ⅛ teaspoon ground allspice

¼ teaspoon plus ⅛ teaspoon ground cinnamon

1 teaspoon dried mint

¼ cup cold water

2 tablespoons butter

¼ cup pine nuts

1 medium yellow onion, chopped

Salt and freshly ground black pepper to taste

5 tablespoons extra-virgin olive oil

1. In a bowl, mix the bulgur and onion flakes together; add the water and set aside to soak for 30 minutes. Drain the bulgur and mix it with 2 pounds of the ground lamb and the parsley, salt, ¼ teaspoon allspice, ¼ teaspoon cinnamon, mint, and water.

2. Melt the butter in a 4-quart Dutch oven. Add the remaining ½ pound of ground lamb, pine nuts, onion, ⅛ teaspoon cinnamon, ⅛ teaspoon allspice, salt, and pepper. Sauté until the onions are transparent. Remove the meat mixture from the pan and set aside.

3. Preheat the oven to 400°F.

4. Coat the bottom of the Dutch oven with 2 tablespoons olive oil. Press half of the bulgur-lamb mixture into the pan. Evenly spread the sautéed lamb mixture over the bulgur-lamb mixture. Spoon the remaining bulgur-lamb mixture on top and use the back of a spoon or a spatula to press it down evenly over the sautéed mixture. Drizzle the remaining 3 tablespoons of olive oil over the top of the casserole. Bake for 20 minutes; reduce the oven temperature to 300°F and bake for another 30 minutes, or until golden brown. To serve, cut into 8 wedges; use a spatula to remove each wedge from the pan.

SHRIMP AND ARTICHOKE FETTUCCINE

You can prepare this entire meal in three steps using the same deep 3½-quart nonstick skillet. Cooking the pasta in less water will leave it a bit starchy, which will help thicken the sauce.

Yields 4 servings

1 pound shrimp in shells

3 cups water

4 sprigs fresh parsley

1 slice lemon

1 teaspoon freshly ground black pepper

8 ounces dried fettuccine or spaghetti

3 tablespoons extra-virgin olive oil

4 cloves garlic, minced

1 9-ounce package frozen artichoke hearts, thawed and halved lengthwise

½ cup dry white wine

2 plum tomatoes, finely chopped

1 cup shrimp broth

1 tablespoon butter

1 teaspoon freshly grated lemon peel

½ teaspoon sea salt

½ teaspoon freshly ground nutmeg

4 slices Italian country loaf bread or other hearty bread, toasted

1 tablespoon fresh Italian parsley, finely chopped

2 lemons, quartered

1. Peel and devein the shrimp, reserving the shells. Add the shells, water, parsley, lemon slice, and pepper to the skillet and bring to a boil over high heat; reduce the heat and simmer, uncovered, for 10 minutes. Strain; set aside and keep warm until serving time.

2. Cook the pasta according to the package directions; drain and set aside.

3. Add 2 tablespoons of the oil to the skillet and bring to temperature over medium heat; add the garlic and sauté for 30 seconds. Add the artichokes and sauté for 1 minute. Stir in the shrimp and wine; bring to temperature and cook until the shrimp turns pink, about 2 minutes. Stir in the tomatoes, broth, butter, lemon peel, salt, nutmeg, and cooked pasta; heat through.

4. To serve, place a piece of the toasted bread in each of 4 shallow soup bowls. Divide the pasta mixture among bowls, adding additional shrimp broth as desired. Garnish with the parsley and drizzle with the remaining oil. Squeeze lemon juice from 1 wedge over each serving, and garnish each with the remaining lemon wedges.

LINGUINI IN RED CLAM SAUCE

You can cook fresh pasta in less water than you'd need to cook dried pasta, which enables you to use the same pan to cook the pasta and then make the sauce.

Yields 4 servings

8 ounces fresh linguini

2 tablespoons extra-virgin olive oil

1 medium yellow onion, diced

1 clove garlic, minced

2 6½-ounce cans minced clams, drained and juice reserved

1 6-ounce can tomato paste

1 cup water

2 tablespoons fresh lemon juice

1 tablespoon fresh parsley, chopped

1 teaspoon granulated sugar

⅛ teaspoon dried rosemary

¼ teaspoon dried thyme

Freshly grated Parmigiano-Reggiano cheese to taste

1. Cook linguini until al dente. Drain, set aside, and keep warm.

2. Wipe out the pan and bring the oil to temperature over medium heat. Sauté the onion until transparent. Add the garlic and drained clams and sauté for 30 seconds. Stir in the clam juice, tomato paste, water, lemon juice, parsley, sugar, rosemary, and thyme. Bring to a boil, then reduce the heat and simmer, uncovered, for 15 minutes. Gently stir in the cooked linguini, and cook until the pasta is brought to temperature. Serve topped with freshly grated Parmigiano-Reggiano cheese.

MACARONI AND CHEESE

Baking this dish does away with the hassles of making a white sauce and then slowly melting the cheese into that sauce.

Yields 8 servings

4 cups dried macaroni

4 tablespoons butter

4 tablespoons all-purpose flour

4½ cups milk

8 ounces Cheddar cheese, grated

8 ounces Colby cheese, grated

8 ounces Monterey jack cheese, grated

Salt and freshly ground black pepper to taste

1. Preheat oven to 350°F.

2. In an ovenproof Dutch oven, cook the macaroni according to the package directions. Drain, set aside, and keep warm.

3. Wipe out the Dutch oven. Add the butter and melt it over medium heat. Whisk in the flour, and then slowly whisk in the milk. Add the macaroni and cheeses to the pan and stir to combine. Add salt and pepper to taste. Bake for 1 hour, or until the cheese is melted and the sauce is thickened.

Enhancing Macaroni and Cheese

To add a punch of extra flavor to Macaroni and Cheese, stir a teaspoon of Dijon mustard and a tablespoon of mayonnaise into the milk mixture before you pour it over the macaroni. For a bread crumb topping, spread a thin layer of plain or Italian-seasoned bread crumbs over the top of the casserole and dot the crumbs with butter or drizzle butter over them.

FLORENTINE LASAGNA

This Florentine Lasagna is one way to hide a vegetable in a meal.

Yields 8 servings

2 10-ounce packages frozen spinach, thawed

Company's Coming Four-Cheese Lasagna (see recipe in this chapter)

1. Squeeze the moisture out of the thawed spinach, and then thoroughly dry it in a salad spinner or between cotton towels.

2. Prepare the Company's Coming Four-Cheese Lasagna recipe. Add the spinach in a layer between the first and second layers. Bake for 50 minutes covered and then 20 minutes uncovered. Remove from the oven, cover, and let stand 20 minutes before cutting.

COMPANY'S COMING FOUR-CHEESE LASAGNA

If you like a bubbly brown top on lasagna, put the pan under the broiler for a few minutes when it's done baking.

Yields 8 servings

1 pound lean ground chuck

1 large yellow onion, diced

3 cloves garlic, minced

4 cups tomato juice

8 ounces fresh button mushrooms, cleaned and sliced

1 6-ounce can tomato paste

1 tablespoon Worcestershire sauce

1 teaspoon dried oregano, crushed

1 teaspoon dried parsley, crushed

½ teaspoon salt

½ teaspoon fresh ground black pepper

Nonstick cooking spray

8 ounces dried lasagna noodles, uncooked

15 ounces ricotta cheese

1½ cups freshly grated Parmigiano-Reggiano cheese

1½ cups Romano cheese, freshly grated

2 cups grated mozzarella cheese

1. Add the ground beef, onion, and garlic to a deep 3½-quart nonstick skillet or large saucepan over medium heat. Stir-fry until the hamburger is browned and the onion is transparent. Drain off and discard any excess fat. Stir in the tomato juice, mushrooms, tomato paste, Worcestershire sauce, oregano, parsley, salt, and pepper. Bring to a simmer, lower the heat, and simmer uncovered for 30 minutes, stirring occasionally.

2. Preheat oven to 350°F.

3. To prepare the lasagna, treat a 9" × 13" nonstick baking pan with nonstick spray; layer half of the noodles, half of the hot prepared sauce, half of the ricotta, half of the Parmigiano-Reggiano, half of the Romano, and half of the mozzarella cheese and then repeat in another layer in that order. Cover with aluminum foil and let rest for 30 minutes.

4. Leave the aluminum foil cover in place and bake for 40 minutes. Remove the foil and continue baking for 15 minutes. Remove from the oven, cover, and let stand 20 minutes before cutting.

Baking a Better Lasagna

This recipe tastes best if you make the sauce in advance and refrigerate it for a day or two so the flavors can blend; the added bonus is that then when you're ready to prepare the lasagna, technically you'll only be using that one pot (well, baking pan) to make your meal.

CHICKEN AND NOODLES

This Chicken and Noodles is great served over mashed potatoes or warm biscuits, or with crackers.

Yields 6 servings

2 tablespoons butter or vegetable oil

4 medium carrots, peeled

2 stalks celery, finely diced

1 large yellow onion, diced

4 cups chicken broth

4 cups water

2 bay leaves

1 teaspoon dried thyme, crushed

¾ teaspoon salt

¼ teaspoon black pepper

1 12-ounce package frozen noodles

1 cup milk

2 tablespoons all-purpose flour

1 large egg

1½ cups frozen peas, thawed

2 cups cooked chicken, cubed

1. Melt the butter or heat the oil in a Dutch oven over medium-high heat. Shred 1 of the carrots and dice the remaining 3; add the carrots and celery to the pan and sauté for 3 minutes. Add the onion and sauté for 5 minutes, or until the onion is transparent and the celery is tender. Add the broth, water, bay leaves, thyme, salt, and pepper; stir to combine.

2. Bring the broth mixture to a boil. Add the noodles; reduce the heat to maintain a gentle boil, and cook for the length of time specified on the noodle package, stirring occasionally. In a screw-top jar combine the milk, flour, and egg; beat lightly with a fork, then cover and shake until smooth. Remove the bay leaves and discard. Stir the milk mixture into the noodles and broth. Bring to a boil and then reduce the heat; simmer and stir until thickened and bubbly. If the mixture becomes too thick, stir in some additional milk or water. Stir in the peas and cooked chicken. Continue to cook and stir until heated through, or for about 1–2 minutes.

LEMON GARLIC SHRIMP WITH PASTA

If you're using a newer skillet you can still make this dish, just squeeze the lemon juice over the cooked pasta, shrimp, and sauce.

Yields 1 serving

½ teaspoon olive oil

¼ small yellow onion, halved and thinly sliced

½ teaspoon garlic powder

Juice from ½ lemon

¼ cup chicken broth

6 medium shrimp, peeled and deveined

1 serving angel hair pasta, cooked

Pinch salt

Fresh cracked pepper to taste

1. Place a small skillet over medium heat and when heated, add the olive oil and onion. Stir frequently and cook for 4–5 minutes. The onion should be translucent and just starting to turn golden brown.

2. Add the garlic powder, lemon juice, and chicken broth to the pan and stir to scrape up the fond. Add the shrimp to the skillet and cook for several minutes until they turn pink.

3. Place pasta on a plate and pour the contents of the skillet over it. Sprinkle with salt and freshly cracked pepper before serving.

PASTA PUTTANESCA

This is a quick dish to make and the ingredients are very affordable.

Yields 4 servings

1 pound dry spaghetti

3 tablespoons olive oil

1 garlic clove, minced

2 anchovies, finely sliced

¼ cup olives, pitted and sliced

2 tablespoons capers

¼ cup fresh parsley, chopped

1 pinch dried chili pepper flakes

1 28-ounce can whole, peeled tomatoes

Salt to taste

1. Cook 1 pound of spaghetti according to package directions. Drain, set aside, and keep warm. Wipe out pan, then place over low heat. Once it is warm, add the oil and the garlic. Cook garlic for 1 minute before adding the anchovies. Cook for 3 minutes, stirring continually. The anchovies should begin to dissolve. Add the olives, capers, parsley, and pepper flakes and toss to combine.

2. Pour in tomatoes and gently chop apart while stirring constantly. Let the mixture come to a boil and reduce heat to medium-low. Cook uncovered for about 15 minutes. Stir frequently to prevent sticking. Taste before seasoning with salt, and pour over the pasta.

SPAGHETTI CARBONARA

This dish has to be made fresh in small batches in order to have its full flavor potential. It is a rich dish, so try it as a side instead of a main dish.

Yields 2 servings

4 ounces dried spaghetti

3 tablespoons prosciutto, pancetta, or bacon

2 eggs

¼ cup Parmesan cheese, grated

¼ teaspoon ground black pepper

Pinch nutmeg

1 cup white wine or vermouth

2 tablespoons butter

1. Cook the pasta in a Dutch oven or stockpot according to package directions. Drain, set aside, and keep warm.

2. Wipe out the pot, then place over medium-low heat. Chop the meat into matchstick-size pieces and add to the pot when it is warm. Cook until crispy. Drain off all but 1 tablespoon of the drippings.

3. In a small bowl, whisk the eggs, cheese, pepper, and nutmeg. Increase the heat on the pot to medium and add the wine. Stir occasionally and let the wine reduce until it is a light syrup. Add the butter and stir it until it melts. Reduce heat to low and let the skillet sit until the pasta is cooked.

4. Drain the spaghetti and pour it into the pot. Toss to coat the spaghetti evenly with the sauce. Pour the egg mixture over the pasta and stir vigorously until the noodles are coated and the egg has set. Serve immediately.

JAMBALAYA

There are as many versions of Jambalaya as there are Southern cooks. Originally created as a dish to use up leftovers, it's a versatile recipe that you can adjust according to your tastes.

Yields 6–8 servings

3 tablespoons bacon fat or peanut oil

1 1-pound bag baby carrots

4 stalks celery, diced

2 green bell peppers, seeded and chopped

1 large yellow onion, diced

6 green onions, chopped

3 cloves garlic, minced

½ pound smoked sausage, thinly sliced

½ pound cooked ham, diced

2 15-ounce cans diced tomatoes, drained

1 28-ounce can heat-and-serve pork or chicken, undrained

3 cups chicken broth

1 tablespoon dried parsley

1 teaspoon dried thyme

½ teaspoon hot sauce, or to taste

¼ cup Worcestershire sauce

2 cups long-grain rice, uncooked

Water as needed

1 pound shrimp, peeled and deveined

Salt and freshly ground pepper to taste

1. Add the bacon fat or oil to a Dutch oven or stockpot and bring it to temperature over medium heat. Shred 8 of the baby carrots. Add the shredded carrots, the celery, and the green peppers to the pan; sauté for 3–5 minutes, or until soft. Add the yellow and green onions and sauté until transparent. Add the garlic and sauté for an additional 30 seconds. Stir in the smoked sausage and stir-fry for 3 minutes; add the ham and stir-fry for 1 minute. Chop the remaining carrots and add them to the pan.

2. Stir in the tomatoes, pork or chicken, broth, parsley, thyme, hot sauce, and Worcestershire sauce. Bring to a boil, and then stir in the rice; reduce the heat, cover, and simmer for 20 minutes. Fluff the rice; add additional water, if needed. If the shrimp are large, cut them in half; otherwise, add the shrimp to the pot, cover, and cook for another 3–5 minutes, or until the shrimp are cooked. If excess moisture remains in the dish, uncover and cook until it's evaporated, stirring often to keep the rice from sticking. Taste for seasoning and add salt and pepper, if needed.

Pressure-Cooked Long-Grain Brown Rice

For 6 servings, add 1 cup long-grain brown rice, 2 cups of water or broth, 1 tablespoon oil, and 1 teaspoon salt to a pressure cooker over high heat; lock the lid, and bring to high pressure. Adjust the burner to maintain low pressure for 20 minutes. Remove pan from the heat and let sit for 10 minutes or until the pressure is released and you can remove the lid; fluff the rice with a fork and serve.

SHRIMP ETOUFFÉE

The secret of a good Shrimp Etouffée is in the sauce, which requires a dark roux. It takes a little extra work, but it's worth the effort. Serve the results over cooked rice.

Yields 6 servings

3 tablespoons bacon fat or peanut oil

3 tablespoons all-purpose flour

1 small green pepper, seeded and chopped

Optional: 1 large carrot, peeled and shredded

1 celery stalk, chopped

1 large yellow onion, diced

4 green onions, chopped

3 cloves garlic, minced

3 tablespoons tomato paste

1¼ cups beef broth

1 cup dry white wine

2 bay leaves

¼ teaspoon dried basil

¼ teaspoon dried thyme

1 teaspoon hot sauce, or to taste

1½ pounds shrimp, peeled and deveined

Salt and freshly ground pepper to taste

3 cups cooked rice

Optional: ¼ cup fresh parsley, chopped

1. Add the bacon fat or oil and flour to a Dutch oven or stockpot over medium heat. Cook, stirring constantly so the roux doesn't burn, for 15 minutes, or until the roux is the color of peanut butter.

2. Stir in the green pepper, carrot (if using), celery, yellow and green onions, and garlic. Sauté for 10 minutes, or until the vegetables are tender. Add the tomato paste, broth, and wine, stirring constantly until the mixture thickens. Add the bay leaves, basil, thyme, and hot sauce; stir to combine. Cover, reduce the heat, and simmer for 45 minutes.

3. Add the shrimp and simmer for 20 minutes, uncovered. Remove and discard the bay leaves. Taste for seasoning and add salt and pepper, additional hot sauce, and herbs, if needed. Serve over cooked rice, garnished with chopped fresh parsley, if desired.

Cooked Long-Grain White Rice

For 8 servings, add 3 cups long-grain rice, 4½ cups water or broth, and salt to taste to a large saucepan; bring to a boil over medium-high heat. Reduce heat to medium-low, cover, and cook for 15 minutes. Remove the lid, add butter or extra-virgin olive oil to taste, and fluff with a fork until the butter or oil is mixed into the rice and all of the liquid is absorbed.

GUMBO

For the broth, backwoods cooks save up chicken gizzards and necks until they have 2 pounds of each, then simmer them in 3 or 4 quarts of water. You can find filé powder at the Spice House (www.thespicehouse.com) if your local grocery store doesn't carry it.

Yields 6–8 servings

4 tablespoons lard or peanut oil

4 tablespoons all-purpose flour

4 stalks celery, chopped

1 large yellow onion, diced

1 green bell pepper, seeded and diced

3 cloves garlic, minced

1 15-ounce can diced tomatoes

¼ teaspoon dried thyme

¼ teaspoon dried basil

3 bay leaves

2 tablespoons filé powder

2 tablespoons Worcestershire sauce

1 teaspoon hot sauce, or to taste

8 cups chicken broth

1 pound smoked sausage, sliced

2 cups cooked chicken, shredded

Salt and freshly ground pepper to taste

4½ cups cooked long-grain rice

1. Add the lard or oil and flour to a Dutch oven or stockpot over medium heat. Cook, stirring constantly so the roux doesn't burn, for 15 minutes, or until the roux is the color of peanut butter.

2. Stir in the celery, onions, green pepper, garlic, and tomatoes; cook, stirring constantly, until the vegetables are tender. Add the remaining ingredients except the sausage, chicken, salt, pepper, and rice and simmer covered over medium heat for 30–45 minutes, or until the mixture thickens.

3. Stir in the sausage and chicken; simmer uncovered for an additional 15 minutes. Taste for seasoning; add salt and pepper, if needed. Serve hot over about ¼ cup of rice per serving.

Cooked Short- or Medium-Grain Rice

For 4½ cups of cooked rice, rinse and drain 1½ cups of rice and add to a large saucepan along with 2½ cups of water and salt to taste. Cover and let set for 30 minutes. Bring to a boil over high heat, reduce heat to medium-low, and cook covered for 15 minutes. Turn off the heat. Leave covered for 10 minutes or until ready to serve, for up to 1 hour.

DIRTY RICE

This dish gets its name from the appearance the chopped chicken livers add to the rice. If you prefer a milder liver taste, use ½ pound chicken livers and ½ pound chicken gizzards instead of all livers.

Yields 4 servings

2 tablespoons bacon fat or peanut oil

1 small green bell pepper, seeded and diced

2 stalks celery, chopped

1 medium yellow onion, diced

1 clove garlic, minced

½ pound lean ground pork

½ pound Italian sausage

3 cups chicken broth

1 pound chicken livers

½ tablespoon Worcestershire sauce

Cayenne pepper to taste

1 tablespoon dried parsley

1 cup uncooked long-grain rice

Water, if needed

2 green onions, chopped

Salt and freshly ground pepper to taste

1. Add the bacon fat or oil to a Dutch oven or stockpot and bring to temperature over medium heat. Add the green pepper and celery; sauté for 3 minutes. Add the yellow onion; sauté for 5 minutes, or until the onions are transparent and the vegetables are tender. Add the garlic and sauté for 30 seconds. Stir in the ground pork and sausage; fry until the meat is lightly browned. Drain off and discard any excess fat.

2. Stir in the chicken broth and bring to a boil. Add the chicken livers, cover, and lightly boil for 30 minutes. Use a slotted spoon to remove the chicken livers; set them aside to cool.

3. Stir in the Worcestershire sauce, cayenne, parsley, and rice; bring to a boil. Reduce heat to medium-low, cover, and cook for 15 minutes.

4. Chop the chicken livers. Stir into the rice-sausage mixture. Cover and simmer for 20 minutes; stir occasionally to keep the rice from sticking. Add water if additional moisture is needed. Stir in the green onion. Taste for seasoning; add salt and pepper, if needed.

HOPPED-UP HOPPIN' JOHN

Hoppin' John is a Southern dish traditionally eaten on New Year's Day. This version is hopped up by adding carrots to make it a one-dish meal.

Yields 6–8 servings

½ pound thick-cut bacon, diced

1 stalk celery, minced

1 1-pound bag baby carrots

1 large yellow onion, diced

2 15-ounce cans black-eyed peas, rinsed and drained

3 cups cooked long-grain rice

4 cups chicken broth

Salt and freshly ground black pepper to taste

Add the bacon to a Dutch oven or stockpot; cook over medium heat until the fat begins to render out of the bacon. Add the celery; sauté for 2 minutes. Shred 4 of the baby carrots and add them to the pan with the celery; sauté for 1 minute. Add the onion and sauté for 5 minutes, or until transparent. Dice the remaining baby carrots by slicing them each into 4 or 5 pieces. Stir in the diced carrots, black-eyed peas, rice, and chicken broth. Bring to a simmer; cover, reduce heat, and simmer for 10 minutes or until the carrots are tender and the black-eyed peas are warmed through. Turn off the heat and let set, covered, for 10 minutes. Taste for seasoning; add salt and pepper if needed.

SPANISH RICE

Adding a pinch or two of brown or granulated sugar when you add the water enhances the flavor of this dish and cuts the acidity of the tomatoes.

Yields 4 servings

1 pound hamburger

1 medium yellow onion, diced

1 green pepper, seeded and diced

1 teaspoon chili powder

1½ cups water

Pinch light brown or granulated sugar

½ cup tomato sauce

1 tablespoon butter

1 cup uncooked short- or medium-grain rice

2 tablespoons Worcestershire sauce

Hot sauce to taste

¼ teaspoon dried thyme

Salt and freshly ground black pepper to taste

Add the hamburger, onion, green pepper, and chili powder to a deep 2-quart or larger nonstick skillet; fry the hamburger over medium to medium-high heat, stirring frequently to prevent the vegetables from burning and to break apart the hamburger. When the hamburger is browned and the onions are transparent, drain off and discard any excess fat. Stir in the water, sugar, tomato sauce, butter, rice, Worcestershire sauce, hot sauce, and thyme; bring to a boil. Reduce heat to low, cover, and simmer for 25 minutes, or until the rice is tender. Taste for seasoning and add salt and pepper, if needed.

STUFFED PEPPERS

This recipe is an excellent way to use up leftover rice. It's also delicious if you use cooked brown rice.

Yields 8 servings

8 medium green bell peppers

2 pounds lean ground beef

2 cups cooked rice

3 large eggs

3 cloves garlic, minced

1 large yellow onion, diced

4 tablespoons butter

Salt and freshly ground black pepper to taste

Optional: pinch allspice or nutmeg

1 cup tomato sauce

2 tablespoons white or white wine vinegar

1 tablespoon granulated sugar

1 cup chicken broth

Nonstick cooking spray

1. Preheat oven to 350°F.

2. Cut the tops off of the green peppers. Remove the seeds from the peppers and discard. Set the peppers in a 9" × 13" nonstick baking pan and set the tops aside.

3. Add the ground beef, cooked rice, eggs, garlic, onion, butter, salt, black pepper, and allspice or nutmeg (if using) to a large bowl; mix well. Divide the meat filling mixture between the green peppers; place the tops on each.

4. In the bowl, mix together the tomato sauce, wine or vinegar, sugar, and broth. Pour into the pan holding the stuffed green peppers.

5. Treat one side of a large piece of heavy-duty aluminum foil with nonstick cooking spray. Put the foil atop the baking pan, treated side down; crimp the edges to form a seal. Bake for 45 minutes. Remove the foil, being careful to avoid being burned by the escaping steam. Return to the oven and bake for an additional 15 minutes, or until the peppers are tender and the filling is cooked through.

Stuffed Pepper Options

You can substitute a cup of bread crumbs or cracker crumbs for the cooked rice. Or, replace some of the rice in the meat mixture with peeled and chopped hard-boiled eggs. Or, use a mixture of ground beef and ground pork or lamb.

PAELLA

Paella, named after the style of pan it's cooked in, is made up primarily of rice, saffron, and olive oil. Saffron is expensive; you can substitute ground turmeric, which will give the dish a similar yellow color but will alter the taste a bit.

Yields 6–8 servings

½ cup extra-virgin olive oil or olive oil

1 red bell pepper, seeded and diced

2 medium yellow onions, diced

2 cloves garlic, minced

1 pound boneless chicken thighs, skin removed and diced

½ pound ground pork

1 cup smoked ham, diced

1 cup chorizo, sliced

2 cups uncooked arborio or converted rice

3 cups chicken broth

⅛ teaspoon saffron threads, crushed

2 tablespoons Annatto Oil (see Filipino Pork with Rice Noodles recipe in this chapter)

1 teaspoon paprika

Salt to taste

1 cup frozen peas, thawed

½ pound shrimp, peeled and deveined

1 6½-ounce can mussels, rinsed and drained

1 10-ounce can boiled baby clams, rinsed and drained

1 cup dry white wine

1 lemon, thinly sliced

1. Bring the oil to temperature over medium-high heat in a 15" paella pan or deep skillet. Stir in the red bell pepper and onion; sauté for 5 minutes, or until the onions are transparent. Add the garlic, chicken, and ground pork; stir-fry until the meat is lightly browned. Stir in the ham, chorizo, and rice; sauté until the rice begins to color.

2. Add the chicken broth and bring to a boil. Stir in the saffron, annatto oil, paprika, and salt. Reduce the heat to medium; cover and cook for 10 minutes, rotating the pan or stirring the contents of the pan occasionally. Check the rice; cover and cook until the rice is tender.

3. Stir in the peas, shrimp, mussels, clams, and wine. Cover and cook for 5 minutes, or until the shrimp is opaque and the mussels and clams are warm. Garnish with lemon slices and serve.

Arborio Rice

Arborio rice is an Italian medium-grain rice. It has a high starch content, which creates a creamy base. This is why the firmer rounded grains are often used in paella and risotto dishes in Mediterranean cuisine.

SWEET-AND-SOUR PORK WITH RICE

This is a variation of a recipe that first appeared on the back of the Uncle Ben's Converted Rice package in 1987. Adjust the sugar in the recipe according to whether the pineapple you use is canned in syrup or its own juice.

Yields 4 servings

1 tablespoon peanut oil

1 pound lean pork, cut into bite-size pieces

1 teaspoon garlic powder

1 13½-ounce can pineapple tidbits

Water as needed

¼ cup white vinegar

1 teaspoon soy sauce

Optional: 2 tablespoons granulated sugar

1 cup uncooked converted white rice

1 green bell pepper, seeded and diced

1 tomato, diced

1 16-ounce bag frozen stir-fry vegetables mix, thawed

1. Bring the oil to temperature over medium-high heat in a nonstick wok or large skillet. Add the pork and garlic powder; stir-fry for 5 minutes, or until the pork is browned.

2. Drain the pineapple, reserving the juice. Set aside the pineapple tidbits. Add water to the pineapple juice to bring the total amount of liquid to 2½ cups. Add to the wok or skillet along with the vinegar, soy sauce, and sugar (if using). Bring to a boil; reduce heat to low, cover, and simmer for 20 minutes.

3. Remove the cover and stir in the rice. Cover and simmer for another 25 minutes, or until all of the liquid is absorbed and the pork is tender. Stir in the green pepper, tomato, and stir-fry vegetables mix. Cover and cook on low for 5 minutes. Uncover and stir-fry until the vegetables are cooked to crisp-tender. Serve immediately.

BAKED CHICKEN SUPREME

If your casserole dish can't withstand a 425°F baking temperature, you can bake this casserole at a lower oven temperature; simply extend the baking time as needed, allowing for up to 1 hour, for example, if you bake it at 350°F.

Yields 6–8 servings

¼ cup butter

1 small yellow onion, diced

⅓ cup all-purpose flour

½ teaspoon salt

⅛ teaspoon freshly ground black pepper

1 cup half-and-half

1 cup chicken broth

2 8.8-ounce pouches Uncle Ben's Long Grain & Wild Ready Rice

2 cups cooked chicken, cubed

⅓ cup pimiento, chopped

⅓ cup fresh parsley, chopped

¼ cup almonds, chopped

1. Preheat oven to 425°F.

2. Add the butter and onion to a 2-quart microwave-safe and ovenproof casserole dish. Microwave on high for 30 seconds, or until the butter is melted. Stir, cover, and microwave on high at 30-second intervals until the onion is transparent.

3. Stir in the flour, salt, and pepper, and then whisk in the half-and-half a little at a time. Once you have a smooth, lump-free mixture, stir in the remaining ingredients.

4. Bake uncovered for 30 minutes.

SOUTHWESTERN CHICKEN AND RICE CASSEROLE

You can assemble this dish the night before, refrigerate it, and then bake it the next day. Just increase the cooking time to 45 minutes.

Yields 6 servings

1 tablespoon extra-virgin olive oil

1 medium yellow onion, diced

1 6.9-ounce package chicken-flavored rice and vermicelli mix

1 14-ounce can chicken broth

2 cups water

2 cups cooked chicken or turkey, chopped

1 15-ounce can diced tomatoes

3 tablespoons canned green chili peppers, drained and diced

1 teaspoon dried basil, crushed

1½ teaspoons chili powder

⅛ teaspoon ground cumin

⅛ teaspoon freshly ground black pepper

2 ounces Cheddar cheese, shredded

1. Preheat oven to 425°F.

2. Bring the oil to temperature over medium heat in an ovenproof Dutch oven; add the onion and sauté for 5 minutes, or until transparent. Stir in the rice and vermicelli mix (including the seasoning packet); cook and stir for 2 minutes. Stir in the broth and water; bring to a boil. Reduce the heat, cover, and simmer for 20 minutes.

3. Stir in the chicken, tomatoes, peppers, basil, chili powder, cumin, and black pepper. Cover and bake for 25 minutes. Sprinkle with the cheese. Let stand for 5 minutes before serving.

CHICKEN AND BROCCOLI CASSEROLE

This is another casserole that can be prepared the night before, covered and refrigerated, and then baked the next day. Simply add 10 minutes to the initial baking time.

Yields 8 servings

1 tablespoon butter

1 teaspoon vegetable oil

1 cup fresh button mushrooms, cleaned and chopped

1 small yellow onion, diced

1 pound boneless, skinless chicken breasts, cut into bite-size pieces

2 cloves garlic, minced

1 10¾-ounce can cream of mushroom soup

1 cup pasteurized processed cheese spread or Velveeta, cubed

13.2 ounces Uncle Ben's Whole Grain Brown or Original Long Grain Ready Rice

1 12-ounce bag frozen broccoli florets, thawed and drained

1 8-ounce can sliced water chestnuts, drained

½ cup sour cream

¼ teaspoon freshly ground black pepper

4 ounces Cheddar cheese, shredded

½ cup bread crumbs or crushed croutons

1. Preheat the oven to 400°F.

2. Add the butter and oil to an ovenproof Dutch oven and bring it to temperature over medium-high heat; swirl the pan to blend the butter and oil. Add the mushrooms; cook and stir for 2 minutes. Add the onion and chicken; stir-fry until the chicken is just cooked through. Stir in the garlic and stir-fry for another 30 seconds. Add the undiluted mushroom soup and the cheese spread or Velveeta. Stir until the cheese is melted.

3. Remove the Dutch oven from the heat. Stir in the rice, broccoli, water chestnuts, sour cream, and pepper. Bake uncovered for 15–20 minutes.

4. Remove from the oven and top with the Cheddar cheese and bread crumbs or crushed croutons. Return to oven and bake for 10 minutes, or until the cheese is melted and the bread crumbs or crushed croutons are lightly browned.

Stovetop Cooking Brown Rice

For 3 cups of cooked brown rice, bring 4 cups of salted water or chicken broth to a boil over medium heat. Stir in 1 cup whole-grain brown rice. Adjust the heat so that the liquid maintains a gentle boil. Cook for up to 1 hour, stirring frequently and adding more liquid if necessary to keep the rice covered, or until tender. Drain; plunge in cold water to stop the cooking process.

SHRIMP AND RICE CASSEROLE

You can omit the peas in this recipe if your family doesn't like them. Serve with a tossed salad instead.

Yields 6 servings

2 cups water

½ tablespoon salt

1 pound medium shrimp, peeled and deveined

2 tablespoons butter

½ green bell pepper, seeded and chopped

1 small Vidalia onion, diced

3 cups cooked rice

1 10¾-ounce can condensed cream of mushroom soup

2½ cups sharp Cheddar cheese, grated

1 cup frozen baby peas, thawed

Salt and freshly ground black pepper to taste

1. Preheat oven to 325°F.

2. Add the water to an ovenproof Dutch oven and bring to a boil over medium-high heat. Add the salt and shrimp; boil for 1 minute. Drain immediately and set the shrimp aside.

3. Wipe out the Dutch oven and melt the butter in it; add the green pepper and onion, and sauté for 5 minutes, or until the onion is transparent. Stir in the rice, soup, 1½ cups of the cheese, the shrimp, and peas. Add salt and pepper to taste. Top with the remaining cheese. Bake uncovered for 30 minutes, or until the cheese is melted and bubbly.

UNSTUFFED CABBAGE ROLLS

Use Italian-seasoned tomatoes and cooked orzo pasta instead of the rice to give this dish a Tuscan flair. If you prefer German flavors, add a teaspoon of caraway seeds and 2 teaspoons of brown sugar.

Yields 8 servings

2 tablespoons extra-virgin olive oil

6 stalks celery, diced

6 large carrots, peeled and diced

1 pound lean ground beef

1 large yellow onion, diced

2 cloves garlic, minced

1 teaspoon salt

¾ teaspoon freshly ground black pepper

1 teaspoon granulated sugar

2 15-ounce cans diced tomatoes

2 cups cooked rice

4 cups coleslaw mix

1½ cups chicken broth

1 cup dry white wine

1. Preheat oven to 350°F.

2. Bring the oil to temperature over medium heat in an ovenproof Dutch oven. Add the celery and carrots; sauté for 5 minutes. Add the ground beef and onion; stir-fry until the beef is browned and broken apart and the onion is transparent. Drain off and discard any excess fat. Add all remaining ingredients; stir into the beef mixture. Use the back of a spoon to press the mixture down evenly in the pan. Cover and bake for 45 minutes. Uncover and bake for an additional 15 minutes, or until most of the liquid has evaporated.

CHICKEN AND SPINACH CURRY

The chicken and spinach create a layer in the pressure cooker that keeps the pasta sauce from burning on the bottom of the pan.

Yields 6 servings

½ cup chicken broth or water

1 pound boneless, skinless chicken, cut into 1" pieces

2 10-ounce packages frozen spinach

1½ cups store-bought pasta sauce

1 tablespoon mild curry powder

2 tablespoons applesauce

Salt and freshly ground black pepper to taste

6 cups cooked rice

Optional: fresh chopped cilantro to taste

1. Add the broth and chicken to the pressure cooker and place the still-frozen blocks of spinach on top. Mix the pasta sauce together with the curry powder and pour it over the spinach. Do not mix the sauce into the other ingredients.

2. Lock the lid in place. Bring to high pressure over medium heat; maintain pressure for 5 minutes. Quick-release the pressure. Carefully remove the lid, add the applesauce, and stir well. If the moisture from the spinach thinned the sauce too much, simmer uncovered for 5 minutes, or until the sauce is the desired consistency. Taste the sauce and add salt, pepper, and more curry if needed. Serve over cooked rice. Garnish with cilantro, if desired.

SPANISH CHICKEN AND RICE

Serve this dish with an avocado salad and baked corn chips.

Yields 4 servings

2 tablespoons extra-virgin olive or vegetable oil

1 pound boneless chicken breast, cut into bite-size pieces

1 large green pepper, seeded and diced

1 teaspoon chili powder

1 teaspoon smoked paprika

¼ teaspoon dried thyme

⅛ teaspoon dried oregano

¼ teaspoon freshly ground black pepper

Pinch cayenne pepper

1 medium white onion, diced

4 ounces fresh button or cremini mushrooms, cleaned and sliced

2 cloves garlic, minced

2 cups chicken broth

1 cup long-grain rice, uncooked

½ cup black olives, pitted and cut in half

Add the oil to the pressure cooker and bring it to temperature over medium heat. Add the chicken, green pepper, chili powder, paprika, thyme, oregano, black pepper, cayenne, and onion; stir-fry for 5 minutes, or until the onion is transparent and the chicken begins to brown. Stir in the mushrooms; sauté for 2 minutes. Add the garlic, broth, rice, and olives. Lock the lid and bring to high pressure; maintain for 3 minutes. Remove from the heat and allow the pressure to release naturally for 7 minutes. Quick-release any remaining pressure. Uncover and fluff with a fork. Taste for seasoning and add salt and other seasoning, if needed.

Spice It Up!

Vary the heat level of the Spanish Chicken and Rice recipe by choosing between mild, medium, or hot chili powder, according to your tastes. In addition, you can substitute jalapeño pepper for some or all of the green pepper.

BASIC RISOTTO

You can add vegetables or meat to this dish as you see fit. About 2 cups of meat or vegetables should be the right balance.

Yields 6 servings

8 cups chicken or vegetable stock

2 tablespoons olive oil or butter

1 medium onion, finely chopped

2 cups arborio rice

½ cup dry white wine

¼ cup shredded Parmesan cheese

Salt to taste

Pepper to taste

1. Pour the stock into a saucepan and place over medium-low heat. Place a Dutch oven over medium-high heat. Once it is heated through, add the oil and onion. Sauté for 5 minutes, or until the onion is translucent but not brown.

2. Add the rice to the Dutch oven and stir constantly until the rice loses its chalky appearance and has just a small white dot in the center of each grain. Add the wine, stirring continually for 2 minutes.

3. Add the stock to the Dutch oven 1 cup at a time and stir almost continually until the stock has been soaked up by the rice. After you've added 6 cups of stock to the pan, taste it to determine if it is done. Add stock ½ cup at a time until the rice is tender but not pasty. Stir in the cheese and taste before adding salt and pepper. Serve warm.

Always Better at Home

Most restaurants don't make risotto individually as ordered. Generally they will start making the dish, and then set it aside. When an order is placed they'll take the half-cooked risotto and finish cooking it. But this means the texture is usually not as good as if you make it at home.

WIENERS AND BAKED BEANS

You can leave the hot dogs whole or cut them into pieces, depending on how you plan to serve the dish. Or you can do a combination of the two: Leave the number you need for sandwiches whole and cut the remaining hot dogs into pieces.

Yields 6–8 servings

1 8-ounce package bacon, cut into pieces

1 medium yellow onion, chopped

3 1-pound cans baked beans

¼ cup light brown sugar, firmly packed

1 tablespoon molasses

2 teaspoons Worcestershire sauce

½ teaspoon dry mustard

½ cup ketchup or barbecue sauce

1 1-pound package hot dogs, cut into pieces

Add the bacon to a deep nonstick skillet and brown it over medium heat. Leave 1 tablespoon of bacon fat in the pan and drain off any excess. Add the onion and sauté until transparent. Add the baked beans, brown sugar, molasses, Worcestershire sauce, dry mustard, and ketchup or barbecue sauce and mix well. Stir in the hot dog pieces. If you are keeping any of the hot dogs whole, lay them across the top of the beans. Cover and simmer for 15 minutes.

SOUTHWEST PINTO BEANS WITH PORK AND CORN

This is an adaptation of a Southwestern dish that uses dried pinto beans and chicos (a type of dried sweet corn). You can prepare this version in minutes rather than in hours. Serve it with corn bread or corn chips and a salad.

Yields 4–6 servings

4 slices bacon, diced

1 large yellow onion, diced

3 cloves garlic, minced

Optional: chopped jalapeño or other hot pepper to taste

1 15-ounce can pinto beans, rinsed and drained

1 12-ounce bag frozen whole kernel corn, thawed

1 28-ounce can heat-and-serve pork in pork broth

Salt and freshly ground black pepper to taste

Add the bacon to a deep nonstick skillet or large saucepan; fry over medium heat until it begins to brown. Add the onion and sauté until transparent. Add the garlic and chopped pepper (if using), and sauté for 1 minute. Stir in the beans, corn, and pork. Bring to a simmer and reduce the heat; simmer for 5–10 minutes to bring the beans, corn, and pork to temperature and to marry the flavors. Taste for seasoning and add salt and pepper, if needed.

PUERTO RICAN CHICKEN AND BEANS

Puerto Rican cooking has Spanish, African, Taíno (pre-Columbian inhabitants of the Bahamas), and American influences.

Yields 8 servings

¼ pound salt pork or bacon, diced

1 large carrot, peeled and shredded

1 celery stalk, finely diced

1 large yellow onion, diced

3 cloves garlic, minced

½ pound Spanish or Mexican chorizo sausage, diced or thinly sliced

½ pound ham, chopped

8 chicken thighs

4 cups water, or more, as needed

2 teaspoons Worcestershire sauce

Hot sauce to taste

4 large russet potatoes, peeled and diced

1 small head cabbage, cored and thinly sliced

2 cups kale, tough stems removed, and thinly sliced

4 turnips, diced

1 15-ounce can white beans, rinsed and drained

Salt and freshly ground black pepper to taste

1. Add the salt pork or bacon to a Dutch oven; cook over medium heat until the fat is rendered from the bacon. Add the carrot and celery; sauté for 3–5 minutes, or until soft. Add the onion and sauté until transparent. Add the garlic and sauté for an additional 30 seconds. Stir in the sausage; continue to stir while it fries for a few minutes, then stir in the ham. Add the chicken to the pan, skin side down, pushing the other ingredients to the side so that as much of the chicken as possible touches the pan bottom. Cover and cook for 10 minutes. Add the water, Worcestershire sauce, and hot sauce, and bring to a simmer; reduce the heat, cover, and simmer for 35–45 minutes, or until the chicken is cooked through. Remove the chicken from the pan and set aside.

2. Add the potatoes, cabbage, kale, and turnips to the pan. Stir to combine with the other ingredients. Cover and simmer for 30 minutes.

3. Shred the chicken, discarding the skin and bones. Stir the shredded chicken into the pan.

4. Stir the beans into the pan. Add additional water if needed to prevent the pan from boiling dry. Cover and simmer for 10 minutes. Taste for seasoning, and add salt and pepper as needed.

FALAFEL

Make the falafel into patties for sandwiches, or into walnut-sized balls to serve them in a salad (accompanied by toasted pita) instead. Use water instead of the chicken broth for a meatless meal.

Yields 24 patties, enough for 6–8 sandwiches

1 cup dried garbanzo beans

1 cup dried shelled fava beans

Water as needed

1 medium yellow onion, minced

3 cloves garlic, minced

1 cup chicken broth or water

½ cup sesame seeds

½ cup garbanzo flour

¼ cup fine bulgur

¼ cup fresh parsley, finely chopped

2 teaspoons salt

2 teaspoons ground cumin

2 teaspoons ground coriander

2 teaspoons baking powder

Cayenne pepper to taste

¼ teaspoon freshly ground black pepper

Vegetable oil, as needed

6–8 pita rounds

6–8 slices tomato

6–8 slices yellow onion

1½–2 cups lettuce, shredded

12–16 cucumber slices

1½–2 cups plain yogurt

1. Add the garbanzo and fava beans to a large bowl. Add enough water to the bowl to cover the beans; cover and let soak overnight.

2. Drain the beans and run through the fine blade in a meat grinder or add to a food processor and pulse until they're a fine mash. Return the beans to the bowl, and combine with the onion, garlic, broth, sesame seeds, garbanzo flour, bulgur, parsley, salt, cumin, coriander, baking powder, cayenne, and black pepper. Cover and let stand for 1 hour.

3. Preheat oil in a deep fryer to 375°F. Form the falafel mixture into 1½" round patties about ⅓" thick). Deep-fry for 4 minutes, or until brown and crunchy on the outside.

4. Fill the pita rounds with falafel patties, tomato, onion, lettuce, cucumber slices, and yogurt.

Cayenne Choices

You can throw in a pinch of cayenne pepper to enhance the flavor or up to ½ teaspoon of it to add a hot punch.

RED BEANS AND RICE

Purists insist that this dish requires pickled pork. If you're not one of them, you can double the smoked sausage or substitute cooked pork.

Yields 6–8 servings

3 15-ounce cans kidney beans, rinsed and drained

2 cups water or chicken broth, or more as needed

1 medium yellow onion, diced

1 bunch green onions, cleaned and chopped

7 cloves garlic, minced

2 tablespoons dried parsley

1 stalk celery, diced

½ cup ketchup

1 green bell pepper, seeded and diced

1 tablespoon Worcestershire sauce

2 teaspoons hot sauce, or to taste

2 whole bay leaves

¼ teaspoon dried thyme

1 pound smoked sausage, sliced

1 pound Pickled Pork, cut into cubes (see recipe in sidebar)

Salt and freshly ground black pepper to taste

3–4 cups cooked rice

Add all of the ingredients except the cooked rice to a 4-quart Dutch oven or stockpot. Add additional water if needed to bring the liquid level to just above the other ingredients in the pot. Cover and simmer for 1 hour, stirring occasionally and checking to make sure the pan doesn't boil dry. Taste for seasoning; add salt and pepper, if needed. Serve over the cooked rice.

Pickled Pork

Add ¼ cup mustard seed, ½ tablespoon celery seeds, 1 tablespoon hot sauce, 2 cups white vinegar, ½ bay leaf, ½ tablespoon kosher salt, 6 peppercorns, and 3 smashed cloves of garlic to a nonreactive pan; boil for 3 minutes. Allow to cool, then pour over 1 pound of cooked cubed pork and cover. Pickled pork will keep in the refrigerator for up to 3 days.

CHICKEN AND GREEN BEAN CASSEROLE

This dish is also good if you substitute 1 cup of cooked wild rice for half of the cooked rice.

Yields 6 servings

2 tablespoons butter or vegetable oil

1 medium yellow onion, diced

3 cups cooked chicken, diced

2 14½-ounce cans green beans, drained and rinsed

1 8-ounce can water chestnuts, drained and chopped

1 4-ounce jar pimientos, chopped

1 10¾-ounce can condensed cream of celery soup

1 cup mayonnaise

2 cups cooked rice

4 ounces sharp Cheddar cheese, grated

Pinch salt

1. Preheat oven to 350°F.

2. Add the butter or oil to an ovenproof Dutch oven and bring it to temperature over medium heat. Add the onion; sauté for 5 minutes, or until translucent. Stir in the remaining ingredients and mix until thoroughly combined. Bake uncovered for 20–25 minutes, or until bubbly. Let stand for a few minutes before serving.

PRESSURE COOKER PORK AND BEANS

There's enough cooked pork in this recipe to serve this as an entrée rather than as a side dish. It goes well with cornbread.

Yields 6 servings

2 teaspoons paprika

¼ teaspoon salt

1 teaspoon garlic powder

¼ teaspoon ground black pepper

½ teaspoon onion powder

⅛ teaspoon cayenne

¼ teaspoon dried oregano

½ teaspoon dried thyme

2½ pounds pork shoulder, cut into 1½" pieces

1½ tablespoons vegetable oil

1 large yellow onion, diced

6 cups chicken broth or water

2 cups dried white beans, such as Great Northern or navy

½ pound salt pork or bacon, cut into pieces

1 15-ounce can diced tomatoes

4 cloves garlic, minced

½ cup packed light brown sugar

2 tablespoons whole-grain or Creole mustard

2 teaspoons chili powder

1 bay leaf

1. Add the paprika, salt, garlic powder, pepper, onion powder, cayenne, oregano, and ¼ teaspoon of the thyme to a gallon-size plastic bag; shake to mix. Add the pork pieces and shake the bag to season the meat on all sides. Add the oil to the pressure cooker and bring it to temperature over medium-high heat. Add the pork and stir-fry for about 2 minutes per side, or until it just begins to brown. Move the meat to a plate and set aside.

2. Add the onions to the cooker; reduce heat to medium and sauté for 2 minutes, or until tender. Add the broth or water. Remove any stones or impurities from the beans, and then stir them into the liquid in the cooker, scraping up any browned bits from the bottom of the pot and stirring to incorporate them into the mixture.

3. Lock the lid into place on the pressure cooker. Bring to high pressure. Lower the heat just enough to maintain high pressure and cook for 15 minutes. Turn off the burner and leave the pan in place for 10 minutes, or long enough to allow it to return to normal pressure. Once the pressure is released, carefully remove the lid to allow excess steam to escape.

4. Add the salt pork, tomatoes, garlic, sugar, mustard, chili powder, bay leaf, the remaining ¼ teaspoon thyme, and the reserved pork to the cooker; stir to combine. Lock the lid into place; bring the pressure cooker to high pressure. Maintain high pressure and cook for 15 minutes. Remove from the heat and let set for 10 minutes, or until the cooker returns to normal pressure. Once the pressure is completely released, remove the lid.

5. Check for seasoning and add salt and pepper, if needed. Remove and discard the bay leaf. Serve.

TOFU STEAK WITH MUSHROOMS

Tofu generally comes in 1-pound blocks. To prepare it for steaks, place it in the microwave for 1 minute. Drain off the water and cut the block into 4 even slices.

Yields 1 serving

2 tablespoons soy sauce

1 teaspoon toasted sesame oil

1 tablespoon rice wine vinegar

Several dashes hot sauce

¼ pound firm tofu steak, pressed

2 tablespoons peanut or olive oil

¼ cup mushrooms, sliced

¼ teaspoon salt

1 green scallion, thinly sliced

1. Combine the soy sauce, sesame oil, rice wine vinegar, and hot sauce in a small bowl. Place the drained tofu steak in the sauce and let it rest in the refrigerator for 1–24 hours.

2. Place a small skillet over medium heat. Once it is heated, add 1 tablespoon of the oil and the mushrooms. Sprinkle the salt over the mushrooms and toss to combine. Cook for 4 minutes.

3. Remove the mushrooms from the skillet and add the remaining oil. Remove the tofu from the marinade and place it in the skillet. Cook on each side for 2 minutes.

4. Return the mushrooms to the skillet. Pour the marinade over the steak and cook until the mushrooms have warmed and the sauce has reduced. Sprinkle with chopped scallion and serve while warm.

Tofu Requires Extreme Flavor

Tofu is very low in fat, very high in protein, but very bland by itself. Marinating firm tofu in a very flavorful sauce and then pan-frying is the fastest cooking technique. When trying to flavor tofu, use a more strongly flavored sauce than you would if using chicken. Many Asian bottled sauces are great as a tofu marinade.

RUSSIAN BEEF STROGANOFF WITH KASHA

Tastes vary, so have extra sour cream at the table for those who want it.

Yields 4–6 servings

1 14-ounce can reduced-sodium beef broth

¼ cup water

½ teaspoon salt

½ teaspoon freshly ground black pepper

4 tablespoons butter

1 cup kasha

1 large egg, beaten

2 large yellow onions, diced

2 pounds beef sirloin, trimmed of fat and cut into thin strips

8 ounces fresh button or cremini mushrooms, cleaned and sliced

Additional salt and freshly ground black pepper to taste

½ cup sour cream, plus extra for serving

Optional: fresh chopped dill to taste

1. In a 4-cup microwave-safe container, bring the broth, water, salt, pepper, and 2 tablespoons of the butter to a boil; microwave it on high for 2–3 minutes.

2. While the broth is coming to a boil, add the kasha and egg to a deep 3½-quart nonstick skillet or wok over medium-high heat. Use a nonstick-skillet-safe utensil to stir, flatten, and chop the kasha; do this until the egg is cooked, and then pour in the boiling broth. Reduce the heat to low, cover, and simmer for 10 minutes, or until the liquid is absorbed and the kernels are tender. Transfer the cooked kasha to a bowl; set aside and keep warm.

3. Wipe out the skillet or wok. Add the remaining 2 tablespoons butter and melt over medium-high heat. Add the onion and beef strips. Stir-fry until the onions are transparent and the beef is cooked and releasing its juices. Add the mushroom slices and stir-fry to wilt them. Taste for seasoning and add salt and pepper, if desired. Remove from the heat and stir in the sour cream. Serve ladled over a serving of kasha, or mix the kasha into the stroganoff if you prefer. Garnish with fresh dill, if desired.

CASSOULET

This dish is traditionally baked in layers—beans and vegetables, tomato sauce, and then some of the meat; the layers are repeated until all ingredients are used up. This version mixes everything together to keep the cooking to one pot.

Yields 12 or more servings

2 pounds white beans

Water as needed

¼ pound salt pork or bacon, diced

2 tablespoons butter

2 tablespoons extra-virgin olive oil

8 chicken thighs

2 pounds pork shoulder roast, trimmed of fat and cut into bite-size pieces

1 large yellow onion, diced

2 large carrots, peeled and shredded

2 stalks celery, finely diced

6 cloves garlic, minced

¼ pound Polish sausage, sliced

4 whole cloves

2 small yellow onions, peeled

1 ham bone or 2 smoked ham hocks

1 lamb shank

1 1-pound bag baby carrots

4 cups chicken broth

10 cups water, or as needed

1 cup tomato purée

Salt and freshly ground pepper to taste

1. Add the beans to a large ovenproof Dutch oven or stockpot. Add enough water to cover the beans; cover the pan and let soak overnight.

2. Preheat the oven to 350°F. Drain the beans in a colander and set aside. Wipe out the pan. Add the salt pork or bacon, butter, and oil to the pan; cook over medium heat until the butter is melted. Stir to entirely coat the bottom of the pan. Remove from the heat. Line the chicken pieces across the bottom of the pan, skin side down. Add the pork, diced onion, carrot, celery, garlic, and Polish sausage in layers. Bake for 45 minutes to brown the meat.

3. Remove the pan from the oven. Stick two cloves into each of the onions. Add the beans, onions, ham bone or ham hocks, lamb shank, baby carrots, chicken broth, and enough of the water to cover the beans. Bring to a simmer; cover and cook for 1½ hours, stirring occasionally and adding more water, if necessary. Remove the chicken, ham bone or ham hocks, and lamb shank from the pot and set aside to cool.

4. Stir in the tomato purée, salt, and pepper. Cover and simmer for 30 minutes. Remove the chicken, ham, and lamb from the bones; discard any skin, fat, or bones. Stir the meat into the beans, adding more water if needed. Cover and bake for 1½ hours, checking every 30 minutes to make sure more water isn't needed.

Rule of Thumb: Cooking Beans

You can usually count on using 7 cups of liquid for each pound of beans. The amount you use can vary according to how hot you keep the simmering liquid and how many times you remove the lid to stir the beans.

BARLEY AND MUSHROOM CASSEROLE

This is a delicious way to use leftover chicken. Most other seasonings go well with the basil and parsley, but you can adjust the seasoning in this recipe according to how the chicken was cooked, if necessary.

Yields 8 servings

6 tablespoons butter

1 large carrot, peeled and shredded

1 stalk celery, finely diced

2 medium yellow onions, diced

2 cloves garlic, minced

1 pound button or cremini mushrooms, cleaned and sliced

1 cup pearl barley

½ tablespoon dried basil

½ tablespoon dried parsley

3 cups chicken broth

2 cups cooked chicken, shredded or diced

Salt and freshly ground black pepper to taste

1. Preheat oven to 375°F.

2. Melt the butter in an ovenproof 4-quart Dutch oven over medium heat. Add the carrot and celery; sauté for 3–5 minutes, or until soft. Add the onion and sauté until transparent. Add the garlic and sauté for an additional 30 seconds. Add the mushroom slices; sauté for 5 minutes or until they begin to brown. Stir in the barley, basil, parsley, broth, chicken, salt, and pepper; bring to a boil. Remove from the heat, cover, and bake for 50 minutes, or until the barley is tender. Serve hot.

QUINOA PILAF

If you can't find quinoa at your local grocery store, you can substitute couscous. Quinoa is a grain, but couscous, like pasta, is made from semolina flour. Follow the cooking times on the package when following this recipe.

Yields 2 servings

1 tablespoon olive oil

½ small onion, chopped

¼ teaspoon ground cinnamon

½ teaspoon ground coriander

½ teaspoon ground turmeric

Pinch red chili flakes

1 cup vegetable broth

1 small garlic clove, minced

½ cup quinoa

½ can red kidney beans, rinsed and drained

1 Roma tomato, chopped

6 olives, chopped

2 tablespoons dried currants or cranberries

1. Place a skillet over medium heat and when warm add the olive oil and onion. Cook for 5–7 minutes, stirring occasionally. The onion should be soft and just starting to turn golden. Add the cinnamon, coriander, turmeric, and chili flakes. Stir continually for 1 minute and then add the vegetable broth.

2. Use your spatula to loosen any spices or onion that may have stuck to the skillet. Add the garlic, quinoa, and beans. Reduce the heat to low, cover the skillet, and simmer for 15 minutes. The water should be mostly absorbed.

3. Add the tomato, olives, and dried fruit. Stir and cook for 5 more minutes, or until the water is evaporated. Fluff with a fork and serve immediately.

Quinoa: Superfood

Quinoa is a grainlike crop from the Andes mountains in South America. Cultivated by the Incas, it was called the "mother of all grains" and is very high in protein and fiber. Quinoa grows with an outer coating, but most quinoa sold in America has this coating removed and is ready to use.

BAKED BARLEY RISOTTO WITH MUSHROOMS, ONIONS, AND CARROTS

Most risotto is made using a starchy, short-grain Italian rice. Even though this dish takes longer to cook than traditional risotto, it requires less hands-on time.

Yields 6–8 servings

1 tablespoon olive oil

3 carrots, chopped

1 medium yellow onion, chopped

8 ounces white mushrooms, sliced

½ cup white wine or vermouth

1½ teaspoons dried thyme

2 cups barley

4 cups chicken or vegetable broth

3 tablespoons fresh parsley

½ cup grated Parmesan cheese

Salt to taste

Pepper to taste

1. Preheat oven to 350°F. Place a Dutch oven over medium heat and add the oil, carrots, and onion once heated. Stir frequently and cook until the onion is brown and the carrots are soft. Add the mushrooms and sauté for 10 minutes.

2. Increase the heat slightly and add the wine, thyme, and barley. Stir continually until the wine is evaporated, 3–4 minutes. Add the broth and bring to a boil.

3. Turn off the heat and cover. Cook in the middle of the oven for 50–60 minutes. Stir frequently until the liquid is absorbed and the barley is tender. Stir in the parsley and cheese. Taste before adding salt and pepper.

Barley Should Not Be Ignored

Barley has been cultivated for thousands of years. Half of the barley grown in the United States is used for animal feed, and most of the rest is used for making beer or whiskey. It contains all 8 essential amino acids, is able to maintain blood sugar levels for up to 10 hours, and has a fairly high concentration of fiber and protein.

CHAPTER 6

POULTRY

CHICKEN TORTELLINI AND BROCCOLI CASSEROLE

To turn this into a Southwestern casserole, substitute ground cumin and a pinch of cayenne pepper for the dried parsley and add a layer of crushed tortilla chips to the top of the casserole before you add the Colby cheese.

Yields 8 servings

1 9-ounce package cheese tortellini

3 tablespoons extra-virgin olive oil

2 cups broccoli florets

1 medium yellow onion, diced

1 red bell pepper, seeded and diced

3 tablespoons all-purpose flour

¾ cup chicken broth

¾ cup milk

1 teaspoon dried parsley

4 cups cooked chicken, diced

6 ounces Monterey jack cheese, grated

4 ounces Colby cheese, grated

1. Preheat oven to 325°F.

2. In an ovenproof Dutch oven, cook the tortellini according to package directions; drain and keep warm.

3. Wipe out the Dutch oven. Add the oil and bring it to temperature over medium-high heat. Add the broccoli, onion, and bell pepper and stir-fry for about 3 minutes, or until crisp-tender. Remove the broccoli from the skillet; set it aside with the cooked tortellini and keep warm. Reduce the heat to low and whisk the flour into the oil and remaining vegetables in the pan, stirring constantly, until smooth.

4. Stir in the broth, milk, and parsley. Bring to a boil over medium heat, stirring constantly; remove from heat. Stir in the chicken, Monterey jack cheese, tortellini, and broccoli. Bake uncovered for 30 minutes, or until bubbly. Sprinkle the Colby cheese over the top of the casserole; return to the oven and bake for 10 minutes, or until the cheese topping is melted.

Grated Cheese

Each ounce of soft cheese like Cheddar or Colby equals ¼ cup of grated cheese. Keep this in mind when you go to the grocery store and pick up the bags of preshredded cheese. They'll tell you the weight but not the measurement in cups, so it's up to you to remember that part.

STUFFED CHICKEN BREAST FLORENTINE

If your family isn't fond of spinach, you can replace it with chopped, steamed broccoli florets. Also, remember to take the saltiness of the cheese into consideration when you season the dish.

Yields 8 servings

8 boneless, skinless chicken breasts

3 tablespoons extra-virgin olive oil

8 ounces button mushrooms, cleaned and sliced

2 cloves garlic, minced

3 tablespoons chopped shallots

2 10-ounce packages frozen spinach, thawed and squeezed dry

4 large eggs, beaten

3 cups bread crumbs

4 ounces Swiss or mozzarella cheese, shredded

2 tablespoons dried parsley

1 cup chicken broth

¼ pound deli ham, thinly sliced

Salt and freshly ground black pepper to taste

4 tablespoons butter

1. Preheat oven to 350°F.

2. Place each chicken breast between 2 pieces of plastic wrap; pound until about ½" thick. Brush the bottom of a 9" × 13" nonstick baking pan with 1 tablespoon of the oil. Arrange half of the chicken breasts over the bottom of the pan.

3. Add the mushrooms, garlic, and shallots to a large microwave-safe bowl. Toss with the remaining 2 tablespoons oil. Cover and microwave on high for 1 minute; stir. Cover and microwave for 1 minute. Let cool and then stir in the spinach. Add the eggs, 2 cups bread crumbs, cheese, parsley, and chicken broth; stir to combine.

4. Arrange half of the deli ham over the top of the chicken breasts in the pan. Spread the spinach mixture over the top of the ham, then top with the remaining ham. Place the remaining chicken breasts over the top of the ham. Season with salt and pepper. Tightly cover the pan with foil. Bake for 45 minutes.

5. Melt the butter and mix it with the remaining 1 cup of bread crumbs. Remove the foil from the pan and sprinkle the buttered bread crumbs over the top of the chicken. Return to the oven and bake uncovered for 15 minutes, or until the bread crumbs are golden brown and the chicken breasts are cooked through. Let set for 10 minutes, then cut into 8 equal pieces and serve.

CHICKEN PAPRIKASH MEDLEY

The chopped red bell pepper usually found in broccoli stir-fry mix gives this dish an unexpected flavor; however, if you don't like the crunch added by the water chestnuts, you can substitute a 1-pound bag of broccoli florets or broccoli and cauliflower mix.

Yields 8 servings

4 cups cooked egg noodles or spaetzle

1 tablespoon butter

1 tablespoon extra-virgin olive oil

1 large yellow onion, diced

1½ pounds boneless, skinless chicken breasts

4 cloves garlic, minced

Salt and freshly ground pepper to taste

4 tablespoons Hungarian paprika

4 cups chicken broth

2 tablespoons all-purpose flour

1 1-pound frozen broccoli stir-fry mix, thawed

16 ounces sour cream

1. In a Dutch oven, cook the noodles or spaetzle according to the package directions; drain. Transfer to a serving platter, cover, and keep warm.

2. Wipe out the Dutch oven, then add the butter and oil; bring to temperature over medium-high heat. Add the onion and sauté for 3 minutes. Cut the chicken breasts into bite-size pieces. Add the chicken to the Dutch oven and stir-fry for 5 minutes. Stir in the garlic, salt, pepper, 3 tablespoons of the paprika, and 3½ cups of the chicken broth; cover the pan. While the chicken broth comes to a boil, mix the remaining ½ cup of chicken broth with the flour. Strain out any lumps, and then whisk the broth mixture into the boiling broth. Boil for 3 minutes. Stir in the broccoli stir-fry mix; lower the temperature, cover, and simmer for 5 minutes.

3. Remove the pan from the burner and stir in the sour cream. Pour the chicken and vegetable mixture over the noodles or spaetzle. Sprinkle the remaining tablespoon of paprika over the top. Serve immediately.

Thickening or Thinning

The temperature at which you simmer the paprikash will affect how thick or thin the sauce gets. The sour cream added at the end of the cooking time will also thicken the sauce. If the sauce is too thin, add more sour cream. If it's too thick, slowly whisk in some additional chicken broth, milk, or water.

CHICKEN SIMMERED WITH OLIVES

If you prefer, you can substitute a cut-up 3½-pound whole chicken for the chicken thighs. When you season the dish, keep in mind that the olives and the preserved lemon will affect the saltiness.

Yields 4 servings

2 tablespoons extra-virgin olive oil

8 small chicken thighs

1 large yellow onion, diced

3 cloves garlic, minced

1 teaspoon ground ginger

½ teaspoon turmeric

½ teaspoon paprika

Salt to taste

½ teaspoon freshly ground black pepper

1 15-ounce can diced tomatoes

1 preserved lemon, rinsed and diced (see recipe in sidebar)

1 teaspoon dried parsley

1 teaspoon dried coriander

1 7½-ounce jar pimiento-stuffed olives, drained

2 cups cooked couscous or rice

1. Add the oil to a deep 3½-quart nonstick skillet and bring to temperature over medium heat. Brown the chicken, frying it for about 5 minutes on each side. Remove the chicken from the pan and keep warm. Add the onions and sauté until transparent. Add the garlic, ginger, turmeric, paprika, salt, and pepper; stir into the onions and sauté for 1 minute.

2. Add the chicken back to the pan; pour the tomatoes over the chicken and sprinkle the lemon over the tomatoes. Cover, reduce heat, and simmer for 30 minutes, or until the chicken is tender. Sprinkle the parsley, coriander, and olives over the top; cover and cook for an additional 5 minutes. Serve warm over cooked couscous or rice.

Preserved Lemons

To make preserved lemons, cut 5 lemons into partial quarters, leaving them attached at one end; rub kosher salt over the outside and cut sides of the lemons, and then pack them tightly in a sterilized 1-quart glass jar. Add 2 tablespoons kosher salt and enough lemon juice to cover the lemons. Seal and let set at room temperature for 14 days, inverting the jar once a day to mix. Store indefinitely in the refrigerator.

ITALIAN STUFFED CHICKEN

Serve this chicken with a tossed salad dressed with Italian dressing. If you don't have anchovies or capers on hand, substitute Italian seasoning to season the potato mixture and use it instead of the rosemary to season the outside of the chicken.

Yields 4 servings

4 medium russet potatoes, diced

10 pimiento-stuffed green olives, chopped

1 tablespoon dried parsley

2 cloves garlic, minced

Optional: 3 canned flat anchovies, mashed

1 tablespoon capers, rinsed and chopped

3 tablespoons olive oil

Salt and freshly ground black pepper to taste

1 3-pound chicken

1 tablespoon butter, melted

Dried rosemary to taste

1. Preheat oven to 375°F.

2. Add the potatoes to a microwave-safe bowl; cover and microwave on high for 5 minutes. Add the olives, parsley, garlic, anchovies, capers, olive oil, salt, and pepper to the potatoes and stir to combine.

3. Rinse the chicken inside and out. Dry the chicken with paper towels, then stuff the chicken with the hot potato mixture. Place the chicken on a rack in a roasting pan.

4. Brush the outside of the chicken with the melted butter. Season with salt and pepper to taste. Sprinkle the rosemary over the chicken.

5. Bake for 80–90 minutes. Remove from the oven and let rest for 10 minutes. Cut into quarters and serve with the potato stuffing.

Improvised Roasting Rack

If your roasting pan doesn't have a removable rack, arrange stalks of celery, curved side down, over the bottom of the pan and place the meat on top of the celery. This adds enough height to allow some of the fat to drain away from the meat.

CHICKEN DIVAN

This is a versatile casserole. You can stretch it to 8 servings by adding 1–2 cups of cooked diced potatoes. You can also substitute American, Cheddar, or Swiss cheese for the Parmigiano-Reggiano.

Yields 6 servings

¼ cup butter

¼ cup all-purpose flour

1 cup chicken broth

1 cup milk

Salt and freshly ground black pepper to taste

⅛ teaspoon ground nutmeg

½ cup freshly grated Parmigiano-Reggiano

3 tablespoons dry sherry

3 cups cooked chicken, cut into bite-sized pieces

1 1-pound bag broccoli florets, thawed

1 cup slivered almonds

½ cup heavy cream

Preheat oven to 350°F. Melt the butter over medium heat in a 2-quart or larger ovenproof skillet or Dutch oven. Add the flour and cook, stirring constantly, for 1 minute. Gradually whisk in the broth and milk; cook for 3 minutes, or until it begins to thicken. Stir in salt, pepper, nutmeg, ¼ cup of the cheese, and sherry; cook until the cheese melts. Remove from the heat and stir in the chicken, broccoli, half of the almonds, and the cream. Sprinkle the remaining almonds and cheese over the top. Bake uncovered for 35 minutes, or until bubbly and golden brown.

Different Chicken Divan

For a lighter sauce, whip the cream until it reaches soft peaks and then fold it into the other Chicken Divan ingredients before you top the casserole with the remaining almonds and cheese. If you don't have heavy cream on hand, you can substitute sour cream or melt 4 ounces of cream cheese into the sauce before you add the chicken.

CHICKEN BRAISED WITH SWEET PEPPERS

If you have fresh Roma tomatoes on hand, you can substitute 2 cups of diced fresh tomatoes for the canned tomatoes called for in this recipe.

Yields 4 servings

1 tablespoon extra-virgin olive or vegetable oil

8 small chicken thighs, skin removed

⅔ cup chicken broth

¼ cup dry white wine or chicken broth

2 cloves garlic, minced

¼ teaspoon dried rosemary, crushed

Salt to taste

¼ teaspoon freshly ground black pepper

1 15-ounce can diced tomatoes

1 small yellow sweet pepper, cut into ½" strips

1 small green sweet pepper, cut into ½" strips

1 small red sweet pepper, cut into ½" strips

8 ounces fresh button mushrooms, cleaned and sliced

2 tablespoons cornstarch

2 tablespoons cold water

2 cups hot cooked noodles or rice

1. Add the oil to a deep 3½-quart nonstick skillet and bring to temperature over medium heat. Add the chicken; fry for about 5 minutes, turning the chicken so it browns evenly. Drain and discard any excess fat. Add the broth, wine, garlic, rosemary, salt, and black pepper to the skillet. Bring to a boil; reduce heat, cover, and simmer for 20 minutes.

2. Add the tomatoes, sweet peppers, and mushrooms to the skillet. Cover and simmer for another 15 minutes, or until the chicken is tender and no longer pink. Transfer the chicken to a serving dish; cover with foil and keep warm.

3. Add the cornstarch and water to a small bowl; stir to combine. Mix in 1 or 2 tablespoons of the hot broth to thin the cornstarch mixture and then gently stir the mixture into the broth and vegetables. Continue to cook for 3 minutes, or until the sauce is thickened and has lost its raw cornstarch flavor. Taste for seasoning and add salt and pepper if needed. Spoon the vegetables and sauce around chicken. Serve with noodles or rice.

CHICKEN DINNER OLÉ

This is a quick and easy meal that's great when served with a tossed salad and some baked corn tortilla chips.

Yields 6 servings

3–3½ pounds chicken pieces, skin removed

¼ cup all-purpose flour

½ teaspoon salt

¼ teaspoon cayenne

2 tablespoons extra-virgin olive oil

1 28-ounce can diced Italian-style tomatoes

4 medium russet potatoes, peeled and diced

1 medium yellow onion, sliced

½ cup pitted ripe olives, cut in half

½ cup dry red wine

Optional: 2 tablespoons capers

1 teaspoon dried basil, crushed

½ teaspoon dried oregano, crushed

2 cloves garlic, minced

1 tablespoon cold water

2 teaspoons cornstarch

1. Rinse and dry the chicken pieces. Add the flour, salt, cayenne, and chicken pieces to a gallon-size food storage bag; seal and shake to coat. Bring the oil to temperature over medium heat in a 4-quart Dutch oven. Arrange the chicken pieces in a single layer in the pan and fry for 10 minutes, turning the pieces to brown them evenly.

2. Add the undrained tomatoes, potatoes, onion, olives, wine, capers (if using), basil, oregano, and garlic to the pan. Bring to a boil; reduce the heat, cover, and simmer for 35–45 minutes, or until chicken is tender and no longer pink. Remove the chicken to a serving dish; cover and keep warm.

3. Add the water and cornstarch to a small bowl; stir to combine. Stir the cornstarch mixture in the contents remaining in the pan; cook, stirring gently, for 3 minutes, or until the pan juices are thickened and the cornstarch taste is cooked out. Taste for seasoning and add additional salt if needed. Pour the thickened mixture over the chicken.

CHICKEN AND VEGETABLE STIR-FRY

Add some extra punch to this dish by topping it with toasted sesame seeds, slivered almonds, or cashews.

Yields 4 servings

½ cup water

2 tablespoons soy sauce

2 tablespoons hoisin sauce

2 teaspoons cornstarch

1 teaspoon grated fresh ginger

1 teaspoon toasted sesame oil

2 tablespoons peanut oil

12 ounces skinless, boneless chicken, cut into bite-size pieces

1 1-pound frozen broccoli stir-fry mix, thawed

1 yellow sweet pepper, seeded and cut into strips

2 cups chow mein noodles or hot cooked rice

1. In a small bowl, make the sauce by stirring together the water, soy sauce, hoisin sauce, cornstarch, ginger, and sesame oil. Set aside.

2. Add the peanut oil to a wok or large skillet and bring to temperature over medium-high heat. Add the chicken pieces and stir-fry for 5 minutes, or until the chicken is cooked through. Push the chicken to the edges of the pan; add the stir-fry mix and pepper strips and stir-fry for 3 minutes, or until the vegetables are crisp-tender.

3. Push the chicken and vegetables away from the center of pan. Pour the sauce mixture into the center of pan; cook and stir until thickened and bubbly. Stir the sauce into the chicken and vegetables. Serve over chow mein noodles or rice.

SLOW-COOKED CHICKEN CACCIATORE

This adaptation of an Italian classic recipe has all of the necessary goodies to become one of your family's favorite meals.

Yields 6 servings

8 ounces fresh button or cremini mushrooms, cleaned and sliced

3 stalks celery, sliced

3 large carrots, peeled and diced

2 medium yellow onions, peeled and sliced

1 large green bell pepper, cut into strips

4 cloves garlic, minced

12 skinless chicken thighs or drumsticks

½ cup chicken broth

¼ cup dry white wine

2 tablespoons quick-cooking tapioca

1 teaspoon granulated sugar

1 teaspoon dried oregano, crushed

2 bay leaves

½ teaspoon salt

¼ teaspoon freshly ground black pepper

1 14½-ounce can diced tomatoes

⅓ cup tomato paste

Hot cooked pasta or rice

1. Add the mushrooms, celery, carrot, onions, sweet pepper, and garlic to a 5- or 6-quart slow cooker. Place chicken on top of vegetables. Mix the broth, wine, tapioca, sugar, oregano, bay leaves, salt, and pepper in a small bowl; pour over chicken. Cover and cook on low for 6–7 hours, or until the chicken is cooked through.

2. Remove and discard bay leaves. Remove the chicken to a serving platter; cover and keep warm. Turn the slow cooker to the high setting. Stir in the undrained tomatoes and the tomato paste. Cover and cook for 15 minutes. Pour the resulting sauce over the chicken. Serve with cooked pasta or rice.

Baked Long-Grain White Rice

In an ovenproof 8-cup saucepan or skillet, sauté 1 medium diced onion in 2 tablespoons of butter. Add 1 cup of rinsed long-grain white rice and 2 cups of chicken broth. Bring to a boil, cover, and then bake at 325°F for 20 minutes. Makes about 3½ cups cooked rice.

SLOW-COOKED CHICKEN WITH CREAMY LEMON SAUCE

For this meal, you simply add the ingredients to your slow cooker. Later in the day, all you have to do is finish the sauce, and you have meat, potatoes, and vegetables all ready to serve and eat.

Yields 4 servings

1 1-pound bag frozen cut green beans, thawed

1 small yellow onion, cut into thin wedges

4 boneless, skinless chicken breast halves

4 medium russet potatoes, peeled and quartered

2 cloves garlic, minced

¼ teaspoon freshly ground black pepper

1 cup chicken broth

4 ounces cream cheese, cut into cubes

1 teaspoon freshly grated lemon peel

Optional: lemon peel strips

1. Place the green beans and onion in a 3-quart or larger slow cooker. Arrange the chicken and potatoes over the vegetables. Sprinkle with the garlic and pepper. Pour the broth over the top. Cover and cook on low for 5 or more hours, or until the chicken is cooked through and moist.

2. Transfer the chicken and vegetables to 4 serving plates or a serving platter; cover to keep warm.

3. To make the sauce, add the cream cheese cubes and grated lemon peel to the broth in the slow cooker. Stir until the cheese melts into the sauce. Pour the sauce over the chicken and vegetables. Garnish with lemon peel strips if desired.

The World's Easiest Vegetable Dish

When they're prepared correctly, you'd swear that freeze-dried green beans taste as good as fresh. About 5–10 minutes before you plan to serve them, pour boiling water over the freeze-dried green beans so that they're completely submerged. When you're ready to serve them, drain and toss the green beans with a little fresh lemon juice, extra-virgin olive oil, salt, and freshly ground black pepper.

CHICKEN DINNER BAKED IN ITS OWN GRAVY

Serve this dinner with a tossed salad or Cucumber Salad (see Hungarian Goulash recipe in Chapter 4).

Yields 6 servings

12 small chicken thighs

¼ cup all-purpose flour

¼ cup butter, melted

6 medium russet potatoes, scrubbed and pierced with a fork

1 cup undiluted evaporated milk

1 10¾-ounce cream of mushroom soup

4 ounces American cheese, grated

Salt and freshly ground black pepper to taste

1 1-pound bag frozen baby peas and pearl onions, thawed

4 ounces button mushrooms, cleaned and sliced

Paprika, as needed

1. Preheat oven to 425°F.

2. Coat the chicken in the flour and arrange, skin side down, in the melted butter in a 9" × 13" nonstick baking pan. Add the potatoes to the pan. Bake for 30 minutes. Use tongs to turn the chicken, reduce the oven temperature to 325°F, and bake for an additional 30 minutes.

3. Add the evaporated milk, soup, cheese, salt, and pepper to a bowl; stir to mix. Remove the potatoes from the baking pan, wrap in foil, and return to the oven. Drain any excess fat from the chicken and discard. Arrange the peas and onions over the chicken, then top with the mushrooms. Evenly pour the evaporated milk mixture over the mushrooms. Sprinkle with paprika. Cover the baking pan with foil, return to the oven, and bake for 20 minutes.

Serving Suggestion

If you want to avoid adding extra butter to the baked potatoes you serve with this dish, put each potato on a serving plate, cut it in half lengthwise, and lightly mash the pulp. Spoon the vegetable-gravy mixture over the potato and place a chicken thigh over the top of each half.

CURRIED CHICKEN WITH AVOCADO

Serve this dish with a Cucumber Salad with Yogurt (see Indian Chicken Vindaloo recipe in this chapter) and pita, Indian, or Euphrates bread.

Yields 6 servings

¼ cup butter

1 pound boneless, skinless chicken breasts, cut into bite-size pieces

1 small yellow onion, diced

Salt and freshly ground black pepper to taste

1 Golden Delicious apple, peeled, cored, and thinly sliced

1 clove garlic, minced

1 tablespoon curry powder

¼ cup all-purpose flour

1 cup heavy or light cream

1 cup chicken broth

3 large avocados, peeled, pitted, and halved

3 cups cooked rice

Melt the butter and bring it to temperature in a nonstick skillet over medium heat. Add the chicken, onion, salt, and pepper; sauté until the chicken is cooked through. Add the apple, garlic, and curry powder; sauté for 2 minutes. Stir in the flour; whisk the cream and then the broth into the chicken mixture. Bring to a boil and boil for 2 minutes. To serve, place an avocado half on top of ½ cup of the cooked rice and spoon the hot chicken curry over the avocado.

Optional Condiments

This dish is good served with chopped hard-boiled egg, chopped peanuts, chutney, coconut, crumbled crisp bacon, preserved ginger, raisins, and sweet pickles as condiments. Try something new or just use whatever you have in your pantry.

CHICKEN AND DRESSING

Serving amounts will depend on the size of the chickens and whether or not you leave the crusts on the bread. Round out this meal with a steamed vegetable and a salad.

Yields 4–8 servings

2 tablespoons butter

3 stalks celery, diced

1 medium yellow onion, diced

1 large carrot, peeled and shredded

1 cup chicken broth

1 loaf white bread, torn into bite-size pieces

5 large eggs

2 small chickens, halved

Salt and freshly ground black pepper to taste

4 medium russet potatoes, scrubbed and halved

1. Preheat oven to 350°F.

2. Add 1 tablespoon of the butter and the celery to a microwave-safe bowl; cover and microwave on high for 1 minute. Stir in the onion; cover and microwave for 1 minute. Stir in the carrot; cover and microwave for 1 minute, or until the onion is transparent. Stir in the chicken broth; set aside to cool.

3. Add the torn bread pieces to a 9" × 13" nonstick baking pan. Whisk the eggs into the cooled broth mixture and pour over the bread; stir, if necessary, to coat all of the bread pieces. Arrange the chicken halves side by side over the bread mixture. Rub the remaining tablespoon of butter over the outside of the chicken halves. Salt and pepper to taste. Arrange the potato halves around the chicken. Bake for 1 hour, or until chicken is cooked through and the potatoes are tender.

Dressing Down the Dressing

While dressing is traditionally made with day-old or dried bread, the Chicken and Dressing recipe will work with fresh bread, too; just keep in mind that if the bread is fresh, it'll take longer for the bread to absorb the broth-egg mixture you pour over it. It calls for a standard loaf of white bread, but it's good when made with a rich sweet bread like challah.

ROTISSERIE CHICKEN WITH BALSAMIC VINEGAR–ROASTED VEGETABLES

The directions for this recipe are based on making the chicken in a Cuisinart Brick Oven Premier. Adjust the instructions according to those recommended for the rotisserie unit you'll be using.

Yields 6 servings

1 3- to 4-pound chicken

1 medium yellow onion, quartered

2 cloves garlic, smashed

3 tablespoons extra-virgin olive oil

3 tablespoons butter, melted

⅓ cup balsamic vinegar

2 cloves garlic, minced

Salt and freshly ground black pepper to taste

1½ pounds fresh Brussels sprouts

1 pound fingerling potatoes, scrubbed

1½ pounds pearl onions, peeled

1. Preheat oven to 400°F. Cover a baking pan with foil. Place the pan in the bottom back position in the oven so that it will catch any juices from the chicken.

2. Rinse the inside and outside of the chicken and pat it dry. Stuff the chicken with the yellow onion and smashed garlic cloves. To truss the chicken, start by cutting a heavy cotton string or kitchen twine to five times the length of the chicken. Place the middle section of the string under the tail and wrap the tail. Next, wrap the ends of the string around the ends of each drumstick. Pull the string to draw the legs together, crossing the strings over one another to secure the legs in this position. Turn the chicken over. Tie the string across the wings to hold them in place. Cut off and discard any excess string.

3. Add the oil, butter, vinegar, minced garlic, salt, and pepper to a bowl and mix well. Rub 2 tablespoons of the mixture over the outside of the chicken. Insert the rotisserie skewer through the chicken; secure the forks with the rotisserie screws to stabilize the chicken and place the rotisserie spit into the oven's spit support and socket. Turn the oven to the rotisserie setting. Roast for 45 minutes.

4. Cut off the brown ends of the Brussels sprouts and pull off any yellow outer leaves. Put the Brussels sprouts, potatoes, peeled pearl onions, and the remaining vinegar-oil mixture in a large plastic bag; secure and shake to coat the vegetables. Pour them onto the pan under the chicken and roast for another 30 minutes. Open the oven door and roast for another 15 minutes to crisp the chicken skin.

5. To serve, drain and discard the excess fat from the potatoes and vegetables. Arrange the potatoes and vegetables on a serving platter, then place the chicken in the center of the platter. Cover with foil and let rest for 10 minutes before carving.

HERB-ROASTED ROTISSERIE CHICKEN WITH OVEN-ROASTED ROOT VEGETABLES

For a simpler meal, pick up a lemon-pepper rotisserie chicken at the supermarket. Roast the potatoes and vegetables for 45 minutes, placing the chicken in the oven with them for the last 15 minutes to heat it through.

Yields 4 servings

1 3-pound chicken

2 lemons

2 cloves garlic, smashed

2 tablespoons extra-virgin olive oil

1 teaspoon dried basil

1 teaspoon dried thyme

1 teaspoon dried parsley

2 cloves garlic, minced

Salt and pepper to taste

¼ pound baby turnips, peeled and stem ends trimmed

¼ pound baby red carrots, peeled and stem ends trimmed

¼ pound orange carrots, peeled and stem ends trimmed

¼ pound baby golden beets, peeled and stem ends trimmed

¼ pound baby beets, peeled and stem ends trimmed

¼ pound fingerling potatoes, scrubbed and halved

1. Set oven temperature at 400°F.

2. Rinse the inside and outside of the chicken and pat it dry. Halve 1 lemon; stuff the chicken with the lemon halves and smashed garlic cloves. To truss the chicken, start by cutting a heavy cotton string or kitchen twine to five times the length of the chicken. Place the middle section of the string under the tail and wrap the tail. Next, wrap the ends of the string around the ends of each drumstick. Pull the string to draw the legs together, crossing the strings over one another to secure the legs in this position. Turn the chicken over. Tie the string across the wings to hold them in place. Cut off and discard any excess string.

3. Juice the remaining lemon and add to a large bowl with the oil, basil, thyme, parsley, minced garlic, salt, and pepper; mix well. Rub 2 tablespoons of the mixture over the outside of the chicken. Insert the rotisserie skewer through the chicken; secure the forks with the rotisserie screws to stabilize the chicken and place the rotisserie spit in the oven's spit support and socket. Cover the baking pan with foil. Place the pan in the bottom back position in the oven. Turn the oven to the rotisserie setting. Roast for 45 minutes.

4. Add the turnips, carrots, beets, and potatoes to the bowl and toss to coat in the herb-oil mixture. Pour them onto the pan under the chicken and roast for another 30 minutes. Open the oven door and roast for another 15 minutes to crisp the chicken skin.

5. To serve, drain and discard the excess fat from the potatoes and vegetables. Arrange the potatoes and vegetables on a serving platter, and place the chicken on the center of the platter. Cover with foil and let rest for 10 minutes before carving.

FUSION STIR-FRY

The steak sauce adds another flavor dimension to this stir-fry, and mixing in cheese tortellini replaces the need for cooked rice or chow mein noodles.

Yields 4 servings

1 3-pound lemon-pepper rotisserie chicken

½ cup water

2 tablespoons soy sauce

2 tablespoons hoisin sauce

2 teaspoons cornstarch

1 teaspoon grated fresh ginger

2 teaspoons steak sauce

Optional: 1 teaspoon honey

1 teaspoon toasted sesame oil

1 12-ounce package frozen cheese tortellini

1 tablespoon peanut oil

1 1-pound frozen broccoli stir-fry mix, thawed

1 red sweet pepper, seeded and cut into strips

1. Remove and discard the skin from the chicken; remove the meat from the bones and shred it. In a small bowl, make the sauce by stirring together the water, soy sauce, hoisin sauce, cornstarch, ginger, steak sauce, honey (if using), and sesame oil. Set aside.

2. Cook the tortellini according to the package directions; drain and keep warm.

3. Add the peanut oil to a wok or large skillet and bring to temperature over medium-high heat. Add the stir-fry mix and red peppers and stir-fry for 3 minutes, or until the vegetables are crisp-tender. Stir in the shredded chicken; stir-fry for 2 minutes, or until the chicken is heated through.

4. Push the chicken and vegetables away from the center of pan. Pour the sauce mixture into the center of pan; cook and stir until thickened and bubbly. Stir the sauce into the chicken and vegetables. Add the tortellini and toss to combine.

OPEN-FACE CHICKEN AND SAUTÉED PEPPER SANDWICHES

Sweet red bell peppers are high in vitamin C, so this recipe gives you an inexpensive and healthful way to stretch a rotisserie chicken to feed a crowd. As a bonus, the sandwich topping could just as easily be tossed with pasta or used to top salad greens.

Yields 8 servings

1 3-pound rotisserie chicken

3 tablespoons extra-virgin olive oil

2 large red bell peppers, seeded and cut into thin strips

2 large orange or yellow bell peppers, seeded and cut into thin strips

2 large green bell peppers, seeded and cut into thin strips

1 large yellow onion, thinly sliced

3 cloves garlic, minced

1 teaspoon dried oregano, crushed

1 teaspoon dried rosemary, chopped

1 tablespoon dried parsley

½ cup dry red wine or ⅓ cup chicken broth and 2 tablespoons balsamic vinegar

Salt and freshly ground black pepper to taste

8 slices bread, toasted

1. Remove and discard the skin from the chicken; remove the meat from the bones and shred it.

2. Bring the oil to temperature in a large nonstick skillet. Add the peppers; sauté for 3 minutes. Add the onion; sauté for 5 minutes, or until the onion is transparent. Stir in the garlic, oregano, rosemary, and parsley. Add the wine or broth and vinegar; simmer for 5 minutes. Stir in the shredded chicken and simmer for 5 more minutes, or until the chicken is heated through, the peppers are tender, and most of the wine is evaporated. Taste for seasoning and add salt and pepper if needed. To serve, evenly spoon the mixture over the top of the toast slices.

Seasoning Suggestions

The herbs used in this recipe go well with an Italian-seasoned rotisserie chicken; however, you may need to adjust the amounts according to how highly seasoned the chicken is. If you're using a lemon-pepper rotisserie chicken, you may wish to omit the herbs suggested in the recipe and replace them with some Mrs. Dash Lemon Pepper Seasoning Blend to taste.

CHICKEN FRIED RICE

How the chicken is seasoned will determine whether the stir-fry sauce will stand on its own or if you'll need to add toasted sesame oil, soy sauce, and/or honey for additional flavor.

Yields 4 servings

1 8.8-ounce microwaveable pouch brown or white rice

1 3-pound rotisserie chicken

1 tablespoon peanut or vegetable oil

2 green onions, sliced

½ cup frozen peas

¼ cup bottled stir-fry sauce

Optional: toasted sesame oil to taste

Optional: soy sauce to taste

Optional: honey to taste

¼ cup sliced almonds

1. Heat the rice pouch in the microwave according to package directions.

2. Remove and discard the skin from the chicken; reserve the breast meat for another meal. Shred remaining meat.

3. Add the oil to a wok or large skillet and bring it to temperature over medium-high heat. Add the onion; stir-fry for 1 minute. Add the rice and stir-fry for 3 minutes. Stir in the shredded chicken, peas, and stir-fry sauce; stir-fry for 3 more minutes, or until heated through. Taste for seasoning and add toasted sesame oil, soy sauce, and honey to taste if desired. Sprinkle with the almonds and serve.

MICROWAVE CHICKEN AND RICE

This is a microwaveable version of the Chicken Fried Rice recipe. You can enhance the flavor by adding some of the optional ingredients or by toasting the almond slices.

Yields 4 servings

1 8.8-ounce microwaveable pouch brown or white rice

1 3-pound rotisserie chicken

1 tablespoon chicken broth or water

2 green onions, sliced

½ cup frozen peas

¼ cup bottled stir-fry sauce

¼ teaspoon toasted sesame oil

Optional: soy sauce to taste

Optional: honey to taste

¼ cup sliced almonds

1. Heat the rice pouch in the microwave according to package directions.

2. Remove and discard the skin from the chicken; reserve the breast meat for another meal. Shred remaining meat.

3. Add the chicken to a covered microwave-safe bowl large enough to hold all of the ingredients; microwave at 70 percent power for 1 minute. Stir. Repeat until the chicken is brought to temperature. Toss the rice, peas, stir-fry sauce, and broth or water with the chicken and microwave for 1 minute at 70 percent power. If the mixture is not sufficiently heated, repeat for 1 more minute. Top with the almonds.

CHICKEN TETRAZZINI

This is an easy one-dish meal, and the leftovers are great warmed over the next day.

Yields 8 servings

1 3-pound roasted chicken

8 ounces dried spaghetti or linguini, broken in half

12 ounces fresh asparagus, trimmed and cut into 1" pieces

2 tablespoons butter

8 ounces small whole fresh button or cremini mushrooms, cleaned and sliced

1 large red sweet pepper, seeded and cut into 1" pieces

1 large yellow sweet pepper, seeded and cut into 1" pieces

¼ cup all-purpose flour

⅛ teaspoon black pepper

1 14-ounce can chicken broth

¾ cup milk

2 ounces Swiss cheese, grated

1 tablespoon finely shredded lemon peel

1½ cups bread cubes

1 tablespoon extra-virgin olive oil

2 tablespoons snipped fresh parsley

1. Preheat oven to 350°F.

2. Remove and discard the skin from the chicken; remove the meat from the bones and shred it.

3. In an ovenproof Dutch oven, cook the spaghetti according to package directions. Add the asparagus during the last minute of the cooking. Drain, set aside, and keep warm.

4. Wipe out the Dutch oven; add the butter and melt it over medium heat. Add the mushrooms and peppers; sauté for 8 minutes, or until the mushrooms are tender. Stir in the flour and black pepper until well combined. Whisk in the broth and milk; cook, stirring frequently, until thickened and bubbly. Add the cooked pasta, asparagus, chicken, Swiss cheese, and half of the lemon peel; toss gently to coat.

5. In a medium-size bowl, toss together the bread cubes, olive oil, and remaining lemon peel; spread on top of the pasta mixture. Bake uncovered for 15 minutes, or until the bread cubes are golden brown. Let stand for 5 minutes before serving. Garnish with parsley before serving, if desired.

Bread Cubes Wisdom

One thick-cut slice of bread will make about ¾ cup of bread cubes. Keep in mind that the cubes will only be as good as the bread you use to make them. Sourdough bread works well in this recipe.

CHICKEN AND CHEESE TORTELLINI MEAL

You can substitute cauliflower or asparagus for the broccoli. All three vegetables have lots of health benefits.

Yields 6 servings

1 3-pound rotisserie chicken

2 9-ounce packages refrigerated cheese tortellini

1 12-ounce package frozen broccoli florets, thawed

1 14½-ounce can diced tomatoes with Italian herbs, undrained

½ cup dried tomato pesto

Optional: Parmigiano-Reggiano, freshly grated, to taste

1. Remove and discard the skin from the chicken; remove the meat from the bones and shred it.

2. In 4-quart Dutch oven, cook the tortellini according to the package directions, adding the broccoli during the last 3 minutes of cooking. Drain. Return to Dutch oven. Stir in the undrained tomatoes, tomato pesto, and chicken. Cook, stirring occasionally, just until heated through. Garnish with freshly grated Parmigiano-Reggiano cheese if desired.

CHICKEN AND VEGETABLES IN HOISIN SAUCE

This recipe omits the chicken breast, which you can save and use for another recipe.

Yields 4 servings

1 8.8-ounce microwaveable pouch brown or white rice

1 3-pound rotisserie chicken

1 medium red sweet pepper, seeded and cut into thin strips

1 small yellow onion, cut into thin wedges

1 clove garlic, minced

Salt to taste

⅛ teaspoon freshly ground black pepper

2 tablespoons orange juice

2 tablespoons hoisin sauce

Optional: kumquats, sliced, to taste

Optional: green onion, sliced, to taste

Optional: sliced almonds, toasted, to taste

1. Heat the rice pouch in the microwave according to package directions.

2. Remove and discard the skin from the chicken. Remove the breast meat; wrap and refrigerate it for a later use, such as for the Chicken Bundles (see recipe in this chapter). Remove the remaining meat from the bones and shred it.

3. Add the sweet pepper, onion, garlic, salt, pepper, orange juice, and hoisin sauce to a large microwave-safe bowl; stir to mix. Cover and microwave on high for 1 minute; stir and microwave at 70 percent power for 1 minute, or until the sweet pepper and onion are tender. Stir in the cooked rice and shredded chicken; cover and microwave at 70 percent power for 2 minutes, or until the entire mixture is heated through. Serve garnished with kumquat slices, sliced green onion, and/or toasted almonds if desired.

HONEY-MUSTARD BBQ CHICKEN SANDWICHES

Stretch a rotisserie chicken to a meal for a crowd by serving these sandwiches with potato chips and tossed salad or coleslaw.

Yields 8 servings

1 3-pound rotisserie chicken

1½ cups bottled barbecue sauce

¼ cup honey

2 teaspoons yellow mustard

1½ teaspoons Worcestershire sauce

8 hamburger buns

Remove and discard the skin from the chicken; remove the meat from the bones and shred it. Add the chicken to a nonstick saucepan or skillet along with the barbecue sauce, honey, mustard, and Worcestershire sauce. Cook and stir over medium heat until heated through. Divide between the buns.

CHICKEN BUNDLES

Serve these with a tossed salad for lunch or with a salad and steamed vegetable for dinner.

Yields 4 servings

1 3-ounce package cream cheese, softened

3 tablespoons butter, melted

Salt and freshly ground black pepper to taste

1 tablespoon mayonnaise

1 tablespoon milk

2 cups cooked chicken, cubed or shredded

1 tablespoon fresh chives or green onion, chopped

Optional: 1 tablespoon pimiento, chopped

1 8-ounce can refrigerated crescent dinner rolls

½ cup bread crumbs

1. Preheat oven to 350°F.

2. Add the cream cheese, 2 tablespoons of the butter, salt, pepper, mayonnaise, and milk to a bowl; whisk to combine. Stir in the chicken, chives or green onion, and pimiento (if using).

3. Separate the dough into 4 rectangles; each rectangle will include 2 connected crescent rolls. Place on an ungreased cookie sheet. Press the perforations holding the sections together to seal. Evenly spoon the chicken mixture onto the 4 rectangles. Pull the 4 corners of dough to the top center above the chicken mixture, twist slightly, and squeeze to seal each bundle. Brush the tops of each bundle with the remaining butter and sprinkle the bread crumbs onto the brushed butter. Bake for 25 minutes, or until golden brown.

INDIAN CHICKEN VINDALOO

If some members of your family like white meat and others like dark, you can substitute a quartered and skinned 3½-pound chicken for the thighs. This makes a rich, spicy stew you can serve over cooked rice or cooked, diced potatoes.

Yields 4–8 servings

¼ cup ghee

8 chicken thighs, skin removed

3 cloves garlic, minced

2 large yellow onions, diced

2 tablespoons fresh ginger, grated

2 teaspoons ground cumin

2 teaspoons yellow mustard seeds, crushed

1 teaspoon ground cinnamon

½ teaspoon ground cloves

1 tablespoon turmeric

1½ teaspoons cayenne pepper, or to taste

1 tablespoon paprika

1 tablespoon tamarind paste

2 teaspoons fresh lemon juice

2 tablespoons white vinegar

1 teaspoon light brown sugar

1–2 teaspoons salt

2 cups water

1. Bring the ghee to temperature over medium heat in a 6-quart Dutch oven. Fry the chicken pieces until browned, about 5 minutes on each side. Remove the chicken from the pan and keep warm.

2. Add the garlic and onion to the pan and sauté until golden brown. Stir in the ginger, cumin, mustard seeds, cinnamon, cloves, turmeric, cayenne, and paprika; sauté for a few minutes. Stir in the tamarind paste, lemon juice, vinegar, brown sugar, salt, and water. Add the chicken pieces. Bring to a boil; cover, lower the heat, and simmer for 45 minutes, or until chicken is tender. Remove the cover and continue to simmer for another 15 minutes, or until sauce thickens.

Cucumber Salad with Yogurt

Chicken Vindaloo is good with a simple cucumber salad. Thinly slice 2 cucumbers; dress the slices with 2 tablespoons fresh lemon juice, ¼ cup extra-virgin olive oil, and salt and freshly ground black pepper to taste. Add a dollop of plain yogurt to each serving of the salad.

MOROCCAN CHICKEN AND VEGETABLES

This is an adaptation of a chicken tagine recipe. It's traditionally served in deep soup bowls over the top of cooked rice, noodles, or couscous.

Yields 4–8 servings

3 tablespoons extra-virgin olive oil

4 chicken thighs, skin removed

2 chicken breasts, halved and skin removed

1 large yellow onion, diced

3 cloves garlic, minced

1 large eggplant

3 cups chicken broth

2 2" cinnamon sticks

1 teaspoon curry powder

1 teaspoon ground cumin

¼ teaspoon turmeric

¼ teaspoon freshly ground black pepper

2 large carrots, peeled and diced

1 large zucchini, diced

1 large white turnip, diced

1 small red pepper, seeded and diced

2 cups tomatoes, diced

½ cup golden raisins

2 tablespoons fresh cilantro, chopped

1. Add the oil to a 6- or 8-quart Dutch oven; bring to temperature over medium-high heat. Add the chicken pieces and brown on both sides. Remove from the pan and keep warm.

2. Reduce the heat to low and add the onion, garlic, and eggplant. Sauté for 5–10 minutes, or until the onion is transparent. Increase the heat to medium-high; stir in the broth, cinnamon sticks, curry powder, cumin, turmeric, and black pepper and bring to a boil. Reduce the heat and simmer for 10 minutes.

3. Add the chicken thighs, carrots, zucchini, turnip, and red pepper. Cover and simmer for 10 minutes. Add the chicken breasts, tomato, raisins, and half of the cilantro; cover and simmer for 10 minutes, or until the chicken is cooked through. Taste for seasoning and add more salt and pepper, if necessary. Garnish with the remaining cilantro.

Eggplant Matters

Some people find the taste of eggplant to be bitter unless it's first salted and allowed to sit for 20 minutes. If you take that step, drain off any liquid after 20 minutes, then rinse the eggplant and let it drain well again.

UNSTUFFED ARABIAN VEGETABLES

Rather than choosing whether you want to stuff tomatoes, zucchini, or green peppers, this option lets you stretch the meal to more servings by using all three veggies. For variety and an additional flavor boost, use 2 green and 2 red bell peppers.

Yields 6–8 servings

2 cups chicken broth

1 cup instant white rice

½ pound ground chicken

½ pound ground beef

⅛ teaspoon ground cinnamon

¼ teaspoon freshly ground nutmeg

¼ teaspoon ground allspice

Salt and freshly ground pepper to taste

3 tablespoons butter

3 medium zucchini, diced

1 cup cherry tomatoes, halved

4 medium green bell peppers

¼ cup water

¼ cup tomato juice

3 tablespoons fresh lemon juice

6–8 tablespoons plain yogurt, drained

1. Add the chicken broth to a deep 3½-quart nonstick skillet and bring to a boil. Add the rice; cover, turn off the heat, and let sit for 30 minutes. Fluff the rice and pour into a large bowl; cover.

2. Add the ground chicken and ground beef to the skillet; brown over medium-high heat, stirring to break apart the meat and mix it together. Pour the cooked meat into the bowl with the rice and mix together with the cinnamon, nutmeg, allspice, salt, and pepper.

3. Melt the butter in the skillet and add the zucchini; stir-fry until the zucchini is crisp-tender and much of the moisture is evaporated. Add the tomatoes and stir-fry until warm. Add to the rice-meat mixture and mix well.

4. Cut the peppers in half lengthwise, and remove the stems, seeds, and white membrane. Pour the water, tomato juice, and lemon juice into the skillet. Arrange the peppers around the bottom of the skillet, cut side up. Spoon the rice-meat mixture into and around the pepper halves. Bring the juice mixture in the pan to a boil over medium heat. Reduce the heat, cover, and simmer for 20–30 minutes, or until the peppers are tender. Top servings with a dollop of plain yogurt.

Extra Flavor

You can make a Middle Eastern–style yogurt sauce by flavoring it with a little lemon juice and some raw, minced, or roasted garlic. The lemon will add a bit of a kick, and the garlic will impart a bit of sweetness to the dish.

CHICKEN STUFFING CASSEROLE

This casserole probably won't need salt because of the sodium content of the stuffing mix, soup, and green beans. You may wish to add freshly ground pepper, however.

Yields 4–6 servings

⅓ cup butter

1 small yellow onion, chopped

2 celery stalks, chopped

1 6- to 8-ounce package of stuffing mix

1⅔ cups chicken broth or water

4 boneless skinless chicken breast halves, cut into 1" chunks

1 10¾-ounce can condensed cream of mushroom soup

⅓ cup sour cream

1 14½-ounce can green beans, drained

Optional: 1 cup Cheddar cheese, grated

1. Preheat oven to 350°F.

2. Melt the butter in a deep 3½-quart ovenproof nonstick skillet; add the onion and celery and sauté until softened, about 5 minutes. Pour the sautéed vegetables into a bowl and stir in the stuffing mix and its seasoning packet, if there is one. Add the broth or water and stir to combine; set aside to allow the liquid to be absorbed.

3. Spread the chicken cubes evenly in the bottom of the skillet. Mix the soup with the sour cream and spoon it evenly over chicken. Spread the green beans evenly over the soup mixture, and then sprinkle stuffing mixture evenly over all. Bake, uncovered, for 45 minutes or until the chicken is cooked through. Add the cheese at the 30-minute mark, if using, then bake an additional 15 minutes, or until the cheese is melted.

STOVETOP CHICKEN CASSEROLE

Adjust the amount of salt in the cooking liquid for the noodles according to the type of cooked chicken and the amount of sodium in the soup you are using in this recipe.

Yields 6 servings

12 ounces dried wide egg noodles

1½ cups frozen mixed vegetables of your choice

1½ cups cooked chicken, cubed

1 4½-ounce can sliced mushrooms, drained

1 10¾-ounce can cream of mushroom soup

1 large egg

1 tablespoon mayonnaise

2 tablespoons milk

1 cup Cheddar cheese, grated

1. In a Dutch oven, cook noodles according to the package directions. Add the vegetables during the last 3 minutes of cooking time. Drain; return the noodles and vegetable mixture to the pan.

2. Stir in the chicken, mushrooms, and half of the mushroom soup. Stir to combine and start to bring the mixture to temperature over medium-low heat. Add the egg, mayonnaise, and milk to the cream of mushroom soup remaining in the can; use a fork to mix thoroughly. Add the soup mixture to the Dutch oven and stir to combine it with the other ingredients. Cook for 5 minutes, stirring occasionally. Add the cheese and mix well. Continue to cook and stir until the cheese is melted.

CHICKEN POT PIE

If you prefer, you can replace the buttermilk biscuits with pie crust.

Yields 8 servings

¼ cup butter

5 large carrots

4 stalks celery, finely diced

2 large yellow onions, diced

2 large cloves garlic, minced

1 teaspoon dried thyme

8 ounces button mushrooms, cleaned and sliced

4 boneless, skinless chicken breasts, cubed

6 cups chicken broth

4 large russet potatoes, peeled and diced

½ cup all-purpose flour

½ cup dry white wine

½ cup heavy cream

1 cup frozen baby peas, thawed

Salt and freshly ground black pepper to taste

1 large egg

2 tablespoons water

8 large refrigerated buttermilk biscuits

1. Preheat oven to 400°F.

2. Melt the butter in a 4-quart ovenproof Dutch oven over medium heat. Peel the carrots; shred 1 carrot and dice the others.

3. Add the shredded carrot, celery, onion, garlic, thyme, and mushrooms to the pan. Sauté until the onions are translucent.

4. Add the remaining carrots, chicken, broth, and potatoes to the pan. Bring to a simmer, reduce the heat, cover, and simmer for 20 minutes, or until the vegetables are tender and the chicken is cooked through.

5. Whisk the flour and wine together in a small bowl or measuring cup. Whisk in 1 cup of the hot broth from the pan. Strain to remove any lumps, then pour into the pan. Stir to mix. Increase the temperature to bring to a low boil. Boil and stir until the mixture thickens and the flour taste is gone, about 5 minutes. Stir in the cream and peas. Taste for seasoning and add salt and pepper, if desired.

6. In a small bowl, beat the egg with the water. Press or roll out the biscuits until they're about ¼" thick. Cut slits in the top of each biscuit to allow steam to escape while they're baking. Arrange the biscuits over the top of the pie and brush them with all of the egg mixture. Bake for 50 minutes, or until the biscuit crust is golden and the gravy is bubbling. Let stand for 10 minutes before serving.

Chicken Upside-Down Pie

Instead of baking the entire pot pie, roll out the biscuits to ¼" thickness, turn a muffin pan upside down, and shape the biscuits over the muffin pan indentations. Bake for 12–15 minutes, or until golden brown. For each serving, place a biscuit "bowl" inside another bowl, ladle the chicken pot pie mixture into the biscuit bowl, and top with grated Cheddar cheese, if desired.

TEX-MEX CHICKEN CASSEROLE

To keep this truly a one pot dish, everything could be stirred into and baked in the Dutch oven, but the presentation is more attractive if this casserole is made as explained in the instructions.

Yields 8–10 servings

2 pounds skinless, boneless chicken breasts, cubed

2½ cups chicken broth

½ cup dry white wine

¼ cup coarsely chopped fresh cilantro leaves

1½ tablespoons fresh lime juice

2 cloves garlic, smashed

1 teaspoon black peppercorns

¼ teaspoon dried Mexican oregano

2 bay leaves

6 tablespoons butter

1 pound white button mushrooms, cleaned and sliced

¼ teaspoon salt

Freshly ground black pepper to taste

4 tablespoons all-purpose flour

1½ cups whole milk

Nonstick cooking spray

12 cups crusted tortilla chips

2 large yellow onions, diced

2 green bell peppers, seeded and diced

2 jalapeño peppers, seeded and minced

8 ounces pepper jack cheese, grated

8 ounces Cheddar cheese, grated

2 teaspoons chili powder

1 teaspoon ground cumin

½ teaspoon paprika

¼ teaspoon freshly ground black pepper

½ teaspoon ground coriander

Pinch cayenne pepper

1 teaspoon garlic powder

Pinch dried red pepper flakes, crushed

1 cup chopped canned tomatoes, drained

1 4-ounce can diced green chilies, drained

1. Combine the chicken, broth, wine, cilantro, lime juice, garlic, peppercorns, oregano, and bay leaves in an ovenproof Dutch oven over medium-high heat; bring to a boil. Reduce the heat to a simmer and cook, uncovered, for 10 minutes. Pour all the contents of the pan into a bowl and allow the chicken to cool in the poaching liquid.

2. Preheat oven to 350°F.

3. Wipe out the Dutch oven. Add the butter and heat on medium until melted. Add the mushrooms, salt, and pepper and cook, stirring occasionally, for 6 minutes, or until the mushrooms are browned and all the liquid has evaporated. Sprinkle the mushrooms with the flour, stir to blend, and cook for 1 minute. Slowly whisk in the milk, scraping up any bits from the bottom of the pan. Cook until the mixture begins to thicken. Stir in about 1½ cups of the chicken cooking liquid; simmer for 10 minutes, stirring occasionally. Remove from the heat.

4. Treat a 9" × 13" casserole dish with nonstick spray; crush the tortilla chips and add them in a layer to the bottom of the dish. Pour the remaining broth over the tortilla chips. Once the broth is absorbed by the crushed chips, scatter the chicken over the top of the tortilla layer. Spread the onions, bell peppers, and jalapeños in layers evenly over the chicken. Top with half of the grated cheeses.

5. Mix together the chili powder, cumin, paprika, ¼ teaspoon black pepper, ground coriander, cayenne, garlic powder, and red pepper flakes; sprinkle over the cheeses. Spoon the mushroom mixture evenly over the top of the spices, then top with the tomatoes and green chilies. Cover with all the remaining cheese. Bake uncovered for 45 minutes, or until the cheese is bubbly and the casserole is heated through. Let sit for 5 minutes before serving.

CHICKEN À LA KING PIE

Adjust the seasoning in this recipe according to how well the cooked chicken and gravy are seasoned. For example, if herbs aren't needed, substitute a finely minced shallot for the Mrs. Dash Onion and Herb Blend.

Yields 4 servings

1½ cups cooked chicken, cubed

1 4½-ounce can sliced mushrooms, drained

1 tablespoon pimiento, chopped

1 cup store-bought chicken gravy

½ cup frozen baby peas, thawed

½ cup heavy cream

½ teaspoon Mrs. Dash Onion and Herb Blend

⅛ teaspoon freshly ground nutmeg

1 15-ounce package refrigerated peel-and-unroll-style pie crusts

1. Preheat oven to 375°F.

2. In a bowl, mix together the chicken, mushrooms, pimiento, gravy, peas, cream, Mrs. Dash Onion and Herb Blend, and nutmeg. Mix well.

3. Line the bottom of a 9½" deep-dish pie pan with one of the pie crusts. Add the chicken mixture to the pan. Cover the pie with the remaining crust; seal and flute the edges. Cut slits in the top of the crust. Bake for 35 minutes, or until the crust is golden brown.

Crust Tips

To prevent the crust edge from burning, wrap a strip of nonstick aluminum foil around it and crimp to secure; remove the foil after the first 20–30 minutes of baking. For a shinier, prize-winning look to the top crust, brush it with heavy cream or some beaten egg mixed with a little water before baking.

GREEK MEAT AND VEGETABLE PIE

Serve this casserole with Cucumber Salad with Yogurt (see Indian Chicken Vindaloo recipe in this chapter).

Yields 8 servings

1 medium yellow onion, diced

2 green onions, diced

2 tablespoons extra-virgin olive oil

1 8-ounce bag baby spinach, torn

1 12-ounce bag frozen steam-in-the-bag
  broccoli florets

8 ounces crumbled feta cheese

2 large eggs

2 cups cooked chicken or turkey, diced

2 tablespoons fresh chives, minced

2 tablespoons fresh dill, minced

½ cup fresh parsley, minced

Freshly ground black pepper to taste

1 16-ounce package phyllo dough

½ cup butter, melted

1. Preheat oven to 350°F.

2. Add the onions and oil to a large microwave-safe bowl. Cover and microwave on high for 1 minute. Stir, cover, and then microwave for 2 minutes, or until transparent. Add the spinach to the bowl and toss with the onions. Microwave the broccoli according to the package directions; drain and add to the bowl along with the cheese, eggs, chicken or turkey, chives, dill, parsley, and pepper; mix well. Set aside to cool.

3. Brush the bottom of a 9" × 13" nonstick baking pan with some of the butter. Layer half of the phyllo sheets on the bottom, 1 sheet at a time, brushing each sheet with butter before adding the next sheet. Evenly spread the meat and vegetable filling over the buttered phyllo sheets. Top the filling with the remaining sheets, brushing each sheet with butter before you add the next sheet. Cut into 8 equal pieces. Bake uncovered for 1 hour, or until golden brown.

GRANDMA'S CHICKEN AND DUMPLINGS

Some grandmas add chopped potatoes and carrots in step 3, and let things simmer until the vegetables are done before proceeding. Thawed frozen peas and carrots can be added before you spoon in the dumplings.

Yields 6 servings

1 3-pound whole chicken

Salt and freshly ground black pepper to taste

1 large yellow or white onion, quartered

4 cloves garlic, crushed

2 stalks celery, halved

2 large carrots, peeled and cut in 1" pieces

Water as needed

2 tablespoons butter or extra-virgin olive oil

1 stalk celery, finely chopped

1 large carrot, peeled and shredded

1 small yellow onion, finely diced

1 clove garlic, minced

2 cups all-purpose flour

1 tablespoon baking powder

1 teaspoon salt

2 large eggs

2 teaspoons lemon juice

¾–1 cup milk or heavy cream

Optional: ¼–½ cup heavy cream

1. Rinse the chicken inside and out in cold, running water. Add the chicken to a Dutch oven or stockpot along with the salt, pepper, quartered onion, crushed garlic, halved celery, and carrot pieces. Add enough water to cover the chicken. Bring to a simmer over medium heat; cover, lower the heat, and simmer for 1 hour, or until the chicken is cooked through.

2. Use tongs to move the chicken to a cutting board or platter; allow to sit until cool enough to handle. Remove and discard the bones and skin. Strain the broth, discarding the vegetables.

3. Melt the butter in the Dutch oven or stockpot over medium heat. Add the chopped celery, shredded carrot, and diced onion; sauté for 2 minutes. Cover, lower the heat, and allow the vegetables to sweat for 5 minutes, or until the onion is transparent and the celery is tender. Stir in the minced garlic.

4. Measure the reserved chicken broth and add enough water to bring it to 6 cups. Pour the broth into the pan. Add the cooked chicken and stir it into the sautéed vegetables and broth. Bring to a simmer over medium heat; reduce heat to maintain the simmer.

5. To make the dumplings, mix the flour, baking powder, and salt together in a large bowl. Make a well in the center of the flour mixture and add the eggs. Use the tines of a fork to pierce the yolks. Add the lemon juice, and lightly beat the juice into the eggs. Add the milk or cream. Mix just until the dough comes together, adding just enough liquid to moisten the batter so that it resembles biscuit dough. Using 2 spoons, carefully drop heaping tablespoonfuls of the dumpling batter into the simmering chicken and broth. Cook for 10–15 minutes, or until the dumplings are cooked through, firm, and puffy. If desired, stir heavy cream to taste into the broth, being careful not to break apart the dumplings. Taste for seasoning and add salt and pepper, if needed.

CHICKEN WITH 40 CLOVES OF GARLIC

Serve this chicken with a tossed salad and heated or toasted slices of French bread. Squeeze the cloves of roasted garlic onto the bread; they'll spread like butter.

Yields 8 servings

⅔ cup extra-virgin olive oil

8 chicken drumsticks

8 chicken thighs

Nonstick cooking spray

4 stalks celery, cut in long strips

2 medium yellow onions, diced

1 1-pound bag baby carrots

1 tablespoon dried parsley

1 teaspoon dried tarragon

½ cup dry vermouth

Salt and freshly ground black pepper to taste

⅛ teaspoon ground nutmeg

40 cloves garlic, unpeeled

8 medium Idaho potatoes, scrubbed

1. Preheat oven to 375°F.

2. Add the oil and chicken pieces to a large plastic bag; seal and turn to coat the meat on all sides. Treat the bottom of a heavy 6-quart casserole with nonstick spray. Spread the celery, onions, and carrots in layers over the bottom of the pan; sprinkle with the parsley and tarragon. Lay the chicken pieces on top of the seasoned carrots. Pour the vermouth over the chicken, and then sprinkle them with the salt, pepper, and nutmeg. Tuck the garlic cloves around and between the chicken pieces. To create an airtight seal for the casserole dish so that the steam doesn't escape, cover it with heavy-duty aluminum foil crimped around the edges of the dish, and top that with the casserole lid. Move the dish to the oven.

3. Rub some of the oil remaining from coating the chicken onto the skins of the potatoes; wrap each one in foil and move to the oven beside the casserole dish. Bake for 1½ hours. Transfer the chicken, carrots, and cloves of roasted garlic to a serving platter. Strain the pan juices, skim off the fat, and serve it alongside the chicken and potatoes.

CASHEW CHICKEN

Bump up the flavor by serving this dish over rice cooked in chicken broth instead of water.

Yields 4 servings

2 tablespoons peanut oil

1 large green pepper, seeded and cut into strips

1 stalk celery, finely diced

1 medium sweet onion, diced

8 boneless, skinless chicken thighs, cut into bite-size pieces

1 tablespoon soy sauce

1 tablespoon cornstarch

½ cup chicken broth

⅛ cup dry white wine

1 teaspoon honey or granulated sugar

Toasted sesame oil to taste

1 cup unsalted roasted cashews

4 cups cooked rice

Optional: 4 cups iceberg lettuce, torn into bite-size pieces

1. Heat a wok or large nonstick pan over medium-high heat. Add the oil, green pepper, and celery; stir-fry 2 minutes. Push to the side. Add the onion; stir-fry for 3 minutes, or until transparent. Push to the side.

2. Add the chicken; stir-fry for 4 minutes, or until cooked through. Mix the green pepper, celery, and onion in with the chicken.

3. Add the soy sauce, cornstarch, broth, wine, and honey or sugar to a small bowl; mix well and strain out any lumps; pour into the stir-fried chicken mixture. Heat and stir until the sauce is thickened and clear. Stir in the toasted sesame oil and cashews. Serve over the rice or a mixture of rice and lettuce, if desired.

Preparing Rice in a Pressure Cooker

To make a tad over 4 cups of long-grain or basmati rice, add 1½ cups of rice, 2½ cups of broth or water, and 1 tablespoon of butter or oil to a pressure cooker. Cook for 3 minutes on high pressure. Remove from the heat and allow the pressure to release naturally for 7 minutes. Quick-release any remaining pressure. Uncover and fluff with a fork.

SENEGALESE CHICKEN

Senegal is a large country on the Atlantic Ocean in West Africa. Many dishes from this area have inspired American soul food dishes.

Yields 6–8 servings

½ cup peanut oil

4 medium onions, roughly sliced

2 lemons, juiced

4 limes, juiced

½ cup apple cider vinegar

2 bay leaves

4 garlic cloves, chopped

2 tablespoons prepared mustard

1 serrano pepper, cleaned and diced

1 teaspoon salt

½ teaspoon black pepper

1 stewing chicken, 5–6 pounds, cut into individual pieces

2 tablespoons peanut oil

½ cabbage, cut into chunks

3 carrots, peeled and chunked

1. Mix everything but the chicken, 2 tablespoons of oil, cabbage, and carrots in a gallon-size sealable plastic bag. Add the chicken and toss to combine. Marinate for 4–24 hours.

2. Place a large skillet over medium-high heat. Once it's heated add 2 tablespoons of peanut oil. Place a few pieces of chicken in the skillet and cook for 4–5 minutes on each side until just browned. Remove the chicken to a dish; you may have to sauté the chicken in batches.

3. Once the chicken is sautéed, remove the onions from the marinade and cook for 10–12 minutes. Add the rest of the marinade and the vegetables to the skillet. Cover and boil for 10 minutes or until the carrots are not quite tender.

4. Place the chicken back in the pot, cover with a lid, and cook for 20 minutes. Stir occasionally. Serve over rice or couscous.

CHICKEN BREAST ROTOLO WITH CURRANT STUFFING

Rotolo *translates from Italian as "coil." It's a common cooking technique used with larger sheets of pasta, or pieces of meat that are pounded flat. This dish works great with chicken breast, but would also work with a tender cut of pork.*

Yields 1 serving

1 chicken breast half

Pinch salt

Pinch pepper

2 tablespoons pine nuts or other nut

2 tablespoons olive oil

½ celery stalk, minced

¼ small yellow onion, minced

1 small garlic clove, minced

¼ cup fresh currants

1 tablespoon fresh thyme or basil, chopped

2 tablespoons fresh parsley, chopped

1. Use the flat end of a meat tenderizer or a rolling pin to pound the chicken breast until it's ⅜" thick. Sprinkle each side with salt and pepper.

2. Place a small skillet over medium heat. Place pine nuts in the skillet and shake every 30 seconds to 1 minute and turn off the heat as soon as you smell them toasting. Transfer nuts to a separate container.

3. Place the small skillet back over medium heat and once it is warm add 1 tablespoon olive oil, vegetables, and garlic. Stir the vegetables frequently for 5–7 minutes. Add the currants and cook for 1 minute until warm. Use the back of a spoon to crush them. Cook for 3–4 minutes. Once most of the juices have evaporated, stir in herbs and nuts.

4. Spoon the mixture onto the widest end of the chicken breast, and roll toward the narrow end. Use kitchen twine or toothpicks to hold it together. Wipe out the skillet.

5. Place the skillet over medium heat and once heated add 1 tablespoon olive oil. Place the chicken in the skillet and cook for 2–3 minutes, make a quarter turn, and cook for another 2–3 minutes. Continue cooking and turning for 8–12 minutes. Remove twine or toothpicks and slice the chicken into ¾" rounds. Serve immediately.

Currants Are Historically Current

Currants are a tiny, tart fruit that grow on a small bush and are very high in vitamin C. During World War II, fruit that was high in vitamin C was incredibly hard to import into Britain so the British government encouraged its citizens to grow currants that were then turned into a syrup and given to children.

CHICKEN BREAST STUFFED WITH RAPINI AND BLACK OLIVES

Rapini is also called broccoli rabe. Even though it grows little broccoli-like buds on its stems, it is more similar to turnip greens. If you can't find rapini, or don't like its nutty, bitter taste, you can substitute chard or spinach.

Yields 1 serving

1 chicken breast

Pinch salt

Pinch black pepper

1 tablespoon plus 1 teaspoon olive oil

2 ounces rapini, chopped

¼ small onion, chopped

1 garlic clove, minced

2 ounces pitted black olives, minced

1 tablespoon shredded Parmesan cheese

1. Preheat oven to 350°F. Place the chicken breast on a sturdy surface. Use the flat side of a meat tenderizer to pound the breast until it is about ⅜" thick. Sprinkle both sides with salt and pepper.

2. Place a skillet over medium-high heat. Once heated, add 1 tablespoon olive oil, the rapini, and the onion. Cook for several minutes until the leaves are wilted and the stems are softened.

3. In a bowl, combine the rapini, the garlic, the olives, and the Parmesan cheese. Place the mixture near the widest end of the chicken breast and roll toward the other end. Use cooking twine or toothpicks to keep in place.

4. Place the small skillet back over medium-high heat. Once warmed, add 1 teaspoon oil to the pan and add chicken. Brown for 1 minute on each side. Transfer the skillet to the middle of the oven and cook for 35–40 minutes.

5. Remove the twine or toothpicks and cut the roll in slices. Serve immediately.

ALSATIAN CHICKEN

This would be a great dish to serve with Pommes Fondantes (see recipe in Chapter 3) and Garlic Soup (see recipe in Chapter 4).

Yields 4 servings

4 tablespoons butter

4 chicken thighs

1 medium onion, sliced

8 ounces mushrooms, sliced

2 tablespoons brandy

1 cup Riesling wine

1 tablespoon ground mustard powder

Salt to taste

Pepper to taste

¼ cup whole milk

1. Preheat oven to 350°F.

2. Place a skillet over high heat. Once it is warmed, add 3 tablespoons butter. When it's melted, add the chicken thighs, skin side down. Cook for 6–7 minutes, or until the skin is golden brown. Turn the chicken over and cook for an additional 5 minutes.

3. Place the chicken on a plate and keep it warm. Reduce the heat to medium, add the sliced onion, and cook for 5 minutes. Sprinkle the mushrooms over the pan and cook for 5 minutes.

4. Add the brandy, wine, and the ground mustard to the skillet and increase the heat slightly. Stir to scrape any stuck-on bits. Once the liquid starts to simmer, turn off the burner and place the chicken back in the skillet.

5. Place the skillet in the middle of the oven and cook for 1 hour and 15 minutes. Then place the chicken onto a clean plate and keep it warm. Place the skillet over a medium-high burner and let the liquid reduce until 1 cup is left. Season with salt and pepper to taste.

6. Stir the milk and 1 tablespoon butter into the sauce. Melt the butter and quickly whisk the sauce before pouring it over the chicken to serve.

Taste Alsace

Cast-iron cookware is common in Alsace, France, a region near Germany. This dish, like many other dishes of the region, combines elements of classic French and German cooking to create a very flavorful one pot meal. You could also add a few chopped potatoes and carrots before step 5.

CHICKEN THIGHS STUFFED WITH APRICOTS AND CHEESE

If you don't have dried apricots, you can use any dried fruit. Dates would work great, as would cranberries or cherries.

Yields 4 servings

2 tablespoons olive oil

1 large onion, thinly sliced

1 carrot, thinly sliced

1 stalk celery, thinly sliced

4 boneless, skinless chicken thighs

½ cup dried apricots, chopped

½ cup provolone cheese, cubed

¾ cup panko or unseasoned bread crumbs

1 tablespoon chopped fresh thyme

Pinch salt

Pinch pepper

1. Place a skillet over medium-high heat. Once it is heated, add the oil and onion and cook for 10–12 minutes. Remove half of the onion mixture from the skillet and put into a bowl.

2. Add the carrot and celery to the skillet and cook for 4–5 minutes, or until the celery is just starting to soften. Turn off the heat.

3. Trim any excess fat from the thighs and lightly pound them so they're flat. Add the apricots, cheese, panko, thyme, and a sprinkle of salt and pepper to the bowl. Toss lightly and add ¼ of the mixture to each thigh.

4. Roll the thigh, starting with the widest edge and rolling toward the smallest edge. Use toothpicks or kitchen twine to hold it together. Place it back in the skillet over medium-high heat. Move the vegetables to the edges of the skillet. Sear the chicken on each side for 3–4 minutes, or until it is lightly browned on all sides.

5. Reduce the heat to medium-low, cover, and cook for 20 minutes, until the center measures 150°F. Turn off the heat and let it rest for 5 minutes before serving.

Chicken Thighs—the New Chicken Breasts?

Boneless, skinless chicken breasts are the most common cut at grocery stores, which means other cuts are often cheaper. Chicken thighs do have about 10 percent more of your recommended daily allowance of fat than breast meat, but they have only about 50 more calories.

TURKEY CASSEROLE

This casserole is gussied-up turkey dressing dinner. Serve it with a tossed salad and then have cranberry juice punch to drink to complete the off-season Thanksgiving feel to your meal.

Yields 8 servings

2 tablespoons butter or extra-virgin olive oil

1 green bell pepper, seeded and diced

6 stalks celery, diced

1 medium yellow onion, diced

1 28-ounce can heat-and-serve turkey

4 large eggs, beaten

½ cup mayonnaise

1 10¾-ounce can condensed cream of mushroom soup

3 cups milk

12 slices bread, crusts removed and torn into bite-size pieces

4 ounces Cheddar cheese, grated

1. Preheat oven to 325°F.

2. Melt the butter or add the oil to an ovenproof Dutch oven over medium heat. Add the green pepper and celery; sauté for 5 minutes. Stir in the onion and sauté for another 5 minutes, or until the onion is transparent and the other vegetables are tender. Stir in the undrained can of turkey, and before the turkey is heated through, stir in the eggs. Add the mayonnaise, soup, and milk; mix well. Fold the pieces of bread into the mixture. Cover and bake for 45 minutes.

3. Remove the cover and sprinkle the cheese over the top of the casserole. Return to the oven and bake for an additional 15 minutes, or until the cheese is melted and the casserole is set.

TURKEY-TOPPED ENGLISH MUFFINS

A twist on the traditional eggs Benedict, this English muffin is topped with lettuce, avocado slices, turkey breast, poached egg, and an easy homemade hollandaise-style sauce.

Yields 1 or 2 servings

1 English muffin, split

⅔ cup water

⅛ teaspoon white vinegar

2 large eggs

¼ cup plain yogurt

2 teaspoons lemon juice

Optional: ¼ teaspoon Dijon or honey mustard

Lettuce leaves

½ avocado, peeled and sliced

4 ounces cooked turkey, heated

Salt and freshly ground pepper to taste

1. While you toast the muffin, put the water and vinegar in a microwave-safe bowl. Crack the eggs into the water. Pierce each egg yolk with a toothpick. Cover the bowl with plastic wrap. Microwave on high for 1½ minutes, or until the eggs are done as desired. Keep in mind that as long as the egg remains in the water, it will continue to cook, so be ready to assemble the dish quickly.

2. To make the mock hollandaise, in a small bowl mix the yogurt, lemon juice, and mustard (if using).

3. To assemble the open-face sandwiches, place the toasted English muffin halves on a plate. Arrange lettuce atop the muffins. Top the lettuce with the avocado slices and then the turkey. Use a slotted spoon to remove the eggs from the water and place them on top of the turkey. Salt and pepper the eggs to taste. Spoon the yogurt sauce over the eggs. Serve immediately.

TURKEY CASSEROLE

This casserole is a great use for leftover turkey. It also tastes great with cooked chicken or leftover roast beef.

Yields 8 servings

1 tablespoon extra-virgin olive oil

1 tablespoon butter

1 large yellow onion, finely chopped

1 green pepper, finely chopped

1 large carrot, peeled and finely chopped

1½ cups celery, finely chopped

½ teaspoon salt

¼ teaspoon freshly ground black pepper

2 cups cooked turkey, chopped

½ cup mayonnaise

1 10¾-ounce can cream of mushroom soup

1 10¾-ounce can cream of celery soup

4 eggs, beaten

3 cups milk

1 loaf white bread, torn into small pieces

1 pound Cheddar cheese, grated

1. Preheat oven to 350°F.

2. Add the oil and butter to an ovenproof Dutch oven and bring it to temperature over medium heat. Add the onion, green pepper, carrot, celery, salt, and pepper and sauté until tender.

3. Add the turkey and lightly sauté it with the vegetables to bring it to temperature. Stir in the mayonnaise, mushroom and celery soups, eggs, and milk; mix well. Add the bread pieces and half of the grated cheese; toss to combine.

4. Cover and bake for 45 minutes. Remove the lid and top with the remaining cheese. Bake for an additional 15 minutes, or until the cheese is melted and the casserole is cooked through. Serve immediately.

A Turkey Casserole Tweak

Add a turkey stuffing taste to your casserole by adding a teaspoon of poultry seasoning, dried sage, or a ½ teaspoon of dried marjoram and a ½ teaspoon of dried thyme.

MOCK BRATWURST IN BEER

The Spice House (www.thespicehouse.com) *has a salt-free Bavarian seasoning blend that is appropriate for this recipe. It's a blend of Bavarian-style crushed brown mustard seeds, French rosemary, garlic, Dalmatian sage, French thyme, and bay leaves.*

Yields 8 servings

2 stalks celery, finely chopped

1 1-pound bag baby carrots

1 large yellow onion, sliced

2 cloves garlic, minced

2–4 slices bacon, cut into small pieces

2 pounds turkey breast

1 2-pound bag sauerkraut, rinsed and drained

8 medium red potatoes, washed and pierced

1 12-ounce can beer

1 tablespoon Bavarian seasoning

Salt and freshly ground pepper to taste

Add all the ingredients to a 4-quart slow cooker in the order given. Note that the liquid amount needed will depend on how wet the sauerkraut is when you add it. The liquid should come up halfway and cover the turkey breast, with the sauerkraut and potatoes being above the liquid line. Add more beer, if necessary. Slow cook on low for 6–8 hours. Taste for seasoning and adjust if necessary. Serve hot.

BAVARIAN-STYLE TURKEY SAUSAGE SKILLET

Rinsed and drained sauerkraut will have a milder flavor. If you prefer more sour-packed punch in your sauerkraut, you can skip rinsing it and only drain it of the packing liquid in the can.

Yields 6 servings

1 tablespoon cooking oil

1 medium yellow onion, sliced

2 tablespoons all-purpose flour

1 cup apple cider or apple juice

½ cup chicken broth

2 tablespoons stone-ground mustard

1 20-ounce package refrigerated red potato wedges

1 pound cooked smoked turkey sausage, cut into bite-size slices

1 14½-ounce can sauerkraut, rinsed and drained

2 packed tablespoons light brown sugar

½ teaspoon caraway seeds

Optional: ¼ cup dried cranberries or raisins

1. Add the oil to a deep 3½-quart nonstick skillet or electric skillet and bring it to temperature over medium-high heat. Add the onions and sauté for about 8 minutes, or until tender. Sprinkle the flour over the onions and cook for 2 minutes, stirring frequently.

2. Slowly whisk in the apple cider, broth, and mustard. Bring to a boil while you continue to stir, then add the potato wedges, sausage pieces, and sauerkraut. Reduce the heat, stir in brown sugar and caraway seeds, and cover the pan; simmer for about 30 minutes, or until the sauce is thickened and the potatoes are tender. If desired, stir cranberries or raisins into the sausage mixture. Serve immediately.

TURKEY, SPINACH, AND ARTICHOKE CASSEROLE

This is an adaptation of traditional hot spinach and artichoke dip. If you want to serve it as a dip or for a light lunch, simply mix all ingredients together in a food processor and bake it according to the recipe instructions.

Yields 10–12 servings

1 14-ounce jar artichoke hearts, drained and chopped

3 10-ounce packages frozen chopped spinach, thawed and well drained

2 cups cooked turkey, finely chopped

2 8-ounce packages cream cheese, cut into cubes

2 tablespoons mayonnaise

¼ cup butter or extra-virgin olive oil

6 tablespoons heavy cream or milk

Freshly ground black pepper to taste

½ cup freshly ground Parmigiano-Reggiano or Romano cheese

1. Preheat oven to 375°F.

2. Evenly spread the artichoke hearts across the bottom of a 9" × 13" nonstick baking pan. Top with the spinach and the turkey.

3. Add the cream cheese, mayonnaise, butter or oil, and cream or milk to a food processor; process until smooth. Spread over the top of the turkey. Sprinkle with pepper, and then the cheese.

4. Bake uncovered for 40 minutes, or until the cheese is bubbly and the casserole is lightly browned on top. This dish can be assembled the night before and refrigerated; allow extra baking time if you move the casserole directly from the refrigerator to the oven.

TURKEY "LASAGNA" PIE

Cook the lasagna noodles in the same Dutch oven in which you'll eventually assemble the lasagna. Baking in a deep Dutch oven means you don't have to worry about the lasagna boiling over, and it cooks more evenly than it would in a rectangular pan.

Yields 8 servings

12 dried whole-wheat or regular lasagna noodles

½ cup basil pesto

1 teaspoon grated lemon peel

1 large egg, beaten

1 15-ounce carton ricotta cheese

2 cups mozzarella cheese, grated

¼ teaspoon salt

¼ teaspoon ground black pepper

Nonstick cooking spray

2 cups fresh spinach, chopped

½ cup chopped walnuts, toasted if desired

2 cups cooked turkey, chopped

1 24-ounce bottle marinara or pasta sauce

1 8-ounce package fresh button or cremini mushrooms, cleaned and thinly sliced

½ cup dry red wine

Optional: fresh Italian flat-leaf parsley leaves

1. Preheat oven to 375°F.

2. Cook the lasagna noodles according to the package directions until almost tender. Drain the noodles in a colander and rinse in cold water to stop the cooking. Drain well and set aside.

3. In a small bowl, mix together the pesto and lemon peel; set aside. Add the egg, ricotta cheese, 1 cup of the mozzarella cheese, and the salt and pepper to a medium-size bowl and mix well.

4. Lightly coat the Dutch oven with nonstick cooking spray. Arrange 4 cooked noodles in the bottom of the pan, trimming and overlapping them to cover the bottom of pan.

5. Top with the spinach. Sprinkle with half of the walnuts. Spread half of the ricotta cheese mixture evenly over walnuts. Spread half of the pesto mixture evenly over the ricotta, then sprinkle half of the turkey over the pesto. Pour half of the pasta sauce evenly over the turkey. Top with another layer of noodles. Top with the mushrooms. Spread the remaining ricotta cheese mixture over the mushrooms. Spread the remaining pesto mixture over the ricotta. Sprinkle the remaining turkey over the pesto, and then pour the rest of the pasta sauce over the turkey. Top with another layer of noodles.

6. Pour the wine into the empty marinara sauce jar, screw on the lid, and shake to mix with any sauce remaining in the jar. Pour over the top layer of noodles.

7. Cover the pan and bake for 45 minutes.

8. Remove the cover. Sprinkle the remaining mozzarella cheese over the top. Bake for an additional 15–30 minutes, or until the cheese is melted and bubbly and the lasagna is hot in the center. Let set for 10 minutes and then garnish with parsley if desired. To serve, cut the lasagna into pizza slice–style wedges.

TURKEY PILAF

Adjust the amount of turkey you add to this recipe according to the number of people you need to serve or the amount of protein you prefer in a meal. Choose the vegetables according to your family's tastes.

Yields 4–6 servings

2 tablespoons butter

Optional: 1 small yellow onion or large shallot, chopped

1 cup uncooked long-grain rice

2 cloves garlic, minced

1½ cups chicken broth

½ cup dry white wine

Salt to taste

1 12-ounce steam-in-the-bag frozen mixed vegetables

1–2 cups cooked turkey, chopped

Freshly grated Parmigiano-Reggiano cheese to taste

1. Add the butter to a Dutch oven or 4-quart nonstick saucepan and melt over medium heat. Add the onion or shallot, if using, and sauté for 2 minutes. Add the rice and brown it in the butter. Add the garlic and sauté for 30 seconds. Pour in the broth and wine. Bring to a boil and then add the salt. Cover; simmer for 20 minutes, or until the rice is tender.

2. While the rice cooks, microwave the vegetables in the bag for 4–5 minutes.

3. Uncover the rice and add the turkey and microwave-steamed vegetables. Stir to combine. Cover and cook on low for 2 minutes. Remove the cover and stir. Cover and continue to cook until the turkey is warmed through, if necessary.

4. Serve warm topped with the cheese.

Veggies Fresh from the Garden Pilaf

This recipe variation will require a second pot, but you can cut up a pound of fresh zucchini, yellow summer squash, and/or sweet peppers and sauté them in butter until tender. Substitute them for the microwave-steamed vegetables in step 3.

TURKEY TORTELLINI STIR-FRY

It's easy to vary this recipe. Simply choose a different vegetable mix and stir-fry sauce. For example, use a peanut stir-fry sauce and use chopped peanuts instead of the cashews.

Yields 4 servings

1 9-ounce package refrigerated cheese-filled tortellini

1 tablespoon peanut oil

1 16-ounce package fresh-cut or frozen stir-fry vegetables (such as broccoli, pea pods, carrots, and water chestnuts)

1–2 cups cooked turkey, chopped

¾ cup stir-fry sauce

½ cup dry-roasted cashews, chopped

1. Cook the tortellini in a Dutch oven or large stockpot according to the package directions. Drain, set aside, and keep warm.

2. Wipe out the pot and add the oil. Bring to temperature over medium-high heat. Add the vegetables and stir-fry for 3–5 minutes for fresh vegetables or 7–8 minutes for unthawed frozen vegetables, or until crisp-tender. Stir in the turkey and cook until it is warmed through. Add the stir-fry sauce and stir it in with the turkey-vegetable mix. Cook until the sauce is heated through. Add the cooked tortellini and toss gently to combine. Sprinkle with cashews and serve immediately.

TURKEY AND BISCUITS

You can punch up the flavor of this dish by adding ½ teaspoon dried sage and 1–2 teaspoons dried parsley when you add the pepper. The style of biscuits you use is up to you; just keep in mind that the bigger the biscuits, the longer they'll take to bake.

Yields 4 servings

1 tablespoon extra-virgin olive oil

1 tablespoon butter

1 medium yellow onion, chopped

1 stalk celery, chopped

3 tablespoons all-purpose flour

1 cup chicken broth

1½ cups milk

1 12-ounce package frozen peas and carrots

2 cups cooked turkey, cubed

Freshly ground black pepper to taste

1 7½-ounce can refrigerator biscuits

1. Preheat oven to 425°F.

2. Bring the oil and butter to temperature in an ovenproof Dutch oven over medium heat. Add the onion and celery and sauté for 5 minutes, or until the onion is transparent. Sprinkle the flour over the cooked vegetables and stir-fry for 2 minutes to cook the flour.

3. Slowly add the chicken broth to the pan, whisking to prevent lumps from forming. Stir the milk into the chicken broth. Increase the temperature to medium-high and bring to a boil. Reduce the heat and simmer for 5 minutes, or until mixture begins to thicken. Add the peas and carrots, turkey, and pepper. Mix well.

4. Arrange the biscuits over the top of the turkey mixture. Bake for 20–25 minutes, or until the biscuits are golden brown.

Ground Turkey and Biscuits

You can substitute 1 pound of ground turkey for the cooked turkey in this recipe. Simply add it when you sauté the onion and celery. Fry it until the turkey is cooked through, using a spatula to break up the turkey as it cooks. You may need to drain off a little excess oil before you add the flour, but otherwise you simply follow the recipe.

OVEN-ROASTED TURKEY BREAST WITH ASPARAGUS

The internal temperature of a baked turkey breast cutlet should be 170°F. The size and thickness of the cutlet can alter the baking time.

Yields 4 servings

4 medium baking potatoes

2 tablespoons butter, softened

1 teaspoon Dijon mustard

1 7-ounce jar roasted red sweet peppers, drained and chopped

4 teaspoons red onion or shallot, finely chopped

¼ teaspoon dried tarragon, crushed

½ teaspoon dried parsley, crushed

⅛ teaspoon salt

⅛ teaspoon freshly ground black pepper

1 pound asparagus spears

2 tablespoons extra-virgin olive oil

Salt and freshly ground pepper to taste

4 boneless turkey breast cutlets

1. Preheat the oven to 325°F.

2. Clean and pierce the potatoes. Place on a microwave-safe plate and microwave on high for 6–10 minutes, or until they can be pierced easily with a knife.

3. In a small bowl, combine the butter, mustard, peppers, onion or shallot, tarragon, parsley, salt, and black pepper; set aside.

4. Clean the asparagus, and snap off and discard the woody bases. Carefully cut the potatoes into quarters. Add the potatoes, asparagus, and olive oil to a large sealable plastic bag. Close the bag and shake to coat the vegetables. Pour the potatoes and asparagus out of the bag into a 9" × 13" nonstick baking pan. Sprinkle salt and freshly ground black pepper over the top.

5. Evenly spread the butter mixture over the top of the turkey cutlets. Place the cutlets on top of the potatoes and asparagus. Bake for 15–20 minutes, or until the turkey is baked through and the asparagus is tender.

THAI TURKEY AND SLAW

This is a dish that is a great way to take advantage of leftover turkey; however, it does require one pot and a bowl. You can save time by using coleslaw mix instead of shredding the cabbage.

Yields 4 servings

2–3 tablespoons Thai green curry paste

¼ cup dry white wine

½ cup unsweetened coconut milk

2 cups cooked turkey, chopped

¼ cup rice or rice wine vinegar

½ teaspoon granulated sugar

6 green onions

2 cups savoy cabbage, napa cabbage, bok choy, or gai choi, finely shredded

3 tablespoons unsalted dry-roasted cashew halves or dry-roasted peanuts, chopped

1. In a large skillet, stir together green curry paste and wine. Stir over medium-high heat for 1–2 minutes or until most of the liquid is gone. Stir in the coconut milk and bring to a boil. Add the turkey. Reduce the heat and continue to cook, uncovered, for about 1–2 minutes or until the sauce thickens.

2. In a serving bowl, stir together the vinegar and sugar; whisk until the sugar dissolves. Using a sharp knife, cut the green onions lengthwise into thin slivers. Add the green onions, cabbage, and cashews or peanuts to the bowl and toss to mix.

3. To serve, divide the turkey and sauce between 4 individual plates and serve the slaw on the side.

Making a Coconut Milk Substitute

If you don't have coconut milk on hand, make a good substitute by mixing unsweetened flaked coconut with an equal amount of milk and simmering the mixture for 2 minutes, or until it begins to foam; strain and use in any recipe that calls for coconut milk.

SLOW-COOKED TURKEY KIELBASA STEW

If you're using reduced-sodium broth, start out with about ½ teaspoon each of salt and pepper. If the broth is not reduced-sodium, skip the salt altogether and taste for seasoning before serving.

Yields 4 or 5 servings

4 cups coarsely chopped cabbage

4 medium russet potatoes, peeled and cubed

1 1-pound bag baby carrots

1 pound fully cooked turkey kielbasa, sliced

½ teaspoon dried basil, crushed

½ teaspoon dried thyme, crushed

Salt and freshly ground black pepper to taste

2 14-ounce cans reduced-sodium chicken broth

Place the ingredients in a 4-quart slow cooker. Cover and cook on low for 8–10 hours or on high for 4–5 hours.

MAKE LIME FOR TURKEY BAKE

Heat-and-eat rice and wild rice are available on the supermarket shelves. Some varieties are also available in the freezer case. This dish is good served with rice or even with dried chow mein noodles. Add a tossed salad or coleslaw and you have a complete meal.

Yields 4 servings

4 turkey breast cutlets

Juice from 1 lime (about ⅓ cup)

1–2 tablespoons extra-virgin olive oil

Salt to taste

Freshly ground pepper to taste

1 teaspoon paprika

1 15-ounce can pitted black olives

1 large yellow onion, chopped

1 medium green pepper, seeded and sliced

1 medium red pepper, seeded and sliced

1½ cups orange juice

1. Marinate the turkey cutlets in the lime juice for 30 minutes.

2. Preheat oven to 350°F.

3. Add the oil to a deep ovenproof skillet and bring to temperature over medium heat. Add the turkey cutlets to the oil. Sprinkle them with salt, pepper, and paprika. Brown on both sides. Add the olives, onion, green pepper, red pepper, and orange juice.

4. Cover and bake for 45 minutes. Serve with the pan juices.

POLYNESIAN TURKEY AND NOODLES

Be sure to have soy sauce, toasted slivered almonds or chopped dry-roasted peanuts, and toasted sesame oil as condiments at the table. This dish also tastes great with crunchy dried chow mein noodles.

Yields 4–6 servings

1 8-ounce package dried egg noodles

1 large egg

¼ cup plus 2 tablespoons cornstarch

2 cups turkey, cubed

2 tablespoons peanut or vegetable oil

1 13½-ounce can pineapple chunks, drained (reserve juice)

½ cup granulated sugar

½ cup cider vinegar

1 medium green pepper, cut in strips

¼ cup cold water

1 teaspoon soy sauce

4 large carrots, peeled, cooked, and cut into 1" pieces

1. In a Dutch oven, cook the egg noodles according to the package directions. Drain in a colander; set aside and keep warm.

2. Add the egg to a small bowl and beat lightly. Put ¼ cup cornstarch in another bowl. Dip each chunk of turkey in the egg, and then roll it in the cornstarch. Add the oil to the Dutch oven and bring it to temperature over medium heat; brown the turkey pieces in the oil. Remove them with a slotted spoon and let them rest atop the egg noodles in the colander.

3. Add enough water to the reserved pineapple juice to make 1 cup; carefully add it to the oil in the Dutch oven along with the sugar, vinegar, and green pepper. Bring to a boil, stirring constantly. Reduce the heat and simmer for 2 minutes. Blend 2 tablespoons of cornstarch with the cold water and add it to the pineapple juice mixture. Heat, stirring constantly, until it thickens and boils; boil for 1 additional minute. Stir in the pineapple chunks, soy sauce, carrots, and turkey. Cook until all the ingredients are heated through.

4. To serve, either divide the noodles between serving plates and spoon the turkey-pineapple mixture over the noodles, or add the noodles to the turkey-pineapple mixture and gently stir to combine.

TURKEY AND NOODLE CASSEROLE

This easy recipe leaves you all evening to enjoy this satisfying comfort food.

Yields 8 servings

1-pound dried extra-wide egg noodles

1 tablespoon extra-virgin olive oil

6 slices bacon or turkey bacon, chopped

2½ pounds ground turkey

1 pound white mushrooms, cleaned and sliced

1 large yellow onion, diced

Salt and freshly ground black pepper to taste

1 tablespoon dried thyme

1 cup dry white wine

2 cups chicken broth

1 cup heavy cream

¼ teaspoon freshly grated nutmeg

8 ounces Gruyère cheese, grated

1 cup plain bread crumbs

2 tablespoons butter, melted

1. Cook the noodles in a Dutch oven according to package directions. Drain, set aside, and keep warm.

2. Preheat oven to 350°F.

3. Wipe out the Dutch oven. Add the oil and bring it to temperature over medium-high heat. Add the bacon and cook for 3 minutes to render the bacon fat and until the bacon begins to brown at the edges. Add the ground turkey; brown the turkey, crumbling it apart. Add the mushrooms and onions; stir-fry for 3–5 minutes, or until the onions are transparent and the meat loses its pink color. Sprinkle with the salt, pepper, and thyme.

4. Stir in the wine, deglazing the pan by scraping up any food stuck to the bottom of the pan. Stir in the broth and bring to a boil; boil for 2 minutes, stirring occasionally. Lower the heat to a simmer and whisk in the cream. Stir in the nutmeg and cheese. Stir in the noodles. Top with the bread crumbs; drizzle the butter over the crumbs. Bake for 30 minutes, or until the crumbs are browned.

STOVETOP MOROCCAN TURKEY CASSEROLE

This recipe is an out-of-the-ordinary way to use up leftover turkey.

Yields 6 servings

1 tablespoon vegetable oil

2 cups baby carrots, halved lengthwise

6 green onions, diced

3 cloves garlic, minced

1 teaspoon ground cumin

1 teaspoon paprika

½ teaspoon turmeric

¼ teaspoon ground cinnamon

⅛ teaspoon cayenne pepper

2 cups chicken broth

⅔ cup quick-cooking couscous

6 pitted dates, quartered

3 cups cooked turkey, cubed

2 cups torn fresh spinach

1¼ cups bran flakes cereal

1. Bring the oil to temperature over medium heat in a Dutch oven. Add the carrots; sauté for 3 minutes. Add the onions; sauté for 3 minutes. Stir in the garlic, cumin, paprika, turmeric, cinnamon, and cayenne; sauté for 30 seconds. Stir in 1 cup of the broth and bring to a boil. Stir in the couscous and dates. Remove from heat, cover, and let stand for 5 minutes, or until the liquid is absorbed.

2. Stir the remaining 1 cup of broth into the couscous mixture. Return to heat and bring to a boil. Stir in the turkey, spinach, and cereal. Reduce the heat, cover, and simmer for 3 minutes, or until the turkey is heated through and the cereal has absorbed the extra broth. Serve immediately.

ENCHILADA CASSEROLE WITH TURKEY

Serve this casserole with shredded lettuce, black olives, avocado slices or guacamole, and sour cream on the side.

Yields 6 servings

1 pound ground turkey

Salt and freshly ground pepper to taste

2 cups picante sauce or salsa

2 teaspoons ground cumin

1 8-ounce package cream cheese, cubed

1 10-ounce package frozen chopped spinach, thawed and squeezed dry

12 6" flour tortillas

1 15-ounce can diced tomatoes

4 ounces Cheddar cheese, grated

1. Preheat oven to 350°F.

2. Add the ground turkey to a microwave-safe bowl; season with salt and pepper. Cover and microwave on high for 2 minutes. Use a fork to break the turkey apart. Cover and microwave on high for an additional 2 minutes, or until the turkey is cooked through. Stir in 1 cup of the picante sauce or salsa, and 1½ teaspoons of the cumin. Microwave uncovered on high for 2 minutes, or until most of the liquid has evaporated. Add the cream cheese and stir the mixture until it is melted into the sauce. Stir in the spinach.

3. Soften the tortillas by placing them on a microwave-safe plate; cover with a damp paper towel and microwave on high for 1 minute. Spoon about ⅓ cup filling down the center of each tortilla. Roll up and place seam side down in a lightly greased 9" × 13" nonstick baking pan.

4. Combine the tomatoes, the remaining cup of picante sauce or salsa, and the remaining ½ teaspoon cumin. Spoon over the enchiladas. Bake for 20 minutes. Sprinkle with the cheese; return to the oven and bake for 10 more minutes, or until the cheese is melted and bubbly.

GRILLED TURKEY CUTLETS AND MANGO SLICES

If you can't find fresh mangoes, fresh or canned pineapple slices can be used instead. If you can't find turkey cutlets, you can use thin slices of chicken breast or pork tenderloin.

Yields 4 servings

½ cup pomegranate juice

2 tablespoons honey

Several dashes Tabasco sauce

½ teaspoon salt, plus more to taste

¼ teaspoon black pepper, plus more to taste

Vegetable oil, as needed

4 thin-cut turkey cutlets (1¼ pounds)

2 large fresh mangoes, peeled and sliced ½" thick

1. Place a small skillet or saucepan over medium heat. Combine the juice, honey, Tabasco, salt, and black pepper and bring to a boil. Boil for 10–15 minutes until the sauce is reduced and thickened slightly.

2. Place a grill pan over medium-high heat and lightly oil the ridges. Spoon the sauce over the cutlets and sprinkle with salt and pepper. Place the cutlets on the grill pan and cook each side for 2–3 minutes.

3. Dip the mango slices in the fruit sauce and place on the grill pan. Cook on each side until there are grill marks. Serve the turkey and fruit over rice or noodles. Pour the leftover sauce on each serving.

GROUND TURKEY TACOS

You can use flour or corn tortillas in this recipe. Flour tortillas are soft, and corn tortillas can be steamed lightly to soften them or fried to make them crunchy.

Yields 16 tacos

1 tablespoon vegetable oil

1 medium onion, chopped

2 jalapeños, minced

3 garlic cloves, minced

1 tablespoon chili powder

1 tablespoon dried oregano

¼ teaspoon powdered cayenne pepper

1 teaspoon salt

¼ teaspoon pepper

2 pounds ground turkey

16 small tortillas or taco shells

Salsa for garnish

Shredded cheese for garnish

Chopped tomatoes for garnish

Shredded lettuce for garnish

Sour cream for garnish

2 limes cut into wedges

1. Place a skillet over medium heat. Once it is warm add the oil, onion, and jalapeños. Sauté 5–7 minutes. Add the garlic and stir frequently for 2–3 minutes. Add the chili powder, oregano, cayenne powder, salt, and pepper and toss to combine.

2. Reduce the heat to low. Crumble the ground turkey over the skillet and stir to cook. Once the outside of the meat is brown, cover the skillet with a lid and cook for 10 minutes.

3. Drain off any grease and discard.

4. Serve with warmed tortillas and top with salsa, cheese, tomatoes, lettuce, sour cream, and limes, if desired.

Homemade Taco Shells

Place a skillet over medium-high heat and add 1" of corn oil. Once the oil is heated, hold 1 tortilla with a pair of tongs and place half of it in the skillet. Hold it in a taco shape. Cook until it is golden brown. Repeat with the other side. When cooked, place over paper towels like a tent to drain.

JUICY TURKEY BURGER

Turkey tends to dry out when it is ground and cooked. But adding the shredded zucchini keeps these burgers juicy and nutritious.

Yields 4

2 teaspoons vegetable oil

½ cup shredded onion

¾ cup bread crumbs

1 teaspoon soy sauce

1 teaspoon Worcestershire sauce

½ teaspoon garlic powder

¼ teaspoon ground mustard

¼ teaspoon ground black pepper

1 teaspoon salt

¼ cup shredded zucchini

¼ cup mushrooms, minced

1 pound ground turkey

1. Place a skillet over medium heat. Once it is heated, add 1 teaspoon vegetable oil and the onion. Cook for 3–4 minutes, or until very soft. Remove the skillet from the heat, and put the onion in a large bowl. Combine all other ingredients, except for the turkey and remaining 1 teaspoon of vegetable oil, and stir until well combined.

2. Break the turkey up over the surface of the bowl. Use your hands to gently massage the meat into the other ingredients. Combine the meat into 4 equally shaped balls.

3. Flatten balls into patties and then wrap them in plastic wrap. Place in the refrigerator to rest for at least 20 minutes.

4. Place a skillet over medium heat and add 1 teaspoon of vegetable oil. Place 2 patties into the skillet and cook for 4–5 minutes, or until well browned.

5. Flip patties, cover the skillet with a lid, and let cook for an additional 4–5 minutes. Check the center to make sure they're cooked through. Repeat for remaining 2 patties.

TURKEY FILLETS WITH ANCHOVIES, CAPERS, AND DILL

Turkey breast is often cheapest after Thanksgiving. If wrapped tightly in plastic, this dish can be frozen for 3 months.

Yields 4 servings

2 tablespoons olive oil

6 anchovy fillets, or 1 tablespoon anchovy paste

4 turkey fillets, 4–6 ounces each, pounded thin

¼ cup chicken broth

1 tablespoon capers, chopped

2 tablespoons dill, chopped

1. Place a skillet over medium heat. Once the skillet is heated, add the oil and the anchovies. Cook for 5 minutes, stirring continually, or until they fall apart.

2. Place as many turkey fillets in the skillet as possible without overlapping. Cook on each side for 3 minutes, or until they're nicely browned. Repeat as necessary and remove the cooked fillets to a plate and keep warm.

3. Add the chicken broth to the pan and use a spoon to scrape up any bits from the bottom of the pan. Stir in the capers. Cook for 1 minute until the sauce reduces.

4. Pour the sauce over the turkey fillets and sprinkle them with chopped dill. Serve while warm.

HERBED DUCK WITH PARSNIPS

If you need something green to complete a meal, crispy duck cracklings will add a delicious dimension to a tossed salad.

Yields 4 servings

1 5-pound duck

2 large parsnips, diced

1 8-ounce bag baby carrots

10 ounces shallots, peeled

2 heads garlic, cloves separated but unpeeled

2 bay leaves

½ teaspoon dried rosemary

Salt and freshly ground black pepper to taste

1 cup water

Optional: fresh parsley to taste

1. Carve the duck so that you have 12 pieces: 2 bone-in breast pieces, 2 breast fillets, 2 legs, 2 thighs, 2 wing drumsticks, and 2 2-part wing pieces. Trim off any superfluous fatty skin pieces and reserve for later use. Freeze the neck to use later for broth, or add it to the skillet along with the other pieces.

2. Place the duck pieces skin side down in a deep 3½-quart nonstick skillet over medium to medium-high heat. Cook for 25 minutes, or until the skin is crispy. Watch the skillet and adjust the temperature, if necessary, to ensure that the duck doesn't burn.

3. Reduce the temperature to low and spread the parsnips, carrots, shallots, and garlic over the top of the duck pieces. Add the bay leaves and sprinkle with the rosemary, salt, and pepper. Cover and simmer for 30 minutes, or until the parsnips and carrots are tender.

4. Discard the bay leaves. Use a slotted spoon to move the duck pieces and vegetables to a serving platter. Pour off the duck fat and reserve it for later use. Place the pan back over medium heat, pour the water in the pan, and bring to a boil while stirring and scraping the bottom of the pan with a spatula. Pour the resulting sauce over the duck. Garnish with fresh parsley, if desired.

Duck Cracklings and Rendered Duck Fat

Cut fatty skin pieces from the duck into ¼" strips. Arrange them in a baking pan and bake at 350°F for 40 minutes, or put them in a nonstick skillet and fry for 30 minutes over medium heat. The cracklings are done when they're crisp and the rendered duck fat is clear. Drain the cracklings on paper towels. The duck fat keeps for months when stored in a covered container in the refrigerator.

BRAISED AND PAN-SEARED DUCK LEGS

This dish is more commonly known as duck confit, but only if you plan on keeping the meat in the jar with the fat in your refrigerator.

Yields 2 servings

2 duck legs with skin on

Salt to taste

Pepper to taste

2 bay leaves, crumbled

1 thumb-size bundle of fresh thyme

Skin from remainder of duck

1. Sprinkle the duck legs with salt and pepper. Place in an airtight container with bay leaves and thyme and refrigerate for 12–24 hours.

2. Place a skillet over medium-low heat. Once it is heated, add the skin to the skillet and cook for 1 hour, stirring occasionally to keep the fat from sticking. Cool for 15 minutes.

3. Preheat the oven to 300°F. Carefully place the duck legs in the skillet with the bay leaves and thyme. Place in the middle of the oven and cook for 2 hours, or until the bone moves independently of the meat. The skin should be crispy.

4. Remove the pan from the oven and set it aside to cool. Remove bay leaves and thyme. Let the oil cool and pour off the fat.

5. Duck fat will keep for up to 2 months in an airtight container in the refrigerator.

The Glory of Duck Fat

Duck fat rivals bacon fat for flavor, but its higher smoke point makes it perfect for frying. Duck fat can be substituted in any vegetable recipe that requires 1–3 tablespoons of oil. French fries cooked in duck fat are the most flavorful you'll come across. They're perfect when served with garlicky mayonnaise for dipping alongside the French or Belgian Steamed Mussels (see recipe in Chapter 8).

SEARED AND BAKED DUCK BREASTS WITH FRUIT COMPOTE

Duck fat is flavorful and has a high smoke point. You can keep the leftover fat in a jar in your refrigerator for a month and substitute it for oil or butter when pan-frying vegetables, potatoes, or even other meat.

Yields 2 servings

1 quart warm water

¼ cup table salt

2 tablespoons sugar

2 boneless, skin-on duck breasts

Savory Fruit Compote, as desired
(see sidebar)

1. Place the water, salt, and sugar in a small saucepan over medium heat. Stir until the salt and sugar have dissolved. Transfer to a large sealable container. Place the duck breasts on a cutting board and drag a knife across the skin in diagonal lines that are 1" apart. Rotate the breast and cut again to create a diamond pattern. Place the duck in the brine in the refrigerator. Let it rest for at least 8 (but no more than 24) hours.

2. Preheat oven to 400°F. Heat a skillet over medium heat. Remove the duck from the brine and pat dry. Place the breasts skin side down in the skillet and cook for 1 minute. Nudge the breasts to loosen them if necessary and cook for 5 more minutes.

3. Turn off the heat and drain the fat. Flip the breasts over so they're skin side up and place the skillet in the middle of the oven for 5 minutes.

4. Remove from the oven. Cover the skillet with a lid, and let sit for 4 minutes. Remove the breasts from the pan and place on a plate loosely covered with foil for 5 minutes.

5. Cut the breasts in ½"-thick slices on an angle. Fan out on a plate before pouring compote over them to serve.

Savory Fruit Compote

Mince 1 shallot and place it in a hot skillet with 2 tablespoons of duck fat. Cook for 3 minutes. Stir in ½ cup fruit jam, ¼ cup sherry, crème de cassis or a similar liqueur, and 2 tablespoons balsamic vinegar. Cook for 1 minute before spooning it out of the pan and over the sliced duck breast.

CHAPTER 7

BEEF, PORK, AND LAMB

YANKEE POT ROAST

New England cooking is traditionally plain and straightforward. If your family prefers a heartier flavor, add ½–1 cup of red wine in place of some of the broth, ½ teaspoon dried thyme, a bay leaf, and 2 cloves of sliced garlic.

Yields 6 servings

⅛ pound salt pork or bacon, cut into cubes

2 stalks celery, diced

1 3-pound chuck or English roast

Salt and freshly ground black pepper to taste

2 large yellow onions, quartered

1 1-pound bag baby carrots

2 cups beef broth

Water, if needed

4 tablespoons butter

4 tablespoons all-purpose flour

1 turnip, diced

6 medium russet potatoes, peeled and halved

1. Add the salt pork or bacon and the celery to the bottom of a 4-quart slow cooker. Place the roast on top of the pork and celery; salt and pepper to taste. Add the onions and baby carrots. Pour in the beef broth. Add water, if necessary, to cover the roast completely, making sure that the water level is not more than ¾ of the depth of the crock for the slow cooker. Cover and cook on low for 6 hours.

2. Uncover the slow cooker and increase the heat to high. Mix together the butter and flour to make a paste. Evenly distribute the paste into the beef broth in ½-teaspoon-size pieces. Add the turnip and the potatoes. Cover and cook for 1 additional hour, or until the potatoes are done. Taste the broth for seasoning and stir in more salt and pepper if necessary.

Mocking the Maillard Reaction

Contrary to myth, searing meat before it's braised doesn't seal in the juices, but it does—through a process known as the Maillard reaction—enhance the flavor of the meat via a caramelization process. Using beef broth (or a combination of beef base and water) mimics that flavor and lets you skip the browning step.

SLOW COOKER BEEF BRISKET WITH APPLES

This is a rich dish. Serve it with a crusty bread and a tossed salad with honey-mustard dressing.

Yields 6–8 servings

1 3- or 4-pound beef brisket

1 large yellow onion, quartered

2 large cloves garlic, chopped

4 large cloves garlic, left whole

1 10-ounce jar apple jelly

3 tablespoons Dijon mustard

Salt and freshly ground pepper to taste

¾ teaspoon curry powder

⅓ cup dry white wine

1 cup apple juice

1 cup water

Add all the ingredients to a 4-quart slow cooker. Add additional water to just cover the meat if needed. Cook on low for 6 hours or until meat is tender.

Adding a Second Step

Brisket will be more tender if you allow it to cool in the broth, so this is a good dish to make the day before you plan to serve it. To reheat it, bake it for 45 minutes at 325°F.

BAKED APPLE BUTTER STEAK WITH SWEET POTATOES

If you prefer your steak very rare, you can either add it to the pan 20 minutes into the baking time or cook the Brussels sprouts and sweet potatoes in the microwave and bake and broil the steak separately.

Yields 4–6 servings

Nonstick cooking spray

½ cup apple juice or water

¼ cup apple butter

2 tablespoons soy sauce

2 tablespoons dry sherry

½ teaspoon fresh ginger, grated

2 green onions, finely chopped

1 1½-pound sirloin steak, thick cut

1 12-ounce bag frozen Brussels sprouts, thawed

2 large sweet potatoes, peeled and diced

Salt and freshly ground pepper to taste

1. Preheat oven to 375°F. Treat a 9" × 13" nonstick baking pan with nonstick spray. Pour the apple juice or water into the pan.

2. In a small bowl, mix together the apple butter, soy sauce, sherry, ginger, and onion. Put the steak in the center of the pan and spread the apple butter mixture over the top of the meat. Arrange the Brussels sprouts and sweet potato pieces around the steak. Salt and pepper to taste.

3. Cover and bake for 45 minutes, or until steak reaches desired doneness and the potatoes are tender.

4. If you wish, uncover and put under the broiler for a couple of minutes to glaze the sauce on top of the meat.

TZIMMES

This dish looks like you slaved in the kitchen all day, but aside from the labor of readying the ingredients and removing the pan from the oven a couple of times, your time is free to get yourself ready to greet your guests.

Yields 8 servings

1 4-pound beef brisket

Salt and freshly ground black pepper to taste

1 large yellow onion, chopped

2 stalks celery, chopped

¼ cup fresh parsley, chopped

3 cups beef broth

3 tablespoons fresh lemon juice

3 whole cloves

1 1½" cinnamon stick

4 large sweet potatoes, peeled and quartered

1 1-pound bag baby carrots

1 12-ounce box pitted prunes

1 tablespoon honey

2 tablespoons white or white wine vinegar

Optional: 2 tablespoons butter

1. Preheat oven to 475°F.

2. Place the brisket fatty side up on a rack in a large roasting pan. Salt and pepper to taste. Bake for 25 minutes to brown the meat. Remove the meat, leaving it on the rack, and set aside.

3. Add the onion, celery, and parsley to the pan. Place the brisket directly on top of the vegetables. Add the broth, lemon juice, cloves, and cinnamon. Cover the pan, reduce the oven temperature to 300°F, and bake for 2½ hours.

4. Take the pan out of the oven and remove the cover. Add the sweet potatoes, carrots, and prunes to the pan. Mix together the honey and the vinegar and pour over the meat. Cover and return to the oven; bake for an additional 1½ hours.

5. Remove from the oven and let the meat rest, covered, for 15 minutes before serving. Remove the cover; adjust the salt and pepper seasoning if necessary. Carve the meat. Serve with the vegetables and the sauce that has formed in the pan. For a richer sauce, after you remove the meat and vegetables to a serving platter, whisk the butter into the pan juices 1 teaspoon at a time before spooning it over the dish.

Recipe Substitutions

Three tablespoons of lemon juice is equivalent to the juice of 1 lemon. Alternatively, you can use Minute Maid fresh lemon juice, available in the freezer case. If you don't have stick cinnamon on hand, substitute ½ teaspoon of ground cinnamon.

SLOW COOKER TZIMMES

Taste the broth before you add the sweet potatoes and carrots. That's the perfect time to add more cloves and cinnamon to taste if you want to add some extra punch to the sauce.

Yields 8 servings

1 3-pound beef brisket

1 large yellow onion, chopped

2 stalks celery, chopped

1 12-ounce box pitted prunes

1 tablespoon dried or freeze-dried parsley

3 cups beef broth

3 tablespoons fresh lemon juice

¼ teaspoon ground cloves

1 teaspoon ground cinnamon

1 tablespoon honey

2 tablespoons white or white wine vinegar

Salt and freshly ground black pepper to taste

4 large sweet potatoes, peeled and quartered

1 1-pound bag baby carrots

Optional: 2 tablespoons butter

1. Add the brisket, onion, celery, prunes, and parsley to a 6-quart slow cooker. Mix the broth, lemon juice, cloves, cinnamon, honey, and vinegar together and pour over the meat. Season with salt and pepper to taste. Cover and cook on low for 6 hours. Add the sweet potatoes and carrots. Cover and cook on low for another 2 hours, or until the brisket and vegetables are tender.

2. For a richer sauce, after you remove the meat and vegetables to a serving platter, whisk the butter into the pan juices 1 teaspoon at a time before spooning it over the dish.

Vegetable Swap

To help flavor the broth, add a few chopped baby carrots during the first 6-hour cooking stage. Omit the remaining carrots called for in the recipe when you add the sweet potatoes. Cover and cook on low for 1½ hours. Uncover and add a 12-ounce package frozen cut green beans to the cooker. Cover and cook on low for another 30 minutes to steam the vegetables.

SLOW-ROASTED SIRLOIN DINNER

Slow roasting is the perfect way to get a beef sirloin tip roast to a succulent rare or medium-rare. Thinly sliced leftovers are perfect for sandwiches.

Yields 8 servings

1 4-pound beef sirloin tip roast

1 teaspoon kosher or sea salt

½ teaspoon freshly ground pepper

1 teaspoon garlic powder

1 teaspoon onion powder

1 teaspoon ground cumin

1 teaspoon dried thyme leaves, crushed

½ teaspoon sweet paprika

2 tablespoons extra-virgin olive oil

2 turnips, peeled and cut into 2" pieces

2 parsnips, peeled and cut into 2" pieces

4 large red potatoes, peeled and quartered

1 1-pound bag baby carrots

1 12-ounce package frozen Brussels sprouts

8 cloves garlic, halved lengthwise

2 large yellow onions, sliced

Extra-virgin olive oil to taste

Salt and freshly ground black pepper to taste

½ cup dry red wine

1 cup water

1. Preheat oven to 200°F.

2. To ensure the roast cooks evenly, tie it into an even form using butcher's twine. Mix together the salt, pepper, garlic powder, onion powder, cumin, thyme, and paprika. Pat the seasoning mixture on all sides of the roast. Heat a medium-size roasting pan over medium-high heat. Add the oil and bring to temperature; place the roast in the pan and sear it for 3 minutes on all sides, or until brown.

3. Arrange the turnips, parsnips, potatoes, carrots, and sprouts around the roast. Distribute the garlic and arrange the onion slices over the vegetables. Drizzle with olive oil. Lightly salt and pepper.

4. Roast, basting occasionally with the pan juices, for 3 hours or until an instant-read thermometer inserted in the center registers 130°F for rare. Remove to a serving platter; cover and let rest for about 15 minutes.

5. Put the pan on the stovetop over two burners on medium-high heat. Add the wine and water. Bring to a boil, stirring to scrape up any browned bits from the bottom of the pan. Cook for about 5 minutes, or until reduced by half. To serve, thinly slice the roast across the grain. Serve drizzled with some of the pan juices.

POT ROAST WITH FRUIT SAUCE

Parsnips go well with the gravy that results from this dish, but you can substitute 8 medium red potatoes, washed and halved or quartered, if you prefer.

Yields 8–10 servings

2 cloves garlic, minced

1 teaspoon dried sage, crushed

½ teaspoon salt

½ teaspoon freshly ground black pepper

⅛ teaspoon cayenne pepper

1 3-pound boneless beef chuck pot roast

2 tablespoons vegetable oil

1 cup beef broth

1 large yellow onion, quartered

1 cup pitted prunes, halved

2 large apples, peeled, cored and cut into thick slices

1 pound parsnips, peeled and cut into ½" pieces

1 1-pound bag baby carrots

½ cup cold water

¼ cup all-purpose flour

1 tablespoon balsamic vinegar

1. In a small bowl, stir together the garlic, sage, salt, black pepper, and cayenne. Spread the garlic mixture over both sides of the meat. Add the oil to a 6-quart Dutch oven and bring it to temperature over medium heat; add the roast and brown it on all sides. Drain off the fat. Pour the broth over the roast and add the onion. Increase the heat to medium-high and bring to a boil. Tightly cover and reduce the heat; simmer for 1½ hours.

2. Add the fruit and vegetables to the pan. Add some water to the pan if needed to cover all the ingredients. Increase heat to return it to boiling, cover, and reduce the heat; simmer for 30 minutes or until the parsnips, carrots, and apples are tender. With a slotted spoon, transfer the meat, fruit, and vegetables to a serving platter.

3. Skim the fat off the juices that remain in the pan. Add water if necessary to bring the pan juices to 1½ cups. Bring to a boil over medium-high heat. In a small bowl, whisk together the cold water and flour until smooth. Slowly whisk the flour mixture into the boiling pan juices. Boil for 1 minute, then reduce the heat to medium and continue to cook and stir until thickened. Taste for seasoning and add salt and pepper if necessary. Stir in the balsamic vinegar. Serve the gravy over the roast, vegetables, and fruit.

Add Some Germanic Flair

Rather than adding the balsamic vinegar at the end, stir several finely crushed ginger snaps into the pan juices before you add the flour mixture. Once it's thickened, stir a teaspoon of red wine vinegar into the gravy.

HERBED POT ROAST

You can stretch this meal to serve more by also preparing a 12-ounce package of steam-in-the-bag frozen green beans or Brussels sprouts. Mix them with the potatoes and carrots.

Yields 8 servings

2 stalks celery, diced

1 3-pound boneless beef chuck roast

Salt and freshly ground black pepper to taste

2 large yellow onions, quartered

2 cloves garlic, minced

2 cups beef broth

¼ cup red wine vinegar

1 teaspoon dried thyme, crushed

8 medium red potatoes

2 pounds baby carrots

Optional: ¼ cup butter, softened

Optional: ¼ cup all-purpose flour

1. Add the celery, roast, salt, pepper, onion, garlic, broth, vinegar, and thyme to a 4-quart slow cooker. Cover and cook on low for 6 hours.

2. Wash the potatoes and peel off a strip of the skin from around each one. Add to the slow cooker along with the baby carrots. Cover and cook for an additional 2 hours on low.

3. If you wish to thicken the pan juices to make gravy, use a slotted spoon to transfer the meat and vegetables to a serving platter; keep warm. Increase the temperature on the slow cooker to high and bring 1½ cups of the strained pan juices to a boil. In a small bowl, use a fork to blend together the butter and flour. Whisk the flour mixture into the boiling juices, 1 teaspoon at a time. Once you've added all of the mixture, boil for 1 minute and then reduce the setting to low. Stir and simmer for 2–3 more minutes, or until the mixture is thickened. Taste for seasoning and add salt and pepper if desired.

Iranian Beef Roast

In step 1, omit the thyme and add a small can of diced tomatoes, ⅓ cup fresh snipped cilantro, ¾ teaspoon freshly ground black pepper, ¾ teaspoon ground cumin, ½ teaspoon ground coriander, ¼ teaspoon ground cloves, and a pinch each of ground cardamom, ground nutmeg, and ground cinnamon. In step 2, substitute thawed frozen green beans for the carrots.

ROAST BEEF WITH HORSERADISH POTATOES

Horseradish gives this beef dish an extra flavor dimension.

Yields 6–8 servings

⅓ cup prepared horseradish

2 tablespoons extra-virgin olive oil

1 teaspoon freshly ground black pepper

1 teaspoon dried thyme, crushed

½ teaspoon salt

1 3-pound boneless beef chuck roast

2 celery stalks, halved

¼ cup dry white wine or beef broth

1¼ cups beef broth

2 pounds small red potatoes

Optional: water as needed

1 1-pound package baby carrots

Optional: 2 tablespoons all-purpose flour

Optional: 2 tablespoons butter

1. In a small bowl, mix together the horseradish, oil, pepper, thyme, and salt. Trim the fat from the roast and cut it into 2" cubes. Rub half of the horseradish mixture into the meat. Add the seasoned roast, celery, white wine, and broth to a 4-quart slow cooker. Cover and cook for 1–2 hours on high, or until the celery is limp.

2. Wash the potatoes and peel off a thin strip of the skin from around each one. In a small bowl or a resealable plastic bag, mix the potatoes together with the remaining horseradish sauce.

3. Discard the celery. Add more water, if necessary, to bring the liquid level up to just the top of the meat. Add the potatoes and carrots to the cooker. Cover and cook on low for 4–6 hours, or until the meat is tender and the vegetables are cooked through. Serve warm.

4. If you wish to thicken the pan juices, remove the meat and vegetables to a serving platter. Cover with aluminum foil and keep warm. Turn the slow cooker to the high setting and bring the juices to a boil. Mix together the flour and butter, and whisk it into the boiling pan juices, 1 teaspoon at a time.

Luck of the Leftovers: Horseradish Hearty Beef Stew

If you have leftovers, you can make a hearty beef stew by cutting the meat into bite-size pieces and adding them to the thickened pan juices. Add a tablespoon or two of ketchup or some hot sauce for an extra punch of flavor, if desired. Reheat and serve with hard rolls, or serve over biscuits.

SLOW-COOKED MUSHROOM STEAK AND VEGETABLES

You can easily make this dish into a complete meal by serving it with ready-made mashed potatoes. Heat the potatoes in the microwave. Add your choice of microwave steam-in-bag vegetables or a salad.

Yields 8 servings

- 2 pounds boneless beef round steak, cut ¾" thick
- 1 tablespoon vegetable oil
- 1 12-ounce jar beef gravy
- 1 1-ounce package dry mushroom gravy mix
- 2 medium yellow onions, sliced
- 3 cups cleaned and sliced fresh button or cremini mushrooms

Trim the fat from the steak; cut the meat into 8 serving-size pieces. Add the oil to a 4-quart slow cooker and bring to temperature on the high setting. Add the meat and brown it while you ready the remaining ingredients. Combine the beef gravy and mushroom gravy mix. Remove the meat from the cooker and spread the onions over the bottom of the crock. Place the meat on top of the onions, and arrange the mushrooms over the top of the meat. Pour the gravy mixture over the top. Lower the temperature to the low setting and cook for 8–10 hours.

GRILLED HERBED TENDERLOIN WITH VEGETABLES

You can "grill" this meal indoors. Grill the steaks on high for 3–5 minutes; remove to a serving platter and keep warm. Lower the grill temperature to medium and grill the vegetables until the tomatoes are heated through and the asparagus is crisp-tender, about 2–4 minutes.

Yields 4 servings

2 cloves garlic, minced

1 tablespoon dried basil

2 teaspoons dried thyme

1 teaspoon dried rosemary

1 teaspoon dried mint leaves

2 tablespoons extra-virgin olive oil

½ teaspoon salt

½ teaspoon freshly ground black pepper

4 4-ounce beef tenderloin steaks, cut 1" thick

2 large yellow tomatoes, cut in half crosswise

1 pound asparagus spears, cleaned and trimmed

1. In a small bowl, mix together the garlic, basil, thyme, rosemary, mint, oil, salt, and pepper. Coat both sides of the steaks and the cut half of the tomatoes with the mixture.

2. Evenly coat the asparagus with the remaining garlic-herb mixture. Divide the mixture among 4 pieces of aluminum foil and fold the foil over to make a packet.

3. Bring the grill to temperature. Add the asparagus packets to the back of the grill. Grill the steaks over direct medium heat for 5 minutes. Turn the steaks and asparagus packets; add the tomatoes to the grill, cut side down. Grill until the steaks reach the desired doneness: another 2 minutes for medium-rare or 3–4 minutes for medium.

COUNTRY MEATLOAF

The grated carrots and butter-style crackers make this a sweeter-tasting meatloaf. It's good served with green beans or carrots and country-style hash browns or mashed potatoes and gravy made from the pan juices.

Yields 6–8 servings

1 pound lean ground beef

½ pound lean ground pork

1¼ teaspoons salt

¼ teaspoon ground black pepper

1 medium yellow onion, finely chopped

1 stalk celery, very finely chopped

½ cup carrot, peeled and grated

1 small green pepper, seeded and finely chopped

1 large egg

½ cup plus ⅓ cup ketchup

½ cup tomato sauce

½ cup quick-cooking oatmeal

½ cup butter-style crackers, crumbled

2 tablespoons light brown sugar

1 tablespoon prepared mustard

1. Preheat oven to 375°F.

2. Add the ground beef and pork, salt, pepper, onion, celery, carrot, green pepper, egg, ½ cup ketchup, tomato sauce, oatmeal, and cracker crumbs into a large bowl and mix well; shape into a loaf and place in a nonstick 2-pound loaf bread pan or in the center of a 9" × 13" nonstick baking pan. In a small bowl, mix together ⅓ cup ketchup, the brown sugar, and mustard; spread it over the top of the meatloaf. Bake for 1 hour.

UNSTUFFED GREEN PEPPERS CASSEROLE

You can use a can of whole tomatoes instead of diced, if you prefer. Just crush or cut up the tomatoes when you add them (and their juices) to the casserole.

Yields 4–6 servings

1 pound ground beef

1 medium yellow onion, chopped

1 14½-ounce can chopped tomatoes

1 8-ounce can whole kernel corn, drained

2½ cups herb-seasoned bread crumbs

2 large green bell peppers, seeded and cut into large dice

1 tablespoon butter, melted

1. Preheat oven to 400°F.

2. Add the beef and onion to a 4-quart ovenproof Dutch oven; brown the hamburger over medium-high heat. Pour off any excess fat. Add the tomatoes, corn, 2 cups of the bread crumbs, and green pepper pieces. Mix well.

3. Cover and bake for 25 minutes, or until the green peppers are tender. In a small bowl, mix the remaining bread crumbs with the melted butter. Remove the cover from the casserole and sprinkle the bread crumbs over the top. Bake for an additional 5 minutes, or until the bread crumbs are golden brown.

SLOW-COOKED MEATBALLS

This is an adaptation of a youvarlakia (Greek-style meatball) recipe. You can serve the meatballs and sauce over pasta, beans, or a combination of both.

Yields 8 servings

1½ pounds lean ground beef

1 cup uncooked long-grain white rice

1 small yellow onion, finely chopped

3 cloves garlic, minced

2 teaspoons dried parsley

½ tablespoon dried dill

1 egg

¼ cup all-purpose flour

2 cups tomato juice or tomato-vegetable juice

2–4 cups water

2 tablespoons butter

Salt and freshly ground black pepper to taste

1. Make the meatballs by mixing the ground beef with the rice, onion, garlic, parsley, dill, and egg; shape into small meatballs and roll each one in flour.

2. Add the tomato or tomato-vegetable juice to a 4-quart slow cooker. Carefully add the meatballs. Pour in enough water to completely cover the meatballs. Add the butter. Cover and cook on low for 6–8 hours, checking periodically to make sure the cooker doesn't boil dry. Taste for seasoning and add salt and pepper if needed.

STUFFED ONIONS

At the end of a long day, few things are better than sweet stuffed onions served with a salad.

Yields 4–6 servings

4 large Vidalia onions, peeled

½ pound ground beef

¼ teaspoon ground allspice

¼ teaspoon dried dill

3 tablespoons fresh lemon juice

2 teaspoons dried parsley

Salt and freshly ground black pepper to taste

1 large egg

1–2 tablespoons all-purpose flour

2 tablespoons extra-virgin olive oil

Water or chicken broth

1. Halve the onions by cutting through the center, not from top to bottom. Scoop out the onion cores. Chop the onion cores and add to the ground beef, allspice, dill, 2 tablespoons of the lemon juice, parsley, salt, pepper, and egg; mix well. Fill the onion halves to overflowing with the meat mixture. Sprinkle the flour over the top of the meat.

2. Add the oil to a deep 3½-quart nonstick skillet or electric skillet and bring to temperature. Add the onions to the pan, meat side down, and sauté until browned. Turn the onions so that the meat side is up. Add the remaining tablespoon of lemon juice and enough water to come up to just the top of the onion. Lower the heat, cover, and simmer for 1 hour, or until the onion is soft and the meat is cooked through.

FRITO AND CHILI CASSEROLE

Corn chips are salty, so consider using a reduced- or low-sodium chili in this recipe.

Yields 4–8 servings

Nonstick cooking spray

3 cups corn chips

1 large yellow onion, chopped

1 cup grated American cheese

1 19-ounce can chili con carne

1. Preheat oven to 350°F.

2. Treat a deep-dish pie pan with nonstick cooking spray. Spread 2 cups of the corn chips over the bottom of the pan. Distribute the onion and ½ cup of the cheese over the top of the corn chips, and then top them with the chili. Add the remaining corn chips and cheese over the top of the chili. Bake for 15–20 minutes, or until the casserole is heated through and the cheese is melted.

SALISBURY STEAK IN ONION GRAVY

Serve as an open-faced sandwich or with mashed potatoes. Add a salad and steam-in-the-bag peas.

Yields 6–8 servings

1 10¾-ounce can condensed onion soup

1½ pounds lean ground beef

½ cup dry bread crumbs

1 large egg

Salt and freshly ground pepper to taste

1 tablespoon all-purpose flour

¼ cup ketchup

¼ cup water

1 teaspoon Worcestershire sauce

½ teaspoon prepared mustard

1. In a bowl, mix together half of the soup with the beef, bread crumbs, egg, salt, and pepper. Shape into 6–8 patties.

2. Add the patties to a deep 3½-quart nonstick skillet or electric skillet; brown on both sides over medium-high heat, then pour off any excess fat.

3. Mix the remaining soup together with the remaining ingredients. Pour over the patties. Cover and simmer on low heat, stirring occasionally, for 20 minutes, or until the meat is cooked through and the gravy is thickened.

All-in-One Salisbury Steak Dinner

After you brown the meat patties, remove them from the pan and add a thawed 12-ounce package of frozen hash brown potatoes to the skillet. Place the meat on top of the potatoes and cook according to the directions. Add a thawed 12-ounce package of frozen baby peas, cover, and cook for an additional 5 minutes, or until the peas are heated through.

LAYERED BEEF CASSEROLE

You can substitute 2 tablespoons bacon bits for the cooked bacon if you prefer.

Yields 4 servings

Nonstick cooking spray

1 cup uncooked long-grain white rice

1 16-ounce can whole kernel corn, undrained

½ teaspoon seasoned salt

¼ teaspoon freshly ground black pepper

¾ cup beef broth, boiling

1 15-ounce can tomato sauce

1 teaspoon Worcestershire sauce

1 teaspoon Italian herb seasoning

1 large yellow onion, diced

1 green pepper, seeded and chopped

2 stalks celery, finely chopped

1 pound lean ground beef

1 cup Cheddar cheese, grated

2 slices cooked bacon, crumbled

1. Preheat oven to 375°F.

2. Treat a 2-quart casserole dish with nonstick cooking spray. Add the rice, corn, half of the salt and pepper, and the broth to the casserole dish and mix together. Mix together the tomato sauce, Worcestershire sauce, and Italian herb seasoning; pour half of it over the rice mixture in the casserole dish. Layer the onion, green pepper, and celery over the top. Mix the other half of the salt and pepper into the ground beef; break the beef apart over the top of the celery. Top with the remaining tomato sauce mixture. Cover and bake for 45 minutes.

3. Remove the cover and sprinkle the cheese over the casserole. Bake, uncovered, for an additional 15 minutes, or until the cheese is melted. Sprinkle the crumbled bacon over the cheese before serving.

Bacon Bits

If you don't want to cook the bacon separately, cut it into small pieces and mix it with the ground beef layer of the casserole. This will save you time, and it will also save you the hassle of cleaning up another cooking vessel.

EVERYTHING SLOPPY SANDWICHES

To serve this sloppy dish as open-faced sandwiches, toast the rolls before topping them with the meat. Instead of stirring the cheese into the meat mixture, top the sandwiches with it and place them under the broiler until the cheese melts.

Yields 6 servings

1 teaspoon coriander seeds

1 tablespoon extra-virgin olive or vegetable oil

1 medium yellow onion, chopped

2 cloves garlic, minced

1 pound ground beef

1 teaspoon ground cumin

Salt and freshly ground black pepper to taste

3 carrots, peeled and sliced in ¼" rounds

1 zucchini, halved and cut into ¼" rounds

½ cup chicken broth

1 8-ounce can whole kernel corn, drained

8 ounces Cheddar cheese, grated

8 onion or Kaiser rolls or hamburger buns

Optional: ketchup to taste

Optional: choice of pickles to taste

1. Add the coriander seeds to a deep 3½-quart nonstick skillet and toast for 1–2 minutes over medium heat, tossing or stirring so that the seeds don't burn. Remove from the pan, cool, and coarsely chop in a coffee mill or crush under the flat side of a knife. Add the oil to the skillet and bring to temperature over medium heat; add the onions and sauté until golden. Add the garlic and sauté for 1 minute. Stir in the ground beef and fry until browned, breaking it apart as it cooks.

2. Stir in the cumin, salt, and pepper. Add the carrots and sauté for 1 minute. Stir in the zucchini, broth, and corn; cover and simmer for 2 minutes. Uncover and simmer until most of the broth has evaporated. Top with the cheese; turn off the heat and cover for 1 minute, or until the cheese is melted. Divide the mixture between the rolls or buns to serve as sandwiches.

GROUND ROUND IN MUSHROOM CREAM SAUCE WITH SPINACH

The heat from the meat and mushroom sauce will wilt the spinach slightly, which makes this meal a salad and main course rolled all into one.

Yields 4 servings

1 pound ground round

Salt and freshly ground pepper to taste

2 tablespoons chopped roasted red pepper

Optional: 1 jalapeño pepper, seeded and diced

Optional: butter or extra-virgin olive oil as needed

8 ounces button or cremini mushrooms, cleaned and sliced

1 cup heavy cream

1 large egg, beaten

4 big handfuls baby spinach

Freshly grated Parmigiano-Reggiano cheese to taste

1. Add the ground round to a nonstick skillet and cook over medium heat until no longer pink, breaking it apart while it cooks. Season with salt and pepper to taste. Stir in the red pepper and the jalapeño (if using). If additional fat is needed to sauté the mushrooms, add some butter or oil to the skillet. Sauté the mushrooms until tender.

2. Mix the cream and egg together, then stir into the meat mixture in the skillet. Bring to a boil, then lower the heat; simmer until heated through and slightly thickened.

3. To serve, put a handful of spinach on each of 4 plates. Spoon the meat and mushroom sauce over the spinach. Top each serving with freshly grated Parmigiano-Reggiano to taste.

MARZETTI CASSEROLE

You can make this casserole the night before. Cover and refrigerate it overnight. To prepare the casserole, preheat the oven to 350°F. Bake uncovered for 45 minutes, or until the casserole is heated through.

Yields 8 servings

8 ounces dried medium egg noodles

1 pound lean ground beef

1 medium yellow onion, chopped

2 stalks celery, diced

Salt to taste

1 16-ounce jar spaghetti sauce with mushrooms

1 green pepper, seeded and cut into thin strips

1 cup frozen peas

1 cup tomato juice

1 tablespoon Worcestershire sauce

½ teaspoon dried oregano, crushed

Freshly ground pepper to taste

8 ounces Cheddar cheese, grated

Freshly ground Parmigiano-Reggiano cheese to taste

1. In a 4-quart Dutch oven, prepare the egg noodles according to package directions. Drain in a colander and keep warm.

2. Brown the beef, onion, and celery in the Dutch oven over medium heat, breaking the beef apart as it cooks. Once the beef has lost its pink color and the onion is transparent, drain off any excess fat. Add the remaining ingredients except for the cheeses. Lower the heat and simmer, covered, for 10 minutes. Stir in the noodles and Cheddar cheese. Serve immediately, adding grated Parmigiano-Reggiano to the top of each serving.

Day Two

If you're baking the Marzetti Casserole the next day, you can add another flavor dimension by mixing 1 cup of dried bread crumbs with 1 tablespoon of melted butter or extra-virgin olive oil. Sprinkle the crumb mixture and some Parmigiano-Reggiano over the top of the casserole; bake until the casserole is heated through and the bread crumbs are golden brown.

IRISH BOILED DINNER

You can substitute beef broth for the lager if you'd prefer to cook without alcohol.

Yields 8–10 servings

2 tablespoons extra-virgin olive oil or butter

3 cloves garlic, minced

2 cups leeks, white part only, chopped and rinsed

1 large yellow onion, sliced

1 3½-pound beef brisket

2 12-ounce bottles lager-style beer

2 cups water, or more as needed

2 bay leaves

10 black peppercorns

½ cup fresh parsley, chopped

2 teaspoons salt

1 1-pound bag baby carrots

1 pound small red potatoes

1 pound turnips, peeled and quartered

2 small heads cabbage, cored and sliced

Salt and freshly ground black pepper to taste

1. Add the oil or butter to an 8- or 10-quart Dutch oven and bring to temperature over medium heat. Add the garlic, leeks, and onion; sauté until the onions are transparent.

2. Add the brisket to the Dutch oven along with the beer, water, bay leaves, peppercorns, parsley, and salt. Add additional water if more is needed to completely cover the meat. Bring to a boil, then lower the temperature to low, cover, and simmer for 3½ hours. Add the carrots and potatoes, cover, and simmer for 30 minutes. Add the turnips and cabbage; cover and cook for an additional 15 minutes, or until all the vegetables are cooked according to desired doneness. Taste for seasoning and add additional salt and pepper, if needed.

Cooking with Cabbage

If you'd rather keep the cabbage in wedges, cut each cabbage into quarters, remove the cores, and secure the wedges with toothpicks. Remove the toothpicks before serving. Cabbage is a cruciferous vegetable that is very high in vitamin C and also has respectable levels of folate and vitamin B_6. .

SUKIYAKI

This is an Americanized dish. Serve it over cooked spaghetti, rice, or thinly sliced lettuce, or a combination of cooked rice and lettuce.

Yields 6–8 servings

2 pounds beef sirloin

½ cup soy sauce

½ cup beef broth

¼ cup beer or dry sherry

2 tablespoons granulated sugar

Freshly ground black pepper to taste

4 tablespoons sesame or peanut oil

1 large Vidalia onion, thinly sliced

1 cup sliced bamboo shoots

8 ounces fresh button, cremini, or shiitake mushrooms, cleaned and sliced

4 stalks celery, sliced

1 cup sliced green onions

1 cup bean sprouts

Optional: toasted sesame oil to taste

1. Cut the meat across the grain in paper-thin slices. In a small bowl, combine the soy sauce, broth, beer or sherry, sugar, and pepper.

2. Add the oil to a deep 3½-quart nonstick skillet or wok and bring it to temperature over medium-high heat. Add the meat and stir-fry for 3 minutes. Stir in half of the soy sauce mixture and stir-fry for 1 more minute. Push the meat to the side of the pan, and add the onion, bamboo shoots, mushrooms, and celery; stir-fry for 3 minutes. Pour the remaining sauce into the pan; add the green onions and bean sprouts. Stir-fry for an additional 3 minutes. Taste for seasoning and add more soy sauce, if needed, and add the toasted sesame oil if desired.

MICROWAVE HAMBURGER AND MACARONI CASSEROLE

Feel free to increase the amount of chili powder, according to your tastes.

Yields 4 servings

½ pound lean ground beef

1 cup uncooked macaroni

1 small yellow onion, chopped

1 8-ounce can tomato sauce

1 cup water

¼ cup ketchup

⅓ cup green pepper, seeded and chopped

1 tablespoon light brown sugar

½ teaspoon salt

½ teaspoon freshly ground black pepper

¼ teaspoon chili powder

1 8-ounce can corn, undrained

Place all the ingredients in a 2-quart glass or otherwise microwave-safe casserole dish. Stir well, making sure the ground beef is broken into small pieces. Cover and microwave on high for 8 minutes. Uncover and stir well. Cover and microwave for an additional 7 minutes. Let the casserole rest for 5 minutes, covered. Stir and serve.

Meaty Alternatives

You can substitute ground turkey for the ground beef in this recipe. If you want a lower-fat dish, microwave the ground meat on high until done. Break the meat apart and drain the fat; blot the meat with a paper towel to remove any fat clinging to the meat. Add the other ingredients and make the casserole according to the recipe instructions.

IMPROVISED SHEPHERD'S PIE

Use beef gravy with shredded roast beef or hamburger, and use chicken gravy if you're using chicken or shredded pork; mushroom gravy works with any of them.

Yields 8–10 servings

4 cups leftover meat or cooked hamburger

1 large yellow onion, diced

1 tablespoon extra-virgin olive oil

1 12-ounce bag frozen peas and carrots, thawed

1 12-ounce bag frozen corn, thawed

1 12-ounce jar gravy

1 cup sour cream

4 cups mashed potatoes

8 ounces Cheddar cheese, shredded

1. Preheat oven to 350°F.

2. Spread the meat evenly over the bottom of a 9" × 13" nonstick baking pan. Mix the onion with the oil and sprinkle the mixture over the meat. Evenly distribute the frozen vegetables over the meat and onions, then spread the gravy over the top of the vegetables. Mix the sour cream into the mashed potatoes; spread the potatoes over the gravy. Cover the pan with foil and bake for 45 minutes.

3. Remove the foil and top with the cheese. Bake, uncovered, for 15 minutes, or until the cheese is melted.

A Kinda Crust

If you prefer a solid "crust" of sorts to the bottom of the Shepherd's Pie, mix the meat with onion, oil, 2 beaten large eggs, and 1 cup corn flakes or bread crumbs. This recipe is your chance to use the vegetable and gravy leftovers you've been hiding in the freezer. Thaw and bring them to room temperature before using them.

TAMALE SPOON BREAD CASSEROLE

This recipe requires one pot for the cooking and a separate casserole dish for the baking.

Yields 8–10 servings

1 tablespoon extra-virgin olive oil

1½ pounds ground chuck

1 large yellow onion, chopped

1 clove garlic, minced

1 green pepper, seeded and chopped

1 cup cornmeal

1 cup water

2 14½-ounce cans chopped tomatoes, slightly drained

1 12-ounce can whole kernel corn

2 teaspoons salt, or to taste

1 tablespoon plus 1 teaspoon chili powder

¼ teaspoon freshly ground black pepper

½ cup sliced, pitted ripe olives

Nonstick cooking spray

1½ cups milk

2 tablespoons butter

1 cup grated mild Cheddar cheese

2 eggs, slightly beaten

1. Preheat oven to 350°F.

2. Add the olive oil to a deep 3½-quart nonstick skillet and bring to temperature over medium heat; add the ground chuck and brown the meat. Add the onion, garlic, and green pepper to the skillet; cook, stirring, until the onion is slightly browned. Mix together ½ cup of the cornmeal and the 1 cup water and stir it into the skillet; cover and simmer for 10 minutes. Stir in the tomatoes, corn, 1 teaspoon of the salt, the chili powder, and pepper; simmer for 5 minutes longer. Mix in the olives and then spoon the meat mixture into a 3-quart casserole treated with nonstick spray.

3. Heat the milk over medium heat along with the remaining 1 teaspoon salt and the butter; once the milk begins to simmer, slowly whisk in the remaining ½ cup cornmeal. Lower the heat and continue to simmer while stirring or whisking until it thickens. Remove from the heat and stir in the cheese and eggs. Pour over the meat mixture. Bake uncovered for 1 hour, or until the entire casserole is hot and bubbly.

Quickest and Easiest

You can assemble this casserole the night before or earlier in the day. Cover the casserole dish with plastic wrap and refrigerate until needed. Remove the plastic wrap and bake for 75–90 minutes. The extra cooking time lets you bake the casserole without letting it come to room temperature before you put it in the oven.

REUBEN CASSEROLE

You can bake the tomatoes in with the casserole if you prefer to have everything in one dish—just omit some of the tomato juice. Another option is to serve the casserole with fresh tomato slices or add tomato to a tossed salad.

Yields 4–6 servings

1¾ cups sauerkraut, rinsed and well drained

Nonstick cooking spray

1 pound thinly sliced corned beef

2 cups Swiss cheese, grated

Optional: 2 fresh tomatoes, peeled and thinly sliced

3 tablespoons Thousand Island or Russian dressing

3 tablespoons mayonnaise

½ cup butter, melted

1 cup rye wafers, crumbled

Optional: sprinkle of caraway seeds

1. Preheat oven to 350°F.

2. Put the drained sauerkraut in the bottom of a 3-quart casserole treated with nonstick spray. Add the corned beef and cheese. Spread the tomato slices in a layer over the cheese, if using. Mix the salad dressing and mayonnaise together and spread over the mixture in the casserole dish. Mix together the butter and rye wafers. Sprinkle the crumbs over the top of the casserole. If the wafers or bread that you used to make the crumbs don't contain caraway seeds, sprinkle some caraway seeds over the top of the crumbs. Bake for 30–45 minutes, or until the cheese is melted and the crumb topping is browned and crunchy.

Well-Drained Sauerkraut

Once you've rinsed the sauerkraut and drained it in a colander, it's a good idea to dump it into a clean cotton towel. Roll up the towel around the sauerkraut and then twist the towel to wring out even more of the liquid.

STEAK AND MUSHROOM PIE

Serve this pie with a tossed salad topped with a sour cream–based salad dressing, like blue cheese or ranch.

Yields 4 servings

4 slices bacon, cut into small dice

2 tablespoons butter

1 small yellow onion, diced

8 ounces fresh button or cremini mushrooms, cleaned and sliced

2 cloves garlic, minced

3 tablespoons all-purpose flour

½ cup Madeira wine or broth

1 teaspoon dried parsley

1 teaspoon Mrs. Dash Original Blend

½ cup beef broth

1 14-ounce bag baby potatoes and vegetables blend, thawed

1 cup cooked sirloin steak or roast beef, shredded or cubed

1 refrigerated peel-and-unroll-style pie crust

1. Preheat oven to 375°F.

2. Add the bacon, butter, onion, and mushrooms to a large microwave-safe bowl. Cover and microwave on high for 1 minute. Stir to mix the melted butter with the other ingredients. Cover and microwave on high for 3 1-minute segments, stirring between each minute. If the bacon has lost its pink color, continue to step 3; if it hasn't, cover and microwave on high for another minute.

3. Add the garlic and sprinkle the flour over the mushroom mixture in the bowl, then stir to combine. Slowly stir in the wine or broth. Cover and microwave on high for 1 minute. Whisk in the parsley and seasoning blend until the mixture is smooth and without lumps. Slowly stir in the ½ cup broth. Cut the baby potatoes in the vegetable blend into quarters, if desired, then stir the entire bag and the beef into the mixture.

4. Pour the beef mixture into a 9½" deep-dish pie plate. Top the filled pie plate with the pie crust. Cut vents into the crust. Place the pie plate on a jellyroll pan (a safety measure to catch any drippings should the pan boil over). Bake for 45 minutes, or until the crust is golden brown. Let set for 10 minutes, and then cut and serve.

Recipe Adjustments

Adjust the seasoning in this recipe according to the seasonings used in your cooked beef. For example, if you're using leftover Beef Bourguignon, use Burgundy instead of Madeira and simply add additional freshly ground black pepper to taste instead of the Mrs. Dash Original Blend.

UPSIDE-DOWN BEEF POT PIE

This recipe is a delicious way to use leftover roast beef and potatoes. The Dijon mustard and mayonnaise are optional flavor enhancers.

Yields 4 servings

¼ cup plus 2 tablespoons butter

1½ cups all-purpose flour

1 cup Cheddar cheese, grated

2 teaspoons granulated sugar

2 teaspoons baking powder

½ teaspoon salt

1½ cups milk

1 medium yellow onion, diced

2 baby carrots, shredded

½ stalk celery, finely diced

2 cups cooked beef, diced or shredded

1 cup frozen peas and carrots, thawed

1 cup diced cooked potatoes

1 cup beef gravy

Optional: 1 teaspoon Dijon mustard

Optional: 2 teaspoons mayonnaise

1. Preheat oven to 350°F.

2. Add ¼ cup of the butter to a large microwave-safe bowl; microwave on high for 30 seconds, or until the butter is melted. Pour the butter in an 8" square baking dish. Add the flour, cheese, sugar, baking powder, salt, and milk to the bowl; stir until blended. Pour into the baking dish.

3. Add the remaining 2 tablespoons of butter, the onion, carrots, and celery to the bowl. Cover and microwave on high for 1 minute; stir to combine the vegetables with the melted butter. Cover and microwave on high for 1 more minute, or until the onion is transparent. Stir in the beef, thawed peas and carrots, potatoes, gravy, and, if using, the mustard and mayonnaise. Pour the beef mixture over the batter. Do not stir. Bake for 1 hour, or until the beef topping is bubbly.

ARMENIAN MEAT PIE

Armenian meat pies are traditionally made using individual serving-size rounds of dough that are filled and folded over. This recipe streamlines that process by turning it into what resembles one large double-crust, deep-dish pizza without cheese.

Yields 8 servings

2 pounds lean ground beef

1 medium yellow onion, diced

1 green bell pepper, seeded and diced

2 cloves garlic, minced

1 teaspoon paprika

½ teaspoon ground allspice

Salt and freshly ground black pepper to taste

Pinch cayenne pepper

1 15-ounce can diced tomatoes, drained

2 tablespoons tomato paste

1 tablespoon dried parsley

1 teaspoon dried mint

Extra-virgin olive oil as needed

2 13.8-ounce cans refrigerated pizza crust

1. Preheat oven to 400°F.

2. Add the ground beef, onion, green pepper, garlic, paprika, allspice, salt, pepper, and cayenne to a large microwave-safe bowl. Stir to combine and break the meat apart. Cover and microwave on high for 3 minutes. Uncover and stir. Cover and microwave on high for 3–5 minutes, or until meat is cooked through. Drain off any excess fat. Stir in the drained tomatoes, tomato paste, parsley, and mint. Taste for seasoning and adjust.

3. Brush the bottom of a 14" nonstick deep-dish pizza pan or 9" × 13" nonstick baking pan with a generous amount of olive oil. Using the tips of your fingers, press one can of the pizza crust over the bottom of the pan. Poke holes in the bottom crust with a fork. Top with the filling. Top the filling with the other pizza crust, carefully pressing it out to the edges of the pan. Generously brush the top of the crust with extra-virgin olive oil. Cut several vents into the crust. Bake for 30 minutes, or until the crust is lightly browned on top and baked through. Let stand for 10 minutes, then cut and serve.

Hamburger Deep-Dish Pizza

To convert the Armenian Meat Pie recipe to a more traditional deep-dish pizza, substitute oregano for the mint and add 1 teaspoon of dried basil. Before you add the meat filling, cover the bottom crust with slices of or shredded mozzarella cheese to taste. You can also mix freshly grated Parmigiano-Reggiano cheese to taste into the hamburger filling.

JAMAICAN MEAT PIE CASSEROLE

Rather than making individual serving-size meat pies, this recipe makes one large double-crust, deep-dish pizza-style casserole. The curry powder and jalapeño give it a taste of the islands. Serve with a salad tossed with a citrus vinaigrette to complete the theme.

Yields 8 servings

2 pounds lean ground beef

1 large yellow onion, diced

2 green onions, finely chopped

1 jalapeño pepper, seeded and minced

2 cloves garlic, minced

1 teaspoon dried thyme

2 tablespoons curry powder

2 teaspoons paprika

Salt and freshly ground black pepper to taste

Dash cayenne pepper

2 large eggs

1 tablespoon white or white wine vinegar

½ cup bread crumbs

½ teaspoon granulated sugar, or to taste

2 13.8-ounce cans refrigerated pizza crust

1. Preheat oven to 400°F.

2. Add the ground beef, the yellow and green onions, jalapeño, garlic, thyme, 1 tablespoon of the curry powder, 1 teaspoon of the paprika, salt, pepper, and cayenne to a large microwave-safe bowl. Stir to combine and break the meat apart. Cover and microwave on high for 3 minutes. Uncover and stir. Cover and microwave on high for 3–5 minutes, or until the meat is cooked through. Drain off any excess fat. Stir in the eggs, vinegar, bread crumbs, and sugar. Taste for seasoning and adjust if necessary.

3. Brush the bottom of a 14" nonstick deep-dish pizza pan or 9" × 13" nonstick baking pan with a generous amount of olive oil. Using the tips of your fingers, press one can of the pizza crust over the bottom of the pan. Brush the top of the crust with extra-virgin olive oil and sprinkle the remaining 1 tablespoon of curry powder over the oil. Poke holes in the bottom crust with a fork. Top with the filling. Top the filling with the other pizza crust, carefully pressing it out to the edges of the pan.

4. Generously brush the top of the crust with extra-virgin olive oil. Sprinkle the remaining 1 teaspoon of paprika over the oil. Cut several vents into the crust. Bake for 30 minutes, or until the crust is lightly browned on top and baked through. Let stand for 10 minutes, and then cut and serve.

NEW ENGLAND BOILED DINNER

Don't tell anyone that you actually simmered this dish and you can still call it a "boiled" dinner.

Yields 8 servings

2 teaspoons butter or vegetable oil

1 3-pound boneless beef round rump roast

2 10¾-ounce cans condensed onion soup

1 teaspoon prepared horseradish

1 bay leaf

1 clove garlic, minced

6 large carrots, peeled and cut into 1" pieces

3 rutabagas, diced

4 large russet or red potatoes, peeled or unpeeled, and diced

1 2-pound head of cabbage, cut into 8 wedges

½ cup water

¼ cup all-purpose flour

1. Bring the butter or oil to temperature in a Dutch oven over medium-high heat. Add the roast; brown on all sides. Add the soup, horseradish, bay leaf, and garlic. Bring to a simmer; lower the heat, cover, and cook for 2 hours.

2. Add the carrots and rutabagas; cover and cook for 30 minutes.

3. Add the potatoes and stir into the broth; add the cabbage wedges as a layer on top. Cover and cook for an additional 30 minutes, or until the cabbage is done.

4. Transfer the meat and vegetables to a serving platter; keep warm. Mix the water and flour together; strain out any lumps and add the mixture to the meat juices in the pan. Increase the heat to medium. When the juices in the pan reach a high simmer, whisk in the water and flour mixture. Continue to cook and stir for 5 minutes, or until the juices are thickened. Remove bay leaf. Serve the resulting gravy alongside or over the meat and vegetables.

CORNED BEEF AND CABBAGE

This recipe isn't just for St. Patrick's Day. It makes a satisfying meal any time of year.

Yields 6 servings

1 2- to 2½-pound corned beef brisket

Water as needed

1 teaspoon whole black peppercorns

2 bay leaves

3 medium carrots, peeled and quartered

2 medium parsnips, peeled and cut into chunks

2 medium red onions, cut into wedges

6 medium red potatoes, cleaned and quartered

1 small cabbage, cut into 6 wedges

1. Trim any excess fat from the meat. Place the brisket in a 4- to 6-quart Dutch oven along with the juices and spices from the package that came with the corned beef. Add enough water to cover the brisket. Add the peppercorns and bay leaves. Bring to a boil over medium-high heat; reduce heat and simmer, covered, for 2 hours. At this point, the meat should be almost tender.

2. Add the carrots, parsnips, and onions to the meat. Return to a simmer; cover and cook for 10 minutes. Add the potatoes and cabbage. Cover and cook for 20 minutes, or until the vegetables and meat are tender. Remove the bay leaves and discard. Remove the pot from the heat, cover, and let the meat rest in the broth for 10 minutes.

3. Transfer the meat to a platter and thinly slice it across the grain. Spoon the vegetables around the meat on the platter and ladle some of the broth from the pan over the meat. Strain some of the pan juices and transfer to a gravy boat to have at the table.

OVEN-BAKED SHORT RIBS AND VEGETABLES

Beef Western ribs work well for this dinner, too.

Yields 4 servings

3 pounds beef short ribs

Salt and freshly ground black pepper to taste

1 1-pound bag baby carrots

4 medium russet potatoes, peeled and halved

1 12-ounce bag green beans, thawed

4 small white onions, halved

1 14-ounce can reduced-sodium beef broth

2 teaspoons mustard

2 tablespoons horseradish

2 tablespoons cornstarch

¼ cup cold water

1. Preheat oven to 350°F.

2. Trim off any excess fat from the ribs, and then arrange them in a 9" × 13" nonstick baking pan; sprinkle with salt and pepper. Bake uncovered for 2 hours. Drain off any excess fat and discard.

3. Distribute the carrots, potatoes, green beans, and onions around the meat. In a measuring cup, whisk together the broth, mustard, and horseradish; pour over the meat. Tightly cover the pan with aluminum foil; bake for 1½ hours, or until the meat is tender. Move the meat and vegetables to a serving platter; cover and keep warm.

4. To make the sauce, strain the meat juices in the baking pan. Skim off and discard any excess fat. Add enough water to the pan juices to measure 2 cups; either return the juices to the baking pan or put in a saucepan. Bring to a boil over medium-high heat. Mix the cornstarch together with the cold water; discard any lumps. Stir the cornstarch mixture into the juices; boil for 1 minute.

Crunchy, Tasty Beans

If you prefer crisp-tender green beans, cook them separately rather than adding them to the baking pan. For this recipe, simmer them in water or broth for 5–7 minutes, tasting to test for desired doneness. For extra taste, sauté 1 clove of minced garlic in oil, then add the green beans, toss to coat, and pour in the liquid.

SWISS STEAK MEAL

If you prefer a thick gravy, thicken the pan juices with a roux or cornstarch.

Yields 6 servings

2½ pounds beef round steak, 1" thick

1 tablespoon vegetable oil

Salt and freshly ground pepper to taste

1 medium yellow onion, diced

2 stalks celery, diced

1 large green pepper, seeded and diced

1 cup tomato juice

1 cup beef broth or water

6 large carrots, peeled and quartered

6 medium white potatoes, scrubbed and quartered

Optional: 4 teaspoons butter

1. Cut the round steak into 6 serving-size pieces. Add the oil to a pressure cooker and bring it to temperature over medium heat. Season the meat on both sides with salt and pepper. Add 3 pieces of the meat and fry for 3 minutes on each side to brown them. Move to a platter and repeat with the other 3 pieces of meat.

2. Leave the last 3 pieces of browned meat in the cooker; add the onion, celery, and green pepper on top of them. Place the other 3 pieces of meat on top and pour the tomato juice and broth or water over them. Place the carrots and potatoes on top of the meat. Close the lid; bring to high pressure and maintain the pressure for 17 minutes. Remove the pan from the heat and allow time for the natural release of the pressure.

3. Once the pressure has dropped, open the cooker and move the potatoes, carrots, and meat to a serving platter. Cover and keep warm. Skim any fat from the juices remaining in the pan. Set the uncovered cooker over medium heat and simmer the juices for 5 minutes. Whisk in the butter, 1 teaspoon at a time, if desired. Taste for seasoning and add additional salt and pepper, if needed. Have the resulting gravy available at the table to pour over the meat. Serve immediately.

Pressure Cooker Warning

Remember that you should never fill a pressure cooker more than ⅔ full. When in doubt about cooking times or other issues, check with the instruction manual that came with your cooker.

BEEF ROAST DINNER

Serve this roast with a tossed salad and warm buttered dinner rolls. Have sour cream at the table. Some people also like grated horseradish on their roast.

Yields 6 servings

1 tablespoon vegetable oil

1 stalk celery, finely diced

1 1-pound bag baby carrots

1 large yellow onion, diced

1 3-pound rump roast

Salt and freshly ground black pepper to taste

Optional: 1 tablespoon Dijon mustard

6 medium Yukon gold potatoes, scrubbed and quartered

3 cups beef broth

Water as needed

1 tablespoon butter

Optional: fresh parsley to taste

1. Add oil to a pressure cooker and bring it to temperature over medium-high heat. Add the celery. Grate 6 baby carrots and add them to the pan; sauté for 3 minutes. Add the onion, stir it into the celery and carrots, and push to the edges of the pan. Put the meat in the pan, fat side up. Season with salt and pepper.

2. Brown for 5 minutes, then turn the roast to fat side down. If desired, spread the mustard over the browned top of the roast. Season with salt and pepper. Spoon some of the sautéed celery, carrots, and onion over the top of the roast. Add the potatoes and the remaining carrots to the top of the meat. Pour in the broth. Add water, if needed to bring the liquid level with the ingredients in the pressure cooker.

3. Lock the lid. Bring the cooker to high pressure; lower the heat to maintain pressure for 1 hour. Turn off the heat and let the pan sit for 15 minutes to release the pressure; use the quick-release method to release any remaining pressure. Move the roast, potatoes, and carrots to a serving platter; tent with foil and keep warm.

4. Skim off and discard the fat from the pan juices. Bring to a boil over medium-high heat; reduce the heat and simmer for 5 minutes, and then whisk in the butter 1 teaspoon at a time. Pour into a gravy boat to serve with the roast. Garnish the roast platter with fresh parsley, if desired.

Making Gravy

If you prefer gravy with your roast instead of jus, increase the butter to 2 tablespoons and blend it with 2 tablespoons of all-purpose flour. When the pan juices come to a boil, begin whisking in the butter-flour paste 1 teaspoon at a time. When it's all added, boil for 1 minute and then reduce the heat; stir and simmer until the gravy is thickened.

BARBECUE POT ROAST

Whether you make it with beef or with pork, this barbecue is a delicious part of a casual supper when you serve it on sandwiches along with potato chips and coleslaw.

Yields 8 servings

½ cup ketchup

½ cup apricot preserves

¼ cup dark brown sugar

¼ cup apple cider or white vinegar

½ cup teriyaki or soy sauce

Dry red pepper flakes, crushed, to taste

1 teaspoon dry mustard

¼ teaspoon freshly ground black pepper

1 4-pound boneless chuck roast or pork shoulder roast

1½ cups water for beef; 2 cups water for pork

1 large sweet onion, sliced

1. Add the ketchup, preserves, brown sugar, vinegar, teriyaki or soy sauce, red pepper flakes, mustard, and pepper to a gallon-size plastic freezer bag; close and squeeze to mix. Trim the roast of any fat, cut it into 1" cubes, and add it to the bag. Refrigerate overnight.

2. Add the appropriate amount of water and the cooking rack or steamer basket to a 6-quart or larger pressure cooker. Place half of the sliced onions on the rack or basket. Use a slotted spoon to remove the roast pieces from the marinade and place them on the onions; reserve the marinade. Cover the roast pieces with the remaining onions.

3. Lock the lid in place on the pressure cooker. Place over medium heat and bring to high pressure; maintain for 50 minutes, or 15 minutes per pound (keeping in mind that you reduce the weight of the roast when you trim off the fat). Turn off the heat and allow 15 minutes for the pressure to release naturally. Use the quick-release method to release any remaining pressure and then carefully remove the lid. Strain the pan juices into a bowl, and set aside. Separate the meat from the onions, and return the meat to the pan. Purée the onions in a food processor or blender.

4. Pour the reserved marinade into the cooker and use two forks to pull the meat apart and mix it into the sauce. Bring to a simmer over medium heat. Stir in the onion. Add ½ cup of the reserved pan juices (skimmed of fat) to the cooker and stir it into the meat and sauce. Reduce the heat to low and simmer for 15 minutes, or until the mixture is thick enough to serve on sandwiches.

CHATEAUBRIAND MEAL

Serve this recipe with a salad tossed with blue cheese dressing and warm dinner rolls with butter.

Yields 4 servings

4 Idaho potatoes, scrubbed

1 24-ounce beef tenderloin, cut from the large end

Freshly ground or cracked black pepper to taste

1 12-ounce package frozen steam-in-the-bag Brussels sprouts

1 tablespoon extra-virgin olive oil

2 tablespoons olive or vegetable oil

2 tablespoons butter

8 ounces fresh button or cremini mushrooms, cleaned and sliced

1 large shallot, minced

1 tablespoon brandy

½ cup Madeira or other red wine

Salt to taste

Optional: additional 1 tablespoon butter

1. Preheat oven to 450°F. Wrap the potatoes in foil and place on the oven rack to bake; allow them to bake for 45–60 minutes before you plan to add the tenderloin to the oven.

2. Remove any membrane from the tenderloin and season all sides with freshly ground black pepper or roll it in cracked black pepper. Prepare the Brussels sprouts in the microwave according to package directions. Open one end of the bag and drain out any excess moisture, then pour in the tablespoon of extra-virgin olive oil; hold the bag opening closed and shake to coat the vegetables in the oil.

3. Bring a cast-iron skillet or ovenproof grill pan to temperature over medium-high heat. Add the oil and 1 tablespoon butter; when it begins to smoke, add the tenderloin and quickly sear it on one side and then the other. Pour the Brussels sprouts around the meat. Move the pan to the oven and roast for about 10 minutes for rare or about 15 minutes for medium. Remove the potatoes from the oven and keep warm. Move the tenderloin and Brussels sprouts to a serving platter; tent with aluminum foil.

4. Move the pan back to the stovetop; add the remaining 1 tablespoon of butter and melt it over medium heat. Add the mushrooms and shallots; sauté for 3 minutes, or until the mushrooms are tender. Add the brandy and sauté until all the liquid has evaporated. Turn the heat to low and pour in the wine. Simmer gently for 1 minute; taste for seasoning and add salt and pepper, if needed. To make a glossier sauce, whisk in the optional additional 1 tablespoon of butter, 1 teaspoon at a time, until it's incorporated into the sauce. Remove the foil from the serving platter, carve the meat, and pour the sauce over the tenderloin and Brussels sprouts. Serve immediately.

BEEF BOURGUIGNON

Serve this dish over buttered noodles or mashed potatoes, along with a salad and a steamed vegetable.

Yields 8 servings

8 slices bacon, diced

1 3-pound boneless English or chuck roast

1 large yellow onion, diced

4 cups Burgundy wine

2 cups beef broth or water

2 tablespoons tomato paste

3 cloves garlic, minced

½ teaspoon thyme

1 bay leaf

Salt and freshly ground black pepper to taste

1 large yellow onion, thinly sliced

½ cup plus 2 tablespoons butter

16 ounces fresh button or cremini mushrooms, cleaned and sliced

½ cup all-purpose flour

1. Add the bacon to a Dutch oven and fry it over medium heat until it renders its fat; use a slotted spoon to remove the bacon and reserve it for another use or use it in the tossed salad you serve with the meal. Trim the roast of any fat and cut it into bite-size pieces; add the beef pieces to the Dutch oven and stir-fry for 5 minutes. Add the diced onion and sauté for 3 minutes, or until transparent. Add the Burgundy, broth or water, tomato paste, garlic, thyme, bay leaf, salt, and pepper; stir to combine. Bring the contents of the pan to temperature; reduce the heat, cover, and simmer for 2 hours, or until the meat is tender.

2. Add the sliced onion to a microwave-safe bowl along with 2 tablespoons of the butter; cover and microwave on high for 2 minutes. Add the mushrooms; cover and microwave on high for 1 minute. Stir, cover, and microwave on high in 30-second increments until the mushrooms are sautéed and the onion is transparent.

3. Stir the mushroom-onion mixture into the pan; cover and simmer for 20 minutes.

4. In a small bowl or measuring cup, mix the remaining ½ cup of butter together with the flour to form a paste; whisk in some of the pan liquid a little at a time to thin the paste. Strain out any lumps. Increase the heat to medium-high and bring the contents of the pan to a boil. Whisk the butter-flour mixture into the meat and juices in the pan; boil for 1 minute. Reduce the heat and simmer uncovered, stirring occasionally, until the pan juices have been reduced to make a gravy.

BAKED STUFFED ROUND STEAK

Serve this dish with garlic bread, cooked pasta, and antipasto or a tossed salad.

Yields 4 servings

3 tablespoons extra-virgin olive oil

2 pounds round steak

Salt and freshly ground black pepper to taste

3 cloves garlic, minced

4 hard-boiled eggs, peeled and sliced

4 large carrots, peeled and grated

1 small yellow onion, minced

1 cup zucchini, grated and squeezed dry

2 ounces freshly grated Parmigiano-Reggiano cheese

1 25-ounce jar pasta sauce

1. Preheat oven to 350°F.

2. Rub 2 tablespoons of the oil over both sides of the round steak. Put the steak between 2 pieces of plastic wrap; pound the meat out flatter. Remove the plastic wrap and season the meat with salt and pepper. Sprinkle the garlic over the meat, then rub it into the meat. Evenly arrange the egg slices, carrots, onion, zucchini, and half of the Parmigiano-Reggiano down the center of the meat. Roll up the steak like a jellyroll, and then place it seam side down in a 9" × 13" nonstick baking pan or casserole dish large enough to hold the meat and pasta sauce. Rub the remaining oil over the top of the meat. Place under the broiler for 15 minutes, or until the meat begins to brown and caramelize. Change the oven setting back to 350°F. Pour the pasta sauce over the meat, cover the pan, and bake for 1 hour.

3. Remove the cover from the baking pan. Sprinkle the remaining Parmigiano-Reggiano over the meat and pasta sauce; bake for an additional 30 minutes, or until the meat is tender and the cheese has melted into the bubbling sauce. Remove from the oven, tent or cover, and let rest for 15 minutes before carving the meat and serving.

Potatoes over Pasta

Instead of serving Baked Stuffed Round Steak over pasta, add 4 medium scrubbed potatoes to the baking dish when you add the pasta sauce. You'll still get your starch, but the flavor will be a welcome change from the norm.

BRACIOLE

The stuffing in the Braciole adds substance to this dish, but you can also serve it with cooked pasta or garlic bread if you wish. Add a salad and a steamed vegetable for a complete meal.

Yields 4 servings

4 tablespoons extra-virgin olive oil

2 pounds flank steak

Salt and freshly ground black pepper to taste

3 cloves garlic, minced

1 cup bread crumbs

1 medium carrot, peeled and shredded

½ stalk celery, minced

1 small yellow onion, minced

1 teaspoon dried oregano

¼ teaspoon dried rosemary

¼ teaspoon dried thyme

2 teaspoons dried parsley

2 ounces freshly grated Parmigiano-Reggiano cheese

2 large eggs

1 teaspoon granulated sugar

1 25-ounce jar pasta sauce

Optional: fresh parsley to taste

Optional: additional freshly grated Parmigiano-Reggiano to taste

1. Preheat oven to 350°F.

2. Rub 2 tablespoons of the oil over both sides of the steak. Put the steak between 2 pieces of plastic wrap; pound the meat to ¼" thickness. Remove the plastic wrap and season the meat with salt and pepper. Sprinkle the garlic over the meat, then rub it into the meat.

3. Add the bread crumbs, carrot, celery, onion, oregano, rosemary, thyme, parsley, Parmigiano-Reggiano, and eggs to a bowl; mix well. Use your hands to shape the mixture into a log and place it in the center of the meat. Roll up the steak like a jellyroll so that when you slice the meat later, the slices will be against the grain of the meat; tie with butcher's twine.

4. Add the remaining 2 tablespoons of oil to an ovenproof Dutch oven; bring to temperature over medium heat. Add the meat roll; brown for 5 minutes on each side.

5. Stir the sugar into the pasta sauce, then pour it over the meat. Cover and bake for 1½ hours, or until the meat is tender. Bake uncovered for 15 minutes if necessary to thicken the sauce. Remove from the oven and let rest for 15 minutes, then move the meat to a serving platter, carve, and spoon the sauce over the meat. Garnish with fresh parsley and serve topped with additional freshly grated Parmigiano-Reggiano, if desired.

BASIC HAMBURGER

This burger actually tastes better when you use ground beef with a fat content of 10–15 percent. Making the burgers thinner creates the crunchy edges that are popular at diners.

Yields 3 or 4 servings

1 pound ground beef

Pinch garlic powder

Pinch salt

Pinch pepper

Dash Worcestershire sauce

1. Place a skillet over medium-high heat.

2. Divide the ground beef into 6 equal-sized portions. Shape them into balls.

3. Place a ball in the skillet. Press down on it with a spatula to flatten it. Sprinkle it with a pinch of garlic powder, salt, and pepper. Add a dash of Worcestershire sauce. Repeat with other meat balls.

4. Cook for 2 minutes then flip. Season the cooked side like the first side. Cook for 2 minutes.

5. Reduce the heat to medium. Cover and cook for 2 minutes. Serve while hot.

Variations on a Theme

Adding cheese is an easy way to add flavor to the average burger. You could also add sautéed onion slices, fried bacon, or a grilled pineapple ring. Or sauté some chopped shallots, mushrooms, and garlic and mix it into the meat before cooking.

BASIC BEEF ROAST

If you can't find an eye of round roast, make sure to substitute with a cut that can handle low, dry heat. Tougher cuts will need to be cooked for a long time in liquid in order to stay moist.

Yields 4 servings

1 3–4 pound eye of round roast

4 garlic cloves, cut into slivers

2 tablespoons vegetable oil

1 teaspoon salt

¼ teaspoon ground black pepper

½ teaspoon smoked paprika

½ teaspoon ground cumin

½ teaspoon onion powder

2 tablespoons brown sugar

1 cup beef or chicken broth

4 medium potatoes, cut in half

4 carrots, peeled and cut into large pieces

2 medium onions, peeled and quartered

1 tablespoon flour

1. Preheat oven to 325°F. Make several 1"-deep cuts into the surface of the roast and slide a garlic sliver into each. Rub the oil over the surface of the roast. Combine the dried spices and brown sugar in a bowl. Rub them over the meat. Place the meat in a large sealable plastic bag and pour the broth into the bag. Refrigerate for 2–24 hours.

2. Place a skillet over medium-high heat. Once it is heated, add the roast and cook on each side for 3–4 minutes. Once the roast is seared on all sides, pour the liquid and spices from the bag over the roast and place in the oven. Cover and cook for 1 hour.

3. Place the vegetables around the sides of the roast in the skillet. Return the skillet to the oven and cook for 45–60 minutes or until a thermometer measures 120°F for medium rare, 130°F for medium, or 140°F for well done. Remove from the skillet and rest for 10 minutes.

4. Place the skillet over medium heat. Use a spoon to scrape the stuck-on bits from the bottom. If necessary, add ¼ cup of beef broth to the skillet. Simmer. Sprinkle in 1 tablespoon of flour and whisk constantly. Pour it into a dish to serve over the beef. Slice the beef thinly and serve with the vegetables.

BEEF SHORT-RIB CHOLENT

This is a traditional Jewish stew that is simmered for 12 hours, beginning before sundown on Friday so it is ready for eating on the Sabbath.

Yields 6–8 servings

3 pounds bone-in beef short ribs

Salt to taste

½ cup dried kidney beans

½ cup dried chickpeas

Water, as needed

1 tablespoon vegetable oil

1 cup dry red wine

1 pound onions, coarsely chopped

1 garlic head, peeled

2 tablespoons brown sugar

1 tablespoon sweet paprika

¼ teaspoon ground cayenne pepper

1 teaspoon cumin seeds

½ teaspoon ground black pepper

1 pound baking potatoes, peeled and quartered

2 large carrots, peeled and cut into chunks

4 large eggs

1. The night before cooking, trim the excess fat off the ribs and cut into sections of 3 or 4 ribs. Sprinkle with salt and refrigerate in a tightly sealed container. Sort the beans and chickpeas and place in a large bowl. Cover with water by 2–3". The day you're serving, place a rack in the middle of the oven and preheat to 200°F. Pat the meat dry with paper towels.

2. Place a 6- to 7-quart Dutch oven over medium heat. Add the vegetable oil and a few of the ribs. Sear each side for 4 minutes. Once all the meat is browned, place on a platter and pour off the fat.

3. Add the wine and scrape the bottom of the pan. Add the onions and cook for 5–7 minutes. Add the garlic cloves, brown sugar, paprika, cayenne pepper, cumin seeds, and pepper. Stir and cook for 2–3 minutes.

4. Drain the beans and chickpeas and spread over the onions. Lay the meat on top of the beans. Layer the potatoes on top and sprinkle the carrots on the potatoes. Nestle the eggs in the carrots. Add 4 cups of water gently so the layers don't move. Cover and place over medium-high heat. Bring to a boil.

5. Cook in the middle of the oven for 8 hours. Uncover the pan and skim off as much fat as possible. Place the layers around the edges of a platter and place the ribs in the center. Peel the eggs and cut in half. Use the braising liquid as a gravy and serve immediately.

Cholent Cook-Off

Many Americans have heard of chili cook-offs, but there has been such a resurgence in cholent popularity that the cholent cook-off has been revived. Various synagogues around the country have annual cook-offs to see who has the best recipe. Just like chili, there are many variations on this basic recipe.

LEAN DIJON STEAK STRIPS

The Cattlemen's Beef Board rates twenty-nine cuts of beef as lean or extra-lean, and any of them would work in this dish. Keep in mind that a serving of beef is only 4 ounces, so read package size information.

Yields 1 serving

1 teaspoon olive oil

¼ small yellow onion, finely chopped

¼ pound eye round steak, fat trimmed

¼ cup beef broth

1 tablespoon fat-free sour cream

½ teaspoon Dijon mustard

½ teaspoon soy sauce

½ teaspoon garlic powder

1. Place a skillet over medium-high heat and add oil. When it is heated add the onion. Stir frequently and cook for 2–3 minutes or until the onion is translucent. Add the steak to the pan and cook for 1 minute on each side.

2. In a small bowl combine the beef broth, sour cream, mustard, soy sauce, and garlic powder. Pour over the beef. Cover the pan, reduce heat to low, and cook for 3–4 minutes for a medium-done steak.

3. Remove the lid, increase the heat to medium-high, and boil for 1–2 minutes until the sauce has reduced. Slice steak into thin strips. Serve immediately.

STANDING RIB ROAST

This meal is also good with a salad tossed with blue cheese dressing.

Yields 8 servings

1 3-pound standing rib roast, trimmed

Salt and freshly ground black pepper to taste

1 teaspoon herbes de Provence

3 medium yellow onions, rough chopped

1 head garlic, cloves separated but unpeeled

2 bay leaves, crumbled

1 2-pound bag baby carrots

8 medium Yukon gold potatoes, scrubbed and quartered

Extra-virgin olive oil to taste

½ cup dry red wine

Beef broth as needed

2 tablespoons butter

1. Preheat oven to 425°F.

2. Place the roast rib side down in the center of a large roasting pan. Rub the salt, pepper, and herbes de Provence into the meat. Bake for 15 minutes. Remove the pan from the oven. Lower the oven temperature to 325°F.

3. Scatter the onions, garlic, and bay leaves around the roast. Spread the carrots around the roast on top of the onions and garlic. Rub the potatoes with extra-virgin olive oil; place the potatoes evenly over the carrots. Salt and pepper the vegetables, if desired. Return to the oven and bake for 75 minutes, or until the roast reaches an internal temperature of 125°F for medium-rare.

4. Remove from the oven. Center the roast on a serving platter; remove the potatoes and most of the carrots and arrange them around the roast. Tent with foil and allow to rest for 20–30 minutes.

5. Strain the juices remaining in the pan, pushing against the vegetables to release the juices from them; discard the vegetables. Skim the fat from the strained juices. Set the roasting pan on the stovetop over medium heat. Add the wine to deglaze the pan, using a spatula to scrape any browned bits from the bottom of the pan. Add enough beef broth to the strained pan juices to bring it to 2 cups. Bring to a simmer and then whisk in the butter, 1 teaspoon at a time. Taste for seasoning and add salt and pepper, if needed. Serve the resulting au jus with the roast.

PORK LOIN DINNER

Serve this dinner with warm buttered dinner rolls and a tossed salad.

Yields 4 servings

1 tablespoon vegetable oil

1 small yellow onion, diced

1 pound boneless pork loin, cut into 1" cubes

Salt and freshly ground black pepper to taste

½ cup dry white wine or apple juice

1 cup chicken broth

1 rutabaga, diced

1 large turnip, diced

4 small Yukon gold potatoes, scrubbed and quartered

4 carrots, peeled and diced

1 stalk celery, finely diced

½ cup sliced leeks (white part only)

½ teaspoon mild curry powder

¼ teaspoon dried thyme

2 teaspoons dried parsley

3 tablespoons fresh lemon juice

2 Granny Smith apples, peeled, cored, and diced

Optional: fresh parsley or thyme sprigs to taste

1. Add the oil to a pressure cooker and bring it to temperature over medium heat. Add the onion; sauté for 3 minutes. Add the pork and lightly season it with salt and pepper. Stir-fry the pork for 5 minutes, or until it just begins to brown. Add the wine or apple juice, broth, rutabaga, and turnip. Add the potatoes, carrots, celery, leeks, curry powder, thyme, parsley, and lemon juice.

2. Lock the lid into place and bring to high pressure; maintain pressure for 15 minutes. Turn off the heat and allow the pressure to drop naturally.

3. Carefully remove the lid and add the diced apples. Bring to a simmer over medium heat; reduce the heat and simmer, covered, for 5 minutes, or until the apples are tender. Serve rustic style in large bowls, garnished with fresh parsley or thyme, if desired.

PORK CHOPS WITH ROASTED RED PEPPERS

There's no need for gravy with this dish. The chicken broth and meat juices combine to make a succulent sauce.

Yields 4 servings

1 tablespoon extra-virgin olive oil

4 boneless pork chops, ½" thick

Salt and freshly ground black pepper to taste

4 medium red potatoes, peeled and diced

1 medium yellow onion, diced

1 teaspoon dried oregano, crushed

1 cup chicken broth

1 4-ounce jar roasted red peppers, drained and chopped

1 12-ounce bag frozen cut green beans

1. Bring the oil to temperature in a deep 3½-quart nonstick skillet or electric skillet over medium heat. Add the pork chops. Season the chops with salt and pepper to taste. Brown for 5 minutes on each side. Remove from the pan and keep warm.

2. Add the potatoes and onion, and sauté for 5 minutes or until browned, stirring occasionally. Add the oregano and broth and stir to mix. Return the chops to the pan. Top with the peppers and green beans. Bring to a boil and then reduce the heat, cover, and simmer for 10 minutes, or until done.

SAUSAGE, BACON, AND BEAN FEAST

The simple step of sautéing the vegetables as you fry the bacon and sausage gives this dish that simmered-all-day, comfort-food flavor.

Yields 6–8 servings

1 8-ounce package bacon, cut into pieces

8 ounces ground pork sausage

3 large carrots, peeled and finely chopped

2 celery stalks, finely chopped

1 large yellow onion, finely chopped

2 garlic cloves, minced

1 bay leaf

½ teaspoon dried thyme, crushed

3 cups chicken broth

2 15-ounce cans cannellini beans, rinsed and drained

Salt and freshly ground black pepper to taste

Optional: hot sauce to taste

1. Add the bacon and sausage to a 4-quart Dutch oven and fry over medium heat until some of the fat begins to render from the meat. Add the carrot and celery; sauté along with the meat, stirring occasionally. When the meat is cooked through, drain all but 1 or 2 tablespoons of the rendered oil. Add the onion and sauté until transparent. Add the garlic and sauté for 30 seconds.

2. Add the bay leaf, thyme, broth, and beans. Stir to combine. Bring to a boil and then lower the heat and simmer, covered, for 15 minutes. Discard the bay leaf and add salt and pepper, to taste, immediately before serving. Add a few drops of hot sauce to enhance the flavor, if desired.

BRAISED PORK ROAST WITH KALAMATA OLIVES

Think of this as a prime rib of pork meal. Have the butcher separate the meat from the rack and tie it to the rack of bones. Serve with a steamed vegetable, dinner rolls, and a tossed salad.

Yields 6 servings

1 tablespoon macadamia nut or vegetable oil

1 3½-pound rack of pork, 6 ribs

1 medium red onion, chopped

5 cloves garlic, minced

3 bay leaves

½ cup red wine vinegar

½ cup red cooking wine

1 cup chicken stock

Salt and freshly ground white pepper to taste

6 medium red potatoes

¼ cup kalamata olives, sliced

1 teaspoon dried parsley

1 teaspoon thyme, crushed

1. Add the oil to a large Dutch oven and bring it to the smoking point over medium-high heat. Add the pork, and sear it on all sides until lightly browned, about 5 minutes on each side. Use tongs and a spatula to remove the meat. Add the onion and sauté until transparent; stir in the garlic and sauté for another 30 seconds. Add the bay leaves, and then deglaze the pan with the vinegar. Stir in the red wine and chicken stock. Season the pork with salt and pepper and return it to the pot. Peel off a strip of skin around each potato and add them to the pot.

2. Cover and cook the pork and potatoes over low heat for about 45 minutes, basting occasionally. Discard the bay leaves. Remove the meat to a platter; tent with foil and let it rest for 20 minutes. Remove the potatoes and keep them warm. Reheat the pan juices and add the olives, parsley, and thyme. Cut the strings around the roast to remove the rack of bones. Carve into 6 servings. Spoon the sauce over each rib, and serve. Put extra sauce in a gravy boat to have at the table.

HAM AND SWEET POTATO CASSEROLE

You can improvise the condensed Cheddar cheese soup by mixing 2 tablespoons of heavy cream and a couple of drops of hot sauce into ½ cup of shredded Cheddar cheese.

Yields 4 servings

1 12-ounce bag frozen steam-in-the-bag California-blend vegetables

1 large egg

2 tablespoons milk

3 tablespoons dry bread crumbs

⅛ teaspoon freshly ground black pepper

¾ pound fully cooked ham, ground

1 15-ounce can cut sweet potatoes, drained

Nonstick cooking spray

½ cup condensed Cheddar cheese soup

1. Preheat oven to 325°F.

2. Cook the vegetables in the microwave according to package directions; drain and set aside. In a bowl, beat the egg together with 1 tablespoon of the milk. Stir in bread crumbs, pepper, and ham; mix well. In another bowl, mash the sweet potatoes until almost smooth; spread onto the bottom and up the sides of a 9" Pyrex pie pan treated with nonstick spray. Spread the ham mixture over the sweet potatoes. Top with the vegetables. Combine the soup and remaining milk; spoon it over the vegetables. Cover with foil and bake for 45 minutes, or until heated through.

PORTUGUESE CALDO VERDE

Kale provides the green in this soup. If kale isn't available, you can substitute collard greens, but it will change the flavor somewhat.

Yields 6–8 servings

1 pound kale

1 tablespoon extra-virgin olive oil

1 large yellow onion, thinly sliced

½ pound linguiça or kielbasa, sliced

4 large russet potatoes, peeled and diced

4 cups chicken broth

2 15-ounce cans cannellini beans, rinsed and drained

Salt and freshly ground black pepper to taste

1. Trim the large ribs from the kale. Slice it into thin strips. Put the kale strips into a bowl of cold water and soak for 1 hour; drain well.

2. Add the oil to a 6-quart Dutch oven and bring to temperature over medium-high heat. Add the onions and sauté until transparent. Add the linguiça or kielbasa and potatoes; sauté for a few minutes. Add the chicken broth, drained kale, and beans. Bring to a boil. Lower the heat; cover and simmer for 1 hour. Taste for seasoning and add salt and pepper to taste.

BUBBLE AND SQUEAK

Adding some ham and bacon to this traditional British dish makes it a complete meal, even if you choose to serve it without a salad. For variety, you can add some chopped celery and grated carrots, too.

Yields 4–6 servings

4 slices bacon, cut into pieces

1 small yellow onion, diced

1 zucchini, peeled and grated

3 large russet potatoes, cut into cubes

¼ cup cooked ham, chopped

1 small head cabbage, cored and chopped

Salt and freshly ground black pepper to taste

1. Add the bacon pieces to a deep 3½-quart nonstick skillet; fry over medium-high heat until the bacon just begins to crisp. Lower the heat to medium and add the onion; sauté until the onion is transparent. Stir in the zucchini and potatoes. Reduce the heat to low, cover, and cook for 5 minutes, or until the potatoes are soft enough to mash. Spread the ham over the potato mixture, add cabbage. Cover and cook for 20 minutes.

2. Uncover the pan and test to make sure the cabbage is tender. Season to taste with salt and pepper. If necessary, leave the pan over the heat until any excess moisture from the cabbage and zucchini evaporates. To serve, invert onto a serving plate.

MEATLOAF WITH CREAMY MUSHROOM GRAVY

Once you've removed the meatloaf from the oven and are letting it rest, you can heat ready-made mashed potatoes, your choice of steam-in-the-bag microwave vegetables, and the mushroom gravy in the microwave.

Yields 8 servings

1 tablespoon extra-virgin olive oil

1 teaspoon butter

3 cloves garlic, minced

1 medium yellow onion, finely chopped

2 stalks celery, finely chopped

½ cup carrots, peeled and grated

8 ounces fresh button or cremini mushrooms, cleaned and chopped

¼ cup dry red wine

½ cup fine bread crumbs

½ cup milk

¾ pound lean ground beef

½ pound lean ground pork

¼ pound mild Italian sausage

1 large egg

1 tablespoon freeze-dried parsley

1 teaspoon sweet paprika

Salt and freshly ground pepper to taste

Optional: Worcestershire sauce

1 10-ounce jar beef mushroom gravy

1. Preheat oven to 350°F.

2. Put the oil, butter, garlic, onion, celery, carrots, and mushrooms in a microwave-safe bowl; cover with plastic wrap and microwave on high for 30 seconds. Uncover and stir; repeat at 30-second intervals until the onions are transparent. Add the red wine, bread crumbs, and milk; cover and wait for 10 minutes or until the crumbs absorb the moisture in the bowl. Mix in the beef, pork, sausage, egg, parsley, paprika, salt, and pepper. Pack the mixture into a loaf pan. Brush the top of the meatloaf with Worcestershire sauce, if desired.

3. Cover the loaf pan with foil and bake for 30 minutes. Remove the foil and bake for an additional 30 minutes, or until a meat thermometer inserted in the center of the meatloaf registers at least 165°F. Remove from the oven and let stand for 10 minutes.

4. While the meatloaf is resting, warm the gravy in a saucepan or in the microwave. Serve with the gravy spooned over the top of the meatloaf or serve on the side in a warmed gravy boat.

Crumb Wisdom

The amount of moisture that remains in the bowl after you microwave the vegetables and mushrooms can affect the amount of bread crumbs needed. If, after mixing, the mixture is too wet to form some of it in a ball that will hold its shape, add more bread crumbs.

CRANBERRY ROAST PORK WITH SWEET POTATOES

This recipe calls for a slow cooker, but if you prefer, you can braise the dish, covered, in the oven at 325°F for 3 hours, or until the internal temperature of the meat registers 175°F. Either way, the meat will be pull-apart tender.

Yields 6–8 servings

1 3-pound pork butt roast

Salt and freshly ground pepper to taste

1 16-ounce can sweetened whole cranberries

1 medium yellow onion, chopped

¾ cup orange juice

¼ teaspoon ground cinnamon

¼ teaspoon ground cloves

3 large sweet potatoes, peeled and quartered

Optional: 1 tablespoon cornstarch

Optional: 2 tablespoons cold water

1. Place the pork, fat side up, in a 4-quart slow cooker. Salt and pepper to taste. Combine the cranberries, onion, orange juice, cinnamon, and cloves in a bowl or large measuring cup; stir to mix and then pour over the pork roast. Arrange the sweet potatoes around the meat. Cover and cook on low for 5½–6 hours.

2. To serve with a thickened sauce, transfer the meat and sweet potatoes to a serving platter. Cover and keep warm. Skim the fat off of the pan juices, leaving about 2 cups of juice in the cooker. Bring to a boil on the high setting. Combine the cornstarch with the water. Whisk into the boiling juices. Reduce the temperature setting to low and continue to cook and stir for an additional 2 minutes, or until the sauce is thickened and bubbly.

Pamper the Pork

Many slow cooker recipes can be changed from cooking on low to cooking on high simply by dividing the cooking time in half. It's trickier with pork, especially when cooking with a sugar-based or fruit sauce. If the dish scorches, the whole taste will change; if you cook on high, monitor it carefully during the last hour of cooking.

PORK AND VEGETABLES SAUTÉED WITH APPLES

Some people love the taste of ginger; others find it tastes medicinal. If you fall within the "love it" category, feel free to increase the amount of ginger according to your personal taste.

Yields 4–6 servings

2 pounds pork steak, deboned and cut into thin strips

2 tablespoons soy sauce

2 tablespoons dry sherry

¼ teaspoon freshly grated ginger

3 tablespoons peanut oil

1 large yellow onion, diced

3 Golden Delicious apples, peeled and thinly sliced

4 cloves garlic, thinly sliced

1 12-ounce package steam-in-the-bag stir-fry mixed vegetables

Optional: 1 teaspoon toasted sesame oil

Freshly ground black pepper to taste

4 green onions, chopped

1. Place the pork steak, soy sauce, sherry, and ginger in a resealable plastic bag. Shake to evenly coat the meat. Let marinate in the bag for 15 minutes.

2. Add the oil to a wok or large, deep nonstick skillet and bring it to temperature over medium-high heat. Drain the marinade from the meat; add the meat to the skillet and sauté for 3 minutes. Add the onion and continue to sauté for another 3 minutes, or until the meat is done and onion is transparent. Add the apple slices and sauté until the apples begin to turn brown. Push the contents of the pan to the side and add the garlic; sauté the garlic for 30 seconds before stirring it into the meat mixture.

3. While the meat and apples are cooking, microwave the stir-fry vegetables according to the package directions for crisp-tender. Drain off any liquid from the vegetables. Add the vegetables, toasted sesame oil (if using), and pepper to the pan and toss with the meat mixture. Garnish with the chopped green onion.

MILK-BAKED PORK TENDERLOIN MEAL

The meat juices and milk in this dish magically combine to create a succulent gravy, so all that's left to do is carry the food to the table.

Yields 4 servings

2 teaspoons light brown sugar

1 teaspoon ground ginger

1 teaspoon ground mustard

4 4-ounce pork tenderloin cutlets, tenderized

Salt and freshly ground black pepper to taste

2 cups whole milk

4 large baking potatoes

4 teaspoons butter or extra-virgin olive oil

1. Preheat oven to 350°F. Treat an 8" square Pyrex baking dish with nonstick spray.

2. Mix together the brown sugar, ginger, and ground mustard. Spread it over the meat. Lay the meat flat in the baking dish. Season with salt and pepper to taste. Pour the milk over the meat.

3. Wash the potatoes. Prick each with a fork. Rub each potato with 1 teaspoon of the butter or oil, and wrap in individual pieces of aluminum foil. Place the potatoes in the dish with the meat. Bake for 1½ hours, or until all the milk liquids evaporate.

STUFFED ACORN SQUASH

The hash browns, peas, and sausage will be easier to mix together if the hash browns and peas are still frozen (broken apart) and the sausage is at room temperature.

Yields 8 servings

4 acorn squash

Nonstick cooking spray, as needed

2 cups frozen country-style hash browns

1 cup frozen peas

1 pound pork sausage

2 tablespoons extra-virgin olive oil, or to taste

Salt and freshly ground black pepper to taste

1. Preheat the oven to 350°F.

2. Halve squash lengthwise, remove seeds, and lay skin side down in a roasting pan treated with nonstick spray. Cut squash in half lengthwise and scrape out the seeds.

3. In a bowl, mix together the hash browns, peas, and sausage. Divide the mixture between the halves. Drizzle 1½ teaspoons of the oil over each of the squash halves. Season with salt and pepper to taste. Tightly cover the pan with heavy-duty foil. Bake for 1 hour. Remove the foil. Return the pan to the oven and bake for another 15 minutes, or until the squash is tender and the sausage is cooked through.

BAKED BRATWURST IN BEER

This makes a great football night supper for those times when you're watching the game at home. It's an easy recipe to double or triple. Simply increase the size of the pan. The baking times won't change. Serve with a salad or coleslaw.

Yields 4 servings

4 bratwurst

4 medium red potatoes, peeled and quartered

1 2-pound bag sauerkraut, rinsed and drained

1 large yellow onion, roughly chopped

1 12-ounce can of beer, room temperature

4 hot dog buns

Stone-ground or Bavarian-style mustard to taste

1. Preheat oven to 425°F. Treat an ovenproof Dutch oven with nonstick spray and lay the bratwurst in the pan. Bake uncovered for 15 minutes.

2. Remove the pan from the oven and arrange the potato wedges around the meat. Add the sauerkraut and onion over the potatoes and meat. Pour the beer into the pan, being careful that it doesn't foam up. Cover and bake for 45 minutes. Remove the cover and bake for an additional 15 minutes, or until the potatoes are tender and much of the beer has evaporated.

3. Serve the bratwurst on buns generously spread with mustard; add some drained sauerkraut and onions to each sandwich. Serve the potatoes and additional sauerkraut on the side.

Baked Bratwurst in Beer for a Crowd

If you'll be serving the bratwurst for a casual meal with potato chips on the side, omit the potatoes. There will be enough sauerkraut for 8–12 sandwiches. Add the desired amount of bratwurst and otherwise follow the baking instructions.

SWEDISH PORK LOIN

Leaner cuts of meat can get dry in a slow cooker. A pork sirloin roast is a good compromise; it's low in fat, yet it cooks up tender and moist. For gravy instead of sauce, mix the reduced pan juices with heavy cream.

Yields 8 servings

15 pitted prunes

12 pitted dried apricots

½ cup boiling water

1 cup chicken broth

1 cup dry white wine or apple juice

1 3½-pound pork loin, trimmed of fat and silver skin

4 large sweet potatoes, peeled and quartered

Salt and freshly ground pepper to taste

1 tablespoon cornstarch

2 tablespoons cold water

1. Add the prunes and apricots to a 4-quart slow cooker. Pour the boiling water over the dried fruit; cover and let set for 15 minutes.

2. Add the chicken broth, wine, pork loin, sweet potatoes, salt, and pepper. Cover and cook on low for 5–6 hours, or until the internal temperature of the roast is 155°F.

3. Remove the meat and sweet potatoes from the cooker; cover and keep warm.

4. Turn the cooker to high. Use an immersion blender to purée the fruit. In a small bowl, mix the cornstarch into the cold water. Once the liquid in the slow cooker comes to a boil, slowly whisk in the cornstarch liquid. Reduce the heat to low and simmer the sauce for several minutes, stirring occasionally, until thickened. Place the pork roast on a serving platter and carve into 8 slices. Arrange the sweet potatoes around the pork. Ladle the sauce over the meat. Serve immediately.

ROAST PORK LOIN WITH APPLES

Herbes de Provence is a mixture of equal amounts of thyme, savory, marjoram, and oregano. It sometimes also includes some sage, rosemary, dried lavender flowers, and/or fennel seeds.

Yields 8 servings

1 teaspoon kosher or sea salt

¼ teaspoon freshly ground black pepper

2 teaspoons herbes de Provence

1 4-pound pork loin, trimmed of fat and silver skin

2 tablespoons butter

1 tablespoon vegetable oil

3 large Golden Delicious apples, cored and cut into wedges

¼ teaspoon granulated sugar

4 large Yukon gold potatoes, peeled and quartered

1. Preheat oven to 375°F.

2. Mix the salt, pepper, and herbes de Provence together and rub it into the meat. Add the butter and oil to a 9-quart Dutch oven, and bring to temperature over medium-high heat. Add the roast and brown it for 2 minutes on all sides, or for about 8 minutes. Remove the meat from the pan and arrange the apple slices over the bottom of the pan. Sprinkle the apples with the sugar. Nestle the meat on top of the apples. Arrange the potato wedges around the meat. Season the potatoes with salt and pepper to taste.

3. Cover and bake for 30 minutes. Remove the cover and baste the meat with the pan juices. Continue to bake uncovered for 45 minutes, or until the internal temperature of the roast is 150°F. Remove the roast to a serving platter and tent with aluminum foil; let rest for 10 minutes.

4. Slice the pork crosswise into 8 slices. Arrange the apples and potatoes around the roast. Ladle the pan juices over the roast. Serve immediately, along with microwave steam-in-the bag Brussels sprouts or baby peas tossed with butter, a tossed salad with your choice of dressing, and dinner rolls.

Pan Size

The amount of air space between the food and the lid may add to the cooking time, but when in doubt, go bigger. It saves you the aggravation of having to move the ingredients to a bigger pot if the one you picked doesn't have enough room to hold all of the ingredients, and it prevents boil-overs in the oven.

PORK STEAKS IN PLUM SAUCE

The first part of the meal does take a little work, so go easy on yourself for the rest of it and serve the pork steak with baked potatoes, a microwave steam-in-the-bag vegetable, a tossed salad, and some dinner rolls.

Yields 4 servings

12 pitted prunes

2 cups boiling water

Optional: ½ cup port

3 tablespoons vegetable oil

2 tablespoons all-purpose flour

½ teaspoon salt

¼ teaspoon freshly ground pepper to taste

4 4-ounce or larger pork steaks

2 large shallots, minced

3 tablespoons red wine vinegar

⅔ cup beef broth

1 tablespoon plum jam

1 tablespoon ketchup

1. At least 2 hours before you plan to cook the pork, put the prunes in a bowl and pour in the boiling water. Tightly cover with plastic wrap right away and set aside.

2. Before you begin cooking, drain the water from the prunes and mix them with the port (if using). Cover and allow the prunes to macerate.

3. Add the oil to a large nonstick skillet, and bring to temperature over medium heat. Put the flour, salt, and pepper in a resealable plastic bag; shake to mix. Add the pork steaks to the bag; shake to coat the steaks in the flour. When the oil is hot, lay the steaks flat in the pan. Cook until the meat is almost cooked through and the floured surface touching the pan forms a crust, about 15–20 minutes; turn the steaks and cook until done, about another 10–15 minutes. Place crust side up on a serving platter; set in a warm oven to keep warm.

4. Add the shallots to the pan and sauté for 30 seconds. Deglaze the pan with vinegar. Add the broth and bring to a gentle boil; cook for about 5 minutes or until the liquid is reduced by half. Whisk in the jam and ketchup. Stir until the jam is melted. Arrange the prunes and pour the sauce over the meat. Serve immediately.

SLOW-COOKED PORK ROAST

This recipe makes enough for 12 sandwiches. You can also serve it with mashed potatoes or along with steamed cabbage.

Yields 12 servings

1 tablespoon vegetable oil

1 3-pound pork roast

1 10½-ounce can French onion soup

1 cup ketchup

¼ cup cider vinegar

3 packed tablespoons light brown sugar

Optional: 12 sandwich rolls

1. Add the vegetable oil to a 4-quart slow cooker. Bring to temperature on the high setting. Add the pork roast, fat side down. Cover and cook for 30 minutes. Turn the roast; cover and cook for another 30 minutes.

2. Mix together the soup, ketchup, vinegar, and brown sugar. Pour over the meat. Reduce the slow cooker setting to low, and cook covered for 8 hours, or until the meat pulls apart and registers 175°F in the center of the roast. Within the slow cooker, shred the meat using 2 forks, and mix it with the sauce. Remove the meat with a slotted spoon, and divide it between the sandwich rolls (if using).

MEXICAN PORK STEAK

Spicy Mexican tortilla filling doesn't always have to have a tomato salsa base. If tortillas aren't to your taste, serve the meat with country-fried potatoes and a salad.

Yields 4 servings

1–2 tablespoons peanut oil

1 1-pound boneless pork steak, cut into thin strips

2 cloves garlic, thinly sliced

1 small yellow onion, sliced

1 green pepper, seeded and diced

¼ teaspoon ground cumin

¼ teaspoon dried Mexican oregano

Salt and freshly ground black pepper to taste

Optional: cayenne pepper or dried red pepper flakes to taste

2 tablespoons beer

4 flour or corn tortillas, heated

Optional: refried beans, heated

Optional: shredded lettuce

Optional: sour cream

Optional: 2 green onions, chopped

1. Add the oil to a nonstick skillet and bring to temperature over medium-high heat. Sauté the pork for 2–3 minutes, and then add the garlic, onion, and green pepper. Continue to sauté until the onion is transparent and the pork is cooked through. Stir in the cumin, oregano, salt, black pepper, and cayenne or dried red pepper flakes (if using). Add the beer and cook until most of the moisture evaporates.

2. To fill the tortillas, spread refried beans on each tortilla. Top with the meat, shredded lettuce, sour cream, and green onion. Roll and eat like a burrito.

PORK AND VEGETABLE STIR-FRY

If you like to keep things simple, use the coleslaw mix. If you prefer to remain traditional, you can substitute a cup of chopped Chinese or napa cabbage and 2 cups of chopped bok choy for the coleslaw mix.

Yields 8 servings

3 boneless pork steaks, cut into thin strips

4 tablespoons soy sauce

3 tablespoons dry sherry or beer

2 teaspoons fresh ginger, grated

2 tablespoons peanut oil

2 cloves garlic, minced

2 medium yellow onions, diced

6 stalks celery, chopped

8 ounces fresh button mushrooms, cleaned and sliced

3 cups coleslaw mix

2 cups bean sprouts

½ cup chicken broth

½ teaspoon granulated sugar

1 tablespoon cornstarch

½ tablespoon toasted sesame oil

1. Put the pork steak strips in a resealable plastic bag along with 3 tablespoons of the soy sauce, the sherry or beer, and the ginger; seal and shake to mix. Marinate for 15 minutes.

2. Add 1 tablespoon of the peanut oil to a wok and bring to temperature over medium-high heat. Sauté the pork for 5 minutes, or until cooked through. Remove the pork from the pan and keep warm.

3. Add the remaining 1 tablespoon of peanut oil to the wok. Add the garlic, onion, and celery; sauté for 3 minutes. Stir in the mushrooms, coleslaw mix, and bean sprouts. Sauté until the vegetables are crisp-tender. Stir the pork back into the vegetables.

4. In a small bowl, whisk together the remaining 1 tablespoon of soy sauce, the chicken broth, sugar, and cornstarch. Add to the wok and stir until the mixture thickens and the cornstarch taste is cooked out of the liquids in the pan. Stir in the toasted sesame oil. Serve immediately.

SLOW-COOKED PORK WITH APPLE AND PRUNE SAUCE

Serve this dish with some mashed potatoes and some steam-in-the-bag green beans.

Yields 6–8 servings

12 pitted prunes

3 pounds boneless pork steaks, trimmed of fat

2 Granny Smith apples, peeled, cored, and sliced

¾ cup dry white wine or apple juice

¾ cup heavy cream

Salt and freshly ground pepper to taste

1 tablespoon red currant jelly

Optional: 1 tablespoon butter

1. Add the prunes, pork steaks, apple slices, wine or apple juice, and cream to a 4-quart slow cooker. Salt and pepper to taste. Cover and cook on low for 6–8 hours. Remove the meat and fruit to a serving platter and keep warm.

2. Bring the liquid in the cooker to a boil over the high setting. Reduce the setting to low and simmer until the mixture is reduced by half and thickened. Whisk in the red currant jelly. Taste for seasoning and add more salt and pepper if desired. Whisk in the butter 1 teaspoon at a time for a richer, glossier sauce. Ladle the sauce over the meat or pour it into a heated gravy boat.

Microwave Baked Potatoes

To serve 8, wash 8 medium baking potatoes and pierce each one twice with a knife. Arrange on a microwave-safe plate; microwave on high for 10 minutes. Test for doneness; microwave longer if necessary. Wrap each potato in foil until it's time to serve them. Have butter and sour cream available at the table.

THREE-CHEESE POLENTA GRATIN WITH ITALIAN SAUSAGES

Think of this dish as an improvisation of a deep-dish pizza, only with a polenta crust. Serve with a tossed salad dressed with Italian dressing.

Yields 4 servings

12 ounces sweet or hot bulk Italian sausage

8 ounces fresh button or cremini mushrooms, cleaned and sliced

1 medium yellow onion, diced

2 cloves garlic, minced

2 cups purchased tomato-basil pasta sauce

1 tablespoon extra-virgin olive oil

1 24-ounce package prepared cornmeal mush

1 cup ricotta cheese

1 cup shredded mozzarella or provolone cheese

½ cup finely shredded Asiago cheese

Optional: fresh chopped basil to taste

1. Preheat oven to 400°F.

2. Add the sausage to a 3- or 4-quart ovenproof nonstick skillet; brown over medium-high heat, breaking apart the sausage as it cooks. When the sausage is cooked through, add the mushrooms, onion, and garlic. Lower the heat to medium and sauté until the onion is transparent. Drain off any excess oil and transfer to a bowl; mix with the pasta sauce.

3. Wipe out the pan and add the olive oil, turning the pan to evenly coat the bottom of the pan. Set the pan over low heat. Drain the liquid off the cornmeal mush; cut it into 1"-thick slices and arrange around the bottom of the pan. As the mush softens from the heat, spread it out evenly over the bottom of the pan to form a crust.

4. Spread the ricotta cheese over the crust. Top the ricotta cheese with the sausage sauce mixture. Spread the remaining cheeses over the top. Bake uncovered for 30 minutes, or until the cheese is melted, bubbling, and lightly golden brown. Remove from the oven and let stand for 10 minutes before cutting into 4 wedges to serve. Garnish with fresh basil, if desired.

GROUND PORK AND EGGPLANT CASSEROLE

If you prefer, this dish will fit in a 2-quart baking dish, but using a 4-quart Dutch oven will give you plenty of room to mix the meat and vegetables together and let you do the stovetop cooking and baking in one pot.

Yields 8 servings

2 pounds lean ground pork

2 tablespoons peanut or extra-virgin olive oil

2 large yellow onions, chopped

3 celery stalks, chopped

1 green pepper, seeded and chopped

6 cloves garlic, chopped

4 medium eggplants, cut into ½" dice

⅛ teaspoon dried thyme, crushed

1 tablespoon freeze-dried parsley

3 tablespoons tomato paste

Optional: 1 teaspoon hot sauce

2 teaspoons Worcestershire sauce

Salt and freshly ground pepper to taste

1 large egg, beaten

½ cup bread crumbs

1 tablespoon melted butter

1. Preheat the oven to 350°F.

2. Bring the Dutch oven to temperature over medium-high heat. Add the ground pork and fry until done, breaking it apart as it cooks. Remove from the pan and keep warm.

3. Drain off and discard any pork fat from the pan; add the oil to the pan and bring to temperature over medium heat. Add the onion, celery, and green pepper; sauté until the onion is transparent. Add the garlic, eggplant, thyme, parsley, and tomato paste. Stir to combine. Cover and sauté, stirring often, for 20 minutes, or until the vegetables are tender. Return the ground pork to the pan. Add the hot sauce (if using), Worcestershire sauce, salt, pepper, and egg; stir to combine. Sprinkle the bread crumbs over the top and drizzle with the melted butter or oil. Bake for 40 minutes, or until the crumb topping is lightly browned and the casserole is hot in the center.

Why Freshly Ground Black Pepper?

Bottled ground black pepper contains anticaking agents that can cause stomach upset for some people and can also change the flavor. That last reason is why dishes always taste more peppery when you grind the pepper yourself.

SWEDISH SAUERKRAUT DINNER

Serve this dinner with crusty rolls or pumpernickel bread and some cheese.

Yields 8 servings

1 pound slab bacon or smoked pork jowl, diced

2 medium yellow onions, sliced

4 large russet or red potatoes, peeled or unpeeled, and diced

1 pound green cabbage, cored and shredded

1 2-pound bag sauerkraut, rinsed and well drained

1 apple, cored and chopped

2 cups dry white wine, apple juice, or chicken broth

1 tablespoon light brown sugar

1 teaspoon caraway seeds

1 teaspoon freshly ground black pepper

Put the bacon or pork jowl in a 6-quart Dutch oven, and fry the meat over medium heat to render out most of the fat. Spoon out some of the excess fat, leaving at least 2 tablespoons of it in the pan. Add the onion and sauté until transparent. Add the potatoes and mix with the bacon and onion. Add the cabbage and cook, covered, for 5 minutes, or until the cabbage wilts. Squeeze any excess moisture out of the sauerkraut and add it to the pan, along with the remaining ingredients. Lower heat, cover, and simmer gently for 1 hour, stirring occasionally.

THREE-PORK PIE

The ham and pork are already salty, which is why there is no salt called for in this recipe. Because tastes are different, be sure to have the salt shaker at the table for those who want more.

Yields 8 servings

3 tablespoons butter

1 medium yellow onion, diced

½ pound bulk pork sausage

3 tablespoons all-purpose flour

¼ cup milk or heavy cream

1 tablespoon dried parsley

¼ teaspoon dried sage or thyme

¼ teaspoon savory

¼ teaspoon freshly ground black pepper

1 28-ounce can heat-and-serve pork

½ cup broth

1 14-ounce bag baby potatoes and vegetables blend, thawed

1 cup cooked ham, cubed

1 15-ounce package refrigerated peel-and-unroll-style pie crusts

1. Preheat oven to 375°F.

2. Add the butter and onion to a large microwave-safe bowl. Cover and microwave on high for 1 minute. Stir to mix the melted butter with the onion. Break the sausage apart into the butter-onion mixture; stir to combine. Cover and microwave on high for 3 1-minute segments, stirring between each minute. If the sausage has lost its pink color, continue to step 3; if it hasn't, cover and microwave on high for 1 more minute.

3. Sprinkle the flour over the sausage mixture in the bowl, then stir to combine. Stir in the milk or heavy cream. Cover and microwave on high for 1 minute. Whisk in the parsley, sage or thyme, savory, and black pepper until the mixture is smooth and there are no lumps. Stir in the canned pork and broth. Cut the baby potatoes in the vegetable blend into quarters, if desired, and then stir the entire bag and the ham into the mixture.

4. Divide the pork mixture between 2 9½" deep-dish pie plates. Top each filled pie plate with a pie crust. Cut vents into the crust. Place the pie plates side by side on a large jellyroll pan (a safety measure to catch any drippings should a pan boil over). Bake for 45 minutes, or until the crust is golden brown. Let set for 10 minutes, then cut and serve.

Blending Starch and Vegetables

You can substitute 1 cup of thawed frozen corn and 1 cup of thawed frozen hash brown potatoes for the potato-vegetable blend. You can also replace the sage or thyme, savory, and pepper with ¾ teaspoon of Mrs. Dash Original Blend. Also, if you only need 4 servings, you can freeze half of the filling mixture to use later.

WELSH PORK PIE

This dish is traditionally served cold or at room temperature, so it's an excellent dish to make ahead to serve at brunch.

Yields 6 servings

1½ pounds lean ground pork

1 medium yellow onion, diced

2 large eggs

Pinch cayenne pepper

¼ teaspoon dried sage

2 tablespoons Worcestershire sauce

Salt and freshly ground black pepper to taste

1 refrigerated peel-and-unroll-style pie crust

1. Preheat oven to 375°F.

2. Add the ground pork, onion, eggs, cayenne, sage, Worcestershire sauce, salt, and pepper to a deep-dish pie pan. Mix well and spread out evenly in the pan. Bake for 30 minutes. Drain off any excess fat.

3. Cover the meat mixture with the pie crust. Cut vents in the crust. Bake for 45 minutes, or until the crust is golden brown and flaky.

CROQUE MADAME

This French sandwich contains hot ham and cheese with a fried egg on top. If you leave off the egg, you have a Croque Monsieur. Croquer is French for "to crunch."

Yields 2 servings

2 tablespoons butter, softened

4 slices sourdough or wheat bread

2 teaspoons Dijon mustard

4 ounces Gruyère or Emmenthaler cheese, thinly sliced

5 ounces sliced smoked ham

2 eggs

Pinch salt

Pinch pepper

1. Butter one side of each slice of bread. Spread the other side of each bread slice with a thin smear of mustard. Assemble 2 sandwiches using half of the cheese and ham on each. Make sure the buttered sides are on the outside of the sandwich.

2. Place a skillet over medium heat. When heated, place the sandwiches in the skillet. Cook each side for 3–4 minutes, or until they're toasted and golden brown. Remove to a plate and keep warm.

3. Place the remainder of the butter in the skillet. Once it has stopped foaming, slowly pour 2 eggs into the skillet. Sprinkle each egg with salt and pepper. Cover and let the eggs cook for 3–5 minutes, depending on how firm you like the yolks.

4. Center an egg on top of each sandwich, or inside for easier eating, and serve while warm.

GARLIC AND LEMON FRESH HAM

Fresh picnic ham is just the uncured portion of the back leg used for making ham. The connective tissue breaks down during the slow cooking to provide a great pork flavor.

Yields 8–14 servings

1 fresh picnic ham, 8–10 pounds

1 cup olive oil

4 tablespoons chopped fresh rosemary

2 tablespoons chopped fresh sage

2 tablespoons fennel seeds

6 garlic cloves, minced

Zest from 3 lemons

½ cup kosher salt

1 tablespoon ground black pepper

2 pounds red potatoes, scrubbed and chopped

Water, as needed

1. Preheat oven to 325°F. Use a sharp knife to score through the skin and fat of the ham in a diamond pattern. Make the cuts about 1" apart from each other. Combine the remaining ingredients except potatoes in a large jar. Rub at least half of the mixture on the ham and place it in a large Dutch oven. Add 1" of water in the bottom of the pan.

2. Cook in the middle of the oven for 2½–3 hours. It should cook for 20 minutes per pound. Be sure the meat near the center of the bone is 160°F. Remove it from the pan, cover with foil, and let rest for 20 minutes.

3. Use a wooden spoon to mix up the contents at the bottom of the pan. Add the potatoes and enough water to cover the potatoes halfway. Place the pan over medium-high heat and cook, covered, for 20 minutes, stirring occasionally. Remove the lid, decrease the heat to medium-low, and stir frequently while the potatoes cook for another 10 minutes. Slice the pork and serve with the potatoes.

Italian Ballpark Food

When Americans go to a ball game or a racetrack they indulge in pretzels, hot dogs, and caramel corn. But in Italy, slow-roasted whole pig is fairly common at racetracks as well as other sporting events. This slow-roasted picnic ham is similar to something you might find at a *rosticcerie* in Italy.

OVEN-BRAISED PORK ROAST

This typical German roast is served on New Year's Day with sauerkraut, crusty bread, potatoes, and apples. Pork butt roast, from the shoulder, is perfect for this dish, but don't use tenderloin.

Yields 8–10 servings

1 4-pound pork roast

1 large onion, cut into thick rings

2 celery stalks, cut into 1" pieces

1 14-ounce can chicken or vegetable broth

2 garlic cloves, smashed

7 whole peppercorns

2 tablespoons salt

1 whole allspice

1 12-ounce bottle dark ale

1. Place a Dutch oven over medium-high heat. Place the fat side of the roast down in the pan. Cook for 4 minutes on each of its four sides. Remove it to a plate and let sit.

2. Place the onions and celery in the pan and cook for a few minutes before adding the broth. Stir to remove the fond from the bottom of the pan.

3. Add the garlic, peppercorns, salt, and allspice and stir to combine. Stir in the ale. Reduce the heat to low. Return the roast to the center of the pan. Cover and simmer for 3–3½ hours. The roast should be tender and easy to cut.

4. Remove the roast to a pan to keep warm. Use a stick blender to purée the vegetables left in the pan. Follow the directions for Chicken Gravy (see recipe in Chapter 2) to create a gravy from the contents of the pan if you wish. Serve with mashed potatoes.

PULLED PORK

To create the shredded texture, use a fork in each hand to pull the pork apart. If it has cooked long enough, it will fall apart easily.

Yields 12–14 servings

1 3–4 pound pork butt

½ cup brown sugar

1 tablespoon paprika

1 tablespoon garlic powder

1 tablespoon onion powder

1 tablespoon ground cumin

1 tablespoon chili powder

1 tablespoon ground marjoram

1 teaspoon black pepper

1. Rinse the pork butt and pat dry with paper towels. Trim off any large pieces of fat. Combine all of the remaining ingredients and stir together. Sprinkle some of the mixture on each side of the pork butt and rub to make it stick. Place it on a plate and cover tightly with plastic wrap. Refrigerate for up to 24 hours, or let it sit unrefrigerated for 2 hours.

2. Place a large Dutch oven in the middle of your oven and preheat to 350°F. Once it has come to temperature, place the pork in the middle of the pan and cover tightly with a lid. Place it back in the oven and cook for 3 hours without opening it. The steam will help keep the meat juicy.

3. Once the meat has cooked, remove it from the pan and let it rest for 10–15 minutes. Use 2 forks to pull the meat apart. Once the meat is shredded, serve with the barbecue sauce of your choice on hamburger buns or rolls. You can also serve with pickled red onions.

Pickled Red Onions

Pickled onions provide a great crunch to complement the pulled pork sandwich. Thinly slice a large red onion and separate the rings. Place them into a large glass jar. Pour in ½ cup water, ½ cup white vinegar, ¼ cup sugar, and 2 bay leaves. Refrigerate for at least 2 days before serving.

BLT SANDWICH

This sandwich became popular after World War II when supermarkets started carrying fresh lettuce and tomatoes year round.

Yields 2 servings

6 slices thick-cut bacon

4 slices sandwich bread

2–3 tablespoons mayonnaise

4 slices tomato

2 lettuce leaves

1. Place a skillet over low heat and layer the bacon in the pan, being careful not to overlap the slices. Use tongs to flip them frequently as they cook for 5–7 minutes, or until some of the fat has rendered out of the slices. Increase the heat to medium-high and cook for another 5–7 minutes, or until the bacon is crisp. Place the slices on paper towels to drain.

2. Toast the bread and spread mayonnaise on 1 side of each slice.

3. Place the bacon on one slice of bread, add tomato and lettuce, and top with the other slice of bread. Serve while warm.

Variations on a Classic

Spread a clove of roasted garlic on the bread instead of mayo, use a flavored mayo instead of regular, add slices of avocado to the sandwich, use basil instead of lettuce, or add cheese to the sandwich.

BACON-WRAPPED PORK TENDERLOIN

If you don't have a meat thermometer, cut into the center of the largest piece. If no red liquid comes out, the meat is done.

Yields 4 servings

1½ pounds pork tenderloin, trimmed

8–10 slices bacon, 1 per pork slice

Pepper to taste

¼ cup maple syrup

2 garlic cloves

1 tablespoon balsamic vinegar

2 tablespoons Dijon mustard

Pinch salt

1. Cut the tenderloin into 1½" slices.

2. Place a skillet over medium-low heat. Once it is heated add 1 bacon slice per pork medallion to the skillet. Cook slowly for about 8–10 minutes. When it starts to brown (not crisp), place on paper towels to drain. Discard all but 2 tablespoons of the bacon fat from skillet.

3. Season the medallions with pepper. Wrap one piece of bacon around each medallion and use a toothpick to keep in place, or tie with kitchen twine.

4. Place the skillet over medium-high heat. Once it is heated place 3 or 4 medallions in the skillet so they're not touching. Cook for 5 minutes on each side. Then balance the medallions on their sides and cook in 1-minute increments, slowly rolling the medallions until the bacon is crispy on all sides and the center of the pork registers at 145°F. Transfer to a plate to keep them warm.

5. Add the remaining ingredients to the skillet, stirring until the browned bits are scraped off the bottom of the skillet. Let it simmer for 35 minutes. The contents should be thickened. Place the pork in the skillet and cook for 1 minute on each side to reheat. Serve with the sauce poured over the pork.

SEARED AND ROASTED PORK BELLY

Pork belly is the cut of meat that is used to make bacon. For this dish it is not cured or smoked.

Yields 4 servings

1¼ pounds skinless, boneless pork belly

¼ cup salt

½ cup sugar

4½ cups water

2 cups ice

½ cup chicken broth

5 garlic cloves

10 peppercorns

1. Rinse the pork belly and remove any loose pieces along the edges. Place the salt, sugar, and 4 cups of water into a small saucepan over medium heat. Stir frequently until the salt and sugar are dissolved. Place the pork belly into a sealable container that is deeper than the pork belly, but not much wider. Stir ice into the pan of water. Once the ice is melted, pour the mixture over the pork. Refrigerate for 12–24 hours.

2. Preheat oven to 300°F. Remove the pork from the brine and rinse it. Pat it dry and cut it into four even pieces. Place them in the bottom of a small Dutch oven. Pour in ½ cup of water and the broth. Sprinkle the garlic cloves and peppercorns around the pan. Cover with a lid, place in the middle of the oven, and cook for 2½ hours. The pork should be very tender.

3. Drain the liquid and peppercorns from the pan. Save the garlic cloves. Turn the pork over so it is fat side down. Smear a garlic clove over the meaty side of each slice of pork. Place the Dutch oven over high heat and cook for about 3–5 minutes, or until the fat is crispy and golden brown. Serve immediately.

Go Belly Up

You may not find pork belly in the butcher case, but your butcher should be able to get it for you. Ask for a piece that is equally fatty and meaty. It may be easier to locate pork belly at a Chinese butcher shop.

JAPANESE PORK CUTLETS

Panko is a Japanese bread crumb used for breading and frying. It creates a much crunchier breading than American-style bread crumbs but doesn't usually have added flavors, so it can be used when frying almost any breaded dish.

Yields 4 servings

2 teaspoons soy sauce

1 teaspoon yellow mustard

1 teaspoon honey

½ cup ketchup

2 teaspoons Worcestershire sauce

½ cup cornstarch

2 large eggs

1 cup vegetable oil

3 cups panko-style bread crumbs

4 boneless pork loin chops, ¼" thick

Salt to taste

Pepper to taste

1. Whisk the soy sauce, mustard, honey, ketchup, and Worcestershire sauce together. Set aside.

2. Preheat oven to 200°F and place a baking pan in the middle of the oven.

3. Place the cornstarch in a wide, shallow bowl. Place the eggs in a second wide, shallow bowl and beat 1 tablespoon of vegetable oil into eggs. Place the panko in a third wide, shallow bowl.

4. Pat the pork dry with paper towels. Season with salt and pepper. Dip pork lightly in the cornstarch and shake to remove any excess. Dip pork in the egg and let the excess drain off. Lay the cutlet in the panko and make sure the meat is covered. Place on a wire rack and let dry for 5 minutes. Repeat with the other cutlets.

5. Once the pork breading has dried, place ½ cup of oil in a skillet over medium-high heat. The oil is hot enough for frying when a piece of breading dropped in the oil sizzles and floats. Place 2 cutlets in the oil and cook them until the bottom side is golden brown, about 2–3 minutes. Turn them over and let them cook for another 2 minutes. Place them on the baking pan in the oven to stay warm. Drain the oil, wipe the skillet, and repeat with the remaining oil and pork.

6. Serve whole or sliced with the sauce.

Sizzling Schnitzel in Japan

This dish became popular after World War II when there were a number of Germans living in Japan. In Japan, this dish is usually served with a bowl of shredded cabbage and rice along with a hot English-style mustard and tonkatsu sauce. It's very similar in technique, if not flavor, to German schnitzel.

OVEN-ROASTED SPARERIBS

This very simple preparation lets the flavor of the spareribs truly shine. If the simple flavor won't make your diners happy, feel free to brush on 2 cups of barbecue sauce during the last 30 minutes of cooking time.

Yields 4 servings

4 pounds spareribs

Salt to taste

Pepper to taste

1. Preheat oven to 350°F. Season the spareribs generously with salt and pepper on all sides.

2. Place the ribs in a large skillet in the middle of the oven. Bake for 30 minutes.

3. Turn them over and bake for another 30 minutes. If the ribs aren't crispy on the outside, increase the heat to 425°F and bake for 10 minutes. Serve while warm.

SWEET-AND-SOUR PORK

This dish is a great way to use leftover pork. To determine how far your leftovers will go, each serving of pork is approximately the size of your fist.

Yields 4 servings

¼ cup ketchup

Juice from 1 lemon

2 teaspoons soy sauce

1 15-ounce can pineapple chunks in juice

1 tablespoon cornstarch

¼ cup cold water

1 pound cooked pork, cubed

1. Place a skillet over medium heat. Combine the ketchup, lemon juice, and soy sauce. Add the sauce to the skillet.

2. Stir in the juice from the can of pineapple. Combine the cornstarch and water in a small bowl. Once the sauce is bubbling, whisk in the cornstarch mixture.

3. Let the sauce simmer for several minutes until it starts to thicken. Stir in the pork cubes and pineapple chunks. Cook until the sauce has thickened again and the pork is warmed through. Serve over white rice.

CHOUCROUTE

This dish is pronounced "shoe-CROOTE," and it is French for "sauerkraut." As the sauerkraut cooks the taste becomes very mild. Because of the acidic nature of sauerkraut, it's better to use an enameled skillet for this dish.

Yields 6–8 servings

4 slices bacon

1 large yellow onion, chopped

3 garlic cloves, sliced

2 apples, cored and sliced

1 quart sauerkraut, fresh, jarred, or bagged

1 bottle nonbitter beer, or ½ bottle Riesling

7 juniper berries, or ½ cup gin

8 peppercorns

2 bay leaves

1 tablespoon brown sugar

¼ pound ham, cubed

1½ pounds German sausages (knackwurst, bratwurst, garlic sausage, kielbasa)

1. Place a skillet over medium heat. Once it is heated, add the bacon to the skillet and fry until is cooked through but not crispy. Add the onion and cook for 5–7 minutes or until the onion starts to brown. Add the garlic and cook for 1 minute, stirring continually.

2. Add the apples, sauerkraut, and beer. Stir to combine. Add the juniper berries, peppercorns, bay leaves, and the sugar. Reduce the heat to low, cover, and simmer for 1 hour.

3. Stir the ham into the skillet and add the sausages. Cook for 1½ hours, covered. Add water to the pan if it seems like it is getting too dry. When the sausages are cooked through, serve while warm with boiled and buttered potatoes.

ROAST LEG OF LAMB

Have your butcher trim the pelvic bone and as much fat as possible from a whole 6-pound leg of lamb to get the 4½ pounds you need. Roast lamb on a rack so that any fat drains away from the meat and vegetables.

Yields 8 servings

6 cloves garlic, minced

Salt and freshly ground black pepper to taste

3 teaspoons dried rosemary

1 4½-pound leg of lamb

3 tablespoons extra-virgin olive oil

24–32 small red new potatoes, scrubbed

1 1-pound bag baby carrots, halved

2 10-ounce packages frozen asparagus spears or cuts, thawed

1½ cups chicken broth or dry white wine

Optional: mint or red currant jelly to taste

1. Move the oven rack to its lowest position. Preheat oven to 400°F.

2. Add the garlic, salt, pepper, and rosemary to a small bowl; mix well. Reserve 1½ teaspoons of the mixture. Use a sharp knife to make 1" deep incisions in the top of the leg and around the meatier parts of the leg. Rub the remaining herb mixture into those incisions and on all sides of the meat. Sprinkle additional salt and pepper over the outside of the meat, if desired. Set the roast top side up on a rack in a large roasting pan.

3. Prepare 2 large sheets of double thickness heavy-duty aluminum foil, one large enough to hold all of the potatoes and the other large enough to hold the carrots. Add the oil, chicken broth or dry white wine, and remaining garlic-herb mixture to a small bowl; mix well. Place the potatoes in the center of one of the foil pieces; drizzle with ⅓ of the oil mixture, rubbing it into the potato skins. Bring the sides of the foil up and over the potatoes and crimp it on top to form a packet; put at one end of the roasting pan. Place the carrots on the other foil piece; drizzle with ⅓ of the oil mixture. Bring the sides of the foil up and over the carrots and crimp it on top to form a packet; put at the other end of the roasting pan. Put the roasting pan in the oven for 30 minutes.

4. Remove the roasting pan from the oven; turn the roast over. Open each of the foil packets. Form 1 or 2 bowls out of doubled sheets of heavy-duty aluminum foil; add the asparagus and drizzle with the remaining oil mixture. Position in the roasting pan. Return the roast to the oven for 45 minutes, or until the thickest part of the leg reaches an internal temperature of 130°F. Remove from the oven and transfer the roast and all vegetables to a large serving platter; tent with foil and let rest for 30 minutes before carving the meat.

5. To make a meat sauce, drain as much of the fat as possible from the roasting pan, then use paper towels to blot any fat that remains in the pan. Put the pan on the stovetop over medium heat. Simmer for 15 minutes, stirring occasionally, then whisk in mint or red currant jelly to taste, if desired. Serve the sauce as is or strained over the meat.

MOUSSAKA

This is a simplified recipe that uses yogurt and cream rather than a béchamel sauce; the extra effort comes from moving ingredients in and out of the pan and then laying the dish before you bake it.

Yields 4 servings

7 tablespoons extra-virgin olive oil

1 medium eggplant, peeled and sliced into ½" rounds

Salt and freshly ground black pepper to taste

1 large white onion, diced

2 cloves garlic, minced

1 pound lean ground lamb or beef

½ teaspoon ground cinnamon

¼ teaspoon ground nutmeg

1 15-ounce can diced tomatoes

4 medium russet or red potatoes, peeled and thinly sliced

1 cup freshly grated Parmigiano-Reggiano

2 cups plain whole yogurt

3 eggs, lightly beaten

¾ cup light cream

Optional: additional ground nutmeg to taste

1. Preheat oven to 375°F.

2. Add 2 tablespoons of the oil to an ovenproof Dutch oven and bring to temperature over medium-high heat. Add the eggplant slices and brown them for 2 minutes on each side; remove and drain on paper towels. Lightly salt and pepper the eggplant slices.

3. Add another 2 tablespoons of oil to the same Dutch oven and bring it to temperature over medium heat; add the onion and sauté for 3 minutes, or until the onion is transparent. Add the garlic and ground lamb or beef; salt and pepper to taste and brown the meat completely, breaking it apart as it cooks. Stir in the cinnamon, nutmeg, and tomatoes; simmer uncovered for 10 minutes. Transfer the cooked meat mixture to a bowl.

4. Wipe out the Dutch oven, add the remaining 3 tablespoons of oil, and bring it to temperature over medium heat. Add the potato slices and brown them for about 5 minutes on each side, or until cooked through; spread the potatoes in an even layer across the bottom of the pan. Lightly season with salt and pepper.

5. Spread the meat over the layer of potatoes, arrange the eggplant on top of the meat, and top the meat with the Parmigiano-Reggiano.

6. Add the yogurt, eggs, and cream to a medium-size bowl; stir to combine and pour over the Parmigiano-Reggiano. Sprinkle additional nutmeg over the yogurt sauce, if desired. Let sit for 10 minutes, and then move to the oven and bake for 40 minutes, or until golden brown and bubbly. Remove from the oven and let rest for 15 minutes before serving.

LAMB BURGERS

Lamb is more common than beef in many Mediterranean countries. The rich flavor holds up well to strong spices.

Yields 4 servings

1 pound lean ground lamb

1 cup fresh bread crumbs

1 teaspoon salt

¼ teaspoon ground black pepper

1 celery stalk, chopped

2 teaspoons Worcestershire sauce

½ teaspoon dried rosemary, crumbled

2 tomatoes, seeded and finely chopped

1 egg, beaten

2 tablespoons olive oil

1. Combine all of the ingredients but the olive oil in a large bowl. Mix together and shape into 6 patties.

2. Place a skillet over medium heat. Once it's heated add the oil and 3 of the patties. Cook on each side for 5 minutes, or until cooked through the middle. Repeat for remaining patties. Serve on trimmed pita bread with fresh cucumber slices.

AZERBAIJANI STEWED LAMB

This dish is traditionally called Bosartma, which translates as stewed lamb. It is traditionally served with cherry plums that are commonly found in central and eastern Europe. A darker-skinned plum is better than a lighter-skinned plum.

Yields 4 servings

3 tablespoons butter

2 pounds lamb, cut into 1" cubes

1 large onion, chopped

4 Roma tomatoes, cubed

3 tablespoons tomato paste

2 plums, pitted and chopped

3 cups chicken broth

1 tablespoon chopped dill

1 tablespoon chopped cilantro

1 tablespoon chopped mint

Juice from 1 lemon

Salt to taste

Pepper to taste

1. Place a skillet over medium-high heat. Once it's heated, add the butter. When the butter has melted, add the lamb and cook for 10 minutes, turning the meat every 1–2 minutes until it's browned on all sides.

2. Remove the meat from the skillet and add the onion. Cook for 8–10 minutes. Add the tomatoes, tomato paste, and plums. Stir until everything is well coated. Stir in the chicken broth and the herbs. Cover the skillet, reduce the heat to low, and simmer for 1 hour, or until the lamb is cooked through and soft. Stir in the lemon juice and then season to taste with salt and pepper.

GREEK LEMON AND OREGANO LAMB

You can easily double this recipe and use an entire leg of lamb. Ask the butcher to trim off the last several inches so it will fit in a large skillet.

Yields 4 servings

1 2-pound bone-in lamb leg roast

3 garlic cloves, sliced

Juice and zest from 1 lemon

1 teaspoon salt

½ teaspoon ground black pepper

2 tablespoons dried oregano

2 tablespoons butter

1 cup hot water

1½ pounds potatoes, scrubbed and quartered

2 tablespoons olive oil

Salt to taste

Pepper to taste

1. Preheat oven to 350°F. Rinse and dry the lamb. Trim off any large pieces of fat or silver skin. Cut small slits into the meat and insert slivers of garlic. Mix the lemon juice, salt, pepper, and oregano in a small bowl. Rub the mixture over the lamb.

2. Place a skillet over medium-high heat. Once it's heated, add the lamb and sear it on each side for 4 minutes. Once it is browned, bake in the center of the oven for 1 hour.

3. Remove the pan from the oven and drain the fat. Rub the butter over the meat and return it to the skillet. Pour the water into the skillet and cook for 45 minutes. Toss the potatoes in the lemon zest and olive oil. Sprinkle liberally with salt and pepper and place around the lamb. Bake for 45–60 minutes, or until the potatoes and lamb are tender. Tent the skillet with foil and let it rest for 15 minutes before carving and serving.

HERB-ROASTED RACK OF LAMB

When you purchase the racks of lamb, ask for them to be frenched. The top of the bone has the flesh removed to create an impressive display when cooked, and to prevent burning. This dish isn't cheap, but it is easy to make and impressive to serve.

Yields 4–6 servings

2 14–16-ounce racks of lamb

2 sprigs rosemary, leaves stripped and chopped

2 tablespoons chopped fresh thyme

2 garlic cloves, minced

¼ cup olive oil

Salt to taste

Pepper to taste

1. Trim all but a thin layer of fat from the lamb. Score the fat layer in a crosshatch pattern, being careful to not cut through to the meat. Combine the herbs and garlic in enough oil to coat the lamb. Sprinkle salt and pepper all over the meat, and rub with the olive oil and herbs. Place in a container and seal tightly. Refrigerate for 8–24 hours.

2. Preheat oven to 425°F. Let the meat come to room temperature while the oven preheats.

3. Place a skillet over medium heat. Once it's heated add 2 tablespoons of oil. Place the lamb, fat side down, in the skillet and cook for 6 minutes, or until well-browned. Repeat with the other rack. Remove the skillet from the heat.

4. Stand the racks in the skillet and lean them against each other with the fat side facing to the outside of the skillet.

5. Cook in the middle of the oven for 15 minutes. Reduce the heat to 325°F and roast for 5–15 minutes. Use a meat thermometer to test the meat's doneness: 130°F for medium-rare, 14°F for medium, and 150°F for well done. Let it rest for 10 minutes before cutting the rack between the bones in sections of 2 and serve.

INDIAN-STYLE LAMB CURRY

It is rare to see dishes in India called curries. The British settlers in India adopted the Tamil word kari, *which means "sauce for rice," to refer to any dish with a sauce that was served over rice.*

Yields 4–6 servings

1 small yellow onion, peeled and halved

1 small garlic clove

½ cup Greek-style yogurt

2 teaspoons lemon juice

1 teaspoon ground coriander

½ teaspoon salt

½ teaspoon cumin

½ teaspoon ground cloves

½ teaspoon ground cardamom

½ teaspoon black pepper

¼ teaspoon ground ginger

¼ teaspoon ground cinnamon

½ teaspoon olive oil

1½ teaspoons cornstarch

1 pound boneless lamb, cut into 1" cubes

1 tablespoon butter

1 tablespoon vegetable oil

1 cayenne pepper

1. Purée half the onion, the garlic, yogurt, and lemon juice in a blender.

2. Place a dry skillet over medium heat. Once it's heated, add the dry spices to the skillet and shake every few seconds. Cook for 2 minutes. Pour the spices into the blender with the olive oil and cornstarch and blend.

3. Pour the yogurt mixture over the lamb cubes in a sealable container. Toss so the meat is coated. Leave the meat at room temperature for 2 hours, or marinate overnight in the refrigerator.

4. Place a skillet over medium heat, and once it's heated add the butter and vegetable oil. Mince the other half of the onion. Once the butter stops foaming, add the onion to the skillet. Cook for several minutes while stirring. Add the meat and the marinade and bring to a simmer. Add the whole cayenne pepper.

5. Reduce the heat to low, and cover and simmer for 2 hours. Stir occasionally to keep the sauce from sticking. After 1 hour, taste the sauce. As soon as it seems hot enough, remove the pepper. Taste and season if needed.

LAMB SHANK WITH CHARD

Part of what makes the flavor and texture of this sauce so rich is the bone marrow from the shank. You can scrape out the marrow and stir it into the final sauce to increase the texture.

Yields 4 servings

4 lamb shanks, 1" of the lower bone exposed

2 teaspoons salt

1 teaspoon ground pepper

2 tablespoons vegetable oil

1 medium onion, thinly sliced

2 celery stalks, thinly sliced

2 carrots, thinly sliced

2 cups red wine

2 sprigs rosemary

2 bay leaves

1–2 cups chicken stock

1 pound Swiss chard

1. Preheat oven to 300°F. Place a skillet over medium-high heat. Sprinkle the shanks with salt and pepper. Once the skillet is heated, add the oil and 2 shanks. Cook for 3–4 minutes on each side or until browned. Repeat with the remaining shanks.

2. Set aside the shanks. Add the onion, celery, and carrots to the pan and cook for 12–14 minutes. Pour the wine into the pan and scrape the bottom. Remove it from the heat and add the rosemary, bay leaves, and the lamb shanks. Fill the pan with chicken stock as necessary to cover all of the meat. Cook in the middle of the oven for 3 hours. Turn the shanks every 30 minutes.

3. Once the shanks are cooked, remove them from the pan and keep warm. Skim off some of the fat before placing the pan over a burner set to high heat. Boil until the sauce is reduced and thickened. Reduce the heat to low.

4. Wash the chard, cut out the stalk, and tear the leaves into large pieces. Add the chard to the sauce, place a cover on the pan, and cook for 2–3 minutes. Pour the sauce and chard over the meat and serve while warm.

LAMB CHOPS WITH ROSEMARY AND WINE SAUCE

Lamb chops tend to be an expensive cut of meat, but are fairly lean and cook quickly. Look for chops that are pink to light red with a fat layer that is thin and white or pink instead of yellow.

Yields 4 servings

8 lamb chops

Pinch salt

Pinch pepper

2 tablespoons olive oil

1 shallot, minced

1 clove garlic, minced

1 cup dry red wine

1 teaspoon fresh rosemary, minced

1 teaspoon butter

1 teaspoon flour

2 tablespoons Dijon mustard

3 tablespoons sour cream

1. Place a skillet over medium-high heat. Season the lamb chops with salt and pepper. Once the skillet is heated, add half of the oil and 4 of the chops. Cook on each side for 3 minutes. Remove them from the pan and keep warm. Repeat with the other 4 chops.

2. Pour off all but 1 tablespoon of the oil. Add the shallot to the pan and cook for 3–4 minutes, stirring frequently. Add the garlic and cook for 1 minute, stirring constantly.

3. Add the wine and scrape the bottom of the pan. Stir in the rosemary and increase the heat to high. Let the sauce boil for 3 minutes or until it has thickened to a syrupy consistency.

4. Add the butter and stir until it melts. Sprinkle the flour over the pan and whisk it until it has thickened. Stir in the mustard and the sour cream. Return the chops to the pan and cook for 1–2 minutes. Taste the sauce and season with salt and pepper as necessary. Pour the sauce over the chops and serve while warm.

American Lamb Versus Australian Lamb

You're just as likely to find Australian or New Zealand lamb at your local grocery as you are American lamb. American lamb is fed grain as well as grass, which reduces the gamey taste sometimes found in Australian lamb. The fat on American lamb is white instead of yellowish.

LAMB SHEPHERD'S PIE

The term "shepherd's pie" wasn't used until the 1870s, when people in the British Isles started eating potatoes. "Cottage pie" has been cited before 1800 and refers to a crust-covered pie filled with beef instead of lamb. On current menus, you're likely to find "cottage pie" referring to dishes with beef and "shepherd's pie" referring to dishes with lamb.

Yields 4–6 servings

2 pounds russet potatoes, peeled and cubed

Water, as needed

½ cup milk

1 large egg

¼ cup sour cream

1 pound ground lamb

Salt, to taste

Pepper, to taste

½ pound lean ground beef

1 large onion, minced

2 medium carrots, peeled and sliced

3 garlic cloves, minced

2 tablespoons all-purpose flour

2 cups chicken broth

1 tablespoon apple cider vinegar

1 tablespoon Worcestershire sauce

1 teaspoon dried thyme

2 teaspoons mustard powder

1 cup frozen peas, thawed

1 teaspoon sweet paprika

1. Boil the potatoes in salted water for 14 minutes. Drain and place in a large mixing bowl. Mash lightly and use a hand mixer to incorporate the milk, egg, and sour cream until the potatoes are smooth. Set aside.

2. Place a large skillet over medium-high heat and when heated, add the ground lamb. Sprinkle with salt and pepper and stir, crumbling the lamb. Cook for 4–6 minutes. Remove the meat, but not any fat, and place in a bowl. Add the ground beef to the skillet and cook for 3–4 minutes, stirring and breaking the meat apart. Add it to the bowl with the lamb. Drain off all but 2 tablespoons of the fat and discard.

3. Add the onion and carrot to the pan. Cook for 5–7 minutes. Stir in the garlic and cook for 1 minute. Sprinkle the flour over the vegetables and toss to coat.

4. In a small bowl combine the chicken broth, vinegar, Worcestershire sauce, thyme, and mustard powder. Stir it into the skillet. Bring to a boil and thicken slightly. Stir in the meat and the peas. Remove from the heat and smooth out the mixture.

5. Preheat the broiler and place a rack in the middle of the oven. Spoon the whipped potatoes over the contents in the skillet. Sprinkle paprika over the potatoes. Place in the oven and broil. Check every 30 seconds and remove when the potatoes are golden brown. Rotate the skillet so the potatoes brown evenly. Remove from the oven and let it rest for 5 minutes before serving.

CHAPTER 8

FISH AND SHELLFISH

ROASTED BLACK SEA BASS

You can substitute snapper or grouper for the sea bass.

Yields 4 servings

2 whole black sea bass, about 4 pounds each

¾ cups kalamata olive purée, divided

1 tablespoon paprika

1 teaspoon onion powder

½ teaspoon cayenne pepper

1 teaspoon dried oregano

1 teaspoon dried thyme, crushed

Freshly ground black pepper to taste

½ cup plus 2 tablespoons capers

2 Meyer lemons, sliced

6 tablespoons extra-virgin olive oil

4 tablespoons dry white wine

2 fennel bulbs

2 eggplants, cut in ½" slices

1 tablespoon chives, chopped

1 tablespoon fresh parsley leaves, chopped

2 tablespoons fennel tops, chopped

1. Heat oven to 450°F.

2. Cut 4 or 5 slits in the skin of the sea bass. Place in a 9" × 13" ovenproof baking pan. Spread ½ cup of the olive purée over the surface of the bass and into the slits of the fish. Mix together the paprika, onion powder, cayenne, oregano, and thyme; sprinkle it and the pepper to taste over the fish. Sprinkle ½ cup of the capers over the fish, arrange the lemon slices over the top, and drizzle with 3 tablespoons of the olive oil. Splash with white wine.

3. Season the fennel and eggplant with salt, pepper, and the remaining 3 tablespoons olive oil. Arrange around the fish. Roast for 45 minutes.

4. Remove the fish from the oven and place on a serving tray. Add the remaining olive purée to the baking pan and mix it with the remaining 2 tablespoons capers and the chives, parsley, and fennel tops. Pour over the fish, fennel, and eggplant. Serve immediately.

SEAFOOD BREAD

You can substitute other canned seafood for the tuna, or use a combination of seafood such as salmon, crabmeat, clams, and tuna; if the bread is deep enough, you can increase the amount of meat in the recipe.

Yields 8 servings

1 10"–12" round loaf of bread

½ cup freshly grated Parmigiano-Reggiano cheese, plus more to taste

4 large vine-ripened tomatoes, peeled, seeded, and diced

½ teaspoon sea salt

4 cloves garlic, minced

2 teaspoons dried minced onion

1 teaspoon dried parsley

½ teaspoon dried oregano, crushed

½ teaspoon dried basil, crushed

1–2 teaspoons granulated sugar (to taste)

Optional: dried red pepper flakes to taste

2 cups cottage cheese, drained

1 large egg

3 cups mozzarella cheese, grated

Extra-virgin olive oil as needed

2 cans 6-ounce tuna, drained

8 ounces fresh button or cremini mushrooms, cleaned and sliced

1. Preheat oven to 400°F.

2. Cut the top off of the loaf of bread. Starting about ½" from the outer crust, cut a circle around the loaf, cutting down to about ½" from the bottom of the crust; be careful not to pierce it. Remove the soft bread from the inside of the loaf; use a blender or food processor to make 2–3 cups of coarse bread crumbs. Mix 1 cup of the bread crumbs with ½ cup freshly grated Parmigiano-Reggiano; set aside.

3. In a small bowl, mix together the tomatoes, salt, garlic, dried onion, parsley, basil, sugar, and red pepper flakes (if using).

4. In another bowl, mix the cottage cheese with the egg and 1 cup of the mozzarella cheese.

5. Use a pastry brush to liberally coat the inside and the outside of the bread with extra-virgin olive oil. Place the bread with its crust side down on a baking sheet. Sprinkle freshly grated Parmigiano-Reggiano to taste over the bottom inside of the bread. Use a slotted spoon to spoon half of the tomato mixture over the top of the grated cheese; avoid getting too much of the tomato juice in this layer. Spread the cottage cheese mixture over the top of the tomatoes, spread the tuna over the cottage cheese mixture, and top the tuna with the mushrooms. Ladle the remaining tomato mixture and juices over the top of the mushrooms. Sprinkle the remaining mozzarella cheese over the tomato mixture. Sprinkle the bread crumb and cheese mixture over the mozzarella, carefully pressing the mixture down over the cheese. Add more bread crumbs, if desired. Liberally drizzle extra-virgin olive oil over the top of the bread crumbs.

6. Bake for 1 hour, or until the bread crumbs on top are deep brown and the mozzarella cheese underneath is melted and bubbling. Serve immediately.

LOBSTER PAELLA

If your budget is tight, you can substitute cooked shrimp for the lobster.

Yields 6 servings

¼ cup extra-virgin olive oil

2 large yellow onions, diced

2 red bell peppers, seeded and sliced into ½" strips

4 cloves garlic, minced

2 cups uncooked white basmati rice

5 cups chicken stock

½ teaspoon saffron threads, crushed

¼ teaspoon crushed red pepper flakes

1 teaspoon sea or kosher salt

½ teaspoon freshly ground black pepper

⅓ cup licorice-flavored liqueur, such as Pernod

1½ pounds cooked lobster meat

1 pound kielbasa, cut into ¼" rounds

1 10-ounce package frozen peas

Fresh parsley, chopped, to taste

2 lemons, cut into wedges

1. Preheat oven to 425°F.

2. Add the oil to a large Dutch oven and bring it to temperature over medium heat. Add the onions and sauté for 5 minutes, stirring occasionally. Add the bell peppers; sauté for 5 minutes. Lower the heat; add the garlic and sauté for 1 minute. Stir in the rice, chicken stock, saffron, red pepper flakes, salt, and pepper; bring to a boil over medium-high heat. Cover, move the pot to the oven, and bake for 15 minutes. Take the pot out of the oven and remove the lid; gently stir the rice using a wooden spoon. Return the pot to the oven and bake uncovered for 10–15 minutes, or until the rice is fully cooked.

3. Move the paella back to the stovetop; add the liqueur. Cook over medium heat for 1 minute, or until the liqueur is absorbed by the rice. Turn off the heat, and add the lobster, kielbasa, and peas, gently stirring to mix in the added ingredients. Cover and let it set for 10 minutes. Uncover, sprinkle with the parsley, garnish with lemon wedges, and serve hot.

DILLED SHRIMP DINNER

If fresh dill isn't available, you can use dried dill. The usual rule of thumb is to use one-third the amount; however, dried dill can sometimes taste a bit stronger, so start with ½ teaspoon, taste the dish, and adjust the seasoning if necessary.

Yields 4 servings

1 tablespoon butter

⅔ cup leeks, well rinsed and thinly sliced

1½ cups peeled and shredded carrots

1 cup sugar snap peas, cut in half

¼ cup chicken broth

12 ounces fully cooked, peeled, and deveined shrimp

2 cups hot cooked white rice

1 teaspoon freshly grated lemon peel

1 tablespoon fresh chopped dill

1. Melt the butter in a wok or deep skillet over medium-high heat. Add the leeks, carrots, and pea pods; sauté for 2–3 minutes, or until the vegetables are crisp-tender.

2. Stir in the broth, shrimp, rice, and lemon peel. Cook about 5 minutes, or until heated through, stirring occasionally. Stir in the dill. Serve immediately.

Using Frozen Precooked Shrimp

The instructions for the Dilled Shrimp Dinner are meant for refrigerated or thawed frozen shrimp. If you'll be using frozen shrimp, thaw them by placing a colander in a large bowl. Rinse them under cold running water for several minutes. Pull the colander from the bowl to drain the shrimp before adding them.

PECAN-CRUSTED FISH WITH VEGETABLES

Adding some oil to the egg wash helps create a crisp crust as the fish bakes.

Yields 4 servings

1 tablespoon plus 2 teaspoons peanut or vegetable oil

4 skinless catfish, whitefish, or orange roughy fillets, ½" thick

½ cup finely chopped pecans

⅓ cup yellow cornmeal, finely ground

½ teaspoon onion salt

¼ cup all-purpose flour

¼ teaspoon ground red pepper

1 egg

2 teaspoons water

1 small red pepper, seeded and quartered

1 small orange or yellow pepper, seeded and quartered

1 medium zucchini, cut into ½" diagonal slices

1 medium yellow summer squash, cut into ½" diagonal slices

¼ teaspoon sea or seasoned salt

1. Preheat oven to 425°F.

2. Line a jellyroll pan with heavy-duty aluminum foil. Pour 1 teaspoon of the oil onto the foil and use a pastry brush to distribute it evenly over the foil; set aside. Rinse the fish and pat dry with paper towels.

3. Stir together the pecans, cornmeal, and onion salt in a shallow dish. Stir the flour and ground red pepper together in another shallow dish. Beat together the egg, 1 teaspoon of the oil, and the water together in a small bowl or shallow dish. Working with 1 piece of fish at a time, dip it in the flour mixture to coat lightly, shake off any excess, dip in the egg mixture, and then in the pecan mixture. Place the coated fish on the foil-lined pan.

4. Put the remaining oil in a plastic bag and add the peppers, zucchini, and squash. Add the salt, close the bag, and toss to coat. Arrange the oil-coated vegetables around the fish, overlapping them as needed to fit in pan. Bake, uncovered, for 25 minutes, or until the fish flakes easily with a fork and the vegetables are tender. Serve immediately.

FLOUNDER BAKED IN SOUR CREAM

You can use other whitefish in this recipe. Sole, haddock, and orange roughy all taste delicious.

Yields 4–6 servings

4 tablespoons butter, melted

4 cups frozen hash browns, thawed

4 skinless flounder fillets

½ teaspoon hot sauce

1 tablespoon paprika

¼ cup freshly grated Parmigiano-Reggiano cheese

1 cup all-natural sour cream

1 12-ounce bag frozen baby Brussels sprouts, thawed

¼ cup fine bread crumbs

Salt and freshly ground pepper to taste

Optional: 1 lemon, quartered

1. Preheat oven to 350°F.

2. Add 2 tablespoons of melted butter to a 9" × 13" nonstick baking pan. Add the hash browns; stir to coat with the butter. Bake for 15 minutes while you prepare the fish.

3. Wash the fillets and pat dry with paper towels. In a small bowl, mix together the hot sauce, paprika, cheese, and sour cream.

4. Remove the pan from the oven. Working fast, stir the hash browns and then push them to the sides of the pan. Arrange the fish fillets flat in the middle of the pan. Distribute the Brussels sprouts evenly over the hash browns. Spoon the sour cream mixture evenly over the fish. Top the fish with the bread crumbs. Salt and pepper to taste. Drizzle the remaining 2 tablespoons of melted butter over the Brussels sprouts and bread crumbs. Bake for 30 more minutes, or until the fish flakes easily with a fork. Garnish each serving with a lemon wedge, if desired.

Watching Your Salt Intake?

Omit the paprika, salt, and pepper in the Flounder Baked in Sour Cream recipe; instead, before you return it to the oven, liberally sprinkle the entire dish with Mrs. Dash Lemon Pepper Seasoning Blend.

TUNA AND FRESH TOMATO PIZZA

This is a quick-and-easy, totally "to taste" recipe. Feel free to use fresh herbs if you have them on hand, but the succulent taste of the fresh tomato stands up to the hearty flavor of the dried seasonings.

Yields 1 serving

1 flour tortilla

Extra-virgin olive oil to taste

1 small vine-ripened tomato

Dash granulated sugar

Dash dried minced garlic or garlic powder

Dash dried minced onion or onion powder

Dash dried oregano

Dash dried basil

Dash dried parsley

Salt and freshly ground black pepper to taste

1 12-ounce can reduced-sodium tuna, drained

Mozzarella cheese, grated, to taste

Freshly grated Parmigiano-Reggiano cheese to taste

1. Preheat oven to 450°F.

2. Coat both sides of the tortilla with the oil. Place on a baking sheet.

3. Peel and chop the tomato. Add it to a small bowl and mix it with a pinch of sugar. Spread the tomato and juices over the tortilla. Sprinkle the garlic, onion, oregano, basil, parsley, salt, and pepper over the tomatoes, to taste. Add as much of the tuna as you wish, and top with the cheeses.

4. Bake for 5 minutes, or until the cheese is melted and bubbly. Drizzle more extra-virgin olive oil over the top of the baked pizza, if desired.

CRAB NEWBURG

Crab Newburg is traditionally served over hot rice. Serve it along with a tossed salad or steamed vegetable and you have a complete meal!

Yields 4 servings

¼ cup butter

2 tablespoons all-purpose flour

⅛ teaspoon freshly ground nutmeg

Pinch cayenne pepper

2 cups half-and-half or light cream

3 egg yolks, beaten

8 ounces cooked crabmeat

Optional: 1½ tablespoons dry sherry

Salt to taste

1. Melt the butter in a medium saucepan over medium heat. Whisk in the flour, nutmeg, and cayenne; stir until smooth. Gradually whisk in the half-and-half, and then simmer for 8–10 minutes, stirring constantly, or until slightly thickened.

2. Temper the egg yolks by slowly stirring ½ cup of the hot half-and-half mixture into them. Then, slowly whisk the yolk mixture into the contents of the saucepan. Add the crabmeat and any juices, and continue to cook, stirring constantly, for another 1–2 minutes, or until the crabmeat is heated through and the mixture is thickened. Remove from the heat and stir in the sherry, if using. Taste for seasoning and add salt, if needed.

SALMON QUICHE

Unless you use steam-in-the-bag spinach, you will have to get a pan dirty along with the bowl you use for the egg mixture. But, because the quiche is baked in the pie shell, you're essentially using one pot to fix this meal.

Yields 6–8 servings

1 10" pie shell

1 15½-ounce can pink salmon

1 9-ounce package frozen chopped spinach

1½ cups Monterey jack cheese, grated

1 3-ounce package cream cheese, softened

Salt to taste

½ teaspoon dried thyme, crushed

4 eggs, lightly beaten

1 cup milk

Optional: 1 tablespoon mayonnaise

1. Preheat oven to 375°F. While you mix the quiche filling, bake the pie shell for 10 minutes.

2. Drain the salmon and remove any skin pieces, if desired. Mash any salmon bones and mix them into the salmon. Spread the salmon in an even layer over the bottom of the partially baked pie shell.

3. Cook the spinach according to package directions; drain well. In a medium-size bowl, mix together the spinach, jack cheese, cream cheese, salt, and thyme. Spoon the spinach-cheese mixture evenly over the salmon. Use the same bowl to mix the eggs, milk, and mayonnaise (is using), together, and then pour it over the salmon-spinach mixture in the pie shell. Bake for 40–45 minutes. Remove from the oven and let stand for 10 minutes before cutting and serving.

Salmon Specifics

Because of the cooked bones, salmon is high in calcium. It is also an easily digestible protein high in heart-healthy omega-3 fatty acids, which also help lower cholesterol. It also contains healthy amounts of vitamins A and B.

FANTASTIC FISH PIE

Because of the generous amount of mashed potatoes that form a meringue-style mound over the fish, this recipe could easily be stretched to 6 servings.

Yields 4 servings

Nonstick cooking spray

16 ounces cod fillets, cut into bite-size pieces

1 14½-ounce can stewed tomatoes

¼ teaspoon dried minced onion

½ teaspoon dried minced garlic

¼ teaspoon dried basil

¼ teaspoon dried parsley

⅛ teaspoon dried oregano

⅛ teaspoon granulated sugar

1 tablespoon freshly grated Parmigiano-Reggiano cheese

4 cups prepared mashed potatoes

¼ teaspoon paprika

1. Preheat oven to 375°F.

2. Treat a 9½" deep-dish pie pan with nonstick spray. Arrange the fish pieces evenly across the bottom of the pan.

3. In a bowl, mix together the stewed tomatoes, onion, garlic, basil, parsley, oregano, sugar, and cheese. Pour over the fish. Pipe or spread the mashed potatoes evenly over the top of the sauce. Sprinkle generously with paprika. Bake for 45 minutes, or until the potatoes are lightly browned and the sauce is bubbly.

LOBSTER BAKE

Lobster bibs will add a bit of whimsy to this romantic dinner for two. Serve it with tossed salads and warmed dinner rolls.

Yields 2 servings

Butter to taste

2 Idaho potatoes, scrubbed

2 ears of corn on the cob, husked

2 1½-pound live lobsters

Sea salt and freshly ground black pepper to taste

2 tablespoons extra-virgin olive oil

½ cup unsalted butter, at room temperature

4 ounces fresh button mushrooms, cleaned and sliced

1 tablespoon minced shallots

½ cup dry-style hard cider or dry white wine

1. Preheat oven to 450°F.

2. Rub the potatoes with a little butter and individually wrap them in foil; place on the oven rack. After the potatoes have baked for 30 minutes, rub butter on each ear of corn, individually wrap them in foil, and place on the oven rack next to the potatoes. Continue to bake for 20 minutes.

3. While the corn is baking, kill each lobster with a sharp-pointed knife stuck into the body behind the head. Remove the bands from the claws, twist the claws and knuckles off the body, and separate the claws from the knuckles. Crack them slightly by lying the flat edge of a chef's knife against them and striking a sharp blow against the knife's flat edge with the heel of your hand. Twist off each tail, carefully split it lengthwise, and remove and discard the intestinal tract. Split each lobster body. Arrange the lobster pieces in a single layer in a 9" × 13" nonstick baking pan, placing the tail and body pieces shell side down. Sprinkle sea salt and black pepper over the exposed meat, and drizzle the oil over them. Bake for 8 minutes, or until the shells are almost uniformly red and the meat is opaque.

4. Add several pieces of the ½ cup butter, the mushrooms, and shallots to a microwave-safe dish; cover and microwave on high for 1 minute. Stir, cover, and microwave on high for another 30 seconds. After the lobsters have baked for 8 minutes, remove them from the oven, and pour the mushroom-shallots mix and the cider or wine over the lobsters. Dot with the butter pieces. Place back in the oven for 3 minutes, or until the butter has completely melted.

5. Arrange the lobster pieces on dinner plates. Unwrap the potatoes, split them each in half, and place 2 halves on each plate beside the lobster. Unwrap the corn and place an ear on each plate. Swirl the baking pan to emulsify the liquid ingredients and spoon the resulting sauce over the plates. Have additional sea salt and pepper at the table, if needed.

HONEY-GLAZED STRIPED SEA BASS DINNER

The extra effort required for this meal comes more from hunting down striped sea bass than from the work required to prepare the meal. If, after checking with your local fishmonger, you can't find striped sea bass, you can substitute salmon, halibut, black sea bass, or cod.

Yields 4 servings

4 10-ounce striped sea bass fillets

3 tablespoons honey

1 tablespoon soy sauce

1 tablespoon sesame oil

2 10-ounce boxes rice pilaf

1 12-ounce frozen steam-in-the-bag
   green beans

1 12-ounce frozen steam-in-the-bag
   asparagus tips

2 tablespoons butter

Salt and freshly ground black pepper
   to taste

8 teaspoons sesame seeds, toasted

1. Rinse the fillets and pat dry. Add the honey, soy sauce, and sesame oil to a gallon-size plastic food bag; seal and squeeze to mix well. Add the fillets to the bag, seal the bag, and, being careful not to break the fillets, turn the bag several times to coat them with the marinade. Refrigerate and let marinate for 1 hour.

2. Preheat the oven to 425°F. Place the fillets side by side on a jellyroll pan or baking sheet. Bake for 12 minutes, or until opaque.

3. While the fish bakes, prepare the rice pilaf, green beans, and asparagus tips according to the package directions. Drain any excess moisture from the bags holding the green beans and asparagus; add 1 tablespoon of butter to each bag, allow the butter to melt, then hold the bags closed and turn to coat the vegetables inside with the butter.

4. Add a fillet to each dinner plate, along with a helping of the rice pilaf, green beans, and asparagus. Season with salt and pepper to taste. Sprinkle 2 teaspoons of toasted sesame seeds over all of the food on each plate.

SMOTHERED WHITEFISH

You can use the Onion Marmalade (see recipe in Chapter 2) in this dish instead of the caramelized onions, if you prefer.

Yields 4 servings

4 6-ounce whitefish fillets

Salt to taste

Pepper to taste

1 tablespoon olive oil

1 cup caramelized onions

1. Preheat oven to 350°F. Sprinkle the fillets with salt and pepper on each side. Place a skillet over medium heat to preheat. Once it is heated add the oil and the fillets.

2. Turn off the heat and cover each fillet with ¼ cup of the onion mixture. Place the skillet in the oven and cook for 20 minutes. The fish is cooked through when it starts to flake apart. Serve hot.

SIMPLE SALMON FILLETS

If you'd like to add a little more flavor to this dish, you can substitute butter for vegetable oil.

Yields 4 servings

4¼ pounds salmon fillets

2 tablespoons vegetable oil

1 lemon

1 teaspoon salt

Pepper to taste

1. Rinse the fillets and remove any loose scales or bones. Pat the salmon dry and rub 1 tablespoon of the oil on the fillets. Squeeze a little of the lemon on the flesh side of the fillets. Sprinkle them with salt and pepper.

2. Place a skillet over medium-high heat and once it is warmed add 1 tablespoon of oil. Place the fillets in the pan flesh side down.

3. Cook for 3 minutes before flipping over. Cook for 2 minutes. Remove pan from the heat and let rest for 1 minute. When it is cool enough to touch, you should be able to grab a corner of the skin and peel it off. Serve immediately.

CURRIED CRABMEAT

This dish is often called Crabmeat Indienne. "Indienne" is the name given to many curried dishes in France.

Yields 4 servings

2 tablespoons butter

¼ small onion, chopped

3 tablespoons flour

2 teaspoons curry powder

2 cups chicken broth

1½ cups crabmeat

1. Place a skillet over medium heat. Once it is heated, add the butter. Once the butter stops foaming, add the onion, stirring frequently for 3 minutes, or until the onion is softened.

2. Stir the flour into the skillet with the curry powder to create a paste. Stir the paste continually for 2 minutes.

3. Slowly pour in the chicken broth, whisking continually to prevent lumps. Bring to a simmer and cook for 3 minutes.

4. Stir in the crabmeat and cook until heated. Remove from the heat and serve over rice.

HALIBUT CREOLE

If the fillet comes with the skin on it, don't try to remove it while the fish is raw. After it cooks, you should be able to carefully grab the skin and pull it off. The skin is edible, but many people find the texture and taste off-putting.

Yields 4 servings

4 tablespoons butter

Juice from 2 lemons

Several dashes Tabasco sauce

4 8-ounce halibut steaks

Pinch salt

Pinch pepper

1 small onion, chopped

½ red bell pepper, chopped

3 large tomatoes, peeled, seeded, and chopped

1. Preheat oven to 400°F. Place a large skillet over medium heat. Add the butter, lemon juice, and Tabasco sauce. Stir until the butter has melted. Turn off the heat.

2. Season the fish on each side with salt and pepper. Sprinkle the onion and bell pepper over the bottom of the skillet. Add the fish to the skillet and pour the tomatoes over the fish.

3. Bake for 20–25 minutes, or until the thickest part of the fish is opaque. Spoon the pan juices over the fish every 10 minutes. Remove it from the pan and spoon the sauce over the fish to serve.

TAMARIND TUNA

Since the price of tuna has gone up significantly in the last few years, you can substitute salmon fillets in this dish, which may be cheaper.

Yields 4 servings

½ cup tamarind pulp

1 cup water

1 pound tuna fillet

½ teaspoon salt

¼ cup peanut oil

1. Place the tamarind pulp in a glass bowl. Heat the water and pour it over the paste. Use a spoon to combine the pulp with the water.

2. Sprinkle the tuna lightly with the salt. Cut it into 1½" strips. Add the tuna to the marinade and toss to coat. Let it sit for 30 minutes at room temperature.

3. Place a skillet over medium-high heat and when it is warmed add the oil. Pat the tuna dry and add to the oil when it's hot. Cook for 2 minutes on each side. The tuna will be dark on each side but still pink in the center. Serve over white rice.

Popularity Isn't Always a Good Thing

Tuna used to be a very cheap fish, but in the last ten years, several types of tuna have been depleted and are close to being endangered. To make sure you're eating responsibly, avoid bluefin or bigeye tuna and ask for yellowtail instead.

TRULY BLACKENED CATFISH

This works best with small catfish fillets instead of large ones. Ideally each fillet should be around 4 ounces.

Yields 4–6 servings

2 sticks unsalted butter

1 teaspoon pepper

½ teaspoon thyme

1 tablespoon spicy paprika

1 teaspoon garlic powder

1 teaspoon onion powder

½ teaspoon oregano

2½ teaspoons salt

1 teaspoon chili powder

¼ teaspoon cayenne pepper

1½ pounds catfish fillets

1. Melt the butter in a shallow bowl. Combine the spices and place on a plate. Dip the fish in the butter and then sprinkle or roll the fish in the spices.

2. Heat up a charcoal or gas grill till hot. Place a cast-iron skillet over direct heat for 10 minutes. Let it sit until white ash forms in the bottom of the skillet.

3. Place the fillets in the skillet. Pour 1 tablespoon of melted butter over each fillet. Be careful of flaming butter. Cook for 2 minutes before turning over fillets and cooking for another 2 minutes. Serve with lemon wedges.

YASA TIBS (ETHIOPIAN SAUTÉED FISH)

"Yasa" means fish and "Tibs" means that the meat is served in large pieces that are reserved for guests and special occasions. Use the Ethiopian Berberé Red Pepper Paste (see recipe in Chapter 2) for this recipe.

Yields 4 servings

Juice from 4 limes

1½ teaspoons Ethiopian Berberé Red Pepper Paste

1 pound cod fillets, cut into chunks

2 tablespoons olive oil

1 teaspoon spicy paprika

3 garlic cloves, minced

1 1" piece ginger, peeled and grated

¼ cup plain tomato sauce

¼ cup fish stock

¼ cup chopped cilantro

1. Mix the lime juice and berberé paste in a glass container. Marinate the fish for 1 hour.

2. Place a skillet over medium heat. Add the oil and paprika and cook for 1 minute. Add the garlic and ginger and cook for 1–2 minutes.

3. Add the fish with the marinade liquid, the tomato sauce, and the fish stock. Cook on the first side for 2–3 minutes. Turn it over to cook on the other side for 2–3 minutes. It is done when the fish is flaky. Pour the contents into a bowl and sprinkle cilantro over top. Serve with rice or flat bread.

CAJUN SHRIMP

You can replace the beer with soda in this recipe.

Yields 4 servings

1 pound shrimp, peeled and deveined

¼ teaspoon cayenne pepper

1 teaspoon black pepper

1 teaspoon salt

1 teaspoon red chili flakes

1 teaspoon thyme

1 teaspoon oregano

1 teaspoon ground marjoram

4 tablespoons unsalted butter

3 cloves garlic, minced

2 teaspoons Worcestershire sauce

1 cup beer, room temperature

1. Rinse the shrimp and shake them dry. Combine all of the dried seasonings in a bowl.

2. Place a skillet over medium-high heat. When it is hot, add the butter and garlic and cook for 1 minute. Add the seasoning mix, Worcestershire sauce, and beer.

3. Once the sauce bubbles, add the shrimp. Cook for 4–6 minutes, stirring so they cook evenly.

4. Once the shrimp is cooked, remove from the pan and place in a serving bowl. Let the liquid simmer for 10 minutes until it is a reduced sauce. Adjust the seasonings and serve with white rice.

GRILLED BARBECUE SALMON

Since salmon is a high-fat fish, it holds up incredibly well when grilling. The Kansas City–Style Barbecue Sauce (see recipe in Chapter 2) is great in this dish, or you can use a bottled sauce.

Yields 4 servings

1 tablespoon vegetable oil

Pinch salt

Pinch pepper

4 6–8-ounce salmon steaks

¼ cup barbecue sauce

1. Brush a grill pan lightly with vegetable oil and place over medium-high heat.

2. Sprinkle salt and pepper over the salmon. Brush one side of the salmon lightly with barbecue sauce. Place that side down on the warmed pan. Brush the other side with barbecue sauce.

3. Cook for 3 minutes on each side, or until it is opaque about halfway up the side of the fillet. Once the salmon is cooked through, brush it again with a light coating of barbecue sauce and serve while warm.

FISH TACOS

You need a firm fish since you'll be pan-frying these. Look for perch, grouper, catfish, or ask your fishmonger for suggestions based on availability. It is fine if the fish has the skin on.

Yields 2 servings

½ pound firm whitefish fillets

2 tablespoons peanut or corn oil

Salt to taste

1 lime

4 corn tortillas and desired toppings

1. Rinse fish and pat dry with paper towels. Place a skillet over medium-high heat. Once it is heated, add the oil and swirl to coat. Add the fillets, skin side up. Shake the skillet to prevent sticking. Cook for 3 minutes.

2. Flip the fish over and cook for another 3 minutes. You should see the side of the fish change from translucent to opaque. Remove the fish from the pan and place it skin side up on a plate. Carefully peel off the skin.

3. Chop the fish into 1" strips and place in a bowl. Sprinkle salt and squeeze the lime over the top of the fish. Toss to coat. Serve in tortillas with toppings.

White Sauce and Toppings

Fish tacos are served in warmed corn tortillas with shredded cabbage, diced tomato, and a white sauce. To make the sauce, you'll need to peel, seed, and mince a serrano pepper. Mix with ¼ cup yogurt, ¼ cup mayonnaise, and 1 teaspoon garlic salt. Refrigerate for 3 hours.

FISH DROWNED IN LEMON BASIL

There are many types of basil. Lemon basil has a delicate lemony flavor and can be hard to find. But any type of basil, other than Thai basil, can be substituted in this recipe.

Yields 4 servings

4 6-ounce fillets tilapia or a similar whitefish

Salt to taste

Pepper to taste

2 tablespoons olive oil

2 small zucchini or yellow squash, sliced

1 cup lemon basil leaves

Zest from 1 lemon

Juice from 1 lemon

1. Rinse the fish fillets and pat dry with paper towels. Squeeze gently to find any remaining bones and remove. Sprinkle lightly with salt and pepper. Set aside.

2. Place a skillet over medium heat and add the oil. Slide 2 fillets into the skillet and cook on each side for 4–5 minutes, or until the center is almost opaque and the fish begins to flake on the tips. Place on a clean plate to keep warm. Cook the remaining fish and add to the plate.

3. If all of the oil is gone from the skillet, add another tablespoon of olive oil to the pan before adding the zucchini rounds.

4. Sprinkle the basil, lemon zest, and a pinch of salt and pepper over the zucchini. Cover the pan and steam for 1 minute before tossing. Place the fish on top of the zucchini and sprinkle with lemon juice. Cover the skillet for 2–3 minutes to warm the fish and finish cooking the zucchini. Serve immediately.

Which Fish Is Best?

For people who rarely eat fish at home, shopping for fish can be overwhelming. But it shouldn't be. Fish is often served as either a steak (a cross section of the gutted fish) or a fillet (meat from one half of a fish). Whitefish tends to have a less fishy taste on its own and picks up flavors from sauces very well.

SEARED TUNA STEAK WITH TANGY CILANTRO SAUCE

Tuna is a low-fat fish and can become dry and bland when cooked through. By cooking it till rare, you get a pleasant combination of cooked and rare textures.

Yields 2 servings

1 bunch cilantro, rinsed and picked over

¼ cup water

2 teaspoons plus 2 pinches salt

¼ cup rice wine vinegar

½ cup safflower or canola oil

1 12–16-ounce tuna steak

Pinch pepper

2 garlic cloves, peeled and smashed

1 tablespoon olive oil

1. Roughly chop the cilantro. Place in a blender with the water, 2 teaspoons salt, and vinegar. Pulse on liquefy for several minutes until the contents are smooth. Pour the safflower oil in slowly while the blender runs. Taste and season with salt as needed.

2. Rinse the tuna under cold water and pat dry. Sprinkle with salt and pepper. Place a skillet over medium-high heat. Once it is heated through, add the garlic cloves and olive oil. Toss to coat and move the cloves to the edges of the pan.

3. Place the tuna in the middle of the skillet and cook for 2 minutes on the first side. Flip it to the second side and cook for 1 minute. This will make it rare.

4. If you prefer a medium-done tuna, cook for 4 minutes on the first side and 3 minutes on the second with the skillet over medium heat.

5. Slice the steak against the grain and drizzle the cilantro sauce over the fish. Serve while warm.

Use the Rest of the Sauce

This recipe makes 1 cup of sauce and you'll likely use ¼ cup or less, but don't discard the remainder. You can use it as a salad dressing, drizzle it over sliced fresh tomatoes, or mix it into potatoes or rice as a side. You can store it in a tightly sealed container for a few weeks in your refrigerator.

TUNA ALMANDINE WITH SUGAR SNAP PEAS

With sugar snap peas you eat the pod and the pea. They're younger than the peas that are shelled and served without the pod. You may want to remove the membranous string on one side of the pod of older peas.

Yields 2 servings

2 tablespoons butter

½ large sweet onion, thinly sliced

½ pound sugar snap pea pods

Salt to taste

Pepper to taste

1 tablespoon olive oil

2 6-ounce tuna steaks

½ cup sliced almonds

1. Place a large skillet over medium-high heat. Add the butter and sliced onions. Stir frequently for 8–10 minutes or until they're tender and translucent.

2. Add the peas to the skillet and season with salt and pepper. Toss them a few times and cook for 2–3 minutes. Move the vegetables to the sides of the skillet. If the butter in the skillet has evaporated, add some olive oil.

3. Place the tuna steaks in the middle of the skillet and cook on each side for 2–3 minutes. You'll want the center to be pink, so cooking to medium-rare is recommended. Divide the tuna and peas between two plates and sprinkle the almonds on top.

"Almondine" Versus "Almandine"

Both of these words refer to the same thing. "Almandine" comes from the French word for almond. It's common in French cooking for green beans and fish to have a garnish of sliced or slivered almonds on top. But in American versions of these recipes the word "almandine" was converted to "almondine." Most English dictionaries will direct you from "almondine" to "almandine."

SHRIMP AND AVOCADO PASTA WITH A TEQUILA TOMATO SAUCE

The avocado purée in the sauce and the addition of butter at the end help to create a richly flavored sauce that has very little fat per serving. This sauce is very good served on fettuccine.

Yields 8 servings

1 avocado, peeled and chopped

1 28-ounce can chopped tomatoes

1 teaspoon salt

¼ teaspoon freshly ground black pepper

1 teaspoon crushed red pepper flakes

3 tablespoons cold unsalted butter

1½ pounds medium shrimp

½ cup tequila

1 pound fettuccine

¼ cup fresh cilantro, chopped

1. Put half the avocado, tomatoes, salt, pepper, and red pepper flakes in a blender and pulse several times. You don't want a thin purée but do want to chop up the tomatoes and avocado and mix with the spices.

2. Place a skillet over medium heat and add half of the butter. Cut the other half into cubes and set aside. Once the butter has melted, add the shrimp and tequila to the skillet. Stir quickly to combine and stir every 2 minutes until the shrimp are slightly pink and the tequila has mostly evaporated. Reduce the heat to low.

3. Cook fettuccine according to package directions. Add the contents of the blender and the remaining butter to the skillet. Stir to combine. Add the remaining avocado and cilantro as garnish on the final dish. Once the pasta is cooked through, drain and divide into bowls. Pour the sauce and shrimp over each dish and garnish with avocado and cilantro.

SHRIMP IN FRA DIAVOLO SAUCE

"Fra" is Italian for "brother" and "diavolo" means "devil." "Fra Diavolo" is often used to name recipes that are spicy. This name seems to be an Italian-American name and is not commonly seen in Italy.

Yields 4–6 servings

1 pound linguini

3 tablespoons olive oil

1 pound deveined and shelled shrimp (31–40 count)

1 teaspoon red pepper flakes

1 teaspoon salt

¼ cup sweet white wine

4 cloves garlic, thinly sliced

1 15-ounce can chopped tomatoes

1 cup dry white wine

¼ cup parsley, chopped

1. Cook the linguini according to the package directions. Place a skillet over medium heat. Once it is heated add 1 tablespoon of olive oil, shrimp, red pepper flakes, and salt. Stir frequently for 2 minutes to keep everything from sticking.

2. Turn off the heat and pour in the sweet wine. Toss and let sit for 2 minutes. The residual heat should cause most of the wine to evaporate. Pour the contents into a bowl and set aside.

3. Return the skillet to the stove over low heat. Once it is heated, add 2 tablespoons of olive oil and the garlic. Cook for several minutes. Once it starts to turn golden brown, remove from the oil and discard or set aside for another use. If the oil gets frothy, lower the heat.

4. Stir in more red pepper flakes if desired, tomatoes, and the dry wine. Increase the heat to medium and simmer for 10 minutes to reduce. Stir in parsley. Divide pasta and top with the shrimp and sauce.

Cooking with Wine When You Don't Drink It

Common advice on choosing cooking wine is "If you wouldn't drink it, then don't cook with it." But what do you do if you don't drink wine? Avoid cooking wine because it is full of preservatives and salt that will clash with many dishes. Look for "dry" or "sweet" on the label and match it to the recipe.

WHITE BEANS WITH SHRIMP

If you can't find Great Northern beans, you can substitute cannellini beans or any other small bean you can find.

Yields 6 servings

1 tablespoon olive oil

1 carrot, peeled, cut in half lengthwise, and sliced

1 small onion, peeled and chopped

2 garlic cloves, minced

1 celery stalk, sliced

2 tablespoons parsley, chopped

2 tablespoons thyme, chopped

Pinch red pepper flakes

4 tablespoons unsalted butter

1 pound large shrimp, peeled and deveined

2 cans Great Northern beans, drained and rinsed

Juice from 1 lemon

1. Place a large skillet over medium heat and once it is heated, add the oil, carrot, and onion. Cook for 5–7 minutes or until the vegetables are softened but not browned. Add the garlic and celery. Stir to combine before adding in the herbs, red pepper flakes, and butter.

2. Stir continually until the butter is melted and starts to turn brown. Swirl the skillet occasionally.

3. Place the shrimp in the skillet and cook on each side for 1–2 minutes. Stir in the beans and lemon juice and cook until warmed through. Serve immediately.

FRENCH OR BELGIAN STEAMED MUSSELS

Some mussels won't open during cooking. They should be discarded before serving.

Yields 2 servings

Water, as needed

1 cup cornmeal

2 pounds fresh mussels

2 tablespoons butter

1 medium yellow onion, thinly sliced

1 large garlic clove, minced

2 cups dry white wine or ale

3 tablespoons fresh tarragon or thyme, chopped

1. Fill a very large bowl half full of water that is cool to the touch. Sprinkle the cornmeal across the top of the water and let it settle. Use a plastic bristle brush to remove any dirt or other unwanted debris from the mussels. To remove the beard, place the back of a butter knife on one side of the beard and your thumb on the other side. Pinch the beard between your thumb and the knife and pull using a side-to-side motion.

2. Place mussels into the bowl. Shake the bowl every few minutes to keep the cornmeal floating. Let them sit in the water for 30 minutes. Every 10 minutes gently nudge the bowl to create waves. The mussels should expel any dirt they have stored and replace it with the cornmeal.

3. Place a Dutch oven over medium heat and add the butter. Add the onions and stir to coat in butter. Stir frequently until they are mostly translucent. Add the garlic and stir. Cook for 3–4 minutes. Add the wine and herbs. Cover and bring to a boil.

4. Remove the lid and gently add mussels to the pan, leaving the dirt in the bottom of the bowl. When all of the mussels are added, increase the heat to high and cook for 3–4 minutes.

5. Scoop the mussels into bowls and keep them warm. Let the liquid in the pan continue to boil for 5–10 minutes until reduced by half. Pour the liquid and onions over the mussels. Serve with crusty bread.

Caring for Your Mussels

Discard any mussels with cracked shells. If you tap an open mussel, it should close; if it doesn't, discard it. Make sure they are wrapped in something damp and placed in a mesh bag since they need airflow. Keep them in the bottom of your refrigerator wrapped in wet newspaper for up to 48 hours, but they're best the same day they're purchased.

OYSTERS ROCKEFELLER

This dish uses the skillet for presentation rather than its cooking abilities. Rock salt is often used during canning and is inexpensive. If you don't want to open the oysters yourself, ask your fishmonger to do it for you.

Yields 2 servings

1 scallion, chopped, white and green parts separated

¼ celery stalk, finely chopped

2 tablespoons fresh parsley, chopped

¼ cup fresh spinach, chopped

2 tablespoons unseasoned bread crumbs

3 dashes Tabasco

¼ teaspoon Worcestershire sauce

2 tablespoons butter

½ teaspoon salt

Rock salt, as desired

12 large oysters on the half shell

1 lemon cut into 8 wedges

1. Preheat oven to 450°F. Combine the white part of the scallion, celery, parsley, and spinach. Chop them together till very fine. Place into a bowl with the bread crumbs, Tabasco, and Worcestershire sauce.

2. Cream the butter and salt into the bread crumb mixture until you get a fine paste. Pour 1" of rock salt over the bottom of the skillet. Nestle the oysters in the salt.

3. Divide the butter and bread crumb mixture over the oysters. Bake for 10 minutes, or until the mixture has melted. Sprinkle a pinch of green scallion on top of each oyster and serve while warm with lemon slices.

Rich Rockefeller

This dish was created at Antoine's in New Orleans, the country's oldest family-run restaurant. It was created in 1899 and named after John D. Rockefeller, who was then the richest man in the country. Snails were popular at the time, but these oysters were a substitute using local ingredients. The recipe has been replicated many times, but never duplicated exactly.

SCALLOPS SEARED IN CLARIFIED BUTTER

Dry-packed scallops will brown and cook better. If you use wet-packed scallops, rinse them and let them drain for an additional 10 minutes.

Yields 4 servings

12 whole scallops

3 tablespoons Clarified Butter (see recipe in Chapter 2)

Pinch salt

Pinch pepper

2 tablespoons butter

2 garlic cloves

1 teaspoon dried thyme

1 cup dry white wine

1 lemon, cut into wedges

1. Use several paper towels to pat the scallops dry. Wrap them in paper towels and let them sit at room temperature for 15 minutes. If there is a tough muscle on the side, remove it.

2. Place a skillet over medium-high heat. Once it is warmed add the clarified butter. Season the scallops with salt and pepper and place in the pan.

3. Cook for 2–3 minutes or until the bottom edges start to turn golden brown. Flip them over and cook for 2–3 minutes, or until the sides are opaque.

4. Remove the scallops from the pan. Add the butter, garlic, thyme, and wine. Scrape the bottom to remove the crust. Let the wine boil for 5 minutes. Pour it over the scallops and serve with lemon wedges.

SEAFOOD PAELLA

There are special pans available for paella, but a large skillet or Dutch oven will also work.

Yields 4–6 servings

2 quarts plus 1 cup water

¼ cup salt plus 2 pinches

¼ cup sugar

Ice cubes, as needed

1 pound large shrimp, peeled and deveined

4 tablespoons olive oil

6 garlic cloves, minced

Pinch pepper

1 red bell pepper, seeded and sliced

1 medium white onion, finely chopped

1 15-ounce can diced tomatoes

1 15-ounce can chicken broth

2 cups white rice

½ cup dry white wine

3 bay leaves

1 large pinch saffron threads

12 mussels, cleaned and debearded

1 cup cleaned squid, sliced in rings

2 cups crabmeat

1 cup frozen peas, thawed

¼ cup chopped parsley

1 lemon, cut in wedges

1. Bring 2 quarts of water to a boil. Stir in ¼ cup salt and sugar until dissolved. Add several cups of ice cubes till chilled. Add the shrimp to the brine, cover, and refrigerate overnight. Remove from the brine and pat dry. Sprinkle with 1 tablespoon of oil, 2 garlic cloves, 1 pinch salt, and pepper. Let it sit at room temperature for 30 minutes.

2. Preheat oven to 350°F with a rack just below the middle position.

3. Place a very large skillet or a Dutch oven over medium heat. Add 1 tablespoon of oil and the bell pepper. Cook for 5–7 minutes. Spoon the pepper out and set aside, but leave as much of the oil in the pan as possible.

4. Add 2 tablespoons of oil to the pan with the onion and cook for 5–7 minutes. Add the remaining garlic, stirring continually for 1 minute. Stir in 1 cup of water, the tomatoes, chicken broth, rice, wine, bay leaves, saffron, and 1 pinch salt. Increase the heat to medium-high and bring to a boil.

5. When the contents boil, cover and cook in the middle of the oven for 15–20 minutes. Gently stir the seafood into the rice. Lay the pepper strips in a pinwheel on top and sprinkle the peas across the top. Cook in the oven for 8–12 minutes.

6. Rest for 5 minutes before serving. Discard any unopened mussels and the bay leaves. Serve with parsley and lemon wedges.

TUNA "FISH STICKS" WITH SESAME SOY SAUCE

Tuna fillet is better for this dish than steaks because the fillet can be cut into four even pieces to cook evenly. The crushed red pepper can be omitted if desired.

Yields 4 servings

1 tablespoon rice wine vinegar

2 tablespoons soy sauce

2 teaspoons toasted sesame oil

1 teaspoon honey

½ teaspoon crushed red pepper

1 tablespoon olive oil

1½ pounds tuna fillet, cut into 4 "sticks"

1. Combine the vinegar, soy sauce, sesame oil, honey, and red pepper in a small bowl. Heat in the microwave until the honey has melted and the sauce can be stirred.

2. Place a grill pan over medium-high heat. Rub the oil over the fish sticks.

3. Place the fish on the grill pan at an angle. Cook on each side for 2 minutes, turning the sticks with tongs. Brush each cooked side with the soy sauce mixture.

4. Once the tuna has seared on each side, remove it from the pan and slice on an angle. Drizzle the remaining marinade over the tuna and serve warm.

MISO-GLAZED SALMON

The ingredients for the sauce should be found in the Asian section of your grocery store, or at an Asian specialty shop. If you can't find mirin, you can substitute ¼ cup of white wine and a tablespoon of honey.

Yields 4 servings

¼ cup rice wine vinegar

¼ cup mirin

¼ cup red miso

4 6-ounce salmon fillets

2 tablespoons vegetable oil

1. Combine the vinegar and mirin in a saucepan until it is very warm but not boiling. Stir in the miso paste and dissolve. Cool to room temperature.

2. Rinse off the salmon fillets, remove any bones, and pat dry. Place them inside a sealable plastic bag. Pour the cooled mixture over the fillets and coat. Place in the refrigerator and let it sit for at least 8 hours, but no more than 3 days.

3. Place your grill pan over medium-high heat. Brush the ridges with vegetable oil. Once the pan is heated, place the salmon skin side up. Cook for 3 minutes. Turn the fish to cook for 3 minutes on the other side. At this point the fish should be medium-rare. But if you prefer the fish cooked more thoroughly, turn the fish flesh side down and place the fish at a different angle. Cook for 2 minutes on each side.

4. Place the leftover marinade in a saucepan over medium-high heat and bring to a boil. Boil for several minutes so it reduces to a syrup and brush or pour over the fish.

Miso Hungry

Miso is common in Japan and is made by fermenting rice, barley, and/or soybeans with salt and a special fermenting agent. The thick paste is used in soups, sauces, and for pickling meats and vegetables. It is high in vitamins, minerals, and protein and was necessary during times of drought since it could be preserved and kept for a long time.

SPICY BAKED FISH

Red snapper can be hard to find. You may be able to substitute trout, grouper, or striped bass depending on what is available in your area.

Yields 4 servings

1 whole 2–3-pound red snapper, cleaned

2 teaspoons salt

4 tablespoons Korean Spicy Red Pepper Paste (see recipe in sidebar)

2 scallions, green part, minced

1 tablespoon toasted sesame oil

1 tablespoon rice wine vinegar

1. Preheat oven to 375°F. Apply a thin layer of oil to the griddle if it isn't well seasoned. Place it in the middle of the oven.

2. Rinse the fish and pat it dry with paper towels. Make 3 or 4 slices through the skin and meat on each side of the fish, being careful not to cut through to the bones. Sprinkle the salt on the outside and inside of the fish evenly.

3. Combine all of the remaining ingredients in a bowl. Smear the sauce on the outside and inside of the fish, being sure to season the slits as well. Bake the fish on the griddle in the center of the oven for 10 minutes or until the fish starts to firm up.

4. Increase the heat to 425°F. The skin should get very crispy. Cook for 3–5 minutes. Check to see if it's done by slicing into the thickest part of the fish; the meat should be opaque. Serve while warm with rice.

Korean Spicy Red Pepper Paste

Combine the following ingredients and store them in an airtight jar in the refrigerator for up to 2 months: 2 tablespoons red pepper flakes, ¼ teaspoon cayenne powder, 4 cloves minced garlic, 1 teaspoon minced fresh ginger, 1 tablespoon soy sauce, 1 tablespoon brown sugar, and the juice from 1 lemon.

WHOLE SALT-CRUSTED RED SNAPPER

If you can't find red snapper, you can use any fish that is about 3–4 pounds.

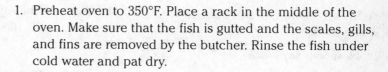

Yields 4–6 servings

1 whole 3–4-pound red snapper, cleaned

¼ cup thyme

1 lemon, sliced

¼ cup parsley, chopped

2 bay leaves

1 small yellow onion, thinly sliced

4 egg whites

1 cup coarse or kosher salt

1. Preheat oven to 350°F. Place a rack in the middle of the oven. Make sure that the fish is gutted and the scales, gills, and fins are removed by the butcher. Rinse the fish under cold water and pat dry.

2. Mix the thyme, lemon, parsley, bay leaves, and onion together in a large bowl. Stuff most of the mixture into the cavity of the fish. Put a few slices of onion on the griddle. Place the fish on top of the onions.

3. Place the egg whites in a bowl and use a hand mixer to whip them to a stiff peak. Fold the salt into the egg whites to create a paste and smear over the fish. Place the griddle in the oven and cook for 35 minutes.

4. Crack the egg white shell and remove the large chunks. If the skin doesn't come off with the crust, peel it away. Use a long, skinny spatula to lift the top fillet off the skeleton. Carefully pull the skeleton off the fish and discard it. Separate the second fillet from the skin. Serve immediately.

DEEP-FRIED TUNA WITH SPICY GARLIC SAUCE

Cooking tuna this way creates a crispy edge on the fish, cooked evenly on all sides. Because the fish seals quickly as it cooks, it doesn't soak up oil and get greasy.

Yields 4 servings as an appetizer, 2 as a meal

2 tablespoons soy sauce

2 garlic cloves, minced

½ teaspoon fresh ginger, grated

½ teaspoon ground black pepper

¼ cup sake

1 tablespoon fish sauce

½ teaspoon chili sauce

1 tablespoon cornstarch

4 4-ounce tuna fillets

Pinch salt

Pinch pepper

1 quart vegetable oil

1. Combine the soy sauce, garlic, ginger, pepper, sake, fish sauce, and chili sauce in a small bowl. Refrigerate overnight.

2. Just before cooking the tuna, stir cornstarch into the cold sauce. Warm the sauce in a microwave or a small saucepan, stirring frequently to thicken. Sprinkle the tuna lightly with salt and pepper.

3. Place a fryer over medium heat and add the oil. Once the oil is heated, add 2 pieces of tuna and cook for 1 minute. Remove them from the oil and pat dry with paper towels. Repeat with the remaining tuna. Slice the tuna into ½" slices and pour the sauce over them. Serve while hot.

BATTERED CATFISH

When purchasing catfish fillets, look for pieces that weigh 3–5 ounces each. The smaller pieces have less fatty tissue, which reduces the fishy taste. Remove any black membranes from the fish before cooking.

Yields 4–6 servings

2 pounds catfish fillets

½ cup yellow cornmeal

¼ cup all-purpose flour

1½ teaspoons salt

¼ teaspoon ground black pepper

Pinch cayenne

2 eggs, beaten

1 12-ounce beer, lager-style

3 cups vegetable oil

1. Rinse the fillets and cut them into 2"-thick slices. Combine the cornmeal, flour, salt, pepper, and cayenne in a wide, shallow bowl. In a separate wide, shallow bowl whisk together the egg and the beer.

2. Dredge the catfish in the flour, then the beer mixture, and then in the flour again. Place on a wire rack and rest for 10 minutes.

3. Place a fryer over medium heat and add the oil. Once the oil is heated, carefully slide 3 or 4 pieces of fish into the oil. Cook until lightly browned. Flip halfway through. Remove them from the oil and dry on a wire rack with paper towels underneath. They will darken as they cool. Serve with tartar sauce, rémoulade, or garlicky mayo.

SALMON WITH PINEAPPLE SALSA AND POLENTA

It's difficult to scale recipes back for one person, but when cooking fish, it's often easy to make a single serving. And with a skillet that can go from the stove to the broiler, it makes it even easier to create a full meal in one pan.

Yields 1 serving

1 6-ounce salmon fillet

Pinch salt

1 teaspoon olive oil

3 tablespoons Pineapple Salsa (see recipe in sidebar)

1 refrigerated tube of premade polenta

2 tablespoons olive oil

1 lime wedge for garnish

1. Preheat broiler to high. Sprinkle the salmon lightly on each side with salt. Place a small skillet over medium-high heat. Once hot, add the oil and place the fillet in the middle of the pan. Cook for 3 minutes on the first side and 2 minutes on the second side. Brush 1 tablespoon of the salsa on top. Place it in the oven about 4" from the flame for 30 seconds, just enough to caramelize the salsa. Place the fish on a plate and let it rest.

2. Place the skillet over medium-high heat. Slice 2 ½"-thick slices from the tube of polenta. Once the skillet is hot, add the oil and slide the 2 patties into the skillet. Don't touch them for 4 minutes. There should be enough crust on the bottom of the polenta to keep it together. Use a spatula to flip the polenta and cook for 5 minutes on the second side.

3. Once the polenta is cooked, drain off excess oil. Place the salmon on top of the polenta, pour the remaining salsa on top of the salmon, and place the skillet back in the oven for 1 minute to warm the fish through. Serve it immediately with the lime wedge.

Pineapple Salsa

To make your own, finely chop 5 pineapple rings and place in a small skillet with 2 tablespoons minced red onion, 2 teaspoons minced red pepper, juice from 1 lime, and 2 teaspoons chopped cilantro. Place over medium heat, salt lightly, and stir frequently for 15 minutes. The juices should evaporate and the onion and pepper should soften.

DEEP-FRIED SHRIMP AND OYSTERS

This breading works and tastes great on shellfish, including clams and scallops.

Yields 6–8 servings

2 quarts safflower or canola oil

1 cup all-purpose flour

2 teaspoons salt

1 teaspoon Old Bay Seasoning

3 eggs, beaten

1½ cups fine bread crumbs or panko

12 ounces shucked oysters, drained and cooled

1 pound medium shrimp, peeled and deveined

Cocktail Sauce (see recipe in sidebar) to taste

1. Place a fryer or Dutch oven over medium to medium-high heat and add the oil. Make sure the temperature is 375°F. Combine the flour, salt, and Old Bay in a wide, shallow bowl. Beat the eggs in another wide, shallow bowl. Add the bread crumbs to a third wide, shallow bowl. Preheat the oven to its lowest setting. Place a wire rack on a cookie sheet in the middle of the oven.

2. Pat the oysters and shrimp dry. Dredge them in the flour mixture with one hand. Dip them in the egg with the other hand. Dredge them in the bread crumbs with the first hand and set on a clean, dry plate.

3. Once you have one layer breaded, slide them into the oil and cook for 2 minutes, or until they're a light, golden brown. Place on the wire rack and sprinkle lightly with salt or more Old Bay. Serve warm with Cocktail Sauce.

Cocktail Sauce

To make your own cocktail sauce combine 1 cup ketchup, 1 teaspoon prepared horseradish, juice from 1 lemon, 1 minced garlic clove, and ¼ teaspoon Tabasco sauce. This easy sauce is great for most fried seafood, and any leftover sauce can be stored for 2 weeks.

CIOPPINO

This is a distinctly San Francisco dish believed to have been created by Italian fishermen as a way to use each day's catch. It goes perfectly with sourdough bread.

Yields 8–10 servings

¼ cup butter or olive oil

2 medium onions, chopped

4 garlic cloves, minced

¼ cup parsley leaves

¼ cup oregano leaves

2 28-ounce cans whole tomatoes, peel removed

2 10-ounce cans of clams

2 bay leaves

2 tablespoons dried basil leaves

2 cups dry white wine

16 fresh clams

16 mussels

1½ pounds salmon cut into bite-size chunks

1 pound fresh crabmeat or imitation crab stick cut into chunks

1½ pounds small bay scallops

Salt to taste

Pepper to taste

1. Place a large Dutch oven over medium heat. Once it's heated through add the butter and onion. Cook for 10–12 minutes. Add the garlic and stir continually for 1 minute. Stir in the parsley and oregano.

2. Add the juice from the tomatoes to the pan. Squeeze each tomato in your hand to break apart. Add to the pan and press each tomato against the side to break it into smaller pieces. Pour the clam juice into the pan and refrigerate the clams for later. Stir in the dried herbs and wine.

3. Cover with a lid, reduce the heat to low, and simmer for 2 hours. (If necessary, you can complete this part up to 2 days ahead and refrigerate. Return it to the pan and bring to a boil before turning the flame to medium-low.)

4. Scrub the clams and mussels with a bristle brush. Remove the beards from the mussels. Soak in cold water for 20 minutes. Gently lift the shellfish and reserved clams into the pan. Stir them into the sauce. Stir in the fish fillets, then the crabmeat. Stir in the scallops. Cover and steam for 5–8 minutes until the clams and mussels have opened.

5. Remove the bay leaves from the pan. Taste and season with salt and pepper if necessary. Serve directly from the pan while hot.

DEEP-FRIED SOFT-SHELL CRAB SANDWICHES

Crabs have shells to protect themselves from predators. But as they grow, they molt to remove an old shell and permit a new shell to grow. Once their shell is gone, the entire crab is edible.

Yields 4 servings

4 soft-shell crabs

¼ cup cornstarch or arrowroot starch

1 quart vegetable oil

4 hamburger buns

4 tomato slices

4 lettuce leaves

4 tablespoons spicy mayonnaise

1. If the crabs aren't cleaned, you'll have to trim a few things before you cook them. Hold the body in one hand and use kitchen shears to cut off ½" of the front of the crab to get rid of the eyes and mouth. Flip the apron, or tail-like piece, up and remove. Scrape out the innards. Lift up each side of the shell and remove the fingerlike pieces of gill.

2. Place the crabs on a plate. Put the cornstarch in a small mesh strainer. Tap the strainer lightly to coat both sides of the crabs. Shake the crabs lightly to remove any extra starch.

3. Place the oil in a fryer over medium heat. Once the oil is heated, slide the crabs into the oil and cook for 4–5 minutes, turning the crabs halfway through. Remove the crab from the oil and let drain for a few minutes before assembling the sandwiches. Serve on hamburger buns with tomato, lettuce, and spicy mayonnaise.

CRAWFISH MAQUE CHOUX

This Cajun dish (pronounced MOCK shoe) can also be served as a side dish. It's best made with the sweetest fresh corn you can find.

Yields 4 servings

2 12-ounce packages frozen crawfish tails, or 2 pounds medium shrimp

½ cup dry white wine

Juice from 1 lemon

½ teaspoon salt

8 ears white corn on the cob

3 tablespoons bacon drippings or olive oil

1 green bell pepper, finely chopped

1 large white onion, finely chopped

¼ cup butter

2 tablespoons heavy cream or whole milk

2 cups chicken stock

1 15-ounce can diced tomatoes, drained

1 teaspoon ground black pepper

½ teaspoon Tabasco sauce

2 tablespoons chopped parsley

1. Place the crawfish or peeled shrimp in a large glass bowl. Add the wine, lemon juice, and salt and toss to combine. Let it marinate for 20 minutes. Stand each ear of corn on end and cut the kernels off. Then run the back of the knife down the cobs to get the corn milk and corn germ out of the cob.

2. Place a large skillet over medium heat. Add the bacon drippings and bell pepper and cook for 2 minutes, stirring frequently. Add the chopped onion and cook until it is translucent and just starting to brown. Remove the vegetables to another bowl.

3. Add the corn, butter, cream, and stock. Stir continuously for 10 minutes until some of the stock has evaporated. Add the tomatoes and cook for 5 minutes.

4. Discard the marinade from the shellfish and add the meat to the skillet. Cook while stirring frequently for 5 minutes. If the mixture seems a bit dry, add some more stock or water. Add the black pepper and the reserved vegetables. Taste before adding Tabasco sauce and salt if necessary. Garnish with parsley. Serve in bowls immediately.

SAUTÉED SHRIMP AND MUSHROOMS

This is great served over rice with a side of Stewed Black Beans (see recipe in Chapter 3) or served over boiled fettuccine.

Yields 1 serving

1 tablespoon butter

1 tablespoon olive oil

¼ cup sliced mushrooms

1 green onion, thinly sliced

Dash salt

1 small tomato, cored and diced

1 garlic clove, minced

Juice from 1 lemon

2 tablespoons dry white wine or vermouth

¼ pound medium shrimp, shelled and deveined

¼ teaspoon Old Bay Seasoning

1. Place a small skillet over medium heat. Once it is heated, add the butter and olive oil. Add the mushrooms, green onion, and a dash of salt. Cook for 4–5 minutes.

2. Stir in the tomato and garlic and cook for 3–4 minutes, or until the garlic smells fragrant and the tomato is starting to break down. Stir in the lemon juice. Cook for 1 minute.

3. Stir in the wine, the shrimp, and the Old Bay. Cook for 3–5 minutes, or until the shrimp turns pink. Serve while warm.

SPANISH GRIDDLE-COOKED SHRIMP

This would be Gambas a la Plancha on a tapas menu. Dishes cooked a la plancha are common on Spanish menus and traditionally cooked on flat cast-iron pans.

Yields 4 servings

3 medium tomatoes, seeded and chopped

3 green onions, thinly sliced

¼ cup chopped cilantro leaves

3 garlic cloves, minced

¼ cup spicy tomato salsa

1½ pounds large shrimp, peeled and deveined

Dash salt

Dash pepper

2 tablespoons oil

Juice from 1 lime

1 lime cut into wedges

1. Toss the tomatoes, green onion, cilantro, garlic, and salsa in a bowl and set aside. Toss the shrimp with the salt and pepper.

2. Place a griddle over medium-high heat. Once it's heated, pour 1 tablespoon of oil in the center of the pan and swirl to coat. Place half the shrimp on the pan so they aren't touching and cook for 1 minute. Remove the shrimp from the pan and place in a bowl. Repeat with 1 tablespoon of oil and the remaining shrimp.

3. Sprinkle the lime juice over the tomato mixture. Pour the mixture into the middle of the griddle and spread it out. Stir gently until the tomatoes are well heated. Sprinkle the partially cooked shrimp on top of the mixture. Cook for 2 minutes or until they're cooked through and hot. Transfer to a large platter and serve with lime wedges.

TAMARIND SHRIMP KEBABS

If you can't find tamarind, substitute equal parts lime juice and brown sugar.

Yields 4 servings

2 tablespoons tamarind paste

½ cup chicken or vegetable broth

2 tablespoons rice wine or dry sherry

1½ tablespoons brown sugar

½ teaspoon salt

4 garlic cloves, minced

1 small yellow onion, minced

1 jalapeño, minced

1 pound shell-on shrimp (31–40 count), deveined

1 teaspoon peanut oil

2 scallions, chopped

¼ cup cilantro, chopped

1. Combine the tamarind paste and broth in a bowl. Let it sit for several minutes and then mash the paste until it has dissolved. Add the wine, sugar, and salt, stirring to combine.

2. Trim wooden skewers to fit your pan. Combine the garlic, onion, and jalapeño, and rub on the cut side of the shrimp. Thread the shrimp onto skewers so they're barely touching. Place the skewers in a large dish and lay flat. Pour the marinade over the shrimp, cover, and place in the refrigerator for 30–60 minutes.

3. Place a grill pan over medium-high heat and brush the ridges with the peanut oil. Remove the skewers from the marinade and place one layer on the pan. Cook for 3–4 minutes on each side. Once they're pink on both sides, place on a serving platter.

4. Sprinkle the scallion and cilantro over the platter for serving. If you want to serve the leftover marinade as a dipping sauce, pour the liquid into a small skillet and bring to a boil and cook for 2–3 minutes. Serve alongside the shrimp.

Tamarind

Tamarind is a fruit that grows in a pod and is common in Southeast Asia, parts of Africa, and Mexico. Its distinct flavor is usually found in paste form. A tablespoon or two can be added to almost any sauce or marinade to add a lot of flavor. It tends to be a bit on the salty side, so taste your dishes before salting them.

GRILLED AND BUTTER-BASTED LOBSTER TAILS

Lobster is expensive, and buying the tails alone is more expensive than buying the whole lobster. But this dish is great for a celebratory meal!

Yields 2 servings

2½ pounds lobster tails

2 tablespoons chives, minced

2 tablespoons olive oil

2 tablespoons butter

2 garlic cloves, minced

¼ cup water

2 tablespoons chopped parsley

1. Place the lobster tail on the cutting board with the shell side down. Cut through the belly shell from the top, through the meat, and through the back shell. Don't cut through the fin portion of the tail. Gently pull the sections of meat away from the shell. Rinse the tails in cold water.

2. Combine the chives and 1 tablespoon of olive oil in a small bowl. Rub the mixture over the meat and shell.

3. Place a grill pan over high heat. Once it's heated through, brush the surface of the pan with the remaining olive oil. Place the lobster, shell side down, on the grill. Cover and cook for 1 minute. Turn the lobster and cook on the other side for 1 minute, covered. The lobster should still be pink in the middle. Remove it from the pan.

4. Lower the heat to medium and add the butter. Once the butter has melted, add the garlic and water and rotate back and forth to combine. Bring to a simmer.

5. Hold the skillet at an angle so the sauce pools to one side. Place the lobster back in the pan on the side farthest away from the flame. Use a long-handled spoon to scoop butter and pour it over the lobster. Baste with the pan at an angle for 5 minutes or until the lobster is cooked through. Sprinkle with parsley, pour the remaining sauce over the lobster, and serve.

CHAPTER 9

DESSERTS

BREAD PUDDING

Because of the eggs and sugar, it's necessary to use a well-seasoned pan or a pan that has had the sides greased with butter to keep this dish from sticking.

Yields 1 loaf or 12 muffins

2 tablespoons butter, melted

¼ cup packed brown sugar

1 teaspoon vanilla extract

1 teaspoon ground cinnamon

½ cup whole milk

3 eggs

6 slices of bread, cubed

1. Preheat oven to 350°F. Place loaf pan or muffin pans on the middle rack.

2. Add the melted butter to a large mixing bowl. Whisk in the brown sugar, vanilla extract, ground cinnamon, milk, and eggs. Add the bread to the bowl and press lightly till cubes have soaked up all of the liquid.

3. Pour the contents into a loaf pan and use a spoon to spread out. Bake for 40 minutes. Or fill the muffin cups about two-thirds with the mix and bake for 30 minutes.

4. Let the pans rest for 10 minutes before running a knife along the outside edge to help dislodge the contents.

OATMEAL MUFFINS

If you wish to make a traditional muffin recipe in a cast-iron muffin pan, reduce the oven temperature by 25°F to prevent the outside from cooking before the center does.

Yields 12–18 muffins

2 cups rolled oats

1½ cups buttermilk

½ cup sugar

2 large eggs

4 tablespoons shortening or butter, small cubes

1 cup all-purpose flour

1 teaspoon baking soda

½ teaspoon salt

1. Place the oats and the buttermilk in a covered bowl and refrigerate for 6–24 hours. Preheat oven to 400°F. Stir the sugar, eggs, and 2 tablespoons of shortening into the oat mixture. Combine the flour, baking soda, and salt, and then fold into the oat mixture.

2. Use the remaining shortening to thoroughly grease each muffin pan cup. Fill the cups two-thirds full with batter. Bake for 20–25 minutes, until an inserted toothpick comes out clean.

3. Once the muffins are cooked through, turn them out of the pan immediately and let cool slightly before serving.

CHERRY ALMOND CAKE

When baking bread in a loaf pan that isn't well seasoned, butter the inside of the pan and cut a piece of wax or parchment paper so it covers the inside of the pan. When it's finished cooking, grab the paper to lift the bread out.

Yields 1 loaf cake

1 cup fresh cherries

¼ cup all-purpose flour

1 cup butter, softened

½ cup and 1 tablespoon sugar

3 large eggs, beaten

¼ teaspoon almond extract

1⅔ cups self-rising cake flour

½ cup finely chopped almonds

⅓ cup milk

1. Preheat oven to 325°F. Pit the cherries and cut in half. Place them on a plate and sprinkle with flour. Toss to coat them evenly and shake to remove the excess.

2. Place the butter and sugar in a mixer bowl and beat until light and fluffy. Add the eggs gradually until well blended. Add the almond extract and combine.

3. Combine the cake flour and almonds. Sprinkle the flour mixture over the wet ingredients and fold in the flour gently. Fold in the cherries and milk.

4. Once the liquid is combined, pour into the loaf pan and bake for 45–60 minutes, or until an inserted toothpick comes out clean.

INDIAN VEGETABLE LOAF

This is like a savory cake baked in the oven. But it is also like a vegetarian meatloaf-style dish that can be served as a main dish or as a side.

Yields 4–6 servings

4 eggs

1 jalapeño, seeded and diced

1½ teaspoons salt

¼ teaspoon pepper

2 tablespoons vegetable oil or butter

1 medium onion, chopped

½ red bell pepper, chopped

½ cup crumbled fresh cheese or Parmesan cheese

1 zucchini, grated

1 large carrot, peeled and grated

1 cup frozen corn

⅓ cup flour

½ teaspoon baking powder

1. Preheat oven to 350°F. Grease a loaf pan. Beat the eggs with the jalapeño, salt, and pepper in a bowl and set aside.

2. Place a skillet over medium-high heat. Add the oil, onion, and bell pepper. Cook for 5–7 minutes, stirring frequently. Add to the egg mixture. Stir the cheese, zucchini, carrot, and corn into the egg mixture.

3. Mix the flour and baking powder together in a large bowl. Stir in the egg mixture until combined but not smooth. Pour the mixture into the loaf pan and bake in the center of the oven for 25–30 minutes. Cool for 5 minutes before slicing and serving.

MEDITERRANEAN OLIVE BREAD

Any type of olive can be used in this bread, but a mixture of black and green olives that have pits will taste best.

Yields 1 loaf

Butter, as needed

1½ cups all-purpose white flour

¾ cup whole-wheat flour

1½ teaspoons baking powder

½ teaspoon salt

¾ teaspoon dried rosemary or thyme

2 large eggs

1 cup milk

¼ cup olive oil

½ cup olives, pitted and coarsely chopped

1. Preheat oven to 350°F. Place a rack in the lower third of the oven. Grease a 6-cup loaf pan with butter.

2. In a medium bowl, whisk together the flours, baking powder, and salt. Coarsely grind the dried herbs. Stir into the flour mixture. In a large bowl, whisk eggs, milk, and oil until the yolks are incorporated. Add the flour mixture and the olives to the liquid mixture. Fold together until the dry ingredients are barely moistened.

3. The thick batter should be scraped into the pan and spread evenly with a spatula. Bake for 40–45 minutes or until a toothpick inserted comes out clean. Cool for 5 minutes before slicing. Serve warm or cold.

GARBANZO BEAN BROWNIES

This recipe makes fudgy brownies. But if you prefer cakelike brownies, divide the mixture into 2 skillets and bake for 45 minutes.

Yields 6–10 servings

4 eggs

1 can garbanzo beans, drained

1½ cups chocolate chips

1¼ cups sugar

1 tablespoon vanilla

¼ cup chickpea flour

¾ teaspoon baking powder

1. Place a skillet in the middle of the oven and preheat to 350°F. Place eggs in a food processor with garbanzo beans. Purée until very smooth. It should have air bubbles, but stop before it starts to look like a meringue.

2. Melt the chocolate chips in a double-boiler or microwave. Add a few tablespoons of chocolate to the processor and pulse. Then slowly pour in the rest of the chocolate. Scrape down the sides as necessary.

3. Once the mixture is a uniform color, add sugar and vanilla. Purée 1 minute. Add flour and baking powder. Purée until incorporated. Pour mixture into the skillet and bake 1 hour. Cool 5 minutes before turning out and cutting.

POPOVERS

Cast-iron muffin or popover pans are best for this recipe because you can heat them before adding the batter. This makes the rising process quicker and the popovers are less likely to flatten when you remove them from the oven.

Yields 6–8 popovers

Butter, as needed

2 eggs, room temperature

1 cup milk, room temperature

1 tablespoon vegetable oil

1 cup flour

½ teaspoon salt

1. Preheat oven to 400°F. Grease each cup of the pan generously with butter or solid vegetable shortening. Place the pan in the oven and bring to temperature.

2. Combine remaining ingredients in a blender and blend for slightly less than 1 minute. Scrape down the sides several times. When the pan is heated through, remove it from the oven and fill the cups halfway with batter.

3. Bake for 35–40 minutes. Popovers should be puffed and golden. To prevent them from collapsing, do not open the oven for 35 minutes. If they seem wet after 40 minutes, pierce with a butter knife, turn off the heat, and return them to the oven for 5 minutes.

EBELSKIVER

This Scandinavian pancake was traditionally made with apple slices, but it can be made with any filling, or served plain with powdered sugar or syrup on top.

Yields 4–6 servings

3 eggs

2 tablespoons sugar

3 tablespoons melted butter

1½ cups buttermilk

½ cup milk

½ teaspoon salt

1 teaspoon vanilla extract

2 cups flour

1 teaspoon baking soda

1 teaspoon baking powder

2 tablespoons canola or vegetable oil

¼ cup fruit syrup, or ½ cup cooked fruit chunks

1. Separate the egg whites from the yolks and place into two bowls. Whip the whites to a stiff peak. Beat the yolks with the sugar, butter, milks, salt, and vanilla. Sift the flour, baking soda, and baking powder together. Stir it into the egg yolk mixture. Fold in the egg whites.

2. Place the ebelskiver pan over medium heat and let it warm for several minutes. Use a basting brush to brush the depressions with oil. Once the pan is hot, fill the depressions halfway with batter. Place ½ teaspoon syrup in the center of the depression and cover with more batter if necessary. Cook for 1–2 minutes on the first side or until there are visible bubbles and the surface starts to look dry.

3. Use a skewer or a crochet hook to lightly pierce the cooked edge of the batter and flip it upside down. Repeat in the same order the depressions were filled. Cook for 1 minute before removing. Oil the depressions again and repeat until all the batter has been used. Serve warm.

FRESH FIG MUFFINS

You can often find fresh figs in grocery stores during the fall. They are also available frozen or dried.

Yields 12 muffins

8 fresh figs

¼ cup dry sherry

1⅔ cups flour

½ cup almond slivers

1 teaspoon salt

1 teaspoon baking soda

1 teaspoon cinnamon

1 teaspoon nutmeg

1½ cups sugar

½ cup vegetable oil

2 eggs

1. Preheat oven 350°F. Remove the stems and cut the figs into ¼" slices and then into ¼" cubes. Place them in a small bowl and add the sherry. Let sit for about 15 minutes.

2. In a medium-size bowl, combine the flour, almonds, salt, baking soda, cinnamon, and nutmeg. In a separate and larger mixing bowl beat the sugar, oil, and eggs. Reduce the mixer speed to low and slowly add the flour mixture.

3. Fold the figs and sherry in by hand, being careful not to overstir. Pour the batter into a well-greased muffin pan. Bake for 1 hour and 15 minutes.

4. When the top has browned and a muffin feels slightly firm, remove them from the oven. Let them sit in the pan for 10–15 minutes. An inserted toothpick should come out clean. Turn onto a rack to cool further.

Rehydrating Dried Figs

Dried figs are easier to find than other types. Place 2 cups of apple juice or water in a small saucepan and bring it to a boil. Place the figs into the liquid and let them sit for 2–4 hours. The figs will be ready for this recipe.

CORN STICKS

Most people love the crunchy edges of cornbread. Using corn stick pans permits everyone to enjoy the crunchy exterior and soft interior.

Yields 2 trays of corn sticks

Vegetable oil, as needed, plus 2 tablespoons

⅓ cup flour, sifted

1 teaspoon sugar

1 teaspoon baking powder

½ teaspoon baking soda

½ teaspoon salt

1⅓ cups yellow cornmeal

1 egg, beaten

1 cup sour cream

¾ cup milk

1. Preheat oven to 400°F. Use a basting brush to thoroughly apply vegetable oil to the corn stick pans. Place the pans in the middle of the oven.

2. In a medium bowl combine the flour, sugar, baking powder, baking soda, salt, and cornmeal. In a large bowl whisk the egg, sour cream, milk, and 2 tablespoons vegetable oil. Once it is thoroughly combined and the egg is completely incorporated, pour the dry ingredients into the wet ingredients. Stir until the dry ingredients are moistened but not smooth.

3. Remove one of the pans. Use a small cup or spoon to fill the pan about two-thirds with batter. Place the first tray in the oven and repeat with the second. The pans should sizzle when you add the mix.

4. Bake the sticks for about 25 minutes, or until golden brown. Carefully remove from the pan immediately. Serve while hot with butter and honey.

CHERRY PUDDING CAKE

This is a modification of the traditional French recipe known as Cherry Clafouti.

Yields 4–6 servings

1 pound cherries, pitted

1 tablespoon butter

1 cup sugar

4 eggs

½ teaspoon vanilla extract

1 tablespoon brandy or amaretto liqueur

1 cup all-purpose flour

1½ cups milk

Optional: powdered sugar

1. Place a rack in the center of the oven and preheat to 425°F. Wash the cherries. Remove the stems and pits.

2. Place a skillet over medium heat. Once it's heated, stir the cherries, butter, and ¼ cup of the sugar in the skillet. Cook for 5–7 minutes. Once the butter and sugar have melted and started to caramelize turn off the heat.

3. Combine the remaining ingredients except the powdered sugar in a blender and pulse for 60 seconds. Scrape down the sides of the carafe. Pour 1 cup of the batter in the skillet and cook in the oven for 5 minutes.

4. Pour the rest of the batter into the skillet and return it to the oven for 15–20 minutes or until an inserted toothpick comes out clean. Slide the cake out of the skillet and let it rest for 10 minutes before slicing. Sprinkle with powdered sugar and serve.

Cherries Are the Pits

It's hard to remove pits from cherries without a cherry pitter, but it isn't impossible. If you don't have one, you can put an icing piping tip, base down, on a plate or shallow bowl and press the cherry over the tip. You can also open a paperclip and use it to cut and scoop out the pit.

CORNBREAD

Sweet cornbread is common in the South. If you prefer your cornbread savory, just eliminate the sugar. You can also mince two jalapeños and add them to the mix if you like it spicy.

Yields 6–8 servings

2 cups yellow cornmeal

1 teaspoon kosher salt

¼ cup sugar

2 teaspoons baking powder

½ teaspoon baking soda

1½ cups buttermilk

2 eggs

2 tablespoons vegetable oil

1. Place a skillet in the middle of the oven and preheat to 425°F. In a bowl combine the cornmeal, salt, sugar, baking powder, and baking soda. Whisk together until well combined.

2. In a large bowl whisk together the buttermilk and eggs. Once the yolks are completely incorporated, pour the dry ingredients into the wet ingredients. Stir gently to combine. Add more buttermilk if necessary to get a pourable consistency.

3. Add the vegetable oil to the skillet and swirl to coat the bottom and sides. Pour the batter into the skillet. You should hear the batter sizzle.

4. Bake for 20 minutes. If you press gently in the middle of the cornbread, it should spring back. Let it cool in the skillet for 10 minutes before serving.

BUTTERED RUM PINEAPPLE

This is similar to the caramelized glaze on the Pineapple Upside-Down Cake (see recipe in this chapter). The addition of rum deepens the flavors.

Yields 4 servings

½ cup brown sugar

¼ cup dark rum

3 tablespoons butter

1 pineapple, cored and cut into ½" slices

1. Place a skillet over medium heat. Once it is heated through, add the brown sugar, rum, and butter and stir until the butter is melted and bubbling.

2. Place the pineapple slices in the skillet one at a time and cook for 3 minutes or until they're warmed through. Serve while hot.

DUTCH APPLE BABY

The "dutch" in this name actually refers to the German-American immigrants known as Pennsylvania Deutsch.

Yields 4 servings

2 Golden Delicious or Granny Smith apples

¼ cup unsalted butter

¼ cup plus 3 tablespoons sugar

2 tablespoons ground cinnamon

¾ cup all-purpose flour

¼ teaspoon salt

¾ cup whole milk

4 large eggs

1 teaspoon vanilla extract

Confectioners' sugar or whipped cream for garnish

1. Preheat oven to 425°F. Core the apples and cut into ¼" thick slices. Place a skillet over medium heat and once it's heated, add the butter and apples. Sauté in the melted butter for 3–4 minutes. Stir in the ¼ cup sugar and cinnamon and cook for 3–4 minutes. Spread the apple slices evenly over the bottom of the pan.

2. Mix the dry 3 tablespoons sugar, flour, and salt in a large bowl. Mix the milk, eggs, and vanilla in a smaller bowl. Once the eggs are whipped and combined, pour into the dry ingredients and stir to combine. Pour the batter mixture over the apple slices, being careful not to move the apples. Bake for 15–20 minutes. The mixture will puff up considerably and the top will brown. A toothpick inserted should come out clean.

3. Remove from the oven and slide a knife along the outside of the skillet to loosen the edges. Place a plate on top of the skillet, and flip the pan upside down to transfer it to the plate. Let it cool for 10 minutes before sifting with confectioners' sugar or serving with whipped cream.

NOT SO FANCY APPLE FOLDOVER

Apples and Cheddar cheese are good together if you like salty and sweet. These flavors meld together in a baked pie.

Yields 8 servings

2½ cups plus ⅛ teaspoon all-purpose flour

½ cup cornmeal

½ cup sugar

2 sticks cold butter, cubed

½ cup cold water in a spray bottle

2 tart apples, peeled, cored, thinly sliced

3 tablespoons cider vinegar

¼ teaspoon ground nutmeg

¼ teaspoon ground mace

2 tablespoons butter

½ cup shredded sharp Cheddar cheese

1 egg white

1. Place the flour, cornmeal, and 3 tablespoons sugar in a food processor and pulse several times. Add half of the butter and pulse 8–10 times to get even-size lumps. Add the rest of the butter and repeat. Spray the top of the flour with water until it is evenly dampened. Pulse 3 times, wait 30 seconds, and pulse 3 more times. Press on the dough. It should come together. Repeat the spraying if it doesn't.

2. Pour the dough into a large sealable bag and mold into a disk. Refrigerate for 30 minutes.

3. Preheat oven to 400°F. Place a skillet over medium heat. When warm, add the apples and toss for 30 seconds. Add the vinegar. Stir for 30 seconds or until the vinegar evaporates. Add ¼ cup sugar and toss to combine. Cook for 2–3 minutes, or until the apples start to soften.

4. Remove the skillet from the heat and add the spices and 2 tablespoons butter. Stir until the butter has melted and coats the apple. Stir in the cheese. Cool apples in a bowl to room temperature. Clean the skillet.

5. Place the dough between two sheets of wax paper. Roll until it is about ¼" thick. Slide the dough into the skillet. Pile the apple mixture onto the center, leaving about 2" of crust on all sides. Sprinkle the apples with ⅛ teaspoon flour. Fold the extra crust toward the center and pinch where the edges meet.

6. Brush the top of the crust with the egg white and sprinkle with 1 tablespoon of sugar. Bake in the center of the oven for 30 minutes. The crust should be golden brown. Let the pie rest for about 20 minutes before serving.

PINEAPPLE UPSIDE-DOWN CAKE

This cake is the perfect dessert to make in a cast-iron skillet. Making the caramel in the pan and then pouring the cake batter on top makes the caramel become part of the cake.

Yields 7 servings

1 18-ounce can pineapple rings

4 tablespoons butter

½ cup plus 1 cup brown sugar

7 maraschino cherries

4 tablespoons cold butter

2 large eggs

½ cup milk

½ cup sour cream

1½ teaspoons vanilla extract

1½ cups all-purpose flour

1½ teaspoons baking powder

½ teaspoon salt

1. Preheat oven to 350°F. Place a skillet over medium-high heat. Drain the juice from the can of pineapple into the skillet. Add 4 tablespoons butter and ½ cup brown sugar. Stir with a wooden spoon as everything melts. Boil to a thick caramel-like consistency. Turn off the heat; lay 6 pineapple rings around the outside and 1 in the center of the skillet with a maraschino cherry in the center of each ring. Place in the oven to preheat the pan while you prepare the cake.

2. Combine the cold butter and 1 cup sugar in a mixing bowl until it is light and creamy. Beat in the eggs one at a time. Make sure the first egg is completely incorporated before mixing in the second. Add the milk, sour cream, and vanilla. Stop mixing once it is combined but not smooth.

3. Sift together the flour, baking powder, and salt. Use a spatula or spoon to fold in the wet ingredients. Remove the skillet from the oven and pour the batter in. Gently shake the skillet back and forth to even out the batter. Bake for 45–50 minutes.

4. Let sit for 5–10 minutes. Place a large plate upside down on top of the skillet. Turn the skillet upside down. If any caramel or fruit sticks, remove with a spatula and place it back on the cake. Let the cake cool for 10 minutes before serving.

The Flip Side of the Pineapple Upside-Down Cake

In 1925, the Hawaiian Pineapple Company ran ads looking for creative pineapple recipes. They received 1,500 recipes for the pineapple upside-down cake. The winning entry came from Mrs. Robert Davis of Norfolk, Virginia, and was published in their cookbook.

IRISH SODA BREAD

The acid in the buttermilk is what causes the loaf to rise and make air bubbles. If you don't have buttermilk, substitute plain yogurt that has half a lemon squeezed into it.

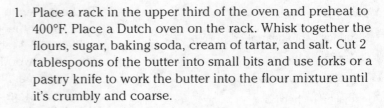

Yields 1 loaf

3 cups all-purpose flour

1 cup cake flour

2 tablespoons sugar

1½ teaspoons baking soda

1½ teaspoons cream of tartar

2 teaspoons salt

3 tablespoons butter, softened

1½ cups buttermilk

1. Place a rack in the upper third of the oven and preheat to 400°F. Place a Dutch oven on the rack. Whisk together the flours, sugar, baking soda, cream of tartar, and salt. Cut 2 tablespoons of the butter into small bits and use forks or a pastry knife to work the butter into the flour mixture until it's crumbly and coarse.

2. Add the buttermilk and stir with a fork until the dough has just come together. Sprinkle some flour onto a surface and knead the dough until everything sticks together and it is still bumpy.

3. Pat the dough into a circle the size of your pan and no more than 2" thick. Cut an X into the top of the dough.

4. Place the dough in the Dutch oven, cover, and bake for 20 minutes. Bake, uncovered, for another 20–25 minutes. Rub the remaining butter on top of the crust and let the loaf sit for 30 minutes or until it has cooled.

UPSIDE-DOWN APPLE PIE

If you prefer, you can substitute vegetable shortening for the butter when making the crust. Peeled apples will give a better texture, and soak up more caramel.

Yields 8 servings

2¼ cups all-purpose flour

¼ cup confectioners' sugar

¾ teaspoon salt

6 tablespoons butter, cold and cubed

1 egg, lightly beaten

2 tablespoons cold water (if needed)

6 tablespoons butter

⅔ cup granulated sugar

¼ teaspoon nutmeg

1 teaspoon cinnamon

½ teaspoon ground cardamom

3 pounds Fuji or Granny Smith apples, cored, peeled, sliced

1. Add the flour, confectioners' sugar, and salt to a food processor. Pulse a few times. Add the cold butter and pulse till it resembles coarse cornmeal. Pour the mixture into a bowl. Stir in the egg until chunks form. If necessary, add a little cold water to get this consistency. Press the chunks together into a disk and wrap in plastic wrap. Refrigerate for at least 1 hour.

2. Place a rack in the middle of the oven and preheat to 375°F. Place a skillet over medium heat. Add the butter and when melted add the granulated sugar. Cook for 5 minutes. Stir in the spices and cook for 1 minute more. Turn off the heat.

3. Layer the apple slices around the outside of the pan so the tips are touching the skillet wall and the thin edge of each slice is under the thicker edge of the slice next to it. Fill in the center with apple slices. Cook over high heat for 12 minutes or until the caramel mixture is very dark and the apples have soaked up most of it. Tilt the pan to cover the apple slices with juice. Cook for 5 minutes. Turn off the heat.

4. Meanwhile, roll the dough between 2 sheets of parchment paper into a 14" circle. Place the dough on the skillet. Tuck the dough edges under so they touch the skillet but are not visible. Cut 4 1" slits in the center of the pie.

5. Bake for 20–25 minutes or until the crust is golden brown. Let cool for 20 minutes. Loosen the edges of the crust with a knife. Place a plate on top of the skillet and invert. Scrape out any apples that stick and rearrange them on top.

BASIC YELLOW CAKE

Serve this staple dessert any way you'd like—topped with icing, a dollop of whip cream or soy whip, or a sprinkling of powdered sugar.

Yields 10–12 servings

1½ cups all-purpose flour

1 teaspoon baking powder

1 cup sugar

½ teaspoon salt

2 eggs, beaten, or 2 mashed bananas

½ cup butter, melted

1 teaspoon vanilla extract

1 cup milk, or soymilk

1. In a medium bowl, mix the flour, baking powder, sugar, and salt. In a large bowl, beat the eggs. Add the dry ingredients to the eggs. Slowly stir in the melted butter, vanilla extract, and the milk.

2. Pour the cake mixture into an 8" round pan. Place the cake in a pressure cooker and lock the lid into place. Cook the cake for 30 minutes over a low flame without the weight in place.

3. Remove the pressure cooker from the heat and carefully remove the cake. Serve with whatever topping that you like.

CORNMEAL CAKE

Serve warm with maple syrup or make a maple-infused butter by whisking pats of chilled butter into heated maple syrup.

Yields 6 servings

2 cups milk or soymilk

¼ cup light brown sugar, packed

1 teaspoon orange zest, grated

½ cup fine yellow cornmeal

2 large eggs or 2 ounces silken tofu

2 tablespoons butter, melted

2 tablespoons orange marmalade

1 cup water

1. Bring milk to a simmer over medium heat. Stir in the brown sugar; simmer and stir until the milk is at a low boil. Whisk in the orange zest and cornmeal. Simmer and stir for 2 minutes. Remove from heat. Whisk together the eggs, butter, and orange marmalade. Stir into the cornmeal mixture. Treat a 1-quart soufflé or heatproof glass dish with nonstick spray. Add batter.

2. Pour water into the pressure cooker and add rack. Place soufflé dish on the rack. Lock lid into place and bring to low pressure; maintain pressure for 12 minutes. Remove from heat and allow pressure to release naturally for 10 minutes. Quick-release any remaining pressure and remove the lid. Transfer to a wire rack.

SPICED CHOCOLATE CAKE

Serve with icing, powdered sugar, or ice cream on top.

Yields 10–12 servings

1½ cups all-purpose flour

4 tablespoons cocoa powder

1 teaspoon cinnamon

1 teaspoon cayenne pepper

1 teaspoon sugar

¼ teaspoon salt

1 teaspoon baking powder

2 eggs, beaten, or 2 mashed bananas

4 tablespoons butter, melted

1 cup milk, or soymilk

2 cups hot water

1. In a medium bowl, mix the flour, cocoa powder, cinnamon, cayenne, sugar, salt, and baking powder. In a large bowl, beat the eggs. Add the dry ingredients to the eggs. Slowly stir in the melted butter and the milk. Pour the cake mixture into an 8" round pan.

2. Add the steaming rack to a pressure cooker and pour in the hot water. Place the cake in the pressure cooker and lock the lid into place. Bring to high pressure, then reduce to low and cook for 30 minutes.

3. Remove the pressure cooker from the heat, quick-release the steam, and carefully remove the cake.

LEMON CUSTARD

You can also prepare the lemon custard by fixing it in a 5-cup heatproof casserole dish that will fit on the rack inside the pressure cooker. Increase the pressure time to 20 minutes. Serve these custards dusted with powdered sugar or topped with fresh or cooked fruit.

Yields 6 servings

½ cup sugar

1 tablespoon cornstarch

2 large eggs

2 egg yolks

1½ cups milk

1 cup heavy cream

2 medium lemons

2 cups water

1. Add the sugar and cornstarch to a bowl. Stir to combine well. Whisk in the eggs and egg yolks. Stir in the milk and cream. Grate the zest from one of the lemons and add it to the batter along with the juice from both lemons (about ¼ cup). Evenly divide between 6 ½-cup custard cups. Tightly cover the top of each custard cup with aluminum foil to prevent any water from getting into the cups.

2. Set the rack in the bottom of a pressure cooker and pour in the water. Place the custard cups on the rack, stacking them if you need to.

3. Lock the lid into place and bring to high pressure; maintain pressure for 12 minutes. Remove the pressure cooker from the heat, quick-release the pressure, and remove the lid.

4. Carefully lift the custard cups from the pressure cooker and place them on a wire rack. Remove the foil.

5. Let custard cool to room temperature. Once cooled, cover each cup with plastic wrap and chill overnight in refrigerator.

CREAMY COCONUT RICE PUDDING

Garnish this pudding with a sprinkling of ground cinnamon and serve with a dollop of whipped cream or soy whip.

Yields 6 servings

1½ cups arborio rice, rinsed and drained

2 cups whole milk or soymilk

1 14-ounce can coconut milk

1 cup water

½ cup sugar

2 teaspoons ground cinnamon

½ teaspoon salt

1½ teaspoons vanilla

1 cup dried cherries, dried strawberries, or golden raisins

1. Add the rice, milk, coconut milk, water, sugar, cinnamon, and salt to a pressure cooker. Cook and stir to dissolve the sugar over medium-high heat and bring to a boil. Lock the lid into place and bring to low pressure; maintain for 15 minutes.

2. Turn off the heat, quick-release the pressure, and remove the lid. Stir in the vanilla and dried fruit. Replace the cover, but do not lock into place. Let stand for 15 minutes. Stir and serve.

BASIC UNSWEETENED APPLESAUCE

There's no need to core the apples to remove the seeds when you'll be using a food mill to process the cooked apples.

Yields 5 cups

1 cup water

12 medium apples (about 3 pounds)

1. Add the water to a pressure cooker. If using organic apples, rinse and quarter the apples. If not, rinse, peel, and quarter the apples. Add to the pressure cooker.

2. Lock the lid into place, bring to high pressure, and immediately remove from the heat; let the pressure release naturally for 10 minutes. Quick-release any remaining pressure.

3. Once the apples have cooled slightly, pass the apples and cooking liquid through a food mill. If you do not have a food mill, add the apples and cooking liquid in batches to a food processor or blender. Refrigerate covered for up to 10 days or freeze for up to 4 months.

Applesauce Notes

Instructions are for a 6-quart pressure cooker. For a yield of 3 cups in a 4-quart pressure cooker, reduce the apples to 2 pounds and the water to ⅔ cup. For a yield of 6½ cups of applesauce in an 8-quart pressure cooker, increase the apples to 5 pounds and the water to 1⅔ cups.

FRUIT COMPOTE

Serve as a topping for plain or soy yogurt.

Yields 6 servings

1 cup apple juice

1 cup dry white wine

2 tablespoons sugar

1 cinnamon stick

¼ teaspoon ground nutmeg

Zest of 1 lemon

Zest of 1 orange

3 apples

3 pears

½ cup dried cherries, cranberries, or raisins

1. Add the apple juice and wine to a pressure cooker over medium-high heat. Bring to a boil. Stir in the sugar until dissolved. Add the cinnamon stick, nutmeg, lemon zest, and orange zest. Reduce heat to maintain a simmer.

2. Wash, peel, core, and chop the apples and pears. Add to the pressure cooker. Stir. Lock the lid into place and bring to high pressure; maintain pressure for 1 minute. Remove the pressure cooker from heat, quick-release the pressure, and remove the lid.

3. Use a slotted spoon to transfer the cooked fruit to a serving bowl. Return the pressure cooker to the heat and bring to a boil; boil and stir until reduced to a syrup that will coat the back of a spoon. Stir the dried cherries, cranberries, or raisins in with the cooked fruit in the bowl and pour the syrup over the fruit mixture. Stir to mix. Allow to cool slightly, then cover with plastic wrap and chill overnight in the refrigerator.

PORT-POACHED FIGS

Serve the figs on top of soy ice cream—or simply on their own—with the syrup.

Yields 4 servings

3 cups tawny port

1½ cups sugar

1 vanilla bean, split and scraped

½ teaspoon cinnamon

¼ cup orange juice

8 whole black peppercorns

12 dried black mission figs

1. Combine the port, sugar, vanilla pod and seeds, cinnamon, orange juice, and peppercorns in a pressure cooker over high heat. Bring to a boil and reduce the heat. Simmer for 20 minutes.

2. Add the figs. Lock the lid into place and bring to high pressure; maintain pressure for 6 minutes. Remove from the heat and allow pressure to release naturally.

PEARS POACHED IN WINE

Use Bartlett, Anjou, or Bosc pears. If you prefer, replace the cinnamon stick, ginger, and orange zest with a whole split and scraped vanilla bean.

Yields 4 servings

4 ripe but still firm pears

2 tablespoons fresh lemon juice

1¼ cups dry wine

½ cup sweet sherry

¼ cup sugar

1 3" cinnamon stick, halved

¼ teaspoon ground ginger

2 teaspoons orange zest, grated

1. Rinse and peel the pears and cut them in half. Use a spoon or melon baller to remove the cores. Brush the pears with the lemon juice.

2. Combine the wine, sherry, sugar, cinnamon, ginger, and orange zest in the pressure cooker. Bring to a boil; stir to blend and dissolve the sugar. Carefully place the pears cut side down in the pressure cooker. Lock the lid into place and bring to low pressure; maintain pressure for 3 minutes. Remove the pressure cooker from the heat, quick-release the pressure, and remove the lid.

3. Use a slotted spoon to transfer the pears to a serving bowl or to place them on dessert plates. If desired, return the pressure cooker to medium heat and simmer uncovered for several minutes to thicken the sauce. Remove and discard the cinnamon stick pieces. Spoon the sauce over the pears. Serve.

Recipe Alternatives

Make this dessert alcohol-free by replacing the wine and sherry with fruit juice; adjust the sugar accordingly. If you prefer to serve whole pears, peel the pears and cut off some of the bottom so they'll stand upright. After you've dissolved the sugar into the sauce, insert the rack into the pressure cooker and stand the pears upright.

CINNAMON POACHED APPLES

Red apples, such as Gala or Red Delicious, complement the cinnamon and ground ginger in this recipe.

Yields 8 servings

5 apples, peeled, cored, and cut into wedges

3 cups water

1 cup white sugar

1 teaspoon ground ginger

1 teaspoon cinnamon

Add all ingredients to a 4-quart slow cooker. Cover and cook on low heat for 4 hours.

POACHED MIXED BERRIES

Poached mixed berries are delicious on their own or served over a scoop of vanilla ice cream.

Yields 8 servings

½ cup blackberries

½ cup blueberries

½ cup strawberries, quartered

3 cups water

1 cup white sugar

1 lemon, juiced

Add all ingredients to a 4-quart slow cooker. Cover and cook on low heat for 3–4 hours.

Frozen Versus Fresh Berries
Frozen berries have a slightly different texture after they're defrosted than fresh berries do, but the texture works well in slow-cooker recipes because of the long cooking time. Frozen berries allow you to use all types year-round, and they're usually cheaper than fresh berries, too.

CREPES

Sweet or savory, filled or simply sauced, crepes are delicate, elegant, delicious, and very easy to make. To make a dessert in a hurry, whisk together this batter, make some crepes, and slather them with chocolate-hazelnut spread.

Yields about 8 crepes

½ cup flour

3 large eggs

1 cup milk

1 tablespoon olive oil

¼ teaspoon kosher salt

Butter

1. Whisk together the flour and eggs until they form a smooth paste. Gradually whisk in the milk, olive oil, and salt.

2. Heat a 10" nonstick skillet over medium heat. Add some butter and spread it around the pan with a brush or the corner of a towel. Add ¼ cup batter to the pan. Swirl the pan around in a circular pattern to evenly distribute the batter.

3. Cook undisturbed until the edges become visibly brown. Using a wooden or rubber spatula, lift the edge of the crepe from the pan. Quickly flip the crepe using your fingers or a wooden spoon. Cook for 30 seconds on the second side, then slide onto a plate; keep warm while you repeat the procedure with remaining batter. Crepes can be stacked 1 atop the other for storage.

CHOCOLATE-ALMOND FONDUE

Fruit is often used for enjoying dessert fondue, but you can also try dipping pretzels or dense yellow cake for a different flavor.

Yields 16 servings

2 14-ounce packages semisweet chocolate chips

2 cups plain soymilk

½ cup butter

½ cup almond pieces

1. Add all ingredients to a 4-quart slow cooker. Cover and cook on low heat for 1 hour.

2. Serve the fondue warm with fruits such as strawberries, pineapples, apples, and bananas.

BANANAS FOSTER

Bananas Foster is usually made from flambéed bananas served over vanilla ice cream, but as this recipe proves, the bananas can be made in a slow cooker, too.

Yields 8 servings

1 cup dark corn syrup

⅛ cup rum

½ teaspoon vanilla extract

1 teaspoon cinnamon

¾ cup butter

½ teaspoon salt

10 bananas, peeled and cut into bite-size pieces

4 cups vanilla ice cream or vegan vanilla ice cream

1. In a medium bowl, stir in the corn syrup, rum, vanilla extract, cinnamon, butter, and salt.

2. Add mixture and bananas to a 4-quart slow cooker. Cover and cook on low heat for 1–2 hours. Serve over a scoop of ice cream.

CHOCOLATE ALMOND BARS

Save your dollar at the grocery store and make an entire batch of homemade candy bars.

Yields 16 servings

2 14-ounce packages semisweet chocolate chips

2 cups almond pieces

1. Add all ingredients to a 4-quart slow cooker. Cover and cook on low heat for 1 hour, stirring every 15 minutes.

2. With a large spoon, scoop out the chocolate mixture and drop it onto wax paper. Allow to cool for 20–30 minutes.

Fun Shapes

Homemade candy bars make easy and budget-friendly holiday gifts, and making them in fun shapes is a festive touch. Spray the inside of a cookie cutter with nonstick spray, then lay it on top of the wax paper before dropping the chocolate on. Pour the chocolate into the cookie cutter and leave it in place until the chocolate is slightly firm.

CHOCOLATE CHIP SKILLET COOKIE

If you don't have a small skillet and still want to make this recipe, bake in a 10" or 12" skillet for 45 minutes. Or you can wrap half of the dough tightly in plastic wrap and freeze it for up to 3 months.

Yields 2 skillet-size cookies

2 cups all-purpose flour

1 teaspoon baking soda

½ teaspoon salt

¾ cup plus 1 teaspoon unsalted butter, softened

½ cup sugar

¾ cup packed brown sugar

1 egg

2 teaspoons vanilla extract

1½ cups chocolate chips

1. Preheat oven to 350°F.

2. Combine the flour, baking soda, and salt in a bowl.

3. Use the paddle attachment of a stand mixer, or use a handheld mixer, to cream ¾ cup butter and sugars until they're light and fluffy. Add the egg and vanilla and blend on low until combined. Add the flour mixture and beat on low until it is just combined. Stir in the chocolate chips by hand.

4. Grease a 4"–6" skillet with 1 teaspoon of butter. Divide the dough in half. Transfer half of the dough to the skillet and press to flatten evenly over the bottom of the skillet. Bake for 30 minutes, or until the edges are brown and the top is golden. Repeat with the other half of the dough.

5. Leave in the pan and rest on a wire rack for 10 minutes to cool. Cut and serve.

ALMOND SHORTBREAD COOKIES

Baking these cookies on a cast-iron griddle will make them crispier, and they'll cook more evenly.

Yields 2 dozen cookies

3 sticks unsalted butter, at room temperature

1 cup granulated sugar

1 teaspoon vanilla extract

1 teaspoon almond extract

3½ cups all-purpose flour

¼ teaspoon salt

1½ cups crushed almonds

1. Preheat oven to 350°F. Using the paddle attachment on a stand mixer or hand mixer, cream the butter and sugar together. Add the extracts and combine.

2. Sift the flour and salt together. Stir the almonds into the flour. Slowly add the flour to the butter while mixing slowly. When mixed, turn onto a floured surface and shape into a flat disk. Refrigerate for 1 hour.

3. Flour a surface and roll the dough until it is ½" thick. Cut into rounds or squares that are no larger than 2½" across. Place the cookies on a griddle, and bake in the middle of the oven for 20–25 minutes. The edges will turn brown. Cool to room temperature and serve.

POUNDED AND FRIED PLANTAINS

Plantains are similar to bananas but are much starchier. Choose plantains that are yellow-gold and firm.

Yields 18–24 pieces

1 cup flour

½ teaspoon baking powder

¼ teaspoon salt

¾ cup cold water

1½ pounds plantains

6 tablespoons peanut oil for frying

Powdered sugar for sprinkling

1. Sift the flour, baking powder, and salt together. Add the cold water to the dry ingredients and stir until it is lump-free. It should coat a spoon when dipped in the batter. Add a tablespoon of flour or water if necessary to get this texture.

2. Cut the ends off the plantains. Cut through the peel lengthwise several times and use the tip of a butter knife to pry off the peel. Cut the plantains in half and again in half lengthwise, and then cut each half into thirds. Use a rolling pin to flatten each plantain.

3. Place a griddle over medium-high heat. Once it is heated, pour 3 tablespoons of oil on the griddle and swirl so the surface is coated evenly. If the oil smokes, lower the heat until it stops smoking.

4. Dip each pounded strip into the batter and let the excess drain off. Place half of the slices of plantain on the griddle so they aren't touching. Fry each plantain for 1–2 minutes per side. They will darken more after they are removed from the oil. Add the rest of the oil and repeat with the rest of the plantains.

5. Sprinkle them with powdered sugar and eat while hot.

STANDARD U.S./METRIC MEASUREMENT CONVERSIONS

VOLUME CONVERSIONS

U.S. Volume Measure	Metric Equivalent
⅛ teaspoon	0.5 milliliter
¼ teaspoon	1 milliliter
½ teaspoon	2 milliliters
1 teaspoon	5 milliliters
½ tablespoon	7 milliliters
1 tablespoon (3 teaspoons)	15 milliliters
2 tablespoons (1 fluid ounce)	30 milliliters
¼ cup (4 tablespoons)	60 milliliters
⅓ cup	90 milliliters
½ cup (4 fluid ounces)	125 milliliters
⅔ cup	160 milliliters
¾ cup (6 fluid ounces)	180 milliliters
1 cup (16 tablespoons)	250 milliliters
1 pint (2 cups)	500 milliliters
1 quart (4 cups)	1 liter (about)

WEIGHT CONVERSIONS

U.S. Weight Measure	Metric Equivalent
½ ounce	15 grams
1 ounce	30 grams
2 ounces	60 grams
3 ounces	85 grams
¼ pound (4 ounces)	115 grams
½ pound (8 ounces)	225 grams
¾ pound (12 ounces)	340 grams
1 pound (16 ounces)	454 grams

OVEN TEMPERATURE CONVERSIONS

Degrees Fahrenheit	Degrees Celsius
200 degrees F	95 degrees C
250 degrees F	120 degrees C
275 degrees F	135 degrees C
300 degrees F	150 degrees C
325 degrees F	160 degrees C
350 degrees F	180 degrees C
375 degrees F	190 degrees C
400 degrees F	205 degrees C
425 degrees F	220 degrees C
450 degrees F	230 degrees C

BAKING PAN SIZES

U.S.	Metric
8 × 1½ inch round baking pan	20 × 4 cm cake tin
9 × 1½ inch round baking pan	23 × 3.5 cm cake tin
11 × 7 × 1½ inch baking pan	28 × 18 × 4 cm baking tin
13 × 9 × 2 inch baking pan	30 × 20 × 5 cm baking tin
2 quart rectangular baking dish	30 × 20 × 3 cm baking tin
15 × 10 × 2 inch baking pan	30 × 25 × 2 cm baking tin (Swiss roll tin)
9 inch pie plate	22 × 4 or 23 × 4 cm pie plate
7 or 8 inch springform pan	18 or 20 cm springform or loose bottom cake tin
9 × 5 × 3 inch loaf pan	23 × 13 × 7 cm or 2 lb narrow loaf or pâté tin
1½ quart casserole	1.5 liter casserole
2 quart casserole	2 liter casserole

INDEX